The Lovemakers

Also by Alan Wearne:

Poetry
The Australian Popular Songbook, 2008
The Lovemakers, Book Two, 'Money and nothing', 2004
The Lovemakers, Book One, 'Saying all the great sexy things', 2001
Out Here, 1987
The Nightmarkets, 1987
New Devil, New Parish, 1976
Public Relations, 1972

Prose
Kicking in Danger, 1997.

The Lovemakers

Alan Wearne

Shearsman Books
Exeter

First published in one volume in the United Kingdom in 2008 by
Shearsman Books Ltd
58 Velwell Road
Exeter EX4 4LD

ISBN 978-1-905700-96-7

Parts 1–8 of this book were originally published in 2001 by Penguin Books Australia Ltd, Sydney, as *The Lovemakers, Book 1*, '*Saying all the great sexy things*'; Parts 9–16 were originally published in 2004 by ABC Books, Sydney, as *The Lovemakers, Book 2*, '*Money and nothing*'.

Copyright © Alan Wearne, 2001, 2004, 2008.

The right of Alan Wearne to be identified as the author of this work has been asserted by him in accordance with the Copyrights, Designs and Patents Act of 1988. All rights reserved.

Acknowledgements
I thank all who helped in the writing, publishing and promotion of *The Lovemakers*, in particular all journals and anthologies that published sections of *The Lovemakers* over the years, and the following organisations: the Literature Board of the Australia Council; the Victorian Ministry of the Arts; the Cité Internationale des Arts, Paris; the English Department at the University of Newcastle; and the Faculty of Creative Arts at the University of Wollongong (particularly for their backing of the Shearsman edition and the work of Miriam Wells); and the School of Communications and Cultural Studies at Curtin University of Technology, Perth.

The lines from William Bronk's poem 'No Way' are published with permission of the Trustees of Columbia University.

The lines from Bronwyn Wallace's poem 'Joseph MacLeod Daffodils' from *The Stubborn Particulars of Grace* are published with permission of Jeremy Baxter, her son and literary executor.

The line from T. S. Eliot's notes to 'The Waste Land' from *Collected Poems 1909–1962* is published with permission of Faber and Faber Ltd.

The lines from 'The Poems of Our Climate' are drawn from Wallace Stevens' *Collected Poems* and are published with permission of Faber and Faber Ltd.

'Lucky Blues', written by Roosevelt Sykes, published by LERIC MUSIC (BMI)/ Administered by BUG, All Rights Reserved, is used by permission.

Continued on p.685.

Contents

Part 1
Jack's Progress (I) — 13
The Kid in St Kilda — 20
Cross QC: Three Villanelles — 29

Part 2
Catholics for Friends (I) — 35

Part 3
Geoff, Julie, St Edwin's and the World — 65
1964: Jack in Love — 73
A Lecture on Love — 76
Out of Trouble: The Baron Hits the Road — 82
Bernie and Jack, Lindsay and Karl — 84

Part 4
Catholics for Friends (II) — 91
'His Majesty Prince Jones smiled
    as he moved amongst the crowd' — 128
1971 — 143

Part 5
Under Fourteen/Under Sixteen — 149
Dave Price Completes His Extension — 152
Barb at Dot's Wedding — 160
Auntie Wynne at Barb's Wedding — 174
The Age of 'Cowboy' Neale — 178
Radio Chook Raffle (I) — 194

Part 6
Lovelife (I) Barb — 199
Lovelife (II) Vivienne, or Seeing Other People/
    Claire and Claire's Poet/The Phil Price Limericks — 211
Lovelife (III) Barb and Neil (I) — 221
Lovelife (IV) Barb and Neil (II) — 245
Mateys — 286
Lovelife (V) Roger, or Of Love and Its Anger — 294

Part 7
Non in spatio sed in muneribus capitus — 309

Part 8
Sophie — 323

Part 9
Radio Chook Raffle (II) — 337
On the Rice Trail: Mr A Cruises North — 338
Nothing but Thunder — 351
Holding the Drug Czar's Hand — 372
Small-Timing: The Alien Returns To Melbourne — 393

Part 10
'The first thing we do, kill all the economists' — 403

Part 11
Night Jasmine — 415
Making the World Revolve (I) — 429
Group Portrait with Benny and Wal — 446
Leo — 488

Part 12
Mister Kim Lacey — 493

Part 13
Stubbsy: A Success — 509
Gibbo's Coast-to-Coast — 550

Part 14
Making The World Revolve (II) — 571
The Kid, The Baron, Mr A
   and The Alien Await The Mini-Series — 589
Bring On The Gerontophiles! — 596
Someone to Make Us Feel Happy — 602

Part 15
'Those Were Strange Days — Strange Days Indeed!' — 625

Part 16
The Horse! — 661
Bunyip at Dave Price's Wake — 666
Lovelife (VI) Barb and Neil (III) — 670
Jack's Progress (II) — 673

For John Forbes (1950–1998)
and
Jas H. Duke (1939–1992)

You know, I am told my tenderness for you
is for me, really, that if I treat you gently,
I replace a harshness I suffered from, the roles reversed.

> William Bronk, 'No Way'

Oh I'm living the life I always wanted to live
Oh I'm living the life I always wanted to live
Instead of begging I've got something to give

> Roosevelt Sykes, 'Lucky Blues'

. . . who actually is The Man?

> Paul Havin to Alan Myers, 1989

You can call it a choice
if you want, but that doesn't change
what we learn to rely on,
the smallest stratagems. Whatever works.

> Bronwen Wallace, 'Joseph MacLeod Daffodils'

Book One

*Saying
all the great sexy things*

Part 1

JACK	AVOIDING TROUBLE
KENT	MURDERER
BERNIE MILLAR	COOK
DENISE	JACK'S GIRL
THE KID	RUNAWAY
DESLEY } IRIS }	WHO HELP THE KID
CROSS QC	BARRISTER

JACK'S PROGRESS (I)

for Rae Desmond Jones

Melbourne, May 1960

  Kent, the friend who said he'll meet him here,
is late, been stopped or given up.
  How many hours has Jack been out?
He'll check when many more get logged.
  *. . . and no use just being 'free', I need to know
I am.*
  Beers and smokes on a damp late morning,
with 'Corner Quiz' from the bar's portable.
  It's quiet, business, and Take five the owner
urges his staff.
    Five what? Jack wonders
Well whatever they are, take fifty.
  So he will read perhaps.
  Someone in the spine-snapped
American paperback loses his name,
has got to find it.
    *If I gave mine away
and never bothered, how long would I last?
A man needs a kid, intelligent and pretty*
and 'honest', 'reliable', the adjectives start melting together
*Yeah and she could take over my name
so as I would never need it. All you can do for years, some years
it seems, is think, read and listen . . .*
  Some queen is flogging corsetry or furs,
how come they finished 'Corner Quiz'?
      ''day Jack.'
It's behind him. 'Jack.'
     He doesn't turn: 'Y' late.'
  Losing my name? That'll keep. Girls? Probably.
  And if he's been numb to it, Jack can always
flirt with forgetting them. But only flirt.

　　　　The rain has blown east. The staff return.
　　'Yes Kent, y' late.'
　　　　　　　　The sun unrolls itself along a wall.

Bernie Millar meets Jack: Sydney, Melbourne Cup Day 1960

　　　　　　　　. . . at fifties. Hi Jinx.
Sure, sure someone should've backed it.
Not Bernie though. For here's what backing's all about
for me, Jack: people, trust, the future;
two out of three, perhaps; three out of three,
Bernie is your bunny.
　　　　　　　Which is why I'm glad
I'm here and meeting you.
　　　　　I've forgotten where but I'm with Kent
and Kent knows you and who you are:
'See him: he's Jack: if he isn't hard
he's pretty hard. But anytime,' says Kent,
'you want someone to trust, trust Jack.
Unlike you, Killer Diller Millar, Jack's
no girl.'
　　　　No girl? 'Well yeah,'
I'm telling Kent, 'let's take that on, except,
except, I'll get things done,
you and this Jack' — pardon Jack —
'couldn't even know or knowing start
to understand'.
　　　　　　Anyone I want, I have them
needing me. And then it's baby time!
There was this one ugly widow, see
(who ought to have been in leopard skins).
'Isn't that a funny coot?' she asks.
'Come over here funny coot.'
And anchors aweigh! I was getting piped
aboard The Good Ship Lollypop out of
Noah's Ark.
　　　　　So what's doing here?
The race was run three hours back,

the party's into headache mode,
whilst you and me just stare at a few
sweet bays, the odd island, headlands and
three or four ferries.
                    Tell us, Jack,
how'd they ever let in coves like us?
A bag o'fruit or two is one thing,
but my guess is they'll try to frisk me
at the door and you'll remind them
*Fellas, this funny coot's with me and I'm
with you aren't I?*
            Don't you love the way it is
up here? How no place slums it quite
like Sydney does. If this lot let in
Bargain Basement Bernie wouldn't they lock out
no-one?
            But matey, Jack, don't they realise how,
one day, I'll do something so special,
how I'll leave everyone looking ridiculous
(I've just one chance to do *that*)
for I'll want them saying (you too Jack,
you too) *So! That's what he meant!
Playing silly buggers wasn't Bernie Millar's
only game!*
            The gee gees?
                            No you can't do much
with them but shout and win perhaps.
Friends took me to the Cup once;
before the race I was staring
at this painting: Carbine. And, I tell you right,
this little prick's beside me,
giving out a tip and, one name sounding good
as any, I take the tip. Which wins!
That's backing enough for Bernie; he's never been more ahead.
            You get out of Melbourne a bit?
I get out of everywhere. You come here,
you go there, you inform the appropriate squad
Just visiting friends which ought to sound good
but often isn't. For Jack, certain people don't enjoy,
don't trust, too much moving around.

    And no-one should of course, unless
it's you and me doing the moving just to annoy
these certain people. I can imagine
telling this walloper tonight *Why am I
in Sydney Sarge? To watch the Melbourne Cup!*
    I still can feel my ears ablaze even if, guess what,
it hasn't happened yet.
        Well Jack, your very first coaxial cable Cup:
how's matey rating it?
        Yeah, I know,
Hi Jinx at fifties: should've been backed
and must've been doped.
        Doing much tonight?

A few tales from my life so far

(1)   A sucker for the nags and their manoeuvres
my father played his life with small debate
*So you miss on the Railway Highweight?
There's bound to be the Second Improvers*
'... for this is not; he'd poke at his chest, 'mug punter
mark one'
   Then, each self-conviction
brimming into the next, each absurder fiction
sustaining the last, our time to leave the Upper Hunter
arrived.
   We always left everything.
        At six,
after The Sisters clipped my skull, forming headaches,
Dad slammed the family's spiritual brakes
right to the floor: quitting being the micks
we hardly were.
     And if our drifting was so-so,
f.a.q., still we drifted: just ask the kids and wife:
it was hardly time for getting on with life:
war days, moving days, twenty years ago.

(II)
  ...and Now I was twenty.
With widgie nights, bodgie days
keeping me learning there were other ways
to turn, to look, to see.
                It's an age of plenty,
I get advised, and so I take
what life's about: living it total, once:
day of the bludger, night of the ponce,
with Jack-on-the-make
at twenty-two running this 'stable'
where they'd only be so young so young.
    And, climbing one extra rung
of respect I go along with the fable;
any balls in a knot
will never be mine,
trusting, perhaps, there'll arrive a time
to get me everything free-with-the-lot.

(III)
 ...and part of me announced as I was grooming my stubble
into a beard Let's play the beatnik/ scientist/ explorer)
Ahh Jack you were born never to be forgotten: like an aurora
        Yeah but now I'm heading one way and trouble
the other. Here's how dumb I was: once, coming south
overloaded with such dreams that ricochet *Whack!* into your chin
...schoolgirls? Who'd I think I was? Errol Flynn?
      I'll tell you what remained but: how my mouth
had tasted hers and hers and hers.
                   The jug is always a shock.
For remember you carry what's called a prick, which might be romantic
but not when it governs your every scheme and antic.
        Now, back on the street what am I after? Christ matey anything
             in a frock.
         Except that this arvo, just as they're running The Cup,
I'm in, of all places, Steak 'n' Kidney
and guess what (he would and he did, wouldn't he didn't he)
Mr Bernie Millar is picking us up.

(IV)
   I'm no 'great man', never was meant to be;
one day but my kind of good might happen;
though not if I stand around plain-yappin'
with you Millar: you're such a poison.
         Y' see,
Bernie isn't merely bland, merely bad, he's so bland –
and bad beyond the bland and the bad of any Mr Bloke.
(Besides, who else but me would have him?)
          And it has got to be a joke
how, tiptoeing the borders of Rockspiderland
he expects to find me there and all I can say is *What?*
Pick up some kid sheila both of us and root her delirious?
Mate I mean y' not this serious?
   But he won't answer and you've still got
That for a friend?
      You sure have.
         For few arrive at the black,
still centre of my heart quite as Bernie does.
   And he says (or may well): 'Whatever this buzz
between us is, it works for mates like us eh? Eh Jack?'

East St Kilda, New Year's Eve 1960

   Look to that first floor flat: a window up,
watching this show that the night plays (water
and lights, a road) it's Jack, his hands over
a woman's shoulders, squeezing them slow
and firm.
    He met Denise through a serving hatch.
  'I'll go to hell for this,' she rather guessed,
the first time they got drunk.
       'If it exists,'
he tried agreeing, 'then I'll join you.'
    Thin, with Betty Boop eyes, she always carries
proof-of-age. The man before called her
Lollypop, pushed her around but
only once.

At noon the heat
(how many days of it?) just split apart
and fled.
      Home after work
Jack kept every door and window open,
showered himself, lay down to hear the rain,
and read, loving the cost of every word,
the working-at-it.
         When Denise arrived,
a best frock over her arm, they went to the window.
Behind them, to follow-on some feather duster gags
(the set's sound down) a throaty 'Ragtime Cowboy Joe'
is mouthed from a dummy.
            Jack spits sharp into the night.
He's wanting something better:
'Hotter Than That', 'Wildman Blues' . . . *aren't I*
nearly hotter, almost wild?
          He's nearly almost anything;
except a kitchen hand's no cook, a cook's hardly a chef.
      Yet who is this in singlet,
thick plain belt and jeans, behind Denise?
Her very own trim bearded hero: our Jackyboy!
Who sounds a sigh. *This is not too bad?* it asks
    No no she likes it . . . Eh?
            And wait, wait
this *Eh?* replies.
      Too right, don't move.
          'All this,'
she's told, 'finds a spot so far inside my head it's
outer space. Do you know that?'
      Do you know what else dazzles him?
Just her standing there; that anyone could.
Or, even simpler, how they might survive.
      'I'm going squarehead from tonight . . . well
part of me might. Yeah . . . I'm Rin Tin Bloody Tin,
who's not? We'll go out soon, there's something,
they reckon it's a cabaret or something,
somewhere.' (The doll stops singing, cackles,
is replaced.) 'Denise,' says Jack. 'Denise.
I can't quite figure what we've started, mate,
but it's unrolling.'

The Kid in St Kilda

        Through their kitchen and onto the back verandah
Desley and The Kid had dragged the mattress.
She'd been known to bring back worse and,
since the lease didn't allow for pets
this way they got around *that*.
                Call it
a sudden snap of weakness, but Des had
wanted to like him: you saw a person,
gulped, took risks. Some paid you to love,
some you almost ordered yourself to enjoy.
He was obviously neither: thanks praise et cetera
hardly a customer, twelve she guessed him, thirteen, fourteen,
young or old enough for those famous
'friendly lectures' Desley almost couldn't help.
      'Saint Bloody Kilda: run away from home,
from any place, you'll find it. What kid
wouldn't?'
        After a few wet days
drains were hopeless, but, till then that's
what people did: some rode round for a root,
others lived in drains.
                'Flat 4 tarum-taraa!'
      Here was her home so where was his?
His name then? No, you're caught with a name.
      'Son, they catch you with a face.
Well I'm Desley, my friend's Iris and here's hoping
she approves.

        Years on, after he'd been
Mr A and The Baron and The Alien
(dealing and taxi-driving to help set himself
back on the rice trail) he'd tell, whoever wanted
or didn't want to hear, how
yes, when he was this tearaway living

in the drains, these St Kilda hookers took him in
(... and how it might have been
right where we are now: 4/9) and how,
yeah anyway at this party there he met,
well kinda met, that sucker Kent.
Then there was Bernie, bit of a mongrel Bern,
who tried interesting him, at twelve,
in grass or whatever it was called;
and Jack who wouldn't let him so as he 'n' Jack
could be friends. Or so it seemed.
Last time, in Bangkok or Manila or wherever,
he thought he saw Bernie, or the ghost of Bernie,
behind a bar, he didn't need to stop.
Jack of course he always saw around, that man
was The Phantom: made to be seen around;
but nothing special now, just someone to nod at.
Then the intros were recalled: you know Jack, Kent?
Well this is Denise his girl; that's Bern
and this is The Kid, he goes with the place for now.
'Know the first law of anything?' Kent wanted to know.
'He's asking you,' Desley prompted.
'Only one law,' Kent advised, 'never be dumb enough.'

    Iris had made a condition:
'You can be here when one of us are home ...'
so a few days on she asked
'What're you doing through the day ...'
(Fish, he thought; or go to town; or read things;
help out.) 'Making trouble or avoiding it?'
Iris knew a stupid question when she
asked one. He kept to his smile.
'You know,' she asked, 'where we work,
Des 'n' me?' The boy had already guessed,
grinning as if he'd known even before
the women had. 'You're not dumb ...'
Iris could enjoy that. 'Girlfriend?'
Stumping The Kid his bravado melted and
he blushed. 'Well not yet. Why should you?

Haven't you friends though, at your age?'
'Friends? Some . . .' He could exist without
them but. Or could he?
'Des,' he shot out fast, 'she's letting me stay . . .'
'On our back verandah, sure. You're not
the first, mind. You heard we have this do
on Saturday?' Flicking his head he showed
he'd heard. 'There'll be Kent,' she told him, 'Jack
and Denise, Paula and her chink, Bernie Millar
(under sufferance), the twins, and now,
by special arrangement, Desley's latest acquisition:
you, The Runaway Kid. We've broadminded
friends, but how do we explain you,
when we have to? Call you my sister's boy?'
Didn't think he'd need that, didn't want to
neither, though Iris buoyed the idea: 'I'll think
of something later . . .' She wouldn't try.

Kent was out. Wouldn't he need a party?
Iris did. It was okay by Des even if
they needed her to accommodate this guest appearance:
The Kid, her kid, late of the drains
with his scrubby sandy hair, his whingey words
and clever words. The drains apart
she wanted to know his home and, truth or fibs,
he mentioned some suburb or country town.
Des thought she'd heard of it; sometimes a customer
might drop a name that sounded familiar,
though in this job, by thirty-four,
you often thought you heard.
Don't expect her to stay trying this
that long. Soon enough she'd quit sitting around
and settle down, with Mr Menzies,
adopting for her boy scout this kid who,
over the past days, ran her a few bobs
worth of messages.
So Kent was out and,
after stocking-up for their party, Iris sagged

into her afternoon. Happy with wanting the lot.
Des of course would give it all away:
they differed over that; but better her than
bible-thumpers, standover ponces, bent cops,
all that these men with Billy Graham jaws could do
was cast blunt spells on those who
wanted to be scared. So what was wrong
in this drooping-off to nothing?
Death might be life's grandest thing (if only
you were certain what it was). 'She went
that way?' acquaintances would ask her friends,
and her friends, proud to have known Iris,
would elaborate. Though of course you'd miss
such admiration.
     And she liked the sound
of what was said: death as life at its grandest.
If only she'd known to inform Kent
(that night or any time) but who would?
For Kent, a trim man under his little hat,
had only eighteen months to live.
In a fortnight he and a mate would
find themselves a job and botch it:
and cornered by two cops would panic:
a cop would get the mate, Kent would get
that cop, then, after next summer,
when nothing but the cricket, the heat and Kent's appeals
made news, they'd string-up Kent,
The Herald having him stroll to the noose
reciting Lawson or Paterson or 'Life is mostly
froth and bubble ...'
     No-one knew an angel
must have been preparing to arrive at
4/9 that evening, this angel malevolent
enough to slap Kent's back, matey style,
with *Welcome home Kent you poor dumb cunt,*
welcome from those of us outside ...
enjoy yourself it's getting late.

        ☙

Jack asked The Kid: 'Told you read a bit?'
And grafting to the man's lean speech
something of his 'When I can. Papers. Anything.'
The Kid replied. The only bearded bloke he'd
met before was Santa Claus.

'Had it a month,' piped Des, 'Jacky's going
Buddhist oooooo!' and waved her hands
like he worshipped Casper The Friendly Ghost.
Should've, she thought, sent The Kid in next door
for 'Hawaiian Eye' and 'Perry Mason' but
Rasmussen was out.

'Me?' Jack looked at The Kid; The Kid
looked back. 'We've got our business . . .'
came an answer pleased with itself.
'Boys aren't my line, you know that. Right Bern?
Go on tell us, Bern . . .'

And Bern told them:
'Makes a decent beer this town don't it?'

Even at his age such phrases shuddered
The Kid: he wouldn't forget it, this exactly:
the very insignificance of Bernie-the-cook.
Jack would be that good smart man he met
a few times at the pros, but Bernie set him
a life-motto: never be anything like that,
an anything that's nothing. A bignoter? Please, if only . . .
for one day he'd become that passenger who
leered back 'Bro? Hey bro?' or Fatso, grinning
to the mates, then goin' down on Crazy Horse pussy
just for them. When someone's getting fucked in
the dark by the wrong guy, Bernie wants to be
that wrong guy: a man and his little little con,
who ceases without it.

'Des, why'd you take me in?' The Kid asked later.
'Why aren't I booted out?'

She explained it:
'Don't think it goes with the job. Iris 'n' me
might have hearts of gold, the next girl

probably hasn't. Of course you'll have to leave one day,
all of us will, but I couldn't have you
caught in a storm, then swept into Port Phillip Bay ...'
Survival was one fact of life, that and love.
There were of course the others, since all that sex-stuff
was living really. You did it or you
read about it and what was the fuss?
*'He saw the outline of her nubile form
swell from behind the negligée* ... It's a bit
like that, but hardly much. It's just
there's something every hour, every minute, second ...'

                       ಶ

          And that day women's problems had Iris
a little peaky. Des was going with her
to the quack, leaving him with Bernie,
their friend, his perhaps, who was humming
'Paper Doll' and 'Ballin' The Jack' now they were alone,
songs The Kid had heard him sing that summer
but knowing *Stay still stay quiet* was the order
of Bernie's eyes, and how it should continue:
Do this, I'll give you that ...
              ('Fourteen maybe, skinny though ...' Iris muttered
as he dozed off his first night there.)
          Now, this arvo, he was being touched
So here's how they start with kids like him
having to shrug-it-through, for money was better but.
Scary when a soft hand pats your face
but near enough to fun, like seeing what
went next, or daring to ask
'What 'm I getting?'
                    'Sheilas feed y' well?'
(In the man's chest something seemed clicking-
up towards his throat.)
                  'What 'm I getting?'
           'They feed y' well?'
                  'What 'm I getting Bernie?'
          He dodged an open hand as, for an answer,
it splayed into a sideboard; half a second

sounded nothing at all, till a pretty cup bombed
onto the floor. *Give us a year I'll be your size,
silly poof you should've got me drunk*
like in the stuff he'd read. Remembering things
he'd heard was great, didn't *You'd fuck anything
Bern* sound wonderful? Might even repeat it.
       'Look . . .' Bernie was blinking, panting. 'Look . . . what . . .'
though with footsteps coming to the door
The Kid could strut out what he liked:
       'Ten. Ten quid and quick, else I tell Des.
She 'n' Iris never believe you!'

       But Bernie had been set-up enough:
during the next few days, wanting to play it right,
he started thinking and a great idea arrived.
It was too risky though: having something pinched
then blaming, no better planting, it on The Kid.
Des adored that boy; Iris would hardly
believe anyone she hated as much as she hated Bern;
whilst he didn't need to imagine Jack
cocking a brow as his eyes drilled for
the little truth left
Know you did it mate, just explain why, Bern.
       It had been a mean idea, but a great one,
just flawed by being clumsy. Yet if Bernie
was bad news, Kent was badder
(even Jack, Cap'n Squarehead himself, seemed
hardly dad material) and how could you
let a youngster stay in St Kilda,
let alone with Desley,
when out where he belonged were paddocks
to run in, plenty of trades to learn?
He wasn't sure how legal it might be but
the right word with the right cop made
everything wonderful. Never was after thanks
but Bernie might be thanked, the girls let off,
praised, even, for their public service:
caring for a runaway best they could,

then giving him up and sending him back
to a loving home and mum's best tucker.
       Equal better Bernie would get his own back.
       So an early morning later, The Kid
looked up from his mattress, recalling the story of
the three wells: for look who'd arrived:
a few of our old mates, the boys and, yes,
even a girl as well, in blue.
Time to give up. But he would leave milking
the situation so that Bernie might cop something:
'Fair go, today's me birthday!'
       Wistfully in tears Desley blanched:
why hadn't he told them?
Muttering 'Learn a trade son'
Bernie sounded, yes, a touch embarrassed; Iris lit up;
and weren't the cops exquisitely uncomfortable?
'Happy returns . . .' the woman offered; and 'Well,'
Jack smiled, as he always seemed to,
'If it is or almost is . . .'
       Des recovered.
She wanted to say something like
No matter even how weird, love's love but 'Crikey Bern,'
she sighed, 'it had to happen sometime,
but today? Y' should've asked us
tell them about the drains son
who's he is this kid needed somewhere, someone.'
       And he wanted to go anywhere now, away from
Bernie shovelling what's-for-the-best
at the bulls. Free country though and no regrets,
when it was decided you move, you moved;
you learnt that knowing Bernie.
Wouldn't he do the same? Had hardly fleeced
this dobber though, that was all.
Next time, even if they never get it,
when someone wants then someone pays.
       Desley came closer: 'Iris sends her love.
Come and see us one day, don't leave
without these, son.' (His *Pocket Compendium
of Australian Statistics; Facts and Figures*
from the SSB.)

He was slightly smiling now
but The Kid had turned into a boy
sloping off with the cops.

Cross QC:

Three Villanelles

for Michael Prideaux

(I) R v Kent: The cross-examination

       ...after what's been said and what's been done
it distresses, I understand, this evidence.
Let's get it right though: *then* he dropped the gun?

      A criminal shot, a colleague dead, Just one-on-one:
life's never been like this before, it's far, far tense
than any courtroom, right? Yet, after what's been done,

after you've heard *I'm gonna get you, son* ...
please constable, take no offence
but get it right: he dropped the gun

and then he aimed it? Where'd you read that? *The Sun?*
     (Your Honour I withdraw.)
                            But what amount of sense
does this make: after all's been said and done,

with a partner dying wouldn't you make a run
(the only thing left to prove your innocence
is time)?
       And yet Kent doesn't. My client drops the gun.
      What guilty men act this way: lots, a few, none?
      (When a life's at risk all words swell immense,
soon as they're said.)
             As for what was done:
we have it right? Then he dropped the gun?

(ii) R v Kent: The summing up

        The case you've heard, with due respects, is bent.
        We may not like him, think he's highly flawed,
yet he's stayed calm my client, Mr Kent,

and that's but a start to show he's innocent.
        Up rose his hands as he howled *Oh Gawd!*
(the case you've heard unravels, it is bent)

having a good idea what *Drop it!* meant
but, for that second, froze: his being gnawed
with staying calm.
        My client Mr Kent's

no saint (what chassis never had a dent?).
It's hardly the point he gambled and he whored
with due respects.
        The case you've heard is bent:

relive this evidence again: the scent
of anger's out, the ground is being pawed ...
still he stays calm my client Mr Kent.

Four! Five! Six! That gun was a long time spent.
Throw it down! somebody implored.
And didn't he?
        The case you've heard is bent:
for he stayed calm my client Mr Kent.

(iii) Some hours after the execution

      I wish I'd had his strength.
                            Now, calm as he was
they've a stronger, calmer Kent to bury
(*perhaps* and *maybe* shall give way to *because*).

      My job requires plain speech, if no applause,
but how could you notify a jury
I crave the strength and calm I thought was

his; how, most nights, dreaming of rowing I haul through mud the oars
of a middle-aged barrister in a hurry?
      Our *perhaps* our *maybe* turned *because*

shaking hands a week ago: 'Thanks Mr Cross.
Had I the know-how I'd syphon off a brewery
and pay you in grog for life!'
                      Calm as Kent was

he knew *doubt* as our one escape (all other doors
were boarded up); knew it had been a puree
of *perhaps* and *maybe*, to taste but once, because

if we have the crimes we have the laws
and have, now, the premeditated fury
of revenge.
      Today, stronger, calmer than even Kent was
(*perhaps* dying, and *maybe*) the state has demanded *because*.

Part 2

NEIL 'GOGO' SPENCER
KIM 'SPACEY' LACY .... HIGH-SCHOOL STUDENTS,
RAY 'FRENCHY' DONELLAN THE SHIRE
HANNAH LITTLE
MARGOT LITTLE .... HANNAH'S MOTHER, SHIRE IDENTITY
FAT DONALD .... NEWSAGENT, SHIRE IDENTITY
LIZ
MONICA .... STUDENTS, THE ACADEMY OF
CHRISSIE MARY IMMACULATE
LOUISE
REVEREND MAC .... OF THE INTER-SUBURBAN
CHRISTIAN CRUSADE

CATHOLICS FOR FRIENDS (I)

... it was reported to me from Sydney, Australia.
T. S. Eliot

Neil

    Driving some winter Sundays they'd get lost.
    Late in an afternoon a market gardener, gazing from
his living room, would see a pale blue Morris Oxford
bouncing through the vegetable rows
to stop at the end of the track where,
with wipers flipping away the drizzle,
a family stared back at a cow.
    'She has us lost; Dad breathing-in accused,
and breathing-out judged: 'the Gregory's ...
you've mis-read, deliberately mis-read, the Gregory's!'
    'Your Gregory's,' she wailed, 'is four years old!
We aren't on this or any bloody page!'
    Her husband lit another Rothmans Plain.
                                 From then,
Neil would hone that moment and its details down
by rote: those puddles by the track, beyond the track:
cabbages and caulies; Mum's tears, his father's smoke',
and the still cow; a verandah light with under it
two men in overalls watching the car reverse;
its windows misting; and then the order
'Bloody wipe them!' with its response
'Who? Wipe bloody what?'
                   Tell Neil
What he was meant to forget and of course
he might; but not, he knew, that afternoon, that hour when
Some sad malevolence of his
Come on, try smiles, everybody, smiles ...
had taken to snap exactly what
the Spencers were; to develop, mount
and caption all their ridiculous despair
Getting lost with Elwyn, Ron and the boys.

Kim

        This midday movie must be thirty years old.
The actors sound like they're in another room:

they arrive some place – a room say – speaking
these muffled words Kim won't be dumb enough to repeat,

and move on. But he'll stay here watching them
because, not that it matters, Neil is with him.

    Today it's sunny in the streets, but The Shire's streets
are quiet, much too quiet for Kim:

During the ads he's in the kitchen attending to
the flapjack mix, and if Neil calls flapjacks 'pikelets',

'pikelets' must be the dumbest word Kim has ever heard.
And isn't it eerie: everyone enjoys being the same as everyone

so everyone's supposed to be happy?
                        The usual things
have continued. There was a property boom, then there wasn't.

Kim's father, Mr Lacy, thought all his shops were going bust,
but the Christmas upturn altered his opinion.

Some hairdresser will marry Kim's sister.
'A Dutch ponce' is the verdict which gets bowled to Neil,

for they're still inside, lowering the flapjack pile,
waiting for the movie to end.

    Last year 'Stinky' Conway and 'Grubbsy' Leaf
recognised this new kid in The Shire as Kim:

'Weren't you in Grade Two? Gee you must get around.'
Neil remembered too, and since Neil likes being liked

Kim will like him, have him around.
Have plenty of kids around, when he wants them.

    Neil's mum thinks Kim needs supervision.
And of course at thirteen you aren't much of anything

(unless you are) 'But look,' he tries to tell his friend
– who'll hardly understand –

'most folks and teachers think they've got something on
What you did. Think of it Neil *What you did*.

Here's how I deal with that one: you must believe
not merely *I didn't* but *What I did never happened.*'

There's little that's easier; unless it's locating short cuts,
or knowing where and when you cave-in,

where and when you don't.
He sees the risks to be taken by other kids

and guesses that, if any story's good enough,
they'll believe the lot.

        No-one is bothering to ask
What's supposed to be in this boy's heart?
Well no-one yet.

    He squints a bit, is growing up tall.
He's not exactly indulged, just gets away with it.

After five or six years here he is back in The Shire,
having new friends and getting more.

Ray

    Where Ambrose Avenue joins Karringal Crescent,
midway through the holidays, Ray, this new kid with skid bars,

was doing wheelies.
    'When you arrive?' asked Neil.
'Week ago.'
   'Where from?'
     Some suburb Neil had never
heard of.
   Why here?
     Because his oldies moved;
they did a few things.
     Like go to church?
   The very latest.

     ☙

   They met again at school:
where everyone stared, for a day, at the new kids.
Ray didn't mind. At the last place
they called him Barnacle Bill: he'd made them.
   Did Neil know this one?:
   It's only me from over the sea
   (Cried Barnacle Bill the sailor).
   I just whop it out when I wanna do wee
   (Cried Barnacle Bill the sailor) . . .
   There was more?
     Of course there was!
   Well, who taught him?
   'My mad uncle from Maduncleland.'
   At the last place someone the school got in
told Ray how *You act like 'this' because, some place*
(most likely here) they treat you like 'that'!
   Ray tried to understand.
Like, you're in line say, and then the next kid
tries to grab your balls: so you try
grabbing his. Not really but you try.
   Everyone reflected off everyone else.
Though at church they told you how everything
reflected back from Jesus
     Nah nah Pastor Wellbeloved,
Ray wished he could announce,
Reflected back from Barnacle Bill!

Pardon me and the way I appeared,
But Mum's a virgin, and that's pretty weird,
'cause Dad's this bloke with a big white beard . . .

❦

    Soon after Ray arrived
Kim Lacy called him 'Squirt'. '"Squirt" Donellan, eh?
Sure you're not a Mormon, "Squirt"?'
                                              It was okay, though,
The Shire: if hardly a place to hear the deep demand
Leave the kid alone. Besides, this kid
attended his way to himself.
                              Lacy had hair which,
lacquered, combed, and rising from his forehead
like the Great Wall of China, announced.
Here, since you aren't a Mormon "Squirt"
is your revenge.'
                Ray was good for looking straight
at people:' A Mormon? No, Squirt's not a Mormon, "China".'
    Poor 'China'. Couldn't quite work out why
(which made it even better). He didn't look
at Ray; he didn't look at anyone too often,
unless something was wanted.
                          They said Kim Lacy
had a girlfriend somewhere. Ray doubted it:
he knew Kim well enough by now, how he slipped around
being Kim, got you to believe things, a bit.
    'We're Catholics, sortov Catholics,'
he admitted. 'Well it's what we put on the forms.'

❦

    That April, everywhere you went
you trod on a Mormon; though pretty nice about things
they prowled The Shire like commandos.
    And, circling these Mormons on his bike,
Barnacle Bill let them know
I won't let a sheila argue the toss,
Or turf me out 'cause she thinks she's boss,

For I get my roots when I visit The Cross . . .
      Would've been thrashed
if someone told his folks. Not that the Mormons
got it; got anything. They came from where?
Salt Lake City? Sure it wasn't Addis Ababa?!

                                                          ❧

      In a back corner of the school yard,
where the cypresses were felled, workmen had left
behind a log. So 'Squirt' with Neil and
half a dozen others formed Ye Loggheads:
'The Dishonourable Order of Ye Olde Loggheads'.
      Then 'Grubbsy' Leaf obtained a mob and,
one lunchtime, got in first behind the log.
      His friends retired
But 'Squirt' remained enraged: pelted with yonnies
but mild-mannered schoolboy Ray Donellan
was returning as Barnacle Bill and, pelting back,
strode towards the log.
                 'Onwards!' he howled.
'Onwards to Addis Ababa!'

Hannah Little (i)
for Rhonda Johnston

      There were few snobs like the snobs
who had to send their kids to State school.
                              And no,
Mother hardly wanted Hannah like those entrants
in the Interhouse Junior Beauty Pageant:
Miss Wattle, Miss Banksia, Miss Waratah,
and the winner . . . Miss Flowering Gum!
      But around the corner from the newsagent,
next to the dentist, down Pacifica Arcade,
came Femline Fashions *More than something to be seen in*
Mother's pitch at haute couture for whatever passed
as a smart set in The Shire:

wives whose husbands asked 'How about it, Margot,
the Progress Association needs a woman's touch ...'
Since Mother had The Shire to cultivate.
                              'Yes'
(she could be only honest with her daughter)
'The Shire ... and though we're merely camping
in this hole till ...' (and Hannah knew that *till*
meant not exactly now) 'it hardly means
that you dress down ...' She paused,
the pause announcing *Young Lady!* and though
she never spoke it, every second sentence closed with that.
            By seven p.m., Mother got to her worst:
feet up for her second cigarette, a sherry,
shooshing Hannah so both might learn
what Mr Menzies did today.
                         After which
a concert, a talk, a variety show, a quiz.
Not that Hannah was Top Forty, who'd want to be,
but Mother, , . Mother was mad, Mother was thirty-eight
and almost didn't care who knew.
                            Speakin' your mind
had this pattern, this rhythm, didn't it?
Whenever gentlemen dropped over Hannah always
thought she overheard *'Oh come now Margot!'*
'Yes come now Ted! / Tom! / Lance! / Lew!'
Next day mother's lips would stop
their pursing long enough to tremble, tremble hard:
'It's unfair unfair unfair!'
                    Some nights Hannah lay
imagining this confession (though whose confession?)
*I wish I could love you, I wish I could love
anyone.*
   You had to watch things.
All right she'd never be a skinny,
but no way was she set to be a fatty.
So you watched things, the good things:
calcium, protein, iron, certain carbohydrates
and the vitamin spectrum.
                      You needed to be smart:
when you were boys would treat you your way.

She knew it was a girl-thing to do
(though what if it was?) to tie up all the baggage
of your accusations by running the boy's name
into one: 'Think you're pretty smart don't you,
NeilSpencer?'
     'Hey sexpot!' RayDonellan yelled
towards Miss Banksia, as if he knew the all
of what it meant.
      And who'd ever want to flounce
like Miss Wattle, to hear 'Hot stuff!'
as KimLacy nudged the boy beside him;
or like Miss Flowering Gum (thinking she was
Brigitte Bardot) dab on beauty spots,
even for school; well who?
Bet Miss Waratah's parents' toilet
didn't seem quite disinfected bet bet bet!
  Even for a bit wasn't it worth thinking all that?
And this book was imagined, one she would write tomorrow
The Naughtiest Girl Does It Again!
      For the naughtiest girl
always did it again; just as a cornered boy always turned
out a giggling boy.

      ❧

     All kids throughout The Shire knew the
     newsagent: knew
and mimicked all Fat Donald's breathy repertoire
Whiskers or *Lad-die* for boys, *Possum* for girls, *Cor-rect money* when the
change got counted out.
     Late one afternoon,
from before it even started, Hannah saw the farce unfold:
these amateurs KimLacy/NeilSpencer were
Casin' th' joint (wasn't that the term she'd read
somewhere?) and if she knew, Fat Donald knew:
just knew NeilSpencer would distract him:
please, where were they kept: the set squares,
compasses, protractors?
     Making his play at help
the man was down the aisle when, turning,

he saw KimLacy: 'Your bag, Whiskers.'
Who didn't have to if he didn't want to,
name him the law.
     Grabbing the bag
Fat Donald was the law. (Plain-dumb, boys,
weren't much more than that, were they?)
And *Sim-sala-bim* this law was magic as, from the bag,
book followed magazine followed book.
  '*Dexter's Fit*,' Fat Donald smirked, holding it to the shop,
'*Man Junior, Rootin' With Angelique*, and wow, man,
Like Mad! Plus all these smokes!'
He turned to NeilSpencer:
'Forget the set squares: Whiskers here
has quite a nice tobacco farm. And you Lad-die
were in this, in this everywhere. Jump ship!'
  On the footpath Hannah caught up with him.
  'I saw you both NeilSpencer. And,
soon as your friend gets pinched he's dumped.'
  And what was done? What boys had always done:
he giggled.

Spencer
for Karlis Terauds

  There's this girl whose brother Spencer knows: Liz.
One day he and Donellan, two of The Shire's
most wayout kids, walk past Liz and her Mary Immaculate friends.
   The boys are
smoking. Cigars. And Donellan, who's primed himself
for this performance, whispers 'These Catholic chicks aren't going
to forget us, ever!'
     'Yeah; thinks Spencer, 'two idiots with cigars.'
 Liz knows she has a really solid tab
on how boys operate: she reckons everything is worth
a mighty peek to size up what's taking off, what's
in flight, what's about to land; and if some things
won't work she'll laugh about it either way.
If that Donellan keeps puffing into that cigar that hard,

Liz knows he'll end up spewing. Spencer's okay
(besides, his cigar's gone out)
and it's better when you vomit, Ray Donellan,
to have a friend around; just to make you even more embarrassed.

❧

    Then there's their friend, Kim Lacy.
All The Shire knows Lacy now: how he hasn't done much,
yet; but soon he should. He must.
You're not meant to trust him, which might be fun
for some girls, though hardly for Liz and her friend,
Monica. Monica calls Kim Lacy 'King Groover',
asks 'Who's he think he is, Mick Jagger?'
And can't you almost hear his reply *Hey girls,
how'd you guess?*

❧

    From a cousin Spencer has recorded,
reel-to-reel, the first two Rolling Stones LPs.
In the sleepout fug of too many fags even for them
he has round Lacy and Donellan.
                      Lacy tells them:
'Every street in The Shire seems to have some band.
Why not this one? Just get ourselves on stage,
then watch out Liz, Monica and every other girl . . . fellas,
fellas, all you have to do is play: at least know how to play . . .'
Learn a bit like Lacy's doing;
he'll have to lead of course' then
to swamp his band with talent, get in 'Stinky',
bring in 'Grubbsy': 'Kim Lacy and the Smelling Salts!'
    But Spencer never combs his hair,
'will never sing in tune, and though he might whack
a reasonable tambourine, Kim has his doubts, big doubts.
Donellan, meanwhile only knows the words to
'I've Been Ev'rywhere' and 'Hello Muddah Hello Faddah';
he's far too neat, his parents are religious:
he'll never get out of the house for midnight gigs, will he?

This main chance goes begging; another,
Kim's solo career, gets planned.

🙢

Lacy, though few people know this,
calls himself a Catholic, in a Lacy kinda way.
It's something the family acquired, he explains
to Spencer: he doesn't go to the schools now,
hasn't been to church, really, since they stopped.
And this is more exotic than if he did
or had. Something to make him special then?
'Well . . . I'm not one of you,' he tells his friends,
'nor either one of them.'
      Lacy, a bullshitter,
has plans for yet another main chance:
'One day,' Spencer and Donellan hear,' courtesy of my old man:
the retail trade.' (Till then of course there's always
that belittling revenge on his mark one bogeyman,
Fat Donald.)
  And The Shire is bulging with teenagers
making plans.
      Everyone knows Donellan's plans:
he's a sex maniac.
        If there are any Spencer plans Neil knows
they'll seem an imitation. He can say plenty though.
A science teacher with over-laconic drawl
tells him, tells the class
'. . . you talk more than a butcher's magpie.'
So Spencer will try imitating *him,* too often.
(And Lacy too, but Lacy does it better.)

🙢

  Everything for Lacy is just-so-easy-enough.
    Until, one day, under her parents' kitchen table
(now how did they get there?)
he puts a hand on one of Liz's breasts,
   Oh how she loves taking it off!
Oh how she loves giving the appropriate lecture!

'Hey,' says Lacy, 'I never meant it that way, Liz . . .'
 Bewildered, but in control, she thinks:
if not *That way* what way could he mean? Is there a further
insult here?
           Then one more order arrives:
Lacy isn't to tell Spencer (really, as if he would!).
Neil, she won't be telling Lacy, sends her letters,
far-too-sweet letters and, although she likes Neil
they're an embarrassment, much more than being
under the table with Lacy.
           So sorry,
but Liz will get attention when she wants it
and from whom.
           After five minutes Lacy
has got over her; just as Spencer will; he'll have to.

Lacy

       'Pay for what you've bought, Whiskers, and then scram!'
After a few years it was real great being back in Fat Donald's again.
And untempted by Errol Flynn's *My Wicked Wicked Ways*
Kim would leave these, the dubious memoirs of Tassie's finest,
           to sex fiends like Donellan.
Besides, there'd never be a prize (Kim had learnt this well)
           for being caught a second time
(there hardly was the first).
           And yet, there is a certain licence
persecution gives you:
Since I haven't done anything he's discovered I may as well.
       Besides, the newsagent needed a lesson,
all newsagents did; and if Kim's fury was always aimed
           anywhere but himself,
at least there was this detachment: the sort to keep him asking
Well, how do you think we should humiliate this toad?
       Easy, the place had to be raided.
       Right now he wanted nothing more.

catholics for friends (i)   47

      Even in other schools throughout The Shire they knew of Lacy.
And yet, of course, the guy had never done much,
much that could be proven. What was he supposed to do:
            wear a cloth cap, mask his eyes
and carry a sack marked LOOT?
                          But every time they met
Kim knew Fat Donald needed a lesson.
Though, till now, he was uncertain what or even why.
All the kids knew the newsagent for a fool:
            now even he would know it!
Last night he'll howl *somebody, I can't prove who ,got inside*
                my business! Isn't that enough?
Except that somebody wouldn't be exactly Lacy. He'd be a half-a-block
away, waiting for his protégés, knowing there were those who
understood
            where all the limits lay
            and those who never would.
Knowing he was liked and Fat Donald wasn't.
    And this would be a very good part of it:
only kids (and even all-of-the-kids)
            would know of the raid.
Not that you need tell everyone in the school, The Shire,
but no-one would ever be denied the knowledge, for, even better,
            Kim knew, no-one could possibly tell.
This would be a truly special event, Lacy style,
a near to invisible production, one that would almost never happen.
            And this was' to be the best of it:
Kim enjoyed giving as much as he liked taking:
            wasn't it who you took things from
            and who you gave things to
that really mattered: who felt bad and who felt good?

      If only the ocean were some marketplace
(sometimes Lacy had to go and look at The Pacific):
          every wave different, every wave the same,
            product interchanging with customers . . .
Of course there were certain things about The Shire
Lacy liked! The Sea; The Fair (well why not,

that's where, his father told him, shopping was headed);
           jacarandas in jacaranda time;
the mick chicks over at Mary Immaculate;
even the fibro cottages half the kids were living in
           – you had to live somewhere;
school, which filled in time and gave you friends;
           even rain rising off the asphalt as steam;
adults with phrases like *Slow horses and fast women*
and the rest of their self-righteous wit
           almost treating you like one of them;
           the simple feeling of safety, of quiet.

           And nothing getting done, ever getting done.
Really, he knew no better reason to raid Fat Donald's.
    'Let's say,' Lacy was unravelling with a skill
Spencer had never heard, 'past midnight, Tuesday next . . .
And did he require 'Stinky' or 'Grubbsy' or Donellan
           in on the act
           running with his glory?
If this one succeeded there would be other shops,
and getting to know two younger kids was working them
           into the action.
           'What'll you take?' asked Spencer.
           Lacy excused his friend,
but there were those who risked things and knew,
and those who never would. (Once you're tall enough
people believe you might have something to say;
so the taller the better; might even want to listen, hey?
           Unless you were merely Spencer.
Who, sure, was Lacy's height, but with little you'd ever want to hear.)
           What would Lacy take?
Anything: fags for the smokers, some magazines for the perves,
books for the rest. The air if necessary.
           The credit and the innocence.

           Known but never proven.
Life and the world would hardly offer better.

Donellan

'Who'd the first TV in your street, Spencer?'
'Well it wasn't us.'
          Donellan, whether they wanted him
or not, had joined them.
                    After Lacy tried to call him 'Squirt'
'Hey Squirt,' advised the phys ed teacher,
'better eat up y'Weeties.'
               Which did it:
adding six inches in a year he almost thought of
growing a moustache.
                    You had to stop avoiding him.
Why? Because you couldn't: doin' wheelies thinking he's
some bikie, shadow-boxing like he's Cassius Clay,
making his pitch to the sickies re-telling
thalidomide jokes.
               'That boy ...'
sighed Pastor Wellbeloved, 'we have to save
that boy!'
          Who adored the attention:
'They think I'm in with the wrong crowd.
What, me? I *am* the wrong crowd!'
                    And then,
one late spring afternoon, he charged over a sand dune,
straight at his friends, breathless with that all-
purpose Donellan war cry 'Let's perve!'
(Spencer and Lacy turned their heads towards
each other.) 'There's sheilas! Sunbaking!'
     'In what?'
     How did Lacy mean *In what?*
Some of the girls were at it: let's perve!
          Unless they were nude, with tits out-to-here
and obviously hot for Kim right now,
he wasn't set on moving. 'Are you, Spencer?'
          'Errgh,' went Donellan, 'you towel-flickers,
you total poofteroonies.'
                    He couldn't quite get through
to them; either that or through to them too much.
          During that summer he was on the phone to Neil just once:

'Guess what? Guess what? I laid my cousin!'
    'Yeah, like an egg.'
    Or 'Please Uncle Buster,' Ray would warble,
'Give my nose a blow . . .' then, sensing more his audience required
'God save our biscuit tin/Don't let the mice get in . . .'
    But these were lesser games.
for Donellan had this unending cache of frenchies,
pinched from his pharmacist uncle,
and every school day arvo he would flog them ('Frenchies!
        Fresh 'n' clean!')
up the line and back.
Know how to liven up a school assembly?
Swap 'Good Golly Miss Molly' for the national anthem,
Frenchy reckoned
reckoning enough to see it done.
                There is a breed of Sir who,
drawing himself a bath of public sarcasm, wallows:
'Ah Mr Spencer oh Mr Lacy oooh Mr Donellan,
hot foot it to your latest icons
(are they The Pterodactyls, The Pea Brains, "Blue" Hills and
        The Hoists?)
and wail your loudest!
Our younger generation? God help us!'
    There is a kind of Miss who'll never get the joke.
'This school has . . .' shame closed her eyes,
'these terrorists, guerillas, who raise female underwear up our flagpole.
On Anzac Day!'
They didn't want to be indignant, Miss, but please, the day before!
The word 'suspect' sounded too honourable and was never used.
No-one of course bothered asking *Who?*
since *Give up give up* everybody knew:
Frrrenchy D., thatzoo!
    Why bother stopping anything about him?
When assembling for the form photo 'Brothers 'n' sisters,' they heard,
'brothers 'n' sisters ahh tell you: there is a devil, truly a devil,
in that Brownie-box!'
Throughout the world in all school snaps,
some dickhead always gives another rabbit's ears.
But Frenchy that year only wanted himself in profile;
turning his head he got caught half way,

and looked like a spaz.
                              Wasn't the only one.
Who was likely to forget the local MLA
(a near-to-no-one with tinted Coke-bottle specs)
urging their bewildered speech night:
'Hitch your wagon to the star of free enterprise
and go! Go! Go!'
        When the Inter-suburban Christian Crusade staked The Shire
'Surely,' they tried suggesting,
'surely surely, Ray, couldn't you give The Lord a try out?'
        'Nah nah I barrack for Buddha . . .'
        Who's that knocking at my door?'
Who's that knocking at my door?
Who's that knocking at my door?
Why it's two young Mormons.
        And then he discovered Dylan . . .

Hannah Little (II)

        Certain things they told you made sense:
The Inter-suburban Christian Crusade. Like the Catholics
hadn't they something to offer, to believe? Sure,
though when Hannah asked those Catholics she knew
exactly what it was most of them went *Huh?*
        No use just changing the world,
Crusaders might advise her, first thing you've to change
is *you;* which all sounded like those diets
Hannah never stopped thinking she might try.
        Then, a few days late, news footage reached
Down Under. Americans (plenty of them Christians)
were changing the world: faced with 'I am the law'
police chiefs, night sticks, German Shepherds, water cannons,
Wanna fight? they taunted. *But your kinda fight?*
they demanded. *Hell no, we'll give you ours:*
let's change, let's change it all!
                        Often relevant,
even-handed when necessary, The Crusade wasn't always absurd;
and if its leaders over-preached,

they'd be saying what they said to those who craved the preaching.
Need you touch a leaf or see the sky
to be entranced by the ever-unfolding pattern of God?
Why not subscribe to *National Geographic!*
    And, though Hannah could accept belief for now,
she had to keep on questioning: there was, she knew,
no better pattern than mankind.
                          And guess who did
the unfolding? Bossy, weight-conscious, curious-minded,
with bold prayers always arriving at crunch time,
'Please God,' she'd proffer, 'let me be no slob like …
like *her* …' and 'Uncertain whether you approve of this one,
Lord, but better a know-all than a know-nothing!'
    Better indeed.
    It was then she turned Hannah-at-her-best
('Come on, aren't we the human race? Let's try things
nice and rational …') the debater.
'Take sex for example: what essentially is it?
Hormones!'
    She'd read about all that;
and, having read for years,
needed to have people gape at words to tease, words to only use when you
were certain of their meaning, and no-one else was:
sodomise and phallic, vaginal and prophylactic.
    All the girls in The Shire were getting
into bed with all the boys; except Hannah,
who'd this exquisite qualification:
'That's right *boys:* Masters Lacy and Donellan.'
Wouldn't it be fab to say *Oh no,*
I'll never have boyfriends, only lovers
(and, even better, some dull cluck to say it to)?
    Given time she'd be found à Paris,
learning to smoke smelly cigarettes,
holding hands with her negro lover.
Then they'd go back to LeRoi's home town where 'Yes,'
she'd tell Mayor Beauregard, 'yes I am a niggerlover.
And proud of it!'
    Later, when their home got torched,
they'd hurry round the world to visit The Shire:
where the only sign of change, of contemplating change, was

Your All New Concept In Sixties Shopping The Fair.
                                             Oh yes
and lovers love and lovers hate and lovers let you say
See, I'm being vulnerable, just for you.
                         Hannah, of course,
would get that hunted out for her one day.
Not yet.

Frenchy!

    Ray told her gags, that's how it went for starters.
Her name was Chrissie, her school was the Academy
and Catholics intrigued him: all their saints, martyrs
and confessions.
                 Though *You won't find a sadder me . . .*
Ray wanted to admit, in words which never arrived:
not now, not after their first kiss/
that first brush against her tits keeping him alive
enough not to ask *Make the joker happy, okay, Chris?*
(A heap of life was starting to unfurl.
Someone or God must've waved a wand.)
    And The Shire might laugh but this was Frenchy's girl.
Did she like Dylan? He'd bring round 'Blonde on Blonde'.
They quipped and giggled, they quarrelled and they bantered.
Ray was dazzled; Chrissie seemed enchanted;
but also canny: 'You'll have to wear the thing,
right Ray? Right? When we . . . when we do it?
True Ray, I'm a goner if ever the sperm goes *ping?*'
Which was sinful, sure, and Chrissie knew it,
but, since everything was, that idea just got shivered-
away; she'd better wars to win: like lining up one more clever missy
and sending her livid:
to announce (as if it wasn't known) 'I'm Chrissie . . .
Ray Donellan's girl?' with this to get taken as read
One day we're getting married?
                         So, after work
that Saturday, they lay down on a bed;
Ray put on the thing. They went berserk!

Their minds just ceased. All reason seemed on strike.'
My God!' they howled, 'so this is what it's like!'

GoGo!

    Neil and Frenchy took Kim to The Crusade
(in any event its softer-edged youth chapter).
Though Hannah was in attendance these three stayed.
Something, it seemed, had spiritually zapped her

and, since she was easy game to cop the raz,
they were rapt! Neil had said 'Hey guys,
remember how Miss Little sure chucks a spaz?'
But being on one of her superior highs

they were ignored. Which did her with them!
(Them battening down – like hell – their wildish oats.)
    Yet the evening held little for Kim. *I mean (ahem!)*
candles melting into flagons, raisin toast, duffle coats

and folk songs?! Makes me wanna order bourbon
on da rocks. What passed for current youth trends
bemused him though: he'd sit through the Inter-suburban
Christian Crusade, just to please his friends.

    Whilst Neil, set on giving an optimist's burl,
told how, after the prayers were sprinted through,
religion hardly happened; even better the odd okay girl
was around. Kim was going to like it, he just knew.

    And yet, Neil also guessed, wherever tonight's fun is,
it's not with Hannah. No matter what made her
such a write-off she was one. And he cast for substitute bunnies . . .
till, enter none other than the chief crusader.

    Now excitement can be one mighty common source
of toothy smiles plus quite wayward spittle.

Well, there he stood beaming with maximum force:
the Reverend Mac, spraying Hannah Little.

    So, 'Go on Frenchy stir Mac, stir him stir him . . .'
Neil sounded frantic; Donellan hardly budged
(once only a cyclone, an earthquake, would deter him).
As through their brains this mini-serum trudged:

'I'm pleased to announce,' glowed the Reverend Mac,
'most pop stars take their bibles . . . everywhere!'
    With little to defend, much less attack,
what could Neil do but shrug *Who'd bloody care?*

and embarrassed ask: 'Micks get it this bad, Space?'
    There was quiet, Lacy slowly smiled
in return the smile he had to: his face
saying most-to-all-of-it *Man! you are getting it mild!*

    'Well . . . this much into The Crusade how's it strike you?'
    It struck Kim that Neil wished to be charmed:
'Since y' something of a groover, and we like you,
I rebaptise thee . . . "GoGo"!'
                      And GoGo got disarmed:
'Compared with you Catholics us lot can only rate
as bland: no buckling knees, guts churning to water.
But Mac's so bad,' Neil promised Kim, 'he's great.
We can say anything, get away with slaughter.

He's not the Pope!'
                 He's not indeed thought Kim
(So how's this other half live? They live as dags.)
and smiled over to this Mac.
                        Who grinned back at him.
Just a few Shire tearaways, a coupla wags,

each one here for the Godstuff the minister understood
whether they know it or not.
    And Ray remained silent. Had he turned goody-good?
Was such little stirring all that the night had got?

Once this had seemed like Frenchy-business: playing that jerk
or two beyond the smartarse (talk about poppin' y' pimples
in public!) He'd let GoGo do that kind of work,
now. Changes were abroad. For it was this simple

(with folks radiant and his mates amazed
that a certain ruthless ease had dispatched
the old Ray, that the full bore Donellan blaze
was lowered more than a touch): The Frenchman was attached!

   'Oh these are grouse days, birds, fellas,'
came the Reverend Mac's well-intentioned ranging
of their culture. 'For, as The Beatles tell us,
the times they are certainly a-changing.'

   What could Neil do (God's man turning pally)
but issue a more than audible moan
Stuff The Beatles! Give us Rudy Vallee!
And cup his hands into a megaphone.

   Hey! Yeah! Kim was going to like it!

Spacey!

(1)
   If anything bewildered Kim the Crusade sure had.
Either that or his friends' response:

sending up their swingin' Reverend Mac
and his already out-of-date brush-back.

Neil and Ray must've known things Kim certainly didn't,
one more full o' shit sky pilot if you asked him.

And you wouldn't want to do this often, I mean
any laughs must get thinner and thinner, eh fellas?

But *No!* GoGo promised and *No!* Frenchy backed him
Just wait for this one, this one's a scream!

    Lapsed holy rollers were weird but.
No wonder they needed their Catholics for friends.

Catholics to ask them: Yeah but where's the actual joke?
You know: the hohoho the hahaha?

And then *Nahnahnah* there was Hannah Little:
faced allcrunchedup with *What? You?* Yep, him, Lacy,

daring you sweetheart to, go on, convert me.
    No, it wasn't his friends that made Kim feel annoyed.

And no, it didn't bore him so much. He just kept thinking:
Yeah but where's the drama? One Sunday evening

you're in this hall beside a church, sitting at a table,
laughing at some silly prick and his attempts

to speak 'a relevant language for today's youth'.
And, as each word of the Reverend's text was added to the next,

Kim understood what relevance, real relevance, was:

throughout The Shire and beyond, with the world turning-on,

there was a life to be led, a living to be made.

(II)
    And, if you had to rebel better it was done

so no-one knew of your rebellion. How about this to finish off
high school then: an inevitable bra run up a flagpole?

Sure he could understand such daggy elan,
but knew it for a Frenchy-GoGo coproduction.

Better you just smile your Lacy smile, keeping in great
with folks, all folks. And if you sat exams,

wondering where you'd land and what you'd land in,
at least out there Kim would be in charge of Kim.

The years were made for him. He hardly required
My my these are fab times from any Reverend *Call me* Mac;

didn't need mates touting certain of his skills either:
'Oh Mac, this is our friend Spacey . . . who plays one mean gui-tar.'

Take little notice Father, or whatever you are,
thought Kim weaving out of embarrassment *it's almost a con job.*

Sure I can pluck more than a few obligatory chords,
but guit-ar? Who doesn't play the gui-tar? Or try to?

And Mac, stop rewriting youth culture. Just make it work for you.
Number One will get what he deserves and feel great!

(III)
      Someone had been hired to work Spacey's father's
latest garden into really something: shrubs and rocks,

all these shrubs and all these rocks.
(They may have owned the place and may have not.)

Then, with the shrubs but not the rocks, they moved.
The Lacys always moved.

      And you know the tale: a circus, a rock group, the world
itself arrives in town, stops for a while then leaves;

and how a young man hurries after them:
he fears remaining *You know who from you know where*

but worse, being asked that moment his life will conclude
What, didn't you do more? That summer,

after the world (let alone The Crusade) had dropped in on The Shire,
where was Kim? Out following the world.

    'Anyone seen Spacey?' Ray wondered/Neil asked.
No-one else was bothering. If he were worth the mystery

there should've been rumours sweeping down from the Gold Coast,
a few sightings traced to the Northern Beaches,

intelligence reports out of The Cross.
                                        The best and worst
About The Shire was its consensus, and if Kim had mattered much

it was allowing such consensus an excuse to spit out *Pest!*
Though once he vanished, provided no girl was pregnant/

there weren't any outstanding debts ... best thing he ever did!

(IV)   Not for Neil it was.

Ditch-digging with the Water Board/
not wanting to attend uni but knowing he must,

'Might've told us where he's gone,' got whined at Ray.
What would The Shire talk about now? Kim's disappearance

if it were worth The Shire's while. Otherwise, GoGo,
nothing, like it always did.
                              The summer had grown this edge

to Ray: now he was stropping it, honing it
on Neil's obsession: Spacey the spaceman?

Even by his absence still the bignoter, still bor-ing:
'What he'll tell us (and he'll tell us) won't be

what happened: jackeroo, pearl diver, contract killer, pimp:
bet he's clearing tables in some pub, slopping-up

after the customers leave. At the most!'
Yes quite an edge.

Must've gone with the girlfriend. And whenever he half-sang
'Under My Thumb' there was only one thing

Ray wanted believed (and no he wasn't ditching Dylan
for The Stones). 'How'd I do it? Sold myself.

Told her *I'm a boy you're a girl
this is what happens.* Bet those nuns

never taught Chrissie *That* . . . Girls?' he elaborated,
'Tell' em we're growing up. Growing up. That's the trick.

And remind yourself GoGo: I'm eighteen,
in possession of the big legal: I can drive, marry, join the army .. .'

(v)
          . . . and one Saturday arvo in early March head to the saloon
bar of the Pacific Inn. Where, prodigal with a pool cue,

there was Lacy. And, though no-one quite said
Hey! like Spacey you could at least try:

'Why like hey! Spaceman! Where've y' been?'
        Where would you like him to have been?

Kim knew his friend not to have the imagination
which would consider *Yeah, but what's he done?*

Here's what *Gone out to see how the world
assembles itself. And then the way it all works.*
                                          So why take Neil

lurching on the high seas of (dare he term it?) truth?
Kim knew much safer shores: Shiretalk:

'Hey! GoGo! Don't dare lie and say you've missed me.
I'll buy the first round, then we can rock 'n' roll!'

Hannah Little (III)

    When her results arrived
Hannah had slowly lowered the needle onto
side two track two and waited till,
    with the Wiener Singverein
she could tell the living, dining and every other room
at 43 Karringal Crescent
    Freude, schöner Götterfunken,
    Tochter aus Elysium . . .
After which she phoned the shop. And
of all the people she had ever known, her mother
    couldn't stop howling
'I am so proud of her, I am so proud of her . . .'
That's right the Deputy Shire President, her mother
    who, whenever the Liberals arrived
(and even the Labor) with *How about it Margot?*
advised them from her disdainful distance
    My vote is my own.

    So much was set to change now:
Hannah was going to read and write
    everything she ever wanted to,
find new ideas, get herself new friends.
She wouldn't leave home yet of course
    but working part time
at The Fair save, and after a few years of that
move into a flat and see where she'd land.
    But now, all she thought of
was what she wanted to start
(and even better what she wanted finished).
    And there would be a man
– yes a man at last; just like her results
God would mean it, mean it to happen.

'I will be disdainful too,'
she found herself announcing. 'Distrustful, disreputable,
the chaser not the chased, full-to-overflowing disproportionate.
I will jettison so much: being just-a-girl
with all those ignorant stumblebum boys
    not really knowing how I feel . . .'
And, after which, how about that pragmatic aura
shimmering from the Reverend Mac?
    But why not sweep all-that-
and-more into the moralising grab bag which was
The Shire? She was sick of the place but worse,
    until her marks,
Hannah had never known. 'The results,' she kept repeating,
'the results have arrived. And so have I!'

Part 3

Geoff	Anglican curate
Julie } Lindsay Price } Margaret }	high-school students, Blackburn South
Jack	Julie's Lover
Julie's Mother	
Bernie Millar	Jack's friend
The Baron	aka The Kid, taxi driver
Karl	Lindsay's friend at university
Dave Price	Lindsay's father

GEOFF, JULIE, ST EDWIN'S AND THE WORLD

And all Fathers, Mothers, Masters and Dames shall cause their children, servants and prentices (which have not learned their catechism) to come to the church at the time appointed and obediently to hear, and be ordered by the curate, until such time as they have learned all that is here appointed for them to learn.

FROM THE INSTRUCTIONS ATTENDING THE ANGLICAN CATECHISM,
The Book of Common Prayer

1
    Err . . . *staying good looks primitive if easy . . .*
Umm . . . *we'll scrub your sins whenever it's requested . . .*
St Edwin's curate, bluff, burly, breezy,
seems bored with such thoughts, hardly interested.

Still, teeners at his confirmation classes
delight him: little palls. Given the on-cue
schedule, seven to eight, their hour passes
brisk as now, August '62.

    So with a modest skim through three girlie mags
(would Christ be blind to this, stone deaf
to the Top Forty?) 'See here Lord . . .' he begs
'a parish that'll call me Father Geoff . . .'

and name a worthwhile priest who, dumped in his shoes,
wouldn't. To heave a stoic Gary Cooper 'yup'
at Blackburn South is why he's here. Given issues
or hoopla ('Four Corners' or 'Sunnyside Up')

the circus wins: the vestry's drone, the manic cluck
of Young Wives. 'All's inevitable . . .' Geoff sighs, 'and I?
A wistful-anxious suburban Friar Tuck
who . . . look, what's my exact lot?' he asks the sky.

'To offer gargles of spiritual Listerine?
To start obscure if semi-risqué bible stories
that finish bland as *Weekend Magazine?*'
Yet who'd jeopardise the full marks earnt for his

firm hand, resounding baritone and flair
with youngsters?
                Grounds awash with teen-talk
'whacker' he catches, 'growly "big deal" square!'
This last word scraping his night like angry chalk

(a mindless term, bigoted, know-nothing)
and, spitting hard at a war cry every novice
conformist never forgets, our pipe-puffing
curate steams, bowl filled, towards his office.

    And how to combat such adolescent mayhem?
J. C. was hip but, hey, did he dig squares!?
Dear Jesus never! He'd outdo Billy Graham,
imagine their gaping mouths, their pop-eyed stares:

Geoff's flipped his wig!
                No, not even Yahweh deflects
St Edwin's calm; if ever the parish trembles
it's more (iconoclasts deferred) an FX
revving. To such a fanfare his group assembles.

2
    Each class, of course, each lesson has 'em:
the unsettlers (one per night doling the grit).
Still, Geoff leaps whenever the chasm
presents.
       Dogs they ain't, can't just 'sit boy sit'.

But silly kid looks as if (whilst he begins
to colour, *if not quite for himself*) *she's driven
by hormones or imagination*. 'Err sins,' he coughs, 'sins
are transient.' *Odd word that*. 'They're forgiven.'

Probably thinks I'm keen. Keep her guessin'
Lust, affection, love, there's always a name for it.
(And this one's Lynne. Her bum improves each lesson.)
'But evil's permanent. Who'll we blame for it?'

    'S-s-satan?' squeaks Beryl, spotty and devout.
    'Kids he ain't on! 'scuse the grammar.
You seen Old Nick? It's man who slogs it out . . .'
In Laos, Geoff reminds them, Alabama.

Oh for that faith-plus-faith with God's insistence
he umpire teenage bouts of pick-the-square.
Then 'Choose Mr K's peaceful co-existence:
err *Man Junior* with . . . *The Book of Common Prayer!*'

he'd suggest (ripples coursing each skirt,
every trouser) cough, smile. And grins never hurt you:
post-class a whopper's planned: Lynne-the-flirt
as target; her confused if randy virtue

almost needs it. *Mine does* he knows *there's such fiction
in abstinence, even celibacy is a form of 'sex'.*
    Then giving part ta-taa, part benediction,
he closes these proceedings till the next.

3
    But a girl (not Beryl not Lynne) Julie approaches.
    Still mourning that parent recently deceased?
Geoff wonders, being a cautious man who broaches
such subjects with reluctance. What has this priest,

and what has his or any faith, for a child
whose father died last March?
Little, he fears.
              And it's hard to get beguiled
by the girl, or her phrases in their starched

and ironed English: 'You see . . . my mother . . .'
                                        'Feel harassed?'
When in doubt Geoff's glib; Julie stares.

This one he thinks *could never get embarrassed,*
'Often the case,' he continues. *Little iceberg's frightful, shares*

in herself since birth. Okay missy, what?
'What? Need to stop?'
                              She wants . . . my mother . . .'
There's a shrug.
              'Give it a week.'
                              And they part: her eyes shot
with pale-grey arrogance.

4
              Clouds commence their cover;

wind snaps out from the paddocks; but winter's closing
and, to show this neighbourhood how to behave
towards clergymen a local crank, hosing,
turns towards the curate, signalling a wave,

which is returned.
              Once more Geoff's popularity zooms
in spite of his requirements. Perfectly credentialled,
for any Ladies Guild summary of eligible grooms,
in him a minister's essences are, it seems, essentialled:

no Man of God's wrist was lesser than limp!
     Then, for comparison, his claque snorted
and tsked over one Molinari, pimp-
to-the-slums, recently deported.

If *there* was a true beast, *theirs* is a real man!
     Well, Geoff's a kind one. Why should *he* snicker
at his parish's day-to-day belief span
(nothing being too worldly for this vicar):

that espresso bars breed darkly-hinted vices,
how the Bombers are firming favourites for the flag?

5
>   But weeks are whirlpooling into the Cuban Crisis
and, leaving his rocking chair, JFK, a stag

craning his head, sniffs the atmosphere,
sensing questions: shall eternity stop dead in
his and the planet's tracks, or, will fate veer
towards life again, Armageddon

cancelled?
>   With such doubling of already-doubled dares
(the stakes demanding brinkmanship implode
into compromise) heeding St Edwin's and all other prayers
(what else is his parish but the globe?)

God, as a muscular padre separating brawlers,
will command *Thou shalt survive.*
And we will, at least, continue (all is
never' on hold' *that* long) breathing again, remain alive;

whilst the combatants, staggering back blotto
with that power of having been themselves, will curl
up in the crib of history.

6
>   Should tonight hold a motto
for Geoff, Julie, St Edwin's and the world

it's sure to sound inevitable *They'll sow it
you'll reap it* as if a crueller deity has found in them
clients for fate or the bomb or some poet
anticipating rhymes and shaping lines around them.

>   So bye-bye the pretty the fair the sweet the nice;
here's what you'll earn, Julie, out of any past/
any future *You may be innocent, that's your price.*
(Like all fatuous dictums designed to last.)

>   For at thirteen who's to understand what can spark
both anger and regret in a spouse? Grief dove-

tailing into irony into the absurd, next year a plaque,
his, St Edwin's first, will read *Ever Loving Ever Loved;*

whilst when her mother states 'It's him we have to thank
for this . . .' she knows why, knows the ferocity
of what he was: a late middle-aged Englishman who drank,
wanted his way and, given the velocity

of such needs, invariably got them. In spite of that insistence
they retain respect, theirs was hardly a Mum, Dad
and the kids existence.
What curate could guess, would understand, how glad

she is, how, only now, she can describe herself as *clean*
or, better, call him *dead man.*
                                And her fears
are re-aligned: with spleen
on hold it's the heart's turn. After what passed for tears

Poor wretch she got told *unable to sup*
on his child's love till her flowers hit the lid.
Later (with that much disposed) Julie raised a small cup
to *dead man,* what he did

as father to daughter, husband to wife.
    Then, heading her list of intentions
is to grab the proverbial swung cat and scythe
'round their cramped, dwelling-at-rear pretensions.

So ''ooddersfield!' she'll mimic. Maybe it's open slaughter
on dreams? With such words to lash her
mother she can survive; being an unplanned only daughter
of a terminal drunk and an immigrant haberdasher,

all bought and sold with a currency of threats,
has points. A hate (distilled, focused)
runs their home; and this hate works: no-one frets,
its generator-chug is hardly noticed;

they can, they will, exist. Tell them any rewards are few
and you're given the blessing-to-curse
ratio of Blackburn South, 1962:
life remains elsewhere, somehow, worse.

7
    Late that afternoon she'd changed from school clothes
into not much: slacks, blouse, jacket;
studied Saturday Russian.
                          Now she's standing with those,
the charmingly intolerant, whose racket

of shouts greet the ever-grinning, light-
weight, bible study chief (a pun
for every occasion: Bildad the Shoe Height . . .
get it? None will.)
                Her hair bunned

back over a damp Yorkshire face
mottled with acne scraps, haughty
if you think she is, you may also trace,
with guesswork, a future: at forty,

at fifty, she won't be very different. Couldn't
be: Julie will rebel, will rule
and, ever failing, know what shouldn't
happen, shall. She'll let events, like curates, drool

upon their Lynnes and Beryls (though, please, not on her).
If kids like these must find excuse
for such attempts, let them. Believe shit? You're a goner,
period. Creation's a scaffold, life's a noose

from which she'll be reprieved, by no miracle
(partner to some mid-twentieth century swoon
of hers) but the entrance of a seedy angel: 'Wait girl,'
it shall announce, 'someone's set to love you soon.'

8
    For nearer town a man who doesn't know
he awaits Julie, waits with a further eighteen months
of baggage to unpack, pack and tow
about. 'Yeah?' he glances, 'What stunts

you got in mind?' There'll be plenty,
and Jack can shiver off any resulting fuss:
Jack always has. Call him this innocent he
may be, though silly, verging to dangerous.

Knowing a world's there for his seizure (given
a failed con-artist of the partial hustle
could escape with it) he's almost driven
to those ideas, stunts, negotiations, muscles,

he'll never exactly use. With books to think on, jazz
to follow, what remains is a lemon, a pup.
    In this shadow she doesn't know she has:
Beware! beware: Julie's growing up!

1964: Jack in Love

    This July after working half a year
somewhere for someone, Bernie's in town again.
And, this Saturday morning, Melbourne's wind
is at its silly-bugger best, stopping a bit
though mostly recommencing.
                            He's staying,
as he always can, at 4/9: Jack's;
moving about is, after all, easy when
everything that's yours fits into less than
two rooms ... like at 4/9: Jack's,
where, back in Iris and Desley's time,
a welcome hardly spread itself for Bernie.
'Yeah, well put it this way ...'
he imagines himself explaining (of course he
never has) 'I over-did things then, yeah ...'
    All right they aren't 'that young' now,
though both seem young enough for challenges,
if they want them.

    Seems Jack wants them: since Bernie's been
up north he's grown himself a beard again:
neat but enough of it. Which hardly is
the challenge Julie is.
Earlier, Jack had mentioned Julie, and now
he'd like to say more. Bernie but
has to talk about his prick:
'A few Fridays back I went out, got very silly
with it, stupid, matey, all weekend.
Damn thing didn't understand how to call it quits ...'
Gave him the flu for a while, there's still
a bit left ... Though at eleven-thirty
or any time, stories that are hardly stories
fuel Jack's impatience. 'Lunchtime,' he interrupts,
'I'm meeting Julie, after her Russian class.'
And 'Sure matey,' Bernie tells him having
heard his fill at breakfast, 'her Russian class.'

Two years before, whilst Jack was up in Brisbane,
what remained of Denise got found in a lane:
a place you moved through, or only stopped
to leak in. Who did it, what they did it with,
will never be 'located', and the chill of such
a neutral word has satisfied Jack.
By now he's getting beyond Denise,
though old friends can still expect things like
'If it's walking, root it . . . your motto? Eh, Bern?'
And Bern will soak this into him as only a mate
would want to. But over April/May, Denise
got a replacement; then Jack went ambitious,
replacing *her*. By now though, ambition or
anything, Bernie has to sigh.
Sure, they've had years alternating sighs:
his concern for Jack, Jack's in return.
This though is a bonus: for with it,
with *Fifteen, Jack* he tries reminding just
how fifteen any girl of fifteen always is.
It's all he seems to be saying, all he
wants to say, that and what he'll call her
Your schoolgirl, Jack; cynically benign in
his dealing out of options, or rather where
she's doubtless headed, given where she's from.
'Dreadful folks? There's always dreadful folks,
in a dreadful home. That more than
goes with the scenery, it *is* the scenery
and Jack, you'll never be that. You mightn't
get caught but she'll go somewhere, Jack,
your schoolgirl will go, she's made to
be lost.' (Though Jack's going to keep at it,
making Bernie quite in excess of
mere bewildered.) 'Never wanted to know
her name. Don't want to know her, Jack,
nor meet her . . .' knowing both will happen.
For Bernie's smart:
honest enough to predict he'll never like Julie,
prick enough to know he'll call her Jools.
Perhaps it's something about her wanting to see
Continental films, the liking to understand

jazz, though over all that Bernie's aware
of her needing to obtain all
the appropriate jargon. And speaking of words:
'You're Jack, right, but what Jack:
Perry? Isaacs? Williams?'
There has to be a smile: Name? Surname?
Won't that depend on the state he's in?
    She could pass for twenty, pass for twelve,
and here, on this city corner
with the winds, the sun-showers,
damp pommy-pale Julie, would be
near invisible, except two men approach her.
She knows one and the other wants to leave.
There's bands around her teeth,
and she's not 'exactly Jack' except
like all of them before she has to be
enchanted. Then Jack can be.
Well they both are.
    Bernie's friend's in love, Bernie's friend's
double her age and more, Bernie's friend's
an idiot. And although Jack can't see
his oscillating concern/despair,
Julie can; whilst her eyes, with all that
proper jargon behind them, tell it simply:
a deadshit is being despised.
    'See you both . . .' they'll need the flat,
he'll see another friend.
'Pleased to meet you Jools.'
    Soon as he's gone her hair's unwound
from its bun. With the wind doing something
near enough to magic for Julie, Jack
is bringing her home.

A Lecture on Love

(1)
     Some afternoons Julie walks home from school
with Lindsay Price: he isn't a friend but he will
listen. Or rather Lindsay would like, would love,
to know.
     And Julie doesn't mind explaining:
how she and Jack first met, how she keeps on
meeting her man, even though her mother is learning
all that the law can do to them.
     Jack is thirty-six;
he works when he has to; reads heaps.
His bookshelf has that heady tang (American paperbacks
seem to possess it) of knowledge brewing; brewing
for Julie. They drink together, and the rest,
he takes her to films, they go out to jazz,
plenty of it.
     Julie isn't cultivating Lindsay,
she doesn't ask *Keep this to yourself*
she only knows how most of their class began
despising her about the time she was returning
the same, and, though Lindsay's tolerated,
when the moment arrives he'll be seen to fall in
with the others.
     But now, at least,
he wants a story and Julie gives it.
   'Does Jack call you?'
                   'Every night.'
   'What does your mother do?'
                         'Not much .. ,.'
    Not much though Julie knows she is about to
carry through those threats. Life in Australia
is closing: byebye the haberdashery business,
an immigrant's attempted better life.
Time to remind your daughter 'home' now
is some other place: Huddersfield.

                    If this were
the kind of film Julie sees with Jack
she might tell Lindsay *I'll live with him, one day.*
    Not now of course. Now they're doomed,
doomed to be discovered.
                    And Julie couldn't
run away: runaways can't stick it out,
runaways never had class; they (alas
for them) don't have Jack to, one day,
conquer all.
    Lindsay, with his shy
but bullish charm, has read somewhere
this etiquette: it's quite okay to ask
a girl how her boyfriend is: that's nice,
it is appreciated.
                    And how is Jack?
Lindsay won't be told but people are always
giving guns and things to Jack
(try telling that to the rest of the world!).
Needing one hidden, he gives it to
the girl he loves.

(II)
        Julie can gossip gossip (her own)
to Lindsay, but no-one in class gets
her respect like Margaret does. She's watched Julie
through it all and understands; is worth it.
        Margaret knows Jack; somehow through her
big brother Julie met the man: at the girls' age
it's starting to be the right time for such patterns:
anyone being connected with everyone: a near virus,
something most adults wish would never occur,
except it gives them someone to blame.
And, Margaret in her sights, Julie's mother
improves her blaming. When your only daughter is
besotted with some ex-crim beatnik
over twice her age, what else is left
but blame the friend and plan to finish everything:
Jack and his liquor, Jack and his books and films;

Jack and his past (yes she's found the gun);
Jack and his jazz (as he calls it,
as they think it is); Jack, Julie and all
their love (as he calls it, as they think it is).

(III)
      Once when Julie stays away
for a week, Lindsay Price asks Margaret
'Jack?'
     'Jack?' She answers:
going on forty, going on fourteen: his name
or names depend on which city he is in.
If ever he goes into business she'd hate
to be the customer. Few his age will
have him: so he gets away with pretty much
the rest of it. Which means Julie, which means
romance.
      Margaret teaches Lindsay Price
about romance, Jack ' n' Julie style: 'Well yes,
there is romance unless another girl is in
Teen Idol's bed ... my brother knows him,
wishes he didn't now ... Julie's mother met him
once, saw the crumb he was and started in
on me! Her daughter may know more,
may have done more, than anyone at this school,
but I've been watching the dumbest show
I've ever seen. And Lindsay,
let's just say it's getting worse.'

(IV)
     The class discussion verges on debate:
and Julie will say, or have prepared,
a few words about those things which matter
a lot, in life.
      Then, some way through,
knowing she wants to shelve the appropriate
low level adolescent gibberish, 'Okay,'
she announces, 'really I have to speak
from experience alone. And it is love!'
She's telling hard:' *You* may not have seen it

but *I* have, *I* have.'
                A lecture on love,
Julie is giving a lecture on love!
   'And if you've seen it,' Margaret wonders,
'what are we meant to think your Jack-love
does? Pilot flying saucers? Why not just
throw out whatever script remains
and announce, as you've announced to me
*One Friday I'll be here, the following Monday
I won't.'*
            No-one wants to look at Mrs, their teacher,
catch how she's reacting; and Lindsay,
who's embarrassed but can't say why,
is thinking 'Must she catwalk her life
and all this Jack to us? Where'd the topic go?
Was there ever one?'
                    This is the topic now:
Julie, or rather Jack: whose girl is hectoring
'A man for a woman, a woman for a man ...'
and 'How could *your* experience ever measure mine ...'
and 'If you have never felt what I have felt
it's your loss.'
            'She hates us.' Lindsay is puzzled
but no longer puzzled. 'Even me, even Margaret:
Julie hates us.'

(v)
     George and Diane, Beryl, Lindsay, Baz:
she wastes a voicebox mouthing so much jazz
at all these has-beens. She'll stick with the has.

     And even Mrs, embarrassed Madam Chair,
who has ideas what is and is not fair,
shuffles herself into a bug-eyed stare.

A progressive teacher, if reasonably well bred,
her tolerance spans a mighty A to Z.
But no-one taught this when she did Dip.Ed.

(The migraine comes later, right now she'd love a Bex.)
    As argument shakes off balances and checks
a barrage of moans erupts from either sex:

give us a break, need we sit through this
too-clever-by-half-then-add-some little miss
A war cry gathers *Let's take out the piss!*

    Then volleys rebounding like Emerson's and Laver's,
Julie's speech turns tirade and oh save us!
disintegrates into these semi-quavers.

For love was hardly anything like she feared
nothing nasty nor approaching weird,
just a lean man, kindly with a beard.

    (How can we tell the mug shot from the mug,
man, you dig? She was asked and dug.
Her trough was full. But mother's pulled the plug.)

    And Mrs glares to see nobody smiles
until this girl is back in the British Isles.
    Set to steam away twelve thousand miles,

Julie, your ship awaits.
                    Well yo heave ho:
girls end like this when Jack becomes your beau.
    Margaret tells herself *I told you so . . .*

(VI)
    oh yes she meant to.
Even if she didn't mean she meant to.
    Margaret knows boys and how to skittle' em.
It's men, men like Jack, she'd prefer
off to the gas chambers one two three!
    Julie phones her friend
and Margaret's told 'If I left home
where would I go? Your place? Jack's?
Jack says they always find you.

Mum, I know, is getting me sent some place soon,
some place for the sort of girl she thinks I am.
Then we'll leave. But Jack will wait I know he will.
They're shutting us out. They think we'll never see
each other. I'm writing him this note, though,
and sending it to you. Get it to him, please.'
  And Margaret reads ... *I'm very happy with you
Darling Jack, but you must know, you must understand
how unhappy, very unhappy they are making me ...*

  He gets the note, but through no love of Margaret's,
Margaret who finds a certain grimy humour in the deal,
Margaret who knows Jack will never be caught.

  And of course the mother found the gun,
it's like a diary, mothers are meant to, and now
she wants the criminal just forgotten, that's understood:
they may be leaving the shop and Australia but,
even in departure, who wouldn't want respect?
  Here comes a Friday,
there goes a Monday; by Wednesday
Margaret is asked to clear out
Julie's locker.
    'And do you know;
Lindsay's told, 'what I found there?
A pamphlet on The Pill! I put that on the top
of the pile and dumped it at the office!'
(Who could dispute Margaret's vindication?
Let Julie's mother, the teaching and the office staff
look on that!) 'I know my worth's beyond
all their blame and judgement. Julie and her love,
Jack and his girls, books, jazz and friggin' gun!
That's the last time I clean up slops for anyone!
Hah!'

Out of Trouble:
The Baron Hits the Road

for Joe Deiacovo

    ...so a man tries making his way in the world
and as (or more likely when) a kid got to know
what trouble could be (or more likely was) then,
for a time, that kid was inoculated.
This, though, was the trouble with trouble: it mutated:
last week's was hardly last year's, last century's.
Just never raise your head, fly low and learn;
fly so close to the ground and, in the taxi game,
they'll call you, just as they called him, The Baron or
The Red Baron (just like in that song).
                                She hated it.
    After their wedding *(And her for a wife*
was the dumbest thing I ever did)
you'd think they survive their drive back
to the flat. Some thought! There'd been a sharp, brief blue,
with half a mile to go. He'd turfed her out,
headed south. And smarting from what her sister said
an hour before, he sucked the bong his wife had packed
and, just past Gardenvale, parked,
taking long breaths in front of the neat dazzle
that was Steve Dodd Toyota; in wedding gear,
downing more mull, his radio snatched some Saturday evening
rock 'n' roll.   Dodd was an almost-proven crook
(who hadn't caught those rumours that it wasn't
merely cars?) but posters of the boss
flanked by all his staff, halted The Baron.
Each smiled and each had his right hand extended;
sure they were crooked (worse still were deadshit dull)
but each, he knew, held some kind of life, *their* kind of life.
    '...and their symmetry!' The Baron croaked.
'That's the human race. Better return to the wedding.'

There'd been a florist's open so, back at Elwood,
the party hardly missing him, he entered,
a dozen red roses in hand, just like in
a song he'd heard; one of her brothers,
or was it one of his, suggesting that he'd be thumped
if he thumped her; only a threat it was the only threat.
No, he wouldn't hit back: skinny
in his wash-over of freckles, The Baron understood
he'd lose any fight with anyone.
       'Doesn't look,'
his best man Jack informed, 'as if she missed you.
Just came in and shrugged and said
she knew what you wanted, you knew what
she wanted and, if you both were good, you'd get it.'
  The noise got stopped. Jack spoke.
Nice things were said about the wife, and even him;
then someone put on The Bloody Red Baron song
and even *she* enjoyed it.
      Too much she did:
over the weeks half-humming
what happened after the century had turned,
half-bleating what the German skies were like,
till it became like a detergent jingle: trouble;
and he preferred being out on the road,
flying low, away from trouble;
trouble which was a marriage that would never last.
From that flat in Elwood to another in Elwood,
to that Richmond cottage and back again to Elwood,
Ten twenty thirty forty fifty times
she hummed and bleated.
      But as Jack explained to him
when he was twelve: 'Kid, women are, thankfully,
what on earth they are; you mustn't hit
or even hit back.'
     And he wouldn't, though
few were surprised when, six months on,
slamming the front door from its hinges,
The Baron left his wife. It was her door now,
he was out of trouble.

BERNIE AND JACK, LINDSAY AND KARL

Jack sees Lindsay hurrying from Bernie's.
Had something happened? *Hey!* he could've yelled
and *Stop!* but given he's avoided trouble since,
being charitable, last week, why start again?
The job's to check, that's why he waited
outside the rooming house. One can handle
trouble or one can't; but jack's loyal, he'll
find out.
    'Your friend in a hurry Bern?'
(Still alive? he feels like saying. *Nothing missing?)*
    'He's twenty-one, why couldn't he relax?'

But Bernie never lies to jack:
always needing new mates, thought he had one in
The Counterlunch Kid. Till a week back they'd both
worked The Whitehorse, Saturdays: him cooking,
the kid clearing; and Jack got shown this polaroid,
last year's Christmas do, started whistling 'Baby face'
then wolfed it: 'Cradle snatching, Bern?'
    'He's twenty-one, why wouldn't he like me?'
    'Because, mate, he mightn't do it.'
                                                    But Bernie
knew better, well a bit better, well thought he did.

'That cook at work ...' Lindsay would tell his friend
and 'This funny derro-type ...' and 'Bernie's a great drinker .
Can he hold it!'
               (But Karl's a snob: a solid
Y 'n' J booze session sounds rather like the first date
he doesn't know it will be: first 'n' only.)
    And Bernie's happy to see him; they're matching
it round for round until a mate, 'Jack,

an old old mate . . .' arrives. 'Got a root lined
up this arvo?'
        'Might've,' and Jack has to smile,
'we all might've.'
            Flushed and buoyed
the student laughs.
                The set-up's pathetic.
(Jack's tragedies are so much bleaker, stronger items):
a good half-dozen pots in you, a chaser or two
and, student, all your chances will've taken
the last train home.
'Nice meeting you Lindsay,
see you Bern, you animal.'

                ❧

              The deal's made
in the taxi: how, later, they can hit
a cat house: 'Don't say you've never been?'
Lindsay has to shrug, Bernie'll shout him.
    ('Waiting till you've left that job?' Jack had near-
admired him, 'you a-grade calculating prick!')
    At his place Bernie wants to wrestle,
Lindsay wants to drink, besides,
isn't the room too small? This place is ugly.
And green, why's everything so green?
    ('And if he won't?' asked Jack. 'But then,
as a big man you get what you're after.')
    So hup hup hup hup: Lindsay's floored.
    (Jack would have mentioned The American Sailor
except that one's a real Bernie special, and, well,
Jack never trusted his mate, so much,
after hearing it. Somewhere, in let's say, Kansas,
someone isn't saying *Mmm, friendly town, Melbourne*.)
    And, getting tumbled over, feeling bristles
scrape his neck, hearing 'C'mon', Bernie moaning
'Come on', Lindsay starts to learn.

                ❧

Karl is having problems with an essay:
tonight he'll drive to the Prices and discuss,
he doesn't know yet, anything but it.
Dave Price is pacing his living room and,
watching him, Mother, Lindsay and Dot
turn to Karl. *Have I?* his face is asking and
How, exactly? and *What combination of
right guy/wrong guy, right time/wrong time
applies here?*

   'Bunyip,' says a sombre Dave,
'please stay.' He gets his son to tell:
what someone tried to do with him; and how he
didn't guess, know, understand this Millar,
this peanut Bernie Millar with his hare lip and
his problems was like that!

  Karl's throat sighs *Errgh* and *Great tale*
he *thinks, glad it's yours*. He knows the Prices,
anticipates that next he'll hear 'Okay son,
we love you son.' He's determined never to be
that kind of naive; to have friends certainly,
but never mates: this is what mates do:
promise to get you pissed then try anything
they care.

   In his room Lindsay says
'It wasn't all. At the pub we wrestled sometimes.
Sometimes grabbed each other. Once a few weeks back,
I cracked this fat, don't know why. He's a deadshit.'

  And, being a snob with words, these phrases
simply gag Karl, though for his friends he suffers them:
revelling in those silent ideas of the quietly pompous:
e.g. when, if ever, will our adolescence end?

∾

  Until further notice Dave gives his family
their mission: they are to sleep with cricket bats,
as a phalanx, it seems of Millars, of Bernie Millars
is heading in battered Valiants east
along Canterbury Rd.

∾

		Jack knows that
after a good half hour of the pity and
the blubber Bernie survives: tough and hopeless,
like gristle but endearing, he'll salvage anything:
he'll 'Shout us both. Like that time in Rocky mate.'
Yeah. Those things you're capable of:
sharing that spaced out underaged chow
in some obscure tropical knockshop.
		'Some call it love, sleep on it Bern.'
But one day on he Crissakes he wants
to call the student, make it up.
Needs jack to do the phoning though.
		They share the earpiece; Lindsay lives at home;
he doesn't answer but a man is sneering
'That you Millar? Millar isn't it . . .'
					And,
very calm for Bernie, he's telling back
'Lins'll say different but your son wanted it,
Dad, wanted it bad.'
				Once, yesterday,
there'd been a master plan to prop his friend's
infatuation: it's all farce now and Jack,
who shouldn't laugh, has to leave the booth:
he's bouncing first one fist, and then the other,
off his forehead.

Part 4

NEIL
KIM
RAY
LIZ   .... YOUNG ADULTS, THE SHIRE AND BEYOND
MONICA
CHRISSIE
LOUISE
HANNAH

JACK .... FACILITATOR
BOB .... LIZ'S FIANCÉ
NAOMI .... SCHOOLGIRL
FAT DONALD .... HER FATHER
TOBY .... POET, FRIEND OF NEIL'S
KARL .... STUDENT POLITICIAN
THE SERGEANT .... ON R AND R
TOBY'S MOTHER
TOBY'S MENTOR
SAL. .... TOBY'S GIRLFRIEND

Catholics for Friends (ii)

for Wendy Smyrk

Prelude: Neil visits Liz. Monday, 12 June 1967, 4.10 p.m.

Of all kids 'GoGo', Neil Spencer, came visiting Liz,
talking about some girl he'd met, Saturday at a dance.
Almost after they'd kissed goodnight ('And, wow,
that was pretty good . . .') he started forgetting what this girl
looked like. By Sunday he'd lost all idea. Small? Yes small
but hardly tiny and yes she wore this cap.
    All else forgotten, 'Liz, I mean,' he asked, 'has it,
anything like it, happened to you?'
                                        She loved being quizzical
and *Mmmmm* told him no but then she could imagine it.
He shouldn't worry, mightn't Neil see the girl again?
Well yes, except earlier today he'd made this call,
which wasn't much of a one, and things had, somehow, stopped;
because he couldn't (this was the point!) recall the face!
    Neil and Liz's brother had 'Frenchy' for a friend,
'Frenchy' Donellan. Two years before Neil had written Liz
something of a love letter and, when there was no reply,
had disappeared; till now. Hell, thought Liz, if I'd taken
'GoGo' and his affections on, it might've been me
he couldn't remember! He was still distressed? Let her
deflect it: What had been his high school? Oh *that* one.
Well, did he know Hannah, Hannah Little, the girl next door
but one? (Sure did, alas.) Liz understood,
but told him how, once you got used to 'Miss Little'
(and *used* was a word Liz somewhat enjoyed)
Hannah seemed okay; even though she'd started uni now
was making friends with them, all of them,
Liz and her Academy friends, hitting it off with Monica,
not Louise so much nor Chrissie. Neil would love Monica,
Monica was too full-on. At Easter,
when they'd gone up to The Show, Liz, Monica,
Chrissie and Louise would pass these couples,

ab-so-lute-ly-be-sot-ted couples and *Young love!*
the four would chorus *Isn't it beautiful!*
Which continued for months.
                        Well Liz should talk.
And she told Neil a lot about Bob, Bob from
'dead centre of The Riverina'; and how 'since I'm sixteen
we could get married now . . . but no, I'll wait, wait
till I'm qualified and twenty. Almost know the date though.'
Some of her brother's friends wouldn't believe her.
She'd even this bet with dumb ol' 'Frenchy'. Ooops!
Wasn't he a friend of Neil's?
                    Something of one.
'But I believe you; Neil reassured, Liz seeming the most
determined girl he'd ever met.
                        Not as determined as her Bob though.
His mother never cared for Catholics, right? (The bush could get
like this.) 'Not that I'm much of a Catholic now.
Almost stopped going to mass . . .' Which doubtless fuelled Bob
even more: he'd joined the army and laid it
to his mother, straight: he was only eighteen, sure,
but he'd joined up to fight nonsense like hers and,
if there was a choice between his old lady
and Liz, this Catholic, it would be Liz.
                    They'd be married,
just watch 'em.   Unis, her mother would tell her,
Put on side. Still, Liz might try one, probably go
to teachers' college. End of '68 she'd be leaving here,
of course, getting a place closer to town,
perhaps with Monica and Louise; like 'GoGo' might
with 'Frenchy' and 'Spacey'. No? Which reminded her:
'Spacey' equalled Lacy, right? And all The Shire knew
why 'Frenchy' was 'Frenchy'. 'GoGo' but?
                        It was just
this name: he'd got it where you got anything
round here: from 'Spacey' of course.
                    'Spacey; he told her,
'can be fun . . .' The oldies, however, didn't like him,
never had.
        'Oh that's them!' She was, it seemed,

an authority on oldies.
 Though with
TEEN STAR ON LOVE DRUG CHARGE AND
4 A.M. PETTING AT DISCO,
life sure could make the oldies wonder,
poor oldies. Didn't understand, really, did they?
She mightn't know much more but Liz seemed certain:
what was on offer, what she wanted.
 'And you?' She became
almost this coach giving the half time rev,
bustling through strategies.
 'Eh?' He'd been caught.
 'And the girl, Neil?'
 'What girl?'
 Only the one
he'd met on Saturday!
 Neil seemed to enjoy his moan of
'Ohhh Saturday!' Nothing was more over.
 'No; Liz demanded,
'look at Bob and his mother. Have it out with her.'
 'Oh,' Neil agreed. (There was little he enjoyed
quite like agreeing.) 'Oh yes. Have it out.'
 Except,
what exactly was *it* and how was *it* to be had?

Theme and Variations: Hannah meets Liz, Monica, Chrissie and Louise. 1967–68.

Here's how, for a while, things went Hannah's way.
Look she'd tell herself *if there's a God there's a God*
but all I seem to have acquired is
this questionnaire: When you were (fill in appropriate age)
you 'got religion' for (ditto time-span)
until being disillusioned with (ditto deity).
 So, for the present, instead of God there'd be friends,
new friends.

            At forty
Hannah would re-imagine it this way:
she'd be looking at the cameras, announcing
. . . not that they were Catholics, total, but here,
if you can bear it, is who I found when I met
Liz, Monica, Chrissie and Louise . . .

⋘

   They were Academy girls, not much younger
than she was, though Liz had remained this acquaintance,
two houses up until, one day, at the bus stop,
anywhere, they got to talking: how Liz had a boyfriend,
a soldier (yes, someone needed to love them).
Then later, just before these kids returned to school,
they met again.
               So what were her subjects? Hannah asked,
suggesting she had books to sell, to lend, to give.
   Soon it was time for Hannah's checklist:
What do Catholics believe *really* believe?
Mightn't you have the grand-goddy of them all?
      'What do you think I am?' Liz laughed, 'a priest?'

⋘

   For the company Hannah arrived at their parties.
   She met Louise, sharp-but-pretty-faced Louise
(hardly much of a bust, who slouched a bit, sometimes).
          'She's good,' Liz said, 'not goody-good
but just that, good. I wish she knew it.'
   I know they're your friends
Hannah wished to tell Louise *and other friends*
can be a baggage, but look: I'm not taking over
right?
        Then there was the pinched pale one who squeaked
'Oh, I'm Chrissie . . .' then, knowing this needed
an elaboration would ask
'Ray Donellan's girl?' hoping to reassure herself
she was. And she was.
             Donellan!

the sound of which caved-in Hannah's stomach.
With Chrissie having a mortgage on *him*,
Neil Spencer, somehow, a friend of Liz,
and all Sydney aware of Kim Lacy,
when would her life stop intersecting with
The Shire's Three Stooges?
       She told Monica:
'Oh I'll end up in the old folks' home
with that lot: GoGo the grandpa, Spacey the senile,
and Frenchy the dirty old man!'
  And here was a girl Hannah could like,
actually like: when Monica Beck said it
she said it straight: 'One day, like our Mum'
I'll be getting my tubes done. If they'd let me now
I would.'
  Monica:
who knew how to use just that much mascara
to get a certain kind of boy, or fella,
going mmmm; and keep them that way . . .
I'd hardly cake-on all that stuff thought Hannah
but gee, it works with her!
       Monica played
a wonderful game; her wonderful game was m.e.n.
Could she help it if, for a father, she'd this
amazing sleaze? After he'd guessed how some of them
had skinny-dipped in his pool 'Girls; he'd pleaded,
'oh girls, girls, why didn't you wait for *meeee!*
. . . sure I'd be a mick,' and Jim Beck winked
his wink, 'a monk! But like you, Hannah,
the devil got me first!'

          ❧

       . . . *so there we were,*
before we got scattered throughout Sydney let alone
the world): surfing or avoiding anything to do
with the beach; hunting boys or shrinking from all
that went with them; coping with Old Man Beck
and his not-so-marvellous sleaze; explaining to Liz
'Sure you try telling my mother No, don't think I'll change

the world exactly, but then, why shouldn't I try?
    Knowing we were doing it all and more
till, one day, one moment, we'd just jolt out
of life, into eternity. Having any god sure helped
with that; unless it didn't.
                      Though it wouldn't require
eternity, yet, merely the years to scatter us:
Liz and Bob (I think Bob's still around)
run this motel somewhere; Louise moved to Melbourne;
Chrissie split from Dickface and doubtless is hitched
with Mark Two Dickface; Monica, so I'm told,
became a madam; and I am forty,
facing imaginary cameras,
constructing what passes for this far of my life.

Arias: Neil becomes friends with Louise, Kim gets to know Jack the barman. Late 1968 into 1969.

(1)
Poor Louise.
(you wouldn't know it, wouldn't want to know it, but
wouldn't-you-know-it!) being voted The Shire Bike!
For someone (not Monica, not Liz) had gossiped so

to Hannah.
Not that *they'd* know, not that you, they or anyone
was meant to. And sometimes hearing 'bike'
would get Hannah to verge on vomiting:

few terms seemed
so relentlessly two-faced. Yet, of course,
certain things made better sense to Hannah now. Poor poor Louise:
acquiring, of all boys, Spencer for a friend.

Insipid Neil Spencer who,
away from his mates Lacy and Donellan,
was so excessively zero. How Hannah dreaded him:
stopping-all-stations to Uni, telling her first off

(only off)
how he'd wait to see what the joint offered, right?
And, after doing that, how him being there was dumb,
mere wish fulfilment for his oldies:

just dumb:
an hour to get there, another to return.
And for what? To sit about a caf with the rest,
thinking how dumb it was, waiting to find out

what was on offer;
what, he supposed, Neil 'GoGo' Spencer was supposed
to study. His whinges tape-worming out he never bothered
to discover Hannah's. Not that she'd offer any.

Was Miss Louise O'Connor
more fortunate? If so: lucky, lucky Missy!
Then Hannah, intent on hi-jacking no-one's friend, paused herself
if (oh God please) I can't be good, let me be consistent!

Which should amuse
the deity, shouldn't it? (Little else about The Shire would.)
But Hannah had it rough? Hardly. Why look at Monica:
with a satyr and a missionary for parents.

(II)
Monica's mother
(when did the woman think they were living?)
disapproved of even netball: that uniform,
making them look like hussies!

So Monica knowing
you are what you wear proposed the team be called
The Hussies. With The Gidgets and The Widgies accommodated
by the competition, what was one more silly name?

Chrissie possibly,
Liz probably, Louise certainly, Mrs Beck would always disapprove:
for some kids just catch that disease none of them ever deserve:
'a reputation.'

(III)
                Often, though she was The Hussies' captain,

Louise felt stupid,
felt The Shire demanding, *What, her?* Felt even more *This better be
                worth it!*
(Which went beyond just boys, school, netball: life better be.)
Then Liz, who loved saying *You'll get on fine*

introduced Louise and Neil.
Who got on fine enough: Neil always telling about that other girl
he was intent on intending if only . . .
Which suited Louise: she'd never feel ridiculous

getting to like *him*
never have to explain *No Neil, we already
know ourselves too well for anything different to start*
since all she hoped to start was *Pardon my French* bugger-all.

Or he'd talk music,
well something like it: his friend Donellan was Dylan-crazed
and Lacy was a guitar natural but lazy with it.
One afternoon Neil improvised their team song

*A Hussy for me,
A Hussy for me,
if you're not a Hussy you're no good for me.
The Gidgets are small,
And The Widgies are tall,
But bonny wee Hussies the pride of them all.*

(IV)
'I'm not exactly
an authority,' Kim admitted, 'but Catholic girls,' he advised,
'either they won't allow you within a country mile,
or else it's full bore total and total again.'

catholics for friends (ii)

What fuss there was
over good Catholic girls and bad Catholic girls
(anyone caught not being good had to be bad, they had to!)
it seemed like a religion defining itself girl-wise,

nothing but;
poor girls! Neil considered The Inter-suburban Christian Crusade,
and how, even with the Reverend Mac's pallid doomed matchmaking:
Jesus with folk-rock, Kim hadn't smiled, Kim, who

as 'a Catholic-sortov',
seemed an authority on the good the bad and the even-more-so.
Being the bullshitter he was. No matter what he'd say
his eyes could look at, into, through and beyond you.

GoGo, they'd signal,
maybe all this is just code, my imagination,
but even if it is enjoy, man, anyway.
'There are good Catholic girls; there are, even better, bad Catholic girls.'

Shouldn't he know?
Or, if he didn't couldn't he, at least, guess?
Neil, by now bewildered, back-footed:
'But aren't they just like us? Err ahh growing up?'

Then Kim looked weird,
Neil might think they were *Just like us. Well* sure
they were, but more so, much more. And Go-mate would never
get it. Oh yes he did; centre of such mumbo-jumbo

(let alone The Shire)
lay The Academy of Mary Immaculate, and his friends, the girls.
But oh GoGo oh GoGo you 'n' your Catholics,
you 'n' your girls! Get yourself a tour of

the real world!
'Spacey' Lacy had. He was out there now, enjoying himself, toolin'
          round,
checking the old man's properties, staying this side of trouble, thinking
Wouldn't it be the greatest to sidle alongside a take-your-pick

of Shire identities
(Fat Donald the newsagent/that midget woodwork teacher
with the bullet head/Spencers' father/Monica Beck's old cheese/
the Reverend Mac) *and announce 'I'd my first deal in a car*

where was yours?'

(v)
Jack the barman had leant cautiously over
('Don't ask why but Kim this is all illegal.')
to open the glove box. You were meant to show

nothing but calm
weren't you? Hardly ever think about it.
'Not everyone rises above the big-noter quota,
so take things es el oh double you

right Kim?'
As packaging this crumpled lunch bag seemed preposterous.
But the product! Smelling so pliant so potent, you just licked and licked
the air around it. All the boy could say was 'It's so . . . it's so . . .'

'Fecund?' Jack proposed.
Who was talking like some crazy dodgy uncle now,
taking you aside for facts, the real world's real facts
This'll make you rich my lad. Count this just the start.

Name the plans, Big Kid.
Okay: well how might Jack suppose Kim could help The Shire become
an extra pleasant place to live in? Join the Foreshore Committee?
'Serious I mean but how we grow this stuff eh Jack?'

'This stuff?'
the barman asked. 'You gotta know when to give and then
not give this, that or any stuff, a stuff.
I wouldn't do it. I'll lend you a book.' Later that night

Kim was on the beach,
his back to the sea, howling 'Hear what I'm hearing GoGo, Frenchy,

you Mary Immaculates,
all you Shire? It's the world's greatest voice telling me *Grow grow grow
your own grow it Kim yours 'n' everyone else's!*

And that voice is mine!
This has been a Sub-Urban Spaceman Production: Kim Lacy speaking.
All his life he's asked *This time: will I give a stuff?*
and I suppose he has and he will until his big until arrives

and I sure won't!'

(VI)
'We've heard his chant *You may not believe this but*
so often now,' (Neil was telling Louise) 'all of us think
what'll it be this time: acid? UFO spotting? drag-racing?

Know Lacy's uncle?
Mr Sin. His cousin? Some centrefold. Remember a few years back
these kids from my school did a night raid on
Fat Donald's, and weren't caught? No? Well it happened:

Kim ran that one.'
Since then The Shire kids had waited for the big bad Spacey event
to even start. Course it wouldn't. Which made him more amazing.
Sure his father owned those Marine Parade apartments

fronting the foreshore,
sure Kim could pick up a guitar, tune it and give you
the beginning of 'Classical Gas' almost all of 'Blackbird'.
Could Louise guess what he said once?

*I'll be camp this week.
I know all the bars, all the phrases. I'll get away with it.*

(VII)
'They're boys,' Liz told Louise. 'Sometimes they make me feel
just a little older.' Which was why she loved Bob; could marry him.

Bob was no boy. Sometimes.
'Neil gets quite intense with things,' Louise told her.
'These girls who won't materialise . . .' ('Never do,' sighed Liz.)
'And after them of course, his friends: Frenchy perhaps, then Spacey:

nothing but Spacey.
What's this Kim like, Liz?' Well, he wouldn't become *her* friend;
but if you were Monica, it'd be great to have him round
just to stir your Mum. Liz liked *her* mum but.

(VIII)
So still each week
more, more about the ever-amazing one (who'd still done little but
remain a bullshitting charmer and get the oldies cringing.
yes please admit it Neil, little remarkable.

Yet. If ever).
Then Louise, assembling and reassembling these patterns she'd
                    received, thought
if Neil and Lacy were girls all I've heard might be infatuation.
She wasn't kidded the least. Who cared if they weren't? It was!

Romanza: Liz and Bob are engaged. At their party Liz introduces Neil to Naomi and Neil introduces Kim to Louise. September 1969.

    Neil had this kinda-luck
(all The Shire knew Neil's kinda-luck) and most weeks
Liz would think *Isn't it time some nice girl
snared him? For his sake?* Well now his luck
would readjust: follow Auntie Liz,
just take things slow and see how they'd land.
She would invite Naomi:
dark round-eyed and still at school,
the Hussies' wing attack with a voice
that found *itself Just sigh-ing* . . . Naomi, yes,
and if Liz had the time (she'd make sure

she had the time) they'd be introduced.
    Some friends were amused. Monica said
Liz should set up 'Cradlesnatchers',
her specialist dating agency; and volunteered
the plan's main flaw: 'Imagine being seventeen again
with *that* for your father': Fat Donald:
Shire identity, community leader, newsagent,
bully-buffoon. *Don't want either of them hurt,*
Monica wanted to warn, if only it didn't sound
such a part of the plot. They hadn't even met!
    Bob had this dag cousin:
he wore a beer-stein on a chain around his neck,
would show you, badly, how to dance the Zorba.
    'A ponce,' said Bob,
'our party will survive without him.'
    'Well Liz,' suggested Hannah, 'who asked Kim?'
    Tagging along, next to Ray, came Lacy.
Liz went to them direct: 'I'll give no dramas
but I want no dramas. Right fellas?'
    'Why'm I here?' Kim confessed to Neil.
'You'd asked me and I'd nothing else to do.'
    Behind them Donellan lectured someone's
younger brother: 'Woddy 'n' orange matey? Leg-opener.
A-one!'
    Kim scoffed hard to Neil:
'Hitched to that thumb merchant Chrissie Thing
what would The Frenchman know?'
(Adopting his targeted breathy hustle)
'Weed matey? Grass matey? Pot matey?
Has matey ever tried *that?* If he hasn't he can,
starting tonight.' Ray might imagine
half the world's legs opening, just give Kim, please,
the doors of perception.
    All parties need
a token gatecrasher. Plus one dumb mate
seeing him in: that was Spencer's job.
But why, thought Monica, did Lacy bother?
Liz was the straightest: that's why she was
Monica's best friend. Lacy though?
There'd be little in tonight for him.

'Reckons he's some hippy,' came her contempt.
'Yeah, hippy as my old man.'
    Though he might turn any gay 'n' hearty
gayer, heartier, Jim Beck wasn't trusted,
hadn't been invited. And, by extension, Mrs Beck
(who'd have hardly come). 'Even us oldies
have our limits' said Liz's mum.
                    Now though,
Bob was thanking everyone he'd ever met,
whilst Monica was muttering, just loud enough for Hannah,
'You are one premium dickhead, Bob.' She knew
the Liz 'n' Bob night would turn her·
extra worldly-wise; though quite concerned
for her friend, thought any engagement nonsense
(even if it had been planned for years).
'Some of us are made to have them, Hannah.
And some are not.'
              She looked at Neil,
now beside Naomi: couldn't you almost lip-read
his prattle: the relentless charm that would
affect no-one but Naomi *Me gosh gosh?*
I'm just a simple suburban lad yuck yuck.
How 'bout you heh heh?
                Monica may've liked Neil
but tonight all she could bring to words was
'Please go GoGo; all of you go.'
She'd never tell Liz but, for her,
engagements went like this: the oldies
put a notice in *The Telegraph;*
the boy bought the ring, his girl wore it;
they had a party; there'd be a wedding.
    Well, she might be a cynic but Monica knew
her bounds. Not Chrissie who, trying to smudge
the evening, was announcing, 'Thought you'd love to know,
Liz, Ray 'n' me are next. In December.
You'll get an invite.'
                If it were Monica's engagement,
and she'd this friend upstaging it,
that friend would cease being a friend.
But Liz was no more Monica than she was

some Vaucluse heiress gushing
Ohh Dahling, how wonderful for you both!
Instead she looked, past Chrissie,
at Chrissie's fiancé, to tell him
'Okay our bet Frenchy. Remember our bet?
You said Bob and me would never do it.'
    'Walk down the aisle, Liz, just walk down
that aisle.'
    Could you call Frenchy a 'fiancé'?
Not quite. Though you could imagine something
even better *I'm Chrissie . . . Ray Donellan's fiancé?*
She was born to say it.
    'Neil meet Naomi,'
Liz held both their hands, 'Naomi, Neil.
You two'll get on fine. My friends always do.'
    And yes they did: 'So you're a Hussy?'
'So you're the famous GoGo?'
We're taking our time with this Neil
warned Neil. *That is total. She hasn't been
all over me, not so much anyway* Though
Come on come on he later urged *Build it
build that excitement!*
    Yet if Naomi mattered
Kim did more. Some time tonight
he had to meet Louise, he had to hear
'Kim Lacy, I'm proud to introduce
Louise O'Connor, Louise, this here's the famous Spacey.'
    And so proceedings opened.
    Where they were
Neil watched, of course; and Monica:
'She'll have a handful'; and Ray:
'This one's sure intriguing'; and Liz:
'Remember Lacy, that girl's my friend and you were
not invited.'
    Which hardly bothered Kim;
no hard word merchant him;
tonight he'd to convince The Frenchman how
life didn't stop at Woddy 'n' Orange; why, matey,
it had hardly begun.
    Outside Kim produced an obese rollie,

and took *You hippies* (Neil, Ray, Chrissie, Louise, Naomi)
down the back fence to smoke it.
 'In a circle,' he demanded.
 'Say,' said Ray, 'Spacey's a pusher and we're
his addicts! Whacko eh.'
    Louise asked
'You grow the stuff?'
    And Chrissie
'Well how's it affect you?'
 Oh just like Kim was now:
'I know I must seem normal; well I am and yet
I'm not.' They should see tonight his way:
Liz's folks, their coloured lights, Bob's army mates,
were all a-maz-ing! 'We call this in the trade
a joint.'
  They knew *that!*
     'Well; urged Neil, 'begin.'
 And when they did, Louise announced
'Liz'll be lonely: Bob's about to save us from
the Viet Cong.' She looked at the sky,
didn't feel ridiculous: all their lives
were starting to be worth it.
    Kim had another ready.
 Naomi was wanting to be hugged,
to crash-on. (So much in fact that Frenchy,
the ex-franger king, would later ask
'Been trying to lift the young one's skirts eh, Go-mate?'
Err not yet.)
   Then everybody started singing
('Twist 'n' Shout' / 'She's Leaving Home' / 'Ob-la-di, ob-la-da')
Chrissie, fancying her voice, trilling above them.
 Louise and Neil asked
did they know 'The Friendship Song'
(which might sound like a Christian Crusade chorus
but wasn't)?
   Well they didn't.
And any 'Friendship Song' stood
chanceless.
   'I'm going; said Donellan,
'to the toilet. The toilet.'

'He's always going
to the toilet the toilet,' Chrissie wailed.
'Ray doesn't love me now, he loves the toilet.'
An urge to improvise surging them,
Neil, Louise and Kim commenced 'The Toilet Song'.

Toccata: Chrissie and Ray get engaged. Neil tries to take Naomi to their party. Saturday, 6 December 1969, 8.30 p.m. onwards.

    For weeks Liz had guessed most of the night's routine:
how she would demand 'Now you're engaged,
Ray, our bet . . . isn't it pay-up time?'
And 'The aisle, right down the aisle,'
Donellan would reply.
    There'd be Monica complaining
about who wasn't there, and Hannah bitching
over who was; speeches interchangeable with
all engagement parties, and the songs
To every thing there is a season . . .
    'Hey!' the drummer ordered, 'Let's hear it for
the thinking man's Pee Wee Wilson . . . Frrrenchy!'
    Chrissie's oldies having hired the reception centre,
Ray (coaxing his friends 'Luvtrip' to perform)
had just completed guest-vocalising a number,
his one number.
    Then Liz noticed Neil,
correction Neil and Naomi, were late.
And though tired of being admirable and stoic
she'd still let everybody ask 'Hi . . .
how's Bob?' (Overseas, alive, she hoped.)
    But that was the currency: Hi Chrissie how's Ray? /
Hi Louise how's Spacey? / Hi Monica how's the latest? /
Hi Hannah how's . . . how's the love-life?
    'Hi Neil,
where's Naomi?'
    For he had arrived, distressed,
heading straight to Liz with his adventures:

the way Fat Donald, newsagent, Naomi's dad,
had had him all but frogmarched to the study,
for the grilling: 'What's your business with her, Whiskers?'
  (And Hannah moved closer to catch it:
this predictable, ground floor gossip.)
  And here was Fat Donald's vision of the evening's business:
just something about Neil, his drug-dealer mates,
and *Us community leaders* ...
       Then The Shire's
premier Michelin Man barrelled Neil through his house
and down the drive, taunting 'Return ...
return and I'll kick it, Whiskers,
I will kick your bum!' With 'Fink!'
the daughter howling at her father, 'Fink! Rat fink!'
  Poor Naomi, Liz imagined,
seventeen and most unlikely to be kissed, much,
for years; and when that time arrived,
disaster.
    Neil, however, wouldn't worry Liz:
with the night set to distract him and him,
the night.
     'Now for you oldies,'
Frenchy informed the throng, 'by oh-so-special request,
the Matt Munro of his generation,
GoGo Spencer!'
      'My love what now/
what now what now ...'
      Drunk already! And
What now?
  Why Neil was martyred and Hannah, furious.
Now he need do absolutely bugger-all
but wail abroad, bailing-up all those sucker enough with
'Does my love grow? You are asking *me*?
Uhh, I dunno. I dunno.'
   ... and a time to every purpose under heaven.

Chorale: Kim gets tired of hearing about Neil's new friend 'this wayout poet' Toby. All summer long 1969—1970.

      Aren't you bored, at least, with lies?
Just a troubadour . . . just a bit if a troubadour
that's what poets always say they are,
or wish they were. Well me and the old man
are set to start my clothing chain:
'Wayout Gear for Fellas 'n' Birds'.
Go-mate, I'm so wayout I've gone completely
round the block to come back through
the front door. Tell you what, though,
it's great to think *I'm almost legit now.*
And don't tell me what your poet looks like.
Anyone can look like what they want to look.
Take Frenchy: ruffle his hair, throw a scarf
around his neck, get him to stare,
if not quite pout and, need I spell it out,
'Blonde on Blonde'! Oh Go-mate Go-mate,
share you the following:
promise not to tell The Frenchman, but,
I hate Dylan: he whinges, he's depressed,
he's never meant a word.
(So who'd I like the world to barrack for?
The Bonzo Dog Doo-Dah Band, what else?)
And here's how you get to be a poet:
pack yourself some acid, head down the coast,
sit under a tree, watch the ants, then return
to amaze everyone. Okay, one day amaze *me,*
bring the poet round.

Intermezzo: Louise is pregnant. Kim dumps Louise. Neil goes shopping with Louise. Hannah sees them. Wednesday, 17 April 1970, 2.30 p.m.

(i)
      Late last year, when Hannah saw Spencer,
'Your friends,' she told him, 'are expecting.'

She'd heard from Liz, and here's what horrified her more:
Louise could really play at being Missy now.

    If only! Kim, performing a cameo one afternoon,
had scooted.
        'Sure won't marry *him*' Louise informed

her friends. 'Won't keep the baby either.'
Stubborn as pregnancy, that's what.

(II)
    As her days trundled, and Kim elaborated excuses
worthy of Kim, Neil turned conduit.

    (Liz told Monica: 'He's more than half in love with her.')
    When you saw Spacey what other words were there

but 'scared' and 'clumsy'? Still, leave it to him and GoGo heard
something about Lacy, Old Man Lacy and plans, certain plans.
    Besides,

as The Frenchman always told them *Ev'rybody must get stoned!*
    Yep, yep and yeah yeah yeah, stoned on bullshit,

stoned on the latest Lacy product,
the latest Lacy promotion.

    'Yes,' Kim was firm, 'I have a product, I have a market.
I can't run out on both. Look,' he glanced a bit,

'you may not believe this, but we're diversifying.
There's plans. Except . . . (sounding fourteen and bad with it)

'except . . . name us the road block, huh? Folks:
hers 'n' mine, right? Put this to Louise then:

she'll live in a bungalow or a sleepout, right?
And pretends she's on a working holiday, okay?

I've friends in Cairns, in Darwin, Tassie. She sends
them cards she writes ... Go-mate?'

He knew some kids, somewhere, who'd done it, once,
and, for a while, it worked.

    Yeah? The idea was stillborn.
Guess why? They knew and weren't so pleased, her folks.

There was a response required: not Neil's this time,
but Kim's, direct. He had a week.

(III)
    By April, the year for a few was caving-in:
some dagged themselves from one end of the Shire to the other;

and some got on with life:
Wednesdays and Fridays Hannah did reception work.

    About to drive home she saw them:
it wasn't the first time Louise and Neil

got rid of their day at The Fair. Wasn't he studying?
Whatever for? With all his relocated honour

Spencer was near enough to a parent now.
    Wet as any puddle the actual father had evaporated

(some reckoned Mount Tom Price, others just The Cross)
until today. *Oh you poor things!* Hannah sighed,

for, inside The Fair, one more Young Australian
was set to make his imprint on The Shire:

placed prime at the foot of the escalators,
in the very belly of the mall,

a sign told *Coming Soon: Mister Kim Lacy's
Wayout Gear for Fellas 'n' Birds.*

In the car park, in her little car, Hannah watched them:
Louise playing at Missy-with-love-chil',

whilst Spencer, like the Duke of Edinburgh, tagged.
    Wait, she began a smile, just wait till you see *That*,

you'll sure say more than *Hey, perhaps Mister Kim Lacy
does a line in maternity smocks!*

Then, knowing how moralising-sour she was *I'm sorry*
Hannah admitted to Hannah,

*but can't they see beyond the fuss?
She went with him, did all she was asked*

(and doubtless more). Then it happened.

(IV)
    Something had arrived in Lacy's way. Something he'd prefer
        ignored.

    'You can take this all the way to her and anyone else,'
Kim had suggested. 'I am sorry, tremendously sorry, but

I mean (youknowwhatImean?) how could I be certain
it's really mine? Blood tests? Where are we? Las Vegas?

I mean it's not she hasn't friends: Liz Whosits,
Monica Whatsits, Donellan's chick, Hannah Little,

my mighty Go-mate.'
        Then, manoeuvring the talk to this knockabout
he'd got to know, some barman, Jack,

Kim turned unfrantic, tidier.
    Jack, as a man, could be any man,

'He's just' and Kim was expanding every neurone
not to be too enigmatic, 'done things. Jack's done things

and knows people. There's contacts: these Americans.
Like they like my product?'
                              Eye-to-eye with Neil,

surer now, Kim had replaced *You may not believe this but . . .*
with *if I were to tell you . . .*

For Go-mate would be told his upcoming fantasy *Los Americanos
and the Great Dope Swap* in all its accompanying dag-code:

lawn clippings for talcum.
        Oh it was just an idea, a oncer,

and Spacey, little but ideas and oncers,
cordoned any speculation the best way: more gossip,

about himself,
                'So Jack takes me to dinner . . . *hey!*
he's not like *that!* and later *hey hey!* we drank

a bit more wine and a bit more wine and a bit more . . .'
        Though he adored such weird music that only could arrive

from Kim, Neil hardly liked his friend smug.
        Plain speaking, though, was crasser. Go-mate might think

*Except to yourself you haven't much commitment
eh, Space?* but never say it

(he'd sound like some Shire oldie denouncing *Our Premier Bad Egg*).
        Since they were twelve this truce had been honed: this pact:

'Let me do the bullshit, you just stay dumb enough to accept it.'
'Sure I'll stay dumb enough, enjoy your bullshit.'

        Best mates? It hardly helped to think *Best mates?*
even if they were. (They weren't.)

Certain people (this Jack the barman?) might want to ask it;
Neil wasn't one of *them*.

(v)   No, if he'd a best mate,

today, she was Louise, and he was with her
patrolling The Fair: picking at items and putting them back.

    They reached the upper level, paraded a bit
(not buying just looking) then stepped on the escalator,

moving down to find it: Kim's announcement
Say Fellas 'n' Birds, who better than Mister Kim Lacy

to flog The Shire their wayout gear?
Sure not quitting this place in a hurry!

    Neil thought of phoning Liz, to ask if she wanted to know,
even now, how remarkable Kim still was. Not really.

And why didn't Spacey call the place plain *Spacey's*
Who else was he? The Shire knew nobody else.

    Louise was crying, and Neil had never seen her cry.
What were the words behind the blubber? Probably

Why won't he just get out and really go?
Ask your friend that, Neil.

(vi)   They returned to the carpark.
                                                It had been months since
            Kim
declared this approximate commitment:

'. . . all right, say, okay tell you what I'll do:
tell her I'll do something about it.'

**Legend: Jack, the barman, talks to Kim. Saturday,
6 June, 1970, 1.15 a.m.**

    Kim, I know what's happening; you better know
what's happening. The manager's suspicious and, since he thinks
I know these things, trust me, I say, Kim's mighty clean.
Doesn't he look it? The manager, of course, knows this
but what's, he asks, what's that boy *do?*
                                Can I keep you
out of trouble? What do you think!
                       Instead,
I'll circle to my point. In Melbourne
I've this mate, this, silly mate. A few weeks back,
whilst I'm down there, Bernie,
who for his sins is something of a poof at times,
Bernie thinks he's met this kid, your age,
who's horny for him. And he is not.
And I was ringside to it: all the set-up,
all the follow-through and final mess, the blubbering threats,
the being mad enough to phone this boy at home,
start to abuse his dad.
                    It's okay, this tale hardly fits
my kind of line (and even if it did
I'd never turn on diamond-eyes for you, young Lacy)
but I like what I'm seeing and my point is:
we have to get to know each other better
(isn't that what Bernie's tiny tragedy is
telling us?) much better.
                      Yes I know a few Americans:
stand back though, look at your actions, look at them again:
we aren't repeat we aren't in Gangland USA.
And even if we were you're no Al Capone.
Courtesy of Dad you're the local semi-rich kid,
thanks to your few plantations (small, discreet)
trying to make the extra quid, liking the idea
of breaking out.
               But the Americans?
Kim cobber, mate, pal, son, old son,
imagine *them* as a more, much more, ridiculous *us,*
and then imagine *us* trying to play at *them;*

ask: where can, when will, such parodies
cease?
   What the Americans are bringing in
they sure aren't bringing out.
         They're certain to like
what you have and,
though the deal's to swap it for something that,
on occasions, kills (I need to tell you, Kim, kills)
the kids love it.
      I won't even look at it:
me who did my stretch ten/ eleven/ twelve
years back, who coped, but hardly needs to do
much of that again.
       Could I keep you out of trouble?
Well there's trouble-trouble and there's
getting-caught trouble. What do you think!
All I can advise is Kim, ask yourself:
how far do I wish to travel; and then take your pick.
   Have *I* killed anyone? Have I *killed* anyone? Have I killed *anyone*?
   We should know each other better.
I find it near impossible to reply:
but there may've been this person, so I'll try.
No, I didn't hate this person, probably loved
this person, but one day I returned from where
I'd been to find out what my trust was worth,
what this person truly, quite and simple,
was, had done. Who never knew how caught
they were. Just once I took this person
behind some building (I was being trusted now) and . . .
left them for dead? Let's say
I haven't seen them since.
       I've killed?
I doubt it.
    Doubts, though; are never enough.
  I hope not.
  You better know what's happening, Kim.

Folkdance: Louise has had her child; Liz, Monica, Neil and Bob visit her in hospital. Saturday, 7 June 1970, 6.00 p.m.

  Like it was some medical drama here they were: young adults, four abreast, sweeping down a corridor.
   Noting that Lacy wasn't mentioned 'Okay. . .' Neil heard Monica complain: Hannah was interstate, being a communist or some such, but wouldn't you think Chrissie, or Mr Chrissie, might've made some effort.
   With Liz's student friends Bob was in a games mood: 'Reckon, Neil, we track down the father *Whatsisface* and break a few essential bones.'
          'Yeah, the father,' Neil had to reply, still having a friend in *Whatsisface*.
    'Let's start,' (even Liz thought Bob was being stupid) 'let's start with kneecaps.'
          'Which would,' Monica knew they knew 'solve sweet fuck-all.'
   Neil liked watching Bob hearing his fiancée's friend, her best friend, announcing that.
        Well Monica had given liking Bob a try, and would again. But most attempts were doomed.
   Liz had been here hours before: 'This way: look like you're going places, pretend we're nurses, even doctors, and, when anyone asks, say Miss O'Connor please.'
   Wearing a Snoopy nightie 'G'day guys,' Louise sighed; she sat up, hugged each girl, said 'Hi Bob' and squeezed Neil's hand.
        Her mother had been in of course but 'I'm fairly lousy . . .' (lonely she almost wanted to admit).
   So how was the kid and where'd they keep it? Would anyone ask *that*? Not now, no more than *what's the matter?* Her whole damn life, that much at least, for the moment.
      Had Liz been in the nightie you could imagine her demanding *Go on, ask us what was for dinner: rissoles 'n' jelly!*
But look who'd be backing her: Corporal Stability, the kneecapper.
     Such an occasion needing a charm to lift itself

the three friends swung into the evening's gossip:
where Hannah was, the Donellans' latest public squabble,
and 'How's the love life, Monica?'
      Little place for fellas in Operation Buck Up,
swamped by girl-talk Neil and Bob turned
each other's way: raising eyebrows together.
There was no attendant deal just *Welcome to the club!*
Had Kim been Bob such a look would tell
*Oh Go Go, just see these rabbits. If you can trust Spacey,
man, there'll be something in this scene for both of us.*
      Of course Kim wasn't here. No, he was everywhere.
Sometimes you just began to turn that corner
you were turning and there he was, pulling alongside, revvin',
easy to like again *GoGo, hey, hop in man!*
as if he couldn't help it any more than Neil, The Shire,
and even history could. Somehow, anyway, Neil would always
intersect with Kim (who'd always find a spot for Neil
in his equations: the mutual bad pennies).
      He knew no-one as smooth,
and no-one who'd done anything as clumsy.
For what it was it was supreme:
an action to keep Neil bewildered for years.
      Going to the carpark Bob asked:
'You know the father then; straight out, what's he like?'
A prick at times but then we all have friends like that.

Tango: Hannah, interstate at the Student Action Conference, meets one interesting and many not so interesting people. Queen's Birthday Weekend, June 1970.

(1) Saturday

... and you're ... Karl? Well Karl, think anyone knows
when us activists are finally meant to act:
the ordinary Josephines 'n' Joes?
That's hardly speculation, mate, it's fact.
And I haven't come how many hundred miles to grapple
vanguard elites. But I have: Maoists and (save us!) Trots.

(Whilst they prepare to paint the Sistine Chapel
we plebs must stay content with join-the-dots,
to sip our Fanta while they groove on daiquiri!)
I shouldn't bitch. When a comrade gets too avid
for some 'common good' it's straight to the knackery!
You asked for an opinion, there you have it;
need any more? Say Karl, what's the banner
you'll be marching under? Sorry, my name's Hannah.

(II) Sunday

. . . know the last time I spent suffering such peasants
for peers? Third form or fourth, at a guess,
when, catty-smart, well into adolescence,
I waited for my boyfriend at recess.
Yep, I had one and yep, then as now
little seems altered: regard this personnel:
hardline, humourless, holier-than-thou,
who (in the fellest of the ideological fell
swoops, thinking the world is theirs to dispose)
have lost (indeed have never known) the plot
As it's occurred so it always goes.
Still, Karl-from-Monash who's after me or not,
second this motion and we'll wipe' em clean:
your Mrs Sparkle to my Mr Sheen.

(III) Monday morning

. . . life's messy. Think the brain's starting to soften.
With self-proclaimed vanguards for my quarry
notice I've been saying *sorry* much too often:
sorry sorry sorry sorry, sorry
about getting us into bed then flaking in a heap;
no I'm not; listen Karl, I never hurl
myself at simply anyone; didn't get much sleep;
did you? I'll say this though: any girl
round here must pretend she's Teresa of Avila
to survive. Still, we lowered our boom
on the crazies and won something. Am I a fellow-traveller?
Maybe, but I'd like to know with whom.

Like, don't ask how, but I've these Catholics for friends.
Friends first is where it starts, where it ends.

(IV) Monday afternoon

... and what's any faith? Just a bigot's crutch.
But one of them's about to have this love chil'.
They'll all be tagging Missy now. Don't like her much.
But I should talk: anything avuncular needs only to smile
and, later, ask 'There, that wasn't too bad
was it?' No, except I'm easily charmed:
like pashing at her party with Monica's dad
(everyone was rooms away) and 'Hannah; he smarmed,
'you kiss, kiss like a married woman!'
Trouble was I always liked his wife,
and where there's trouble there's fun. Oh man,
and all that goes with man, exit my life!
Still, I think you're understanding, Karl;
and we sure clobbered the Trots. Ta-taa, darl.

Danza: Ray and Chrissie are married. On their living room floor they hunt for misplaced Serepax crumbs, Saturday, 20 June 1970, circa 10.15 p.m.

                The relic
might have been a continuing subscription to
'June and School Friend' The Complete Mary Grant Bruce/
that teddy bear, but Chrissie took her slippers
Leftee and Rightee her floppy, sloppy slippers
into the marriage.
                Of course there'd be other problems
but Donellan, who liked his Kitten silly, sometimes,
approved.
            Weekends might stall.
She never liked Neil, he didn't like Monica,
and, this evening, every time she turned
a corner of their flat, there was her husband
proposing 'Let's get ourselves a bit to drink,

some Serepax, some Dylan, and drift into Sunday.'
  She concurred:
'One Saturday but let's do Chinese with
Liz 'n' Bob. Bob's fine, for a soldier.'
  'Sure.' Ray tuned to his brutal *Yer reckon?* mode:
'If he's in Australia, on leave, hasn't been maimed
or killed.'
  Brutal enough; though whatever the mode
Dylan was certain to have the appropriate song;
and Ray would know that song.
  She thought of *Nebraska Nights, Dakota Days*
this Dylan album only Chrissie knew because,
to fool him, she'd imagined it. Would ask herself
*Know what love is? To lie back after one of
half-a-dozen-things-with-you and sigh
God this is fun, Donellan!*
  The next few minutes were simple:
he'd nick round to the rubbity, she'd
unwrap the Serepax crumbs. Unwrap the Serepax crumbs.
  Too simple.
  'Ooops!' she howled, and 'oop-oop-ooops!'
bracing for the rat-a-tat-tat
of her aggrieved spouse
I don't know how you could be so . . .
Because, Donellan, there were these crumbs.
And they spilt, Donellan.
    Who had returned.
  Trapped to explain, hardly knowing what exactly,
Chrissie glanced now at Rightee, now at Leftee.
Just then, whilst he was down the road,
she'd been distracted, let's call it scatty,
and didn't know how, but after she'd unwrapped it,
from the foil, the stuff seemed to . . .
seemed to jump?
  Jump? didn't bother Ray, rather
'Why crumbs, Chrissie, and why foil?'
    'We had them,
Donellan, because we had them . . .'
  And the Serepax was, somehow, on the floor;

her husband was annoyed, for now;
but such was Ray: one minute his hands
were down your slacks, the next,
he just required a cuppa.
    As if there'd be any crumbs under the bean bag,
Ray lifted the bean bag (and she didn't need
'Nashville Skyline' tonight, either;
put on some Kris Kristofferson, watch him squirm).
    'Well you were where, Chrissie?'
    'Here by the table.'
    They crawled under the table, though,
in the soft brown lamplight, their hunt turned difficult;
as a match flared she sought, briefly,
to taunt him *I don't know* got considered
I don't know how you could be so . . .
                      'Found some!'
    'Found some? Are you sure?'
                      'Found some!'
    And they were big crumbs!
    'Big enough. Put out your tongue.'
                      One day
the world would hear about their first whopper:
their Serepax crumb argument; no she told a lie: wasn't it
the stuffed zucchini argument?
                  'Not,' he asked,
'the *aren't we going to fuck tonight?* umm discussion?'
    'Don't be rude or I'll be ruder . . .' and she set
to charm her man. It wasn't getting that late
but Chrissie put the slippers on her hands,
prowling them proudly over his legs: 'These,
have a life of their own!'
           Ray yawned
the kind of yawn she knew he'd yawn
when they were sixty:
'Kitten remembers how I like my Sunday morning
toast and Vegemite?'
        Yes Donellan, Kitten remembered.

Finale: Louise and Neil go to Monica and Hannah's flat-warming. Chrissie sings 'The Universal Soldier'; Louise and Neil sing 'Friendship' and the 'Toilet Song'. Saturday, 5 September 1970, 8.30 p.m. onwards.

    One day Louise would tell a friend
All I wanted was getting the hell outa
The Shire; me with my
fucked-up head, bouncing from trauma to trauma.
Now though, in the midst of that, she was itemising:
Hannah was brilliant, Monica together,
Liz everybody's friend and Chrissie . . .
'Well at least she's married!'
                          Yeah, thought Neil,
to Manhood Inc.: swingin' Frenchy, the Dylanfreak.
'Look,' he told her, 'Monica's great and Liz,
who wouldn't love Liz? But anything else, tonight,
Louise, you're blabbing and blabbing r.s.
Hannah? Plenty commitment, plenty zeal,
plenty doin' the right thing:
little charity though, Hannah.'
                          Next she'd be on
about being Catholic. What other religion
bred such self-absorption? All those guilty Micks
guilty about being guilty Micks. Sorry Catholics,
there's a few more faiths in town
devoted, total, to fucking us round.
When all God's chillun got problems
there's just one question to ask
Got my mojo workin' . . . what've you got?
    As if Neil could parade such bravado,
spending close to a year boring The Shire
with his Naomi saga!
                    But not tonight.
There was the flat-warming: 'Well then,
are we going?'
              They were: 'First we get primed.'
    'Come on,' he caught her, 'it's only
Monica's.'
          'And Hannah's. And Chrissie will be there.'

'And Liz.'
   'And Donellan.'
        Anyway they'd go someplace,
have drinks. But not remain all Saturday night
in that dinky bar, then stagger off, well hardly
into bed, she wasn't going with anyone anywhere
except with Neil to Monica's.
      Going through all that
thought Neil *going through all that to give it away.*
Because of Kim? Catholics, perhaps, did things like that?
Well, not because they were Micks.
If he'd the chance Neil might try saying
Spacey dumps you, I don't get it, I wouldn't have.
Though he did get it: the essential Spacey:
Kim dumped people.
      Yet the man was fun, charming fun
for a big-noter, still driving into The Shire
to check out his 'clothing chain'
ho ho: two stores Old Man Lacy bought him
that wouldn't see themselves past 1972:
just another part of Kim's bullshitting grace:
last month a rock hero, today a drug dealer,
by Christmas a multi-millionaire ... meaning
he played a guitar, had a few ounces of leaf
on occasions, tried to make money.
  And he'd dumped Louise.
  When these two arrived tanked nicely
Hannah knew some time, that night,
they'd be singing the 'Friendship' or the 'Toilet' song.
Still, it wasn't just her party and bracing herself
with 'Hi Louise, hi Spencer,' accepted a few
'Hi Hannah's in return.
      I'm trying, she wanted to tell,
very very very hard, but sorry everyone
why the big fuss over last year's Missy
who threw herself at Lacy; at being careless?
Hannah could hear them:
Monica, Liz, Chrissie and Louise recalling Sister Bernardine's
Virginity, girls, there's nothing like it! What a pup what a lemon.
  What a way to finish part of your life!

Louise went through it again:
that night a few years back
when she walked to the beach with someone
she hardly even liked. But it was okay,
hardly much.
    Given a year she'd tell Monica
'Look, I've been sleeping with all these boys
and no-one knows anything about it.'
            'They will,'
her friend could only offer, 'when you're pregnant.'
 Now, with Neil, arms around each other
In Genesis from six to ten
When sailed the world-will-end ship
Noah took to sea a her and he
Now that indeed was friendship.
    But no,
she told herself, I'll never have a friend
like Liz (who might pass for Karen Black;
who lost it at fifteen with Bob
before he joined the army) who snuck in
to see Louise only hours after the boy
was born; who'd never be in all this
good girl's mess I've been in and still am.
  Up the duff? We'll still have puff!
  'Know the sanest form of sex?' Monica had asked.
'I've worked it out: be a twenty-four-carat callgirl.
and guess what? One day I might.'
  In the toilet? That won't spoil it.
     'Now listen everybody!'
It was Hannah, and time to clear
a space in the evening for Chrissie-
with-gee-tar: all parties need one.
  'Sure,' agreed Frenchy, 'what my missus wants
let's say she deserves. I might've wed another
Joan Baez. Let's play, Chrissie!'
       Play? Strum maybe.
  But Chrissie couldn't sing,
and what was worse she couldn't sing
'The Universal Soldier'. Oh please,
Hannah had to agree, pay us, at least,

to sit through this . . . till,
one song over, and Chrissie pausing,
Missy and Spencer weighed in with
yes, their toilet number
God spake to Noah, 'if nature calls,
Please don't let modesty spoil it . . .'
      He turned to Chrissie: 'C'mon Buffy,'
Spencer urged, 'more Buffy? Buffy Sainte-Marie?'
She'd be treated like this
throughout the night (give him the chance
throughout her life). 'Hey hey,
don't go, don't go. Ever tried busking, Buffy?'
Give forth a lash and make that splash,
The whole world is your toilet.
                No,
Hannah fumed, pity could only go so far
for Missy and her love chil'.
      And where was Donellan? By the fridge,
watching them kick one pretty sick dog:
Mrs Donellan.

Coda: The Sergeant from Seattle.
Monday, 7 September 1970, 9.30 p.m.

      That evening, who is present? Kim a front man
for his father's two-bit clothing chain,
wanting to quit The Shire fast, and, even faster,
wanting to be very rich; and Jack:
squarehead-by-experience: dealing in nothing/
correction very little (the man just likes
arranging things).
                Between 'My old friend Jack . . .
my new friend Kim . . .' their host:
the Sergeant from Seattle, whose presumption
would have to be far better or far worse
to qualify for sleaze. Still . . .
      'Let's not be anything like coy,'
comes his advice, 'know what's become the fashion,

Stateside? Bringing it all back home in body bags:
with the cadavers, or what remains of them.
Hey! Pleas-ant!' And that's why he likes Down Under:
Aussies have limits, even standards.
                            Which are?
    'Hard-ons first,' he laughs, trust him though, he knows.
        Says who?
                    Says the sergeant,
(well, that's who they're told he is) says him
with the Dave Clark Five hairdo.
                            Whilst Jack,
who likes to believe he's part of what history is,
thinks *Even if it's maybe new if hardly new,*
or even if it happens every empire,
whenever the future sets itself to do the judging,
this'll be our baseline.
Why should anyone get hurt? And, if they are,
what had they been worth? Everybody wants it,
the lot.
        One more not-exactly-glib American
on R and R proposing *Shift it for me . . .*
isn't sex. And hardly love, but Kim could live
on the kick of such a suggestion/ plea/
demand for . . . name the time span.
                            Walking to his car
he hopes he knows his market. Jack is sure
he does: 'At your age, Kim, we never had it . . .
Youth culture!'
            And wanting to ask *Yeah?,*
and wanting to laugh (at what he doesn't know)
Kim glances to Jack: *Well?*
                        Jack returns the glance:
I just know people. For something like a public service,
all the world gets introduced. Then I step back,
looking at what I've made. And walk away.

'HIS MAJESTY PRINCE JONES SMILED AS HE MOVED AMONGST THE CROWD'

EPISODES IN THE LIFE OF AN ARTIST

for Laurie Duggan

> *what do they go about like that for only getting themselves and their poetry laughed at*
> JAMES JOYCE, *Ulysses*

These were the salad days of R and R;
no more some twentieth-century Artful Dodger,
Kim had grown up;
and still saw Neil.
         *Well, who'd have thought
for over a decade, the old firm:
GoGo 'n' Spacey. Oh I need you mate,
you're kinda like my cut-rate shrink,
so cut you're free. Sure, I want to tell you
whatever I'd love you to believe,
but would you believe a half of even that?*
         Of course he could say how, last week,
he'd met Joe-Bob (who knew Stu
who knew Troy who knew that Sergeant from Seattle)
and how, helped by all their beautiful cipher
I know what I'm saying and I know what you're hearing
Kim was getting richer, quicker.
         *Retail, GoGo?
Managing two stores of wayout gear for fellas 'n' birds?
Anyone can 'retail'. But deal?
Maybe I am a minor league, non-lethal,
fun-stuff dealer, but the best type: young.*
         And did Kim want to brag how Joe-Bob
took a taxi all the way to The Shire
just to meet Spacey? He'd opt
to save that one.

     Dealing? Bullshitting?
If they shared an horizon he would walk it;
with all that ambiguity, speculation, rumour,
there'd always be those punters seeing him try,
everyone liked to think they knew a dealer,
and there, bullseye of The Members, sat Neil,
the ol' GoGo.
          Sure Kim wanted to taunt
I can say 'just watch me do it' cause that's
exactly what you do: watch me do it.
Except, what have you been seeing? Two men shaking hands
in a carpark of the Pacific Inn?
You've seen nothing like it in your life!

     After turning twenty Neil still attended parties,
hoping to try to get to meet and know that girl who,
for an hour, day, week, lifetime after any party,
might lighten-up his dimming prospects.
There weren't enough such girls? Of course not,
and the time you got to know that, was the time
you met those other kids, like Toby:
Toby who, gliding to the punchbowl, told how
of all the parties he'd been at (not that Toby went
to many now) this was the most ... the least ... the 'Neil,
it doesn't? man you know? gel?' (For it seemed required
you understood, like Toby did, how parties gelled,
or didn't.)
          At nineteen, with patches of facial fluff,
his filled-out puppy fat, Toby wrote, acted and lived
With my ol' lady Sal in a loft,
and 'Oh Sal,' he added with off-handed vanity,
'she's twenty eight ...'
                    On visits though
you'd never see Sal live:
only one photo: passing for Paddo's probable reply
to Grace Slick: peek-a-boo sly from under
one enormous hat.

      Err twenty *what? twenty-come again?*
Now what seemed more exotic than ol' Sal?
Only, Neil presumed, Sal and Toby.
Then what's the use, he wondered, knowing me?
Well if you thought there had to be a *use,*
why yes, one day there'd be one.

       ❦

 Toby wrote poems, a play,
said he was successful (had tried acting)
but come with him, please, to meet his mother
(his grandmother, a poet-friend of mother's,
whoever else arrived) just to let him show
*Sans drugs sans Sal, plenty of poems but,
this is Neil and I am normal!*
 The poet-friend was fat.
His back was turned to everyone.
       'This . . .' the mother cried,
'this is Toby's . . . this is Toby's mentor?'
 'Please!' asked the poet-friend,
her son required so little, just a weeny leg-up
from admirers, up into the system
and glory!
    What a rattlesnake what a toad,
and the mentor turned: 'You?'
 'Me,' Neil confessed; 'suppose I'm hardly talented.
But I like stuff 'n' all.'
 Wanting to be ignored he was
and spent the hour aiming at this mentor-ponce who,
as the recital closed, pleaded '. . . if I may misquote
the Blessed Bogie *Read it again, Tobe!*
That one about Dante, ejaculations and car horns!'
 About?
 Someone had to realise it was
like-man-y' know about *art?*
     And, walking to the bus stop
     Neil was told.

       ❦

dec 6 (2.19 p.m.)
now it was time to start on the *(hey!)* sequence since,
outside his loft, having floated south,
the Summer of Love was anchored to a cloud.
So Toby wrote

```
         (hey!)
    this is a loft
    cloud
    why bother to
              knock?
```

&

Neil brought him Kim, Kim brought his guitar.
'What's that piece you play so well, Kim?'
'Which one, Tobe, Beatles or Mason Williams,
        "Blackbird"
or "Classical Gas"?'
            'Beatles are shit, Kim. I'll take
the other guy.'
        They got to know each other.

&

Out from Toby's typewriter spilled his latest

```
thank-u note & storm warnin' for a
    craz-ee lady

              (hey!)
no shit craz-ee lady/thanx for yr
    carnations
              but
              just
              be
              ware
              the
              pigs
              arent
                   cause
they're after ShelleyRimbaudCheHo all us
    goodguyz
and always have
              but
              (hey!)
we still dig each other craz-ee lady!

              (sunrise, spring equinox)
```

Returning to the loft late one afternoon Toby had this idea: 'Why not come to bed, Kim? No?' Kim and a chick maybe?

Kim was good at pulling funny faces: 'Err yes Tobe, me 'n' a chick maybe. First but find one. Go on man, tell us a chick.'
     A few got mentioned whilst Kim sat plucking 'Mellow Yellow'.

'Yes?' asked Toby. 'No?'
       No yes, no no.

'It's getting late,' Toby got informed.

You had to grasp how Toby would be never angry (even better violent) but being put upon, or utilised,

or asked to do anything, he could swell up,
exquisitely annoyed; so his genius as read and,
bar his opinions, leave him alone when asked and ask him
for nothing.
    Then, after hearing him out,
just approve his talent and all its train
of style; he'd let you admit a few things as,
slow to begin, his encouragement unrolled:
'Well yes, this is basically correct; Mister Neil,
this is essentially good . . .' meaning
Thanks, but since today's performance has been mine
(for you and no-one else, man) appreciate me,
I grow on people.

    Neil had these two friends
(one who hardly 'dealt', the other
who rarely 'used'). They'd simply met.
    But was it meant to be this way: '
the moving people around, the stepping back
to size up perspectives, adjust appropriate shadings
and, even better, get your dreams the daylight
they deserved; to do anything the artist does
except the art: well was it?
All right all right they'd been introduced;
he thought, like, they'd get on? And,
each offering the other heaps, they did so
absolutely.
    With Sal in her poster shop
    Toby lay in their loft
    spinning his life into poetry
    poetry into an approximate fame
    as Kim's friends kept coming
    to town
        Joe-Bob 'n' Troy
        Stu 'n' Leroy
            Hi I'm Kim
was about all you needed to say
Chuck he may've mentioned . . .

ooh yeah sure had.
                    Sometimes
he'd pass a few hints on to Neil
who'd think them bullshit poor GoGo
so decidedly stop stop
how Spacey would love to ask him
know what it is with h-freaks?
(No, what?) None were sceptics
unlike you pal.
                    Hardly unlike him pal.
 'Yes, even here in The Shire,' Neil's mother reported,
'hippies are getting married.' There was at least
one couple she'd heard of.
                    Hippies? In The Shire?
Like Toby 'n' Sal?
                    She didn't know *them*
but *these* were hippies; with dawn vows
on an ocean headland it was a hippy wedding.
        'With some hippy minister?'
                                Apparently yes.

    Though Toby would leave Sal often
once he climbed out of their loft
he needed to be numb to most of it
(the husband and wife academics:
We feel we love you very much ...
some teenybopper from Bondi
I didn't know, no shit, poets were so much fun ...).
    It was great enough being back with Sal,
you just reminded her 'Like get it right,
like *Let it be* Sal, right?'
    She'd be looking at him, into his eyes
and out the other side; you had to say it
again: 'Right?'
            Last week,
when his *Dinkum Nirvana* manuscript
had been accepted, Sal fussed.
Right now she was telling Toby

'Well well well, lookee lookee lookee:
aren't *you* the last of the five-star groovers!'
For she was dressing up her man-boy for
his *play (one)* premiere.
                        As centrepiece,
set to comet-through the youth festival,
it was bound to scatter all appropriate
cosmic dust.

                    ಞ

        'I told you GoGo it's my shout. *play (one)*?
What in the fuck's *play (one)* and when's it start?'
Kim glanced about the auditorium: a twenty-five minute delay,
was that par for youth festival theatre,
and if so why? 'Well who's that:
Fatso the glad-hander?'
                        'Some poet. Now Space,
really, I have to pay.'
                        'You only get so stroppy
when you're drunk? I can afford it.
Business is berserk. I am a patron of the arts.'
        'Drunk?' asked Neil. 'Were you there
the first time I got drunk?' (Kim had
heard about it.) 'Remember going to dances
and there'd always be those little fat thirteen-year-olds
with oversized belt buckles and cigarettes and yet,
for whatever reason, they like you? Anyway this time
one of them comes up to me saying
*Tonight, if anyone messes with my mate GoGo
just let me know.* It was "Stinky" Conway.
Remember "Stinky"? "Grubbsy's" cousin. So I think:
a thirteen-year-old offering protection,
that deserves a drink! And, a bottle of cider on
(that's right cider) I'm *B'lukb'luk B'laaaak!*
cluckin' like a chook. Who'd ever want
to be a hippy? Ever done that on acid?
I was eighteen and *B'luk B'laaaak!* the happiest boy
in The Shire.'
            'Jeez Neil, I can excuse you being drunk

but how old are you, thirty-five?
Who's Fatso again?'
      'Some poet,
Toby's mentor. Same dance,
there's me little mate: Kellee Brown
queen bopper of 3B. Remember Kellee?
So I wave hi and *Bblaaaak* and she's with this boyfriend
who stares back bristling. *No no no,*
she explains, *he's all right he's GoGo Spencer,*
GoGo's growly. Boyfriend smiles, shakes my hand,
and we're enrolled: buddies for life.'

 'Neil, when I want the story of *my* life,
you're enrolled. Mmmm *play (one).*'
Kim was beginning to enjoy the name. 'Think they'll
ever start *play (one)?*'
      Better not ask GoGo:
'B'lukb'luk b'laaaak!'

      ❧

 Enter a crazy scientist carrying a fruit bottling jar;
now, what was in the fruit bottling jar?
        'Give up?'
and he pointed to the jar. 'Shit. But not *just* shit,
my *magic* shit which I'm gonna serve to heehee …'
      The Pope
      An Asio spook
      Doris Day
      and the board of BHP
 Then to finish *play (one)* why not crackernight?
And Neil saw what Toby saw: how, if you really want it,
war would be over.
Just take a nutty professor brewing up his supercrap,
stir in this brace of tom thumbs skittling over
the performance space and ea-sy! the Viet Cong had won!

      ❧

 Under his floppy Renaissance merchant's hat
came the granny-shades, a shy smile and a sly smile,

a green velvet smoking-jacket;
his mother at one elbow, her mother at the other;
playwright/poet/dreamer/leave him just th' fuck alone
Toby flowed through the foyer.
 Quite right, thought Neil, for the codpiece and the mandolin
to stay at home, though he had to hear himself ask
'Where've *you* come from Toby, the "Satanic Majesties" cover?'
 Half a decade younger Good Neil recoiled
He's a very sensitive artist!
Bad Neil was half a decade older
Umm yeah well mmm aren't we all?
See, you're ignored already . . .
      For Toby,
grinning his grin of a dope was asking
'Like it Kim?'
     'Oh man *play (one)* I'll never forget *play (one)*.
There's gotta be *play (two)*.'
      And Neil,
who needed to ask anything by now, asked
'That kid in the top hat playing the kazoo?'
  'Jules is a poem.'
    'A poet?'
      'No a poem. Jules says
he wants to be a poem.'
    'Oh.'

 Dinkum Nirvana had been assembled:
gallery and caterer booked, The Mentor primed
to launch it, friends invited to buy.
 Friends, thought Toby, you can't do
without friends: dedicating *Loftpoems* to Sal,
Squaresville Double Two Three Oh to Neil,
and *Big Deals* to K—, my pusher.
 If Neil hadn't contributed much he had
supplied some symmetry: as Kim was Neil's
'other' friend, so Toby was Neil's
'other other' friend; by now Toby was mad
about Kim: like Kim turned Toby on,

right? Not this way no nor that way neither:
just turned-him-on?
                        Like the book should be
For Kim but a jealous bitch called Sal
refused to let him. Okay, for whom? Hell man,
wasn't he for what it's worth an Aussie?
He'd fix her: *Pro Patria!* The very thing.
        'Darling,' she whined, 'your friend is mistletoe,
a toadstool. You're the one with talent,
daring.' And Kim? Some jeans salesman
who'd discovered turning-on and how to play
a bad guitar.
                '. . . and who,' The Mentor asked,
'was this fascinating young man?'
                [Someone who knows what he likes, thought Kim.
                Someone who's going to do the lot, thought Neil.
                Just a boy-genius, thought Sal.]
                                And The Mentor surged:
'. . . groping and fanatical as only the young can be
he dispatches *Shows promise* to the cliché bin
where it belongs. Does anything remotely resemble
the young at the height of their powers?
Such fecundity! Why in America he'd be . . .'
        If only his countrymen would halt their cringe;
if only we weren't some cut-rate Coca-Colony!
Ahh but we had *Dinkum Nirvana*
and a fury had been loosed upon the land!
        'I'm happy,' Toby's mother said, 'so very happy.'

        But no, it wasn't meant to be this way.
Neil phoned his father, said he was confused.
        'I'll put your mother on.'
                        Neil hoped to join
the public service, sort things out;
hadn't done much for eighteen months.
                        Some Saturdays later
The Australian led with Toby's second book,
but The Mentor, still at his high velocity florid,

had U-turned:
>
> *It pains me that my friend young Icarus . . .*
> and *acclaim damages as much as any drug . . .*
> but *his generation (which is almost mine)*
> *is now a laughing stock, in short betrayed!*

Neil phoned Toby: 'Sal?'
'Yes this is Sal.' *Port Jackson Vespers*
wasn't getting launched. Toby needed a rest.
Neil knew Fatty? Well he was very cross.
Seems Toby, having gone satiric, created a certain
Oz E Bard *Who shares adjacent urinals with the muse . . .*
Now who could that be? Well it wasn't Judith Wright!
'And Neil, who copped the three a.m. bad-mouthing,
how he would *execute* our Toby?'
     Sal of course . . .
>
> [Fatty would bail up youth fests with his grief:
> 'Oh Tobe Tobe Tobe didn't I say
> don't publish *that*? And what's buddy-boy do?
> Not what he was told!']
> and Sal was growing old.

What with over a dozen heirlooms hocked or lost
or worse, and Kim always arriving
when Toby was unwell. Had Neil met Kim?
Sal thought she might move to Armadale, nice people
lived in Armadale.

   play (two)? This had become *play (two)*:
Sal Kim Neil Fatso mother
all put on a show for Toby.
Well not exactly Kim, who reminded him
'You owe and I owe,
but I owe what you owe . . .' and he wasn't,
despite appearances, that well off, yet.
                              'Oh yeah?
Which of your cars are you driving today,
Lacy, dealer to the stars?'
     Kim had to like that: 'Okay, star;
he followed through, 'go out, get it, and bring it back.
Bring back anything!'

☙

So there's a lot of teen-rubble about?
Well hasn't there been a youthquake?
That's where fellas like Kim were indispensable.
Whenever Toby, Aussie, or this tiny speck of blue
somewhere in the Milky Way requested
make um smile, this is what you always said
There's enough about and I can get it.
    For here was the bottom line: Kim was heading at
the main chance.
              'You know about
the main chance, Toby?
That's where all systems are go go go.
You need a job? I could have
the country's foremost junkie/youth-playwright/poet-
cult-figure working for me You could learn the act,
just listen to the wail of it:
in these tartan slacks, pressed to knife point,
sir looks a million smackeroos. So where
are we headlining tonight? What, you're *not*
a pop star? And do you know
that dumb ol' me was set to announce:
hey fans! Look who's back in town:
Let's give the boy a hand / on your make-believe bandstand!

☙

    Seeing Neil, months later, in the street, Toby told him
how Kim was a prick, really, but they still saw each other.
Sure sounds familiar, Neil didn't add, knowing he wouldn't be heard,
for Toby was explaining how, for a while after Sal,
he'd lived above a butcher's shop with an ex-rock star
who, fucking him round, had run off with their fridge.
They'd met through Kim, who was a prick, really,
though weren't they all, now, not merely Kim but '... me,'
Toby volunteered, and the ex-rock star and 'Mister Neil, even you.
Why bring that real prick Kim to my loft, huh?'
To which (not even *huh?*) there was no answer.

They of course still saw each other Toby 'n' Kim;
why not be a club of pricks together really huh?

❧

'... Sal was great, wasn't she?
Take it from Tobe: he's never found a better trouper.
My mother but, that review quite shattered her.
Wasn't he her friend, my mentor? And why but?
How could I tell that, just for once,
Toby wouldn't come across, that's why.
play (two)? I burnt *play (two)*.
Don't we all need a new break? I suppose
that's mine. And start ruling a line
through 'the theatre': in ten years there'll be none.
Great you found me and called. I'm hitching out:
Melbourne first: check what they have, shops 'n' that.
Perhaps I'll meet some sweetchick in her micro
(better still meet two) and oh Jehoshaphat!
I'll be telling them why hey man
this is Toby Nicholson, that's right
Dinkum fuckin' Nirvana You bought it?
You *bought* it! Gee,
hope there's some scene down there,
gotta be *some* scene. Y' know how shit
is always stronger just over the hill?
(No shit of course, everyone knows that.)
Well Mister Neil that's what a troubadour
acts upon. There's a poet-child in us all.
Try it sometimes.'

❧

So Neil became a public servant, tried living
with a married hippy couple.
                    Law drop-out, pretty as quiche,
'Ooh mate,' boy-half would near-sob over
what he thought passed for the very latest,
'ooh mate, it's so good, so-o-o good!'

> Neil, meanwhile,
was teaching himself how *not* to live with a married hippy couple:
tanked after a Friday evening bull-session, you arrived back
to commence a set of chin-ups in our/your/their living room
doorway; this refining a most alternative style of
neutral aggression:
> > by our silence ye shall know that we,
> > supplicants at the court of King Crimson,
> > are determined to tolerate, be tolerated.
>
> 'He doesn't like us,' girl-half discovered, 'why not Neil?'
having enough sweet' n' gentle loving in her to wish
that any passing Billy Jack might get their house-mate maimed
powpow! so-o-o good!
> > The only person
who could despise these two more than Neil was Kim and
what a feast! He'd adore them!

1971

(I)
    ... here came his final friend
and the ritual since Toby died was closing.
After each call she'd wait for people walking down
her drive to ring the bell, cart in
their lump of shock, refine it, fashion-out
whatever Toby fitted to their lives:
bound as they were by kinda/sorta/like y' know.
The times and him seemed so approximate,
there went her son, a kid waving his hand around
and not much more. Oh much of course,
but when you haven't cried for months,
the boys are with their father and
you're ready to move, hate can truly
straighten things to how you'd like them.
Dickheads, she thought, I still read, I am a teacher,
fuckwits, I know today's vernacular.
News still trickles to the provinces,
she'd improvise, another train of subjects for
the dowager. So you took to a thought,
making it worthwhile, as guests tried salvaging
whatever he had offered. Which, if they knew,
was life and life had gobbled Toby.

(II)
    The final friend came loping to the porch,
glanced to the window, waved a hand;
someone moved behind the curtain gauze.
    The sun today had ambled from a cloud,
warmed you a bit then sought out another.
    One earlier August, kinda drunk in some host's laundry:
'Your old lady knows you get this way? Mine does.
I'm Tobe,' and after a mannered pause 'you're ...'

(III)
    'You've kick-started me,' she seated him.
'Something to do. His brothers are propping with
my ex.' (It needed footnotes.) 'Toby's.' (The name cracked
through its shell.) 'At their father's.'
Clouds ganging up to one cloud now, shadows
were disappearing. 'You heard through . . . them?'
She let it fall. 'Too late for photographs,
they're packed. You're doing studies still?'
Not much, part-time like. 'Sherry then?
Now that's unpacked. Students know
it's necessary, never too early.
Some circle round to a degree
others just take aim and ffft: BA.
Toby would have been a circler.
You two went to films, which ones?'

(IV)
    Tobe got firm for once: 'When I
get out she'll never know or have to.
Meet the old lady though, we sorta like her.'

(V)
    A car drove in across the street.
'There must be an hour when too early turns too late.
Won't be stars tonight, moon'll be lucky.'
She felt deliberate now: today I'll finish angry.
So who's this nice boy at the wrong time
with all his words to choose and then arrange?
    'I've been here once, we were . . . close acquaintances.
We'd different friends, never saw each other much.
We phoned.'
    Grief had idled for weeks.
Was she expected to sigh *I understand?*
Look,' she may have known his name.
'What's my son given? He left three years back
and still there's too much Toby.
No-one should believe a lot.
This sucker's renting out and travelling light.'

Eyes closed, some muscles flicked.
      'But jeez,' he tried, paused, 'Tobe 'n' all.'
      Brainful of schemes to save a friend
he heard her words ricochet the home:
'You're forty-three, this dead man's your child,
he knew you before anyone, that was a life
and you face these mirrors thinking
this isn't me, I'm not doing this!
And dying *that* way! You knew him much?
Well this was him:
*I'll get more fun than any one of you
it'll kill me. Full stop.* That's Tobe . . .'
she stared into her lids,
'as you call him.' And lids flung apart,
the head got jolted back. 'Toby was ratshit!'

Part 5

DAVE PRICE	A PUBLIC SERVANT
WYNNE	HIS WIFE
LINDSAY } DOT	THEIR TWO OLDEST CHILDREN
BARB 'THE LITTLE GOER' } SHANE CLAIRE VIVIENNE PHIL	LINDSAY AND DOT'S COUSINS
TREVOR	DOT'S HUSBAND
ROGER HEATH	BARB'S HUSBAND
KARL	LINDSAY'S FRIEND, A WOULD-BE POLITICIAN
DIGBY 'GIBBO' GIBB	TREVOR'S FORMER FRIEND
LINDSAY'S GRANDFATHER	DECEASED
SYD } DICK KELLY	TEACHER COLLEAGUES OF LINDSAY'S
JANE	STUDENT
SYD'S COUSIN	POLITICIAN
JOANNE	LINDSAY'S GIRLFRIEND

Under Fourteen / Under Sixteen
THE SHANE PRICE RECOLLECTIONS

Sometimes it rates as a rather dull dream;
Dad and Phil shouting, Mum, Barb, Vivienne waving things
Carna Dragons! The mighty red 'n' green!
   . . . so I've this assignment: to play both wings

a quarter about; and Claire, wouldn't you know it?
follows me.
            'Who's her?' my opponent asks.
                              'No-one. A sister.'
   If he thinks he's a *real* boy and wants to show it
let's be prepared for *What? That human blister?*

(Claire's twelve, yells and is fat)
You poor jerk . . .
                  Nothing like this occurs. By lemon time
(let's not consider the finals now!) we're rearguard, flat-
to-the-board, and all is getting simpler: we've one crime,

the score, one punishment, disgrace.
                                 'Fellas, much too lax,'
our coach pleads, 'try like Shane here, harder . . .' (I'm his pup,
his toy, and blush of course.) 'You backs and halfbacks,'
(angry in that nice guy way) 'man up! Man up!'

   So ten goals down we man up. And still lose.
   Yet something I want to make me is in my blood,
it seems forever, now; and hardly mine to refuse:
that tang of liniment, sweat, grass and yes, even mud.

                       ❦

   We'll never know the how or why but (as she fills
out/he grows up) choices invade us: all just a matter of when.

Next week Barb brings this boy along *Oh thrills for dills!*
After which she never turns up again.

Phil starts playing, badly, with another club.
And Vivienne only wants to sprawl in front of the box.
Claire? The butterfly still remains a grub
At fifteen (time's getting on) I'm set to join the crocks.

&

It's then the stupid part arrives: adults getting unstuck.
For the new coach bewilders us: he and our old one seem vast poles
apart. (Mind you here's something approaching luck:
my folks just sit in their car now, tooting the goals.)

So 'Boil' em,' we get advised prematch,
'fry 'em, scramble 'em, omelette and poach . . .
an egg's an egg.'
    Eyes are rolled, scalps given a scratch.
All games now we try ignoring the coach,

each embarrassment overdoing his last.
 It's reckoned there's missus trouble: the man's jumpy,
game by game disintegrating fast
'til, cracking, he hurtles onto the ground, trying to job the umpy.

&

Why had us Dragons bothered to arrive
(dry weather experts stuck in this winter game)?
With four in a fogged-up Toyota it was a sullen drive
from home; but even after a week of rain,

the match still sets itself a start (our grave's dug:
gallons have fallen, the ground's become this marsh)
a start, four quarters and an end . . .
       Well I'm on this thug,
Tombino, my age, with a moustache;

who whacks me places he wouldn't dare last year.
And, as my dodging lowers his hit rate, each melee

finds him rummaging for my balls, must be queer
or something. (And it doesn't help Tombino's smelly

but, heading the final change, all things being equal, who isn't?)
Then, ducking a coat-hanger, I grab my chance to stage
and 'coming to' can hardly believe the sequel:
a losing coach gagged in full throttle rage

rushing the umpire with (straight from his vault
of invective): 'This boy is dead! What would you expect,
woglover?! It's all your fault
white maggot! Cop this!' He swings, doesn't connect,

trips over himself and, beyond scared shitless
now, blubbers softly, fit to be sacked.
   Later, since Tombino's charged, guess who's a witness?
   'Yes, I was staging ...' gets confessed, 'no I wasn't whacked ...'

never getting my chance to add
Yeah, well, it wasn't for lack of trying . . .
   The season's final farce choofs away. Jeez I'm mad
sometimes, I mean, why didn't I try lying?

Do I really believe *It's just a game?*
          After the tribunal
Tombino calls me 'mate' and shakes my hand.
   In the gents our fellas big-note it: sheer urinal-
talk: a sort of revenge is getting planned:

how, next year, that prick'll miss the odd eye tooth or molar.
   Yeah, if Tombino plays.
        And of course Dad's right
saying I did the proper thing.
        Sipping Coca-Cola
I take a back seat come presentation night,

there's enough heroes to hog it
(I never sliced through thousands, never fell on my sword).
Best afield once I proudly admit to 'dogged'
and snag the team's Encouragement Award.

DAVE PRICE COMPLETES HIS EXTENSION

At home, even in winter, he wore those same
inevitable shorts, two decades old;
for that night though, he swore he wouldn't;
since the idea: an evening to celebrate
with more than the usual casks
had started with Wynne, the War Office.
 'Dave,' she tried to tell him,
'The extension's special, isn't it?'
 Yes it had been but, by now,
there was a new garage to consider, and
how to re-lay the drainage.
                    This night
might promise an amount of fuss for a wife
to revel in, 'But,' he'd sigh to their children,
'That's your mother.'
She belonged everywhere, Dave just joined
what he had to.
              An ex-serviceman he preferred
being thought of as a public servant:
but, as it was the age of the public servant
it was the age of the ex-serviceman;
it was also the age of the housewife,
and, twenty-five years before, all three
it seemed had started their suburb after
suburb siege of Melbourne, of everywhere;
and had won something.
         Dave had a younger brother, baffled-affable,
who, marrying an RC, became, when he got
round to it, a friend of the Groupers. No,
he wasn't invited this time, nor his wife:
there were a few locals, a few from work,
a few more from the tennis club, Wynne's sisters
and, by unstated obligation, the family:
Lindsay, down from teaching in the bush.
Dottie with Trev (in a few months Dave would hold
their wedding here in his extension)

dave price completes his extension

David Junior, armchair-pontiff-in-waiting
(a pest) and, still at school, Nicola
(who tried running the home and him
and almost succeeded).
      Dave said things like
'Full o' beer!' or 'End of transmission!';
and gave anyone younger nicknames only he
would use.
    Karl, Lindsay's friend and 'Bunyip',
told Dave how he looked like a koala
from *The Magic Pudding.*
        'A fifty-two-year-old koala,' Dave moderated,
who had a game: taking Bunyip so many steps further till his ideas
(theories, words, air, CO_2) begged to be, at least, fine-tuned.
 'During my lifetime . . .' Karl opined.
 'Such as it is . . .' came the adjustment.
 'Yes . . . as it is . . . Aussie, now, has never seemed . . .'
(how might it be said?) 'Happier?'
 'Not exactly,' the honing increased,
'the Australia that *you* know.'
        There were
other Australias: Dave had hardly needed them.
The nation was set to turn Labor but
eight hundred preferences would help scrape back their
local Lib: a one-time acting deputy
Chairman of Committees given to free enterprise
and Rhodesia, a boozy rhetoric-filled cog,
someone to ignore over the next three years.
Sure, this was a species that flowered throughout
the world, though no better (or worse which
stood for better) than in the West.
Communists?
You had to *think* with communists or,
at least, sometimes Dave thought of them:
whingeing union heavies, florid students
at the end of megaphones, and those old men in berets,
like Pop, his late father-in-law who,
each Christmas, lay down under the stars
and worried over the world. Though never feeling
quite the need Dave understood this; 'Pop,'

he still wanted to tell him, 'Pop, the place just gets stupider . . .
Certain things stop being believed,
but they're replaced.'
     Some time
(ten years back? fifteen?)
there was this local family who'd been
to Sweden for a year; and though
the husband was something of a boffin
Dave admired him. They had returned with slides,
the kindergarten auxiliary inviting her
to speak. But it was, after all, Sweden;
there had to be a meeting, then a vote.
Winnie had gone: they'd won as much
as they could: the slides were shown,
certain people weren't talking, some kids
had been withdrawn.
  'These communists,' a neighbour told him,
'have planes, see, and they're flying . . .'
(as he pointed skywards *Where else?* Dave muttered)
'flying and flying and dropping bombs,
invisible flu bombs.'
     'I've had the flu,'
Dave confessed, 'loved the lot of it.'
  This was as much nonsense as his hearing
could accept; to goad him, though,
just mention the RSL and all that oompah-oompah
expected from ex-servicemen.
He liked to say it once only
(though argument forced otherwise):
'I went to war: it got me my job,
got me my home; I'd do it again and
I never want to do it again.
End of transmission.'
     One day
something to believe beyond anything he knew
would hunt him out: though probably not
in those Friday evening sessions, shout-after-shout,
with Pat the Grouper:
'If you can trust a country that believes
in Nixon . . . be my guest!

dave price completes his extension

What side am *I* on? Not that one!'
    He had to accept too much sometimes.
On occasions he had even talked of
throwing in his deal, handing it on to
the students; not that they needed him,
the future never did; and something about the future,
or was it the past,
could get Dave shivering; you needed a drink, then
after that a nap to ease the chill.
But, on waking, what future had arrived?
Students were becoming teachers;
questions were getting answers;
he was being lectured;
and Dave knew no way to forgive *that*.
Their moodiness? He appreciated moodiness.
No, they just hadn't allowed for misjudgement (theirs)
and he wasn't man to be misjudged;
some days, Dave had to demand,
if only for himself *No, not this bloody time!*
    As one more crank at another parish pump
the most you risked was ridicule:
negotiating the city council's approval
to plant natives on his nature strip,
he made the front page of *The Gazette*.
Hard up for news (that week as most)
they refurbished Dave (someone doing something)
into the little man as hero.
    Thanks they never knew the epic
of his extension: how, Christmas Day,
six years back, he and Lindsay measured out
its limits, started the foundations.
Service and tolerance, courage and scepticism,
he could and did believe the lot
(along with anyone else who wished to)
but measured out from there to there to there
and back again, this building would be his!
    Sure, you might believe what hocus-pocus
your mum and dad stewed you in,
whilst the latest butterfly fluttering over
the back fence might be enough of a god

as anyone would ever need.
But when that became religion, as it would,
then religion bloomed to what it always was:
weaponry; and you didn't believe in JC or
butterflies then, but being what someone
said you were and who you barracked for:
Allah or the man in the moon or Chairman Mao.
    You could say *Yes!* or *No!* by yourself like Dave,
or yes-and-no en masse like Pop or Pat.
Commos were rebels who'd never got what
they were after, not here, not in Australia;
whilst Micks were rebels who had, pretty much,
got what they wanted, and didn't even seem
to wish for more, or believe in more.
He could attempt (it would only end
as an attempt) the following with Pat:
God's like me:
he doesn't care how anybody votes.
You Groupers are Groupers because you
are Groupers: end of transmission.
But he never said it, Dave already knew
the replies; knew the frustration
of confronting a closed mind in a good man;
and by then Dave would want to be obeyed.
He remembered Pop and how all rebels
craved obedience; all rulers those rebellions
that made them rule. In the one nation,
in the one person, fewer things seemed
less opposed; that much Dave knew (almost
understood) even if he didn't have
to live by it.
    You arrived in the world
believing nothing, how could you leave it
in a similar fashion?
    He still sought
that something to make him stay alive
which, in any case, he would. And this much
seemed completed: Wynne and their kids,
his home and this extension;
with one foot in the Second Division door

(enough to say he'd done *that*) Dave could take
a bit more work, a bit more promotion.
Then came, so he enjoyed telling a few,
the time to get out, grow a beard,
learn to sail, and circumnavigate the world!
(All right then, maybe.)
    But he knew what wasn't in any sense heroic.
Name him that idiot who, coming to Lindsay's
and Dottie's party, drove straight up Dave's drive
to the back door, blasting his horn:
Gooey was it, or Pooey?
Lucky for this Gooey, Dave was elsewhere;
and any wonder other idiots-in-authority
had wanted the lot shipped off to Puckapunyal
and beyond. (Though Gooeys 'n' Pooeys
never made it into battle because, like the Americans,
nowadays, they lost them.)
    'Dottie,' he asked
when more relaxed, weeks later,
'Dottie, who was that Pooey?'
    His daughter sighed: 'His name is Gibb, Dad,
Digby Gibb. Gibbo was a friend of Trevor's,
once.'
    Liking the 'once' (though why the 'once'
he didn't care) Dave Price had backed
the right team, his, again.
    And thankfully
this Digby Gibb wasn't around to answer this:
'So Gooey, you're asking me to break you,
eh Pooey? Well . . . *snap!*'
    At least Dave's boys had a resilience:
'Let's see,' they'd indicate, 'if you can break me
this time.' And 'Sure,' came his reply, 'I'll see
if I can break you this time/any time/
name-the-time . . .' and he might or he mightn't;
but to try and break his girls, Dave knew,
set him on course to something so much different:
when their ultimatum arrived: 'This is what
I want to do, try stopping me if you like but,
one day, I'll do it . . .' you knew they'd won.

Jeez over half the block would sigh,
that Pricey's a moody bastard: as complimentary
if they only knew, as was required from *them;*
there'd always be that minority of worthwhile
others; those to court with charm deserved
his charm.
    No, if moodiness
was to be admired (as it should be)
this was what he hated:
being thought by over half of any block
as useless, anything remotely useless.
And there, of course, Dave fooled Dave:
no opinion (except his own) could ever reach
the outer suburbs of that fantasy town.
(Was that why he'd extended? Maybe,
but as families grew you either had to
build-on or buy again.)
      After he had been
demobbed (becoming a clerk, married,
and four times a father) Dave hardly considered
the hypothetical (him as an engineer, an architect,
a builder?) until the time arrived
for this extension and yes, Dave discovered,
on his domain he could, with help, be
builder, architect, even engineer.
        Though tradies
over-talked, first explaining then re-explaining:
'See? This is what I'm doing, see? You're learning,
brother. Now, tell me, after earthquakes,
what men are most required? Give up?'
  'Not public servants!'
        'Too bloody right,'
the tradie grinned, 'plumbers first, then doctors.'
  And as Dave was this bright-fella:
'Hardly necessary 'round here am I brother?'
  But if you believe you only start learning at fifty
then tradesmen had their uses: a plumber
showing those finer points only a plumber knows,
same with electricians (Dave could almost become
an apprentice neurosurgeon); for he didn't know

and didn't want to know, what went with being
an old man, he knew already what being
the old man entailed: anyone who married Dot,
or later Nicola, hadn't a brain cell in their scones
(though after a few years married to the Price girls,
they might obtain some).
 He had a book
he'd love to write: *How Dave Price Manages People*.
No, too many would learn too much
so why not this lesser saga, if still a saga,
How I Completed My Extension?
 'Tonight, Wynne, everyone,' the man announced,
'all extending's finito. Can you believe there isn't
one more bloody thing to do? I can't. Tomorrow,
I'll be starting on a new garage, in which case
forgiveness shall be offered in advance. Thank you.'
 It was just eleven and his audience were
settling into that kind of stake-out only a raconteur
knows how to impose.
 They needn't have bothered,
he'd had enough: '. . . well everyone, tonight,
like every night, I'm full o' beer so listen to what
the beer's saying: *We're off to bed Dave and me*.
You got it? End of transmission.'

Barb at Dot's Wedding

for Helen St John

April

    When Lins was down for Easter his cousin
Sexy little Barb told him she was pregnant,
sure she was, to her boyfriend Roger.
                            No-one that arvo
(not her parents, not even Heathy) knew. Well,
there was a doctor and now, because she needed him,
her cousin.
            Why Lindsay? Being this close/this far
Barb understood that, for these few hours, this was
what she wanted: someone who knew her; someone, though,
who wouldn't judge.
                   By the next evening, of course,
the parents had brokered their part truce/part celebration:
Roger Heath and Barbara Price were to be married. Soon.

    Dot was out
when Rog arrived: telling Trevor he was set
to be a dad, wanting him for best man.
Marriage? he inquired, almost to himself, *it might be
an adventure.*
             And Barb?
                      Her folks had fixed it with
some church, some priest. '... *then I met him,
the man knows bugger-all. Why soon*
he was beside himself *Why very soon
you might present both parents with a wee surprise,*
Yeah I thought, sooner than you bloody think.'
    Dot arrived: 'Bit sudden, Heathy.'
    'No more than it was for me.'
                      'How's Barb?'

'We had this row.'
         'The first?'
                  'Yeah.'
Rog was grinning. 'There's nothing like your first.
Mind if I dial the hot line?'

&

    Barb trusted Lindsay and, as if for her,
each weekend he'd be back in Blackburn,
where they'd sit in his father's garden, Lins listening,
she prepared to explain something, anything:
like how she didn't know (all that much)
what she was doing; like how was this
for just 'going out' with someone:
all you trusted to stay private was going public;
like marrying Roger, Roger *Heath,* who is
Roger Heath? 'Tell us Lins, no don't,
let me find out ...'
         She so liked her cousin,
knowing he was not some *Nah wuz*
she'll be apples ocker-Pollyanna.
                  Not quite.
Roger had said they'd be going bush to teach
next year, and telling Lins he could only answer
'Three years at Woop-woop Consolidated, Barb?
you'll love it!'
         Rog, she knew, would love it
(their Karen-or-Sam wouldn't even remember).
    'You women,' Lindsay told her,
'some women ... a few ... tell me things
at times ... I'll never stop them.'
                  'Thanks', she said.
'Here I am *getting married* and treating you
like a teacher, a parent, the adult I'm
supposed to be.'
         'Don't worry Barb,
it's how you're made and so am I.'
    With this much of nothing to say he was thinking
When life moves, boy how it moves and

Not much could've slowed our little goer.
And how, were he to bail up Heath,
all he could say would be some fatuous
Yer in for the long haul, son two planks' worth.
      And who was Heath?
A friend of the brother-in-law's, someone
who snuck into his sister's wedding.
      While later this would hit him: Jeez!
If Karl had moved in first! *You missed your chance*
he wrote overseas *'cause, after he lowered th' boom*
boy how things went kah-boom! But Roger-dodger's
DOIN' THE RIGHT THING! And so ho ho he should.

Last December

      Even with his flat miles in towards the city
('Up early enough I might try walking to work ...')
Karl was still a fixture at the Prices';
though now, with Lindsay teaching in Gippsland,
it might be months before the crew convened;
until they did, not having much to do
and fewer to do it with; Karl just stayed content
to hear himself breathe out a long nostalgic
Jeez! sighed for those two/three years before
when, pickling themselves in chilled plonk
(and who'd forget those brilliant things cheap flagons
did to you or, even better made you do?)
they'd massacre the next few thousand brain cells.
      Then there was Dot:
sure, calling each other Uncle Karl and Auntie Dot
precluded any overload of sentiment; still,
Karl would tell himself *She's very good,*
Dot Price is very good.
(Wasn't there a time, not so far back,
when every Australian seemed to have their Auntie Dot,
or should have?)

Karl had this friend some years before
whom Lindsay didn't like. Doubtless worse the bumptious,
smelly, self-obsessed St Cloud had been Dot's boyfriend;
for a night. *I had a pleasant evening being mauled.*
   Next day, with the faintest echoes
of a logic Karl never guessed existed, St Cloud reported:
'When we ran out of things to talk about, I talked
about myself.' Mmmmmm.
                  Dot got one more call but everything
just stopped, as always with St Cloud and girls it stopped.
   'The old man's pleased,' Lindsay informed Karl
who, repeating *Pleased* confessed he somehow understood
most fathers would be.
                  'But know why?'
                              'Surely,' Karl
hardly asked, 'St Cloud's the *Why.* Err no?'
   And life never containing that much logic,
more started to unravel: 'Don't take offence,
him being a friend of yours 'n' that,
but Dad reckons he's a poofter.'
So where's the danger? Karl thought it kind to ask.
And kinder not to.

☙

   Now they were more than four years older,
Dot was marrying Trevor and, after the reception,
their cousin Barb would stay a while. Eighteen;
just out of Matric, even before she arrived mischief
was blossoming in Lindsay.
                  As it would often:
when his father wasn't present going in for pseudo-ocker
overkill: saying those things best said when every mouth
at dinner was awash with soup:
'What *him?* Doubt if that ponce ever
cracked a fat!'
            Now, teasing his mother, he asked after
'Sexy Barb . . .' and 'My yummy little cousin . . .'
adding to titillate his mate: Just wait till you meet *her!*'
   Whilst 'Lind-say . . . Lind-say . . .' his sister wailed,

bemused in protest.
                          Karl knew how,
except for harmless Trevor Greene,
little remained which didn't bring the cynic out
in Dottie. And how, even at her wedding,
he and Lindsay would perform for her:
'Plurry good, boss . . .' sliding into
Jacky-Jacky mode:' . . . errgh, you're a whiteman,
son.'
        'Next,' Dot explained to Barb,
'they'll be doing Gough impersonations. Uncle Karl
does bad ones and so does Lins, but badder.'
            'Trust yer Auntie Dot,' Karl advised,
'ev'ry girl deserves her Auntie Dot.'
                'Where do you live?' the cousin asked.
                                            A flat.
Soon though he'd be going o.s., after that, buying something.
Home had been East Brighton: this little piece of
not-quite-kosher heaven, just past Tommy Bent,
and Craig Stubbs' Real Livin' Toyota.
                            Karl had been
at school with Stubbs: 'If I'd any charity remaining
a one-dimensional charmer . . . otherwise, a prick.'
And he told how, for a real livin' government,
Stubbs shaking hands with the latest Liberal hack
made the election special in his parents' local rag
(playground equipment or something).

❧

    Now, from the extension, Karl saw Barb
with Roger Heath stroll into the dark.
Mmmm he decided *quick and the dead stuff;*
better cross us off; still, if she's the girl next door
she's a bloody sexy girl next door;
yippee when you get it; history is being made.
He liked her, though; couldn't stop watching.

❧

'The little goer!' On the patio
Lindsay was dancing with his sister when he saw,
if no-one else did, cousin Barb strolling down the back
with Heath. 'You just missed,' Dot was informed,
'our little goer go. She 'n' The Dodger must be
up to mischief.'
   'Lind-say!' she replied, meaning
Must the bride's big brother be such an ocker perv?
Though meaning, even more, *Tell us again? Barb and who?*
Where?
   For she liked her cousin
and couldn't help taking a moment from the reception
to calculate how Roger Heath was twenty-one or -two
(like her and Trevor) and Barb had just completed school.
Then, sort of approving,
Dot checked herself they'd just met tonight,
weren't anything like 'a couple', whilst only Lins
had seen them wander off behind the shed.
For what? Some getting-to-know-you quickie?
Not even Lindsay for all his *Whoo-hoo-hoo!*
would bother guessing that hard.

       ❧

       Oh yes,
the afternoon and evening hadn't let Dot down;
someone else (she didn't care exactly who)
might appropriate the tears and tantrums;
she had her guests to charm.
       But more a cynic than
she'd let anybody guess tonight, if you presumed to ask
what this wedding meant to Dot,
there'd be a pause to gather in *What, right now?*
and imitating her father, issue a way of life
Get on with it, teach, have kids, teach some more,
get grandkids and get on with it. Together!

       ❧

'I hardly dance,' Roger shrugged at Barb.
'Me neither,'
adding a simpler 'let's leave here.'
'Yes, let's.'
Down the yard they turned, looked, he sounding dry:
'Patio's rockin'.'
Almost heading to a sneer?
Too bad, the boy was company, if need be
just tonight.
To where they'd stepped
the party seemed that touch absurd,
you saw enough of floppy hats and micros,
body shirts and flares, to know one day
you'd ask *We wore, we looked like that?*
Hearing these night sounds: cicadas, side one
of 'The White Album', a sprinkler (was it?) over
the back fence, her head turned up, Barb breathed in
and kissing with him 'What's this?' she murmured.
'Just initiative,' (that slight-corny style amusing her).
Voices: a groomsman, Dot, Trevor's parents, lapped
up from the babble of the patio.
'Barbara ...' was mentioned. But why
attend to that when you could just stand,
under the night, sharing something wonderful-stoopid:
to kiss and hear the lean, sandy boy call it initiative.
Ho? What movie gave that line?
She'd other, better words *Basic* say
*Even if he doesn't know me much,
even if there's someone else, I'm liked again
and that's how 'basic'!*

So who are you lean, sandy boy? Roger,
still studying, just one more from the uni.
And what, he asked, next year?
Art school, she hoped, telling him where she lived.
'What time you going home?'
'I'm not,
I'm staying here.'
He might come round
tomorrow then?
'Initiative,' she answered,

lighting first his cigarette then hers.
    But who kept up that fanfare to 'The Lonely Bull'?
Lindsay of course: Dot and Trevor were going.
    'Better appear.' Roger seemed annoyed. 'You first . . .'
making it sound like war, that they should grenade
the babbling patio.
        The wedding couple
circling their friends, Barb stood by Roger,
wanting to touch and hold this slim boy,
discover what she might be saying next.
Yes with the slightest shrug *He's fine. Roger Heath's
okay. Mightn't come round of course. Always others.
Not tonight though.*

        Beer cartons were soccered
through the extension and 'Bun-yip!' Uncle Dave
commanded, 'Goalie!'
Two attempts then three, four, five,
as Karl-the-Bunyip kept on saving.
        'Hard feelings Dave?'
    'None . . .' but wringing his opponent's hand,
'just pay up you Bunyip, pay!'
(Who, near bored, waited.)
    It all, Barb saw, had been played before
and her uncle relaxed himself into the truce
of cavemen-cobbers: 'Okay? Hard feelings, son?'
    How could there be with Dot's wedding
winding down to a final 'cleansing ale'
from Lindsay's 'secret half dozen'?

        By Roger's car
she leaned against him, saying nothing wasn't easy,
saying *Must meet you soon* too easy and his quiet,
crisp 'I'll come by . . .' got matched as
'Great,' she croaked out: never asking when.
    The night seemed wrapped in scent,

as if all flowers in the suburb had
orders to burst. Windows and curtains open,
the moon over Dot's walls (well her former walls)
over portraits of Trevor, Gough, Butch, Sundance
and Katharine Ross, Simon and Garfunkel;
a reproduction of 'A Breakaway!'
    She'd get some sleep. Hope, ideals,
even infatuations, some things were surely fragile.
Tonight, though, would never lie.
You kiss thought Barb *and you are kissed.*
Kissed too many times. But call it fun call it
being liked, call it she smiled *initiative.*

    Something had been mumbled about
the agricultural pipes, and near where she'd kissed
with whosits, Roger, Uncle Dave was digging.
The Dutch help stacking the dishes
Barb sat with her aunt in the extension.
A warm late-morning draping over Hangover Towers
brought in Lindsay and, soon enough, Karl:
for a brunch dedicated to Deadshits We Have Known!
    'Remember Gibb: here: this room?' Lins puffed
into the role. *'Not just a good fwend Mrs Pwice,*
Twevor's my best mate. Remember Gibb, Mum?
My fwend, my best fwend Twev! Agh!'
(choking on the thought of Gibb, his declaration,
and Trevor's embarrassed acceptance) 'Deadshit!'
If Gibb had never waddled, Lindsay was set
he should've. *'Ooohh . . .'* up the extension
his mimicry went *'Miss-us Pwice . . .'*
    She laughed, but tried rejecting it:
'He was never *that!*'
                    'Yeah? Give him a week
the word is out 'n' hard for Dot:
and Gibb is pissed of course. Remember, Mum?'
    'Plus,' Karl volunteered, 'Gibb *believed* that slop.
He needed to. What remained? Can't have Trevor
like he *really* wants him: gets tanked,

lines up the girlfriend. Best mates?'
(voice rising, Karl's smile just begged
Ready for this?) 'Best? None better.
Gibb was infatuated.
There. Full stop.' He looked about.
'Even if the pack's so shuffled and all conceivable
hands are ready to be dealt, the Ace of Love exists.
It must. What else was it?'
       'Where's Gibb?' Barb asked.
 'Now?' shrugged Karl. 'The near-legendary Gibb?
Advertising, dig?'
       'Real estate, mate?'
 (The terrible two with their catalogue of
dingbat occupations.) '... a stockbroking, Liberal-
voting, A-one poofteroonie!'
 And, having exhausted Gibb,
'Who brought the nineteenth man last night?' asked Karl.
 'Yeah, well ...' Lindsay raised his eyebrows,
'he's something like a friend of Trevor's.
Roger Heath can always get himself invited.'
 There! Nothing to chorus over with
that one. No impersonations for him!
And Barb had hardly to guess what remained:
the following dickheads are brought to you by
Lindsay and Karl, fellas.
And smiles between herself and Auntie Wynne
Aren't they predictable? seemed enough;
for Barb knew guys (well thought she did)
no, call that understood the chants and gags,
their getting the hustle done. *Well perhaps,
since we're supposed to 'love' them, sometimes.
Everything is qualified.*
Yes all-of-it (love or mere attraction)
would never fully measure, would it?
Why try to 'go' with Karl, who wouldn't even
look at you, when someone like her Mr Initiative
(their Mr Immaterial) seemed available.
If he called.

          ❧

          Well, Roger called.
As if to measure how she'd cope
into the afternoon Barb had anticipated his words
as so beyond the spectacular
I want to see you I haven't slept
I've forgotten your face meet me please
But this century (this country)
no boy talks a girl into a swoon
she wouldn't miss. Plenty enough were
doubtless around to like him as, perhaps,
she did.
          So partly braced for *I need . . .*
I haven't . . . I've forgotten . . . (and
Oh come now . . . her over-languid rejoinder)
'I'm Roger,' she heard croak out, 'you doing much?'
          'Come round?'
                    'Go out?'
                              'Where?'
                                        'Where'd y' like?'

May

          Lindsay was waiting to tell Barb how, down where he taught,
these schoolkids and these women came up, told him things:
many things and really told him. And though it wasn't Victoria's
smallest town, the place could be a damn size bigger.
          'You're a good man,
all these women would say.
                              Okay then, what made good men 'good'?
Heathy doing-his-right-thing? Perhaps.
If Karl was a better person, and he was,
Lindsay also knew him as quite an opportunist,
near perverse with it; he thought of warning Barb
Once you're hitched and if Karl's about, watch out:
you'll be even more than a hit with him!
The not quite totally attainable were made for Karl:
that slice of someone else's pie which might,
just once, be Karl's. (Even as fantasy a difficult man's

difficult design. Jee-sus mate, what could be bleaker?)
    Then Lindsay considered Gibb:
for him all men were best mate fodder,
each best mate's girl potential for a silly bugger's
hard word; Gibb: that kind of clown sticking himself up your drive,
your parents' drive, his hand flat on the horn *P'parp p'parp
I'm here I'm here!* wanting all your neighbourhood to understand
*I'm rootin' my car ha-ha ha-ha, that's right shitkickers,
rootin' it!*
    And Roger Heath was not like that.
    But clipped, lean-lipped with flaky, freckled skin,
Roger hardly pleased Barb's cousin: who told himself *She's stuck.*

ও

    Lindsay thought up book titles, err well one:
My Sexy Schoolgirl Cousin and Other Rellies.
    'Kid-ding,' he explained to Dot, 'just kidding.'
    'Sexy? Sexy?' his sister grilled. 'Oh oh,
Lins Lins, come on come on.'
Barb was cuddly, she could grin. You could pick her up,
put her in your pocket and take her home. But that was
'sexy' Lindsay? One year ago what would she have known?
Smiles, hugs and kisses if she were lucky; if she weren't:
maulings from *her* St Clouds, *her* Gibbs hardwording it.
'So Barb's with Heathy now? The world has worse.'
She could trust him; would have to though.
                        Oh Dot was fine,
Lindsay knew, she just had it not right that's all.
Now if Karl were here . . .

ও

          Lindsay asked 'Remember Karl,
    Barb?'
Yes Barb remembered both of them, over-enunciating like
Mr Whitlam *It wasn't a spi-dah / Who sat down besi-dah* . . .
Well he was in England now' . . . chucking a mental
at the Poms, and know what he's written back?
So how's your sexy little cousin?'

❧

In a few Saturdays she'd be Mrs Roger, that was how.
Mrs What? Mrs Doesn't-feel-so-sexy-now.
You were too late, Karl; nice of you to ask,
a jumbo flight away; but here I'm trying to love
someone I've to know first, must save any 'mentals'
for my dreams.
                She'd been ambushed: if let's-call-it-sex
had cornered her first, time did the pummelling now;
she felt sprawled, their victim.
Very soon (a someone, somewhere on display)
at Holy Redeemer, North Ringwood,
I'll turn into Barbara Heath.

❧

                      By now the atmosphere
was fogged with sweetest sacrifice: Barb hunting
tide-us-over work, Roger shelving his honours thesis;
and, packing away all prejudice for the moment,
every possible adult loving them. If there was time
for a crisis, they'd be getting married in crisis;
time, though, held. Barb only knowing
she never wanted anything so clumsy again.

❧

                          Roger had this friend
who had a flat in Murrumbeena. They snuck there for an afternoon,
fucked on the mattress and fell asleep.
                        As if she'd finally moments
to consider *It's something like . . . like . . .* Barb dreamt a waterfall,
woke up knowing how, today, her body held just that waterfall.
Tomorrow, as with all tomorrows now, it would alter,
though still remaining Karen-or-Sam.
                    Then, hardly knowing this boy she
signed on and grappling, lay beside, *Who is he?* the girl kept trying
to ask *Who?*

But, as she rearranged her memories, Barb started a smile:
Lindsay was conjured, guessing correct and shouting
Who? You are asking who???
It was Roger!/ The lodger!/ The sod!

AUNTIE WYNNE AT BARB'S WEDDING

  I'm sure you know, I'm sure I'll never tell you,
Barb, if any passion's built on just mere passion
then passion's built on even less than wind.
  There's little use in feeling *Some weddings make me
even older than those times my parents died*
for if there are events which seem as permanent shunting yards,
many, like today's, are junctions:
guests who've never met before or have, solo,
or in duets, but nearly always chorusing *Let's meet again eh?* /
Weren't they quick, Barb and young Heathy there . . . /
Hey, let's know when we can help!
         But if
in all this faces-to-names-to-faces routine, if
as an example I know him as your husband, Roger, Roger Heath,
who is he though? A boy a touch younger than Lindsay,
doing what he believes he knows he must:
marrying my niece; and a man whose kids
might one day deduce *So, this is how they, they
and all their folks kept up appearances*:
how dumb how noble how sad how strange how apt!
  Not that your children won't continue learning
about their own, all parents do. Today,
driving me here, Lindsay, I rediscover, can still annoy me:
still turns too silly for his age:
'At Holy Redeemer,' he erupted, 'the Little Goer's taken
another one almighty screamer!'
        I passed this nonsense,
knowing there was worse.
       Few prejudices hurt
more than those of any who should know better.
It would've been one life-long campaign
getting *my* father into any Holy Redeemer.
For all his puffed-out tolerance (so vain at being
such a humanist) father knew not merely 'best'
but often, it would be discovered and discovered,
not so much at all.

Yet I never knew a better man.
　　Each Christmas, turning depressed, Dad
would take a blanket into his backyard,
spread it out, lie down, count the stars
and hunt out sputniks: as if such contemplation
might out-stare all the seasonal crass.
　　　　　　　　　　　　It was a time,
it was always a time, to fit his forehead
into that rebel's frown: always prepared, always
hoping to become a fellow-traveller martyr.
　　　　　　　　　　　　　His wife
barely mattered: Mum simply trusted that, somehow,
he might outgrow this fashion: barracking for the Russians.
　　In each once-upon-a-time,
no matter where, someone is adjusting and someone
isn't. Today Barb's father accustoms himself
to those he'd never bother with: his daughter's
in-laws; his wife is not so ashen-faced
though such events as have ensured her past few months
won't go unremembered; under sufferance
Lindsay is a groomsman; my husband who believes
the only worthwhile weddings were and will be his daughters'
still attends; and, as if to give the rest of us
a benchmark, Roger and Barb are married now.
　　　　　What a small melodrama it seems today:
my father lying down in all his Christmas fury;
or even *my* Christmas fury:
when, choosing no better day to remember, David
had to start on his extensions.
For it was hardly the dinner kept on hold, rather
that everyone we were supposed to have around
had to arrive and watch him, him and our sons
stripped to shorts, digging trenches or anything.
Maybe this day I knew my guests were thinking
is Christmas, but that over there is Old Man Price!
　　　Sure he was extending: my patience.
　　　One Christmas? That building must've taken four.
　　　But 'David,' I demanded, though years later,
'we are having Dot's reception *here*.'
　　　Who told me: 'Never said we weren't!'

But only a few might love more than an angry wife,
unless she's an angry mother. All mothers surely,
have to be annoyed, sometimes; either that or not
too easily impressed. And, each time
you find something you've done fails the kids, that,
even that, goes with the job: the job
or whatever it is.
    One day, soon, Barb,
you'll find yourself announcing *Of course I must
employ all my tact, guile, and all my love.*
Though, almost as soon, you'll realise, that until
they and you are adults (oldies together) for kids
the only real questions have to be *their* questions.
('How old,' Dottie asked at six,
'How old must I be before I kiss a boy?'
Well not right now dear.)
     And, even sooner,
you'll be found telling yourself
*I can't, shan't, won't be bothered with simply
all of that!* And yet, of course
you can, you shall, you will:
for it's *you* who have the facts, and it's *you* who can
approve or, doubtless better for them and all their schemes
as rebel or complier, disapprove;
and it will be you, wanting to go into your backyard,
wanting to forget everything that's left inside.
 And you won't.
     For here's the pride there is in families:
the knowledge that the rest of the world accounts
for just so much of your time, anyone's time;
that if each house is a cell, each home is
an empire.
    Where you have, at least, this luxury:
what to name your provinces.
      Twenty years ago
(when it seems all of us had stepped from
knitting pattern booklets: their 'Bobby', 'Ivan',
Janet' and 'Cherie' staring into middle distance)
we dealt out 'Lindsay', 'Dorothy', 'David'
(yet again) and 'Nicola'. (Or 'Barbara', 'Shane',

'Claire', 'Vivienne' and 'Philip'. Or 'Trevor'.
Or 'Roger'.)
               Now, as always, as forever,
the names disperse and merge, merge and disperse:
sealing themselves in homes as families, as empires:
somehow stoic with their hand-me-overs, all mod cons,
all their unending extensions.
                          And love maybe,
or something like we hope it is: luck perhaps?
    If I've had my love, my luck,
here is all this aunt can hope to hand over:
better, even stronger, luck: i.e. Barb
all that this woman wishes she still had this far,
yet never quite.
               Your loving Wynne.

THE AGE OF 'COWBOY' NEALE
SCENES FROM THE LIFE OF LINDSAY PRICE

I.M. Greg St John 1948–1977

Grand-dad

    My mother's father tried to make the bush
stay in the suburbs. His land is a sanctuary now,
his home, council-nurtured flora and fauna.
Poofter developers tried to bribe him off his
seventeen acres: deadshits! The old bugger
told these greasers that, thank you, but
he was a socialist: his body would be given
to science, his land to the people.
Shrewd-naive, cranky, though never faddish, his last years,
like all his life, tendered him issues: his vegetables,
Viet Nam. *Yet,* he said, *brought the game
into the outer.* But even the Americans surprised:
by early '68 he, who always believed,
was justified: 'Johnson is losing his popularity . . .'
Then, just after New Hampshire, the old fella
spread himself over his kitchen floor.
Now with no face, no voice, we simply
had to remember. Tangibles remained of course:
his gardening journalism, fruit promotions, a friend's
humanist elegy. When my sisters and I helped
clear his home we found objects, van loads of them
among the fluff: the shelves were row-on-row
of bottled fruit (those cartons of unreadable
fine print verse we gave to Karl) Fabian tracts
and Russian grammars. Ahh to be a crank
that Menzies would abhor, to be that cranky!
The man gave thoughts, was acts,
this believer believed: the Unitarians, somehow
the Masons, the United Nations, the mighty Saints.

How'd we go?
for Brendan Ryan

  Hitting The Valley to teach I needed company and found Syd:
staff equivocator with that dumb cunning of almost-not-a unionman.
  'After this,' he waved a hand about the school yard,
'I'll be up, off and into real estate.'
  Three of my drinking crowd, art teacher desperadoes,
lived out in Kelly Country: this weatherboard farmhouse:
flagons of plonk, slabs of steak, and if you didn't mind flaking
on their vinyl couch or beanbags, flake away.
  And I would but always found myself most weekday nights
home in town, on my patch with Syd,
watching the local relay channels or whatever fuzzed its way
from Melbourne.
    Or hearing how, still a bushie shucks at heart,
one day Syd would retire here. 'Plans,' he urged, 'Lindsay, plans!'
Relatives lived in The Valley: name anything, they sold or
owned it: one had the town's first laundromat.
'Cents make dollars make sense,' Syd continued. Or *Land!*
he'd mantra *Land! Land!* There was so much still to own,
let alone to sell.
    Whatever the man was he was
serious with it.
    Dot met him once. 'That Syd,'
her verdict snapped, 'has a small mouth
and the face of a rat!' (Which he kept in check with a stinky
electric razor and primed with isobars of aftershave.)

  Kelly Country, having certain limits (no, just one: men,
plain-and-only men) Syd advises how they hold,
every first Saturday at the Showgrounds, a not-so
old style dance (this cow-cocky end of The Valley
little else could get as hip). 'First we'll mildly tank ourselves
(bundy 'n' coke say) then the night is ours and,
if they're lucky, someone else's.' The hospital auxiliary
turns out a decent spread: 'Sangers, cakes . . .' even, to be adventurous,
savouries, and 'Can't wait, eh?' I am elbowed.

'Women, Lindsay, women.'
                    (I'll always wonder what he truly
            thinks they are.)

                       ❧

        I can do a passable barndance but Syd
in all his virginal sleaze (two-stepper, foxtrotter,
fifty/fifty charmer) knows every move
Hey girls, better bring your armour!
                        I sit out lots as,
by the numbers, chatting if not chatting-up
A-one / and-a-two / and-a-three / and-a-four . . .
he does it his way: keeping a watch on me doing it mine.
        And soon he tows across to meet/inspect/be smiled at,
Lynne, a preschool teacher.
                        And what's Syd muttering?
'She hasn't a car mate . . . hasn't a car . . .'
And what's he mouthing? *In, boy. You are in!?*
And what is signalled from his open-eyed mock innocence?
I stand by mates so take her, you take her.
Lynne and Lindsay eh?
                    And how am I looking?
Like I've seen much that's crass but nothing
such as this has happened *In The Valley? In the World?*
        It worsens: Syd flapping his hand is waving ta-taas:
he's really dumping her on me, me on her.
And what are we to talk about? Not Syd, although
I'm tempted to announce *Lynne, you've just met*
The Valley's premier dickhead, him and his dumb mate.
        'Tea?' I ask. 'Coffee? They serve them here . . .'
        She's tall, has angles, probably needs some specs;
and shares, I'm answered, with a girlfriend.
        Oh so do I at least a boyfriend no a friend no
with him that one over there, Syd;
the one who's going to return, isn't he?
                            He must.
He does. For here in The Valley it's getting late
and I am braced for *Eleven-thirty? Bedtime eh!*
        No, he just yawns. But is insistent:

'Lynne we'll take you home, Lindsay and me.
No-one else is.'
     If only I could say
It's a small town, nothing will happen,
trust me, I want you to, please let's salvage
something, Lynne. Be dumb enough.
        She is.

     ಳ

  In my rearview Syd's settling in: settling in and
nodding off (after all his efforts so he should).
  Oh Lynne Lynne you may be this planet's most
adorable doll for someone. I only hope we never meet again;
or, if we do we'll know how (except for him there
snoring in the back) nothing unites us.
  '. . . err,' I'm told, 'you don't have to see me up
the drive. Goodnight, Lindsay.'
        Fine!
  '. . . err goodnight, Lynne.'
        She firmly shuts the door.
  Then, as I rev off, Syd jolts awake.
        And the man is urgent:
'How'd we go mate? How'd we go?'

1974
for Kieran Caroll

  Over the fireplace,
in the farmhouse living room, a sign reads
Welcome To Kelly Country, Girls!
  When I arrived Dick Kelly,
art teacher, year ten coordinator,
him with a reputation for rooting his way
up The Valley and back *Err not exactly yet, Lins*
told me: 'Been here three years, find us better
and I'll leave. You won't though.'
       Now

it's a Sunday afternoon: I've been marking assignments
and, glancing up to catch some VFA bloodbath
in a mudbath, gird myself for a newsflash.
And it is Snedden, Billy *Wavelength of his generation*
Snedden, smuggest of aspirants, enunciating
'An election ... any day now any day.'
    Dick knows the only way to combat
such petulant bonhomie is telling it straight:
'You make me wanna hit 'n' spit 'n' shit!'
    It's fun to be a teacher:
somehow you're certain Snedden won't be
walking over us!
                   And my old man,
thinking he has the only handle on the works of life,
keeps telling me, us, anyone who'll attend
and anyone who won't: 'This, alas, is The Age of Teachers.'
And relishing he warns: 'Bloody well much more it won't be.'
    Later, when he knows
full-as-a-goog is not the entire Dave Price,
he tries to make a reasonable scene:
'Readjust,' he says, 'not everyone's a teacher,
even amongst you teachers. There's plenty,
even in your valley, who still believe
commos invented the flu and worse.
And really what have commos, Aussies commos,
done? Lived in some past and place
that isn't now and isn't here,
tried altering the present and over-believed
their future. In other words they've been,
like your Grand-dad, pests.'
    Though he finds it a certain compensation
this isn't The Age of Snedden, yet.
    One of the staff's Americans asks:
'Don't you guys ever stop having elections?
Say, is this the national sport?'
    Were he worthwhile I'd take him to Moorabbin,
let him observe *my* national sport:
'Cowboy' Neale, hip 'n' shoulder almost nothing but
hip 'n' shoulder, bullock it with the best,
enjoying himself.

When I applaud
I want to applaud all those things I could never do.
I can't abide anyone (members, cheer squad,
the outer) who loves to see just whacks behind
the play, cartings off and nothing more.
My reason's plain: any idiot can walk out
his door, into the street and clock
the first poor sap he meets. I could?
Sure I could.
        No I'd rather announce
Geez 'Cowboy', this game you've been useless.
And still you're better than anyone of us!
    But who'd ever trust me after that?
    Well I wouldn't say anything like that to Snedden!
    Bugger The Age of Snedden!
    It's The Age of 'Cowboy' Neale!

Price and son

    At my folks' Dick noticed a dent in the fridge;
which was? 'The old man, the old man's fist.'
And seeing a hole in the wall Karl got told
'You wouldn't want to know . . .' and understood.
    Later, not too later, I am watching this man,
over fifty, take a twenty-two-year-old's hand and,
trying to pulp it, demand
'All in fun? No hard feelings Bunyip? All in fun?'
    Blue eyes getting wilder as they aged,
thirty years of flat feet and
Outa my way this is a man getting things done
yet so at ease ad-libbing one-liners
he should have been running quiz shows should've
except, mind and body brining away in piss,
who would be allowed to tolerate him?
    Never mention the desert;
don't even think of the islands; who'd you think
he was: Colonel 'Tub' Thumper, RSL loudmouth?
Not only *You wouldn't understand my war,*

you aren't to consider understanding.
     Spluttering back to A after a keg at B
how'd he arrive home total,
how'd he fail to add to the state's increasing
road trauma?
              One summer, at Christmas,
the year's most memorable day,
he started his extension: 'We will not forget this,
son, we are going to get things done!'
He turned to Mum: 'Woman, no complaints!'
     She simmered for years:
'Nothing was more deliberate! Just to spoil
my plans entirely!'

     Dad wouldn't talk, really.
He only made you imagine things.
Like this? It's Cairo you are twenty and a soldier
but still twenty; and in you wander to some place
where blokes cheer on this Arab sheila,
fucking a donkey. Wouldn't you think you were joining
the greatest evil, whether you wanted to
or not?
     And (even though I've only read *that* somewhere,
only imagined it since) later wouldn't you want to sleep
with cricket bats the time deadshit Bernie Millar
planned on paying all of us a visit?
     Why had I bothered with Millar's
matey insinuations, had never considered simple
checking? Why had I never known just what
to check? Why do I keep imagining
the old man demand the old lady answer:
How did Lindsay get himself in that?
and neither parent replying *Because,
with some queer curiosity, he wanted to?*
     Why has Mum stayed with it?
Whatever her why it's what gets the woman
telling her kids: 'There's things which have to stay
within these walls.'

(Certain things,
but not her children: one sets up home with
Mr Okay, one turns armchair boffin,
one just leaves home early, and this one, heading bush,
tries, for a season, to be the 'Cowboy' of
the Woop Woop League.)
    Not that I've asked for it
but why have all these women told me things?
    How come Karl spends year upon year
mock-pining for The Little Goer
(until you're more than guessing he really means it)?
    What makes The Little Goer suffer
the not infrequent moods of Roger Heath?
    What made Dick chat up half the Matric girls
in The Valley, hoping to bring them home to
Kelly Country?
        Why did some of them?
                And why,
some day will I be sitting down in a North Sea oil rig
non-stop laughing at the lot of this?

Theme song

    It's well into another Sunday morning:
yesterday I listened to 'Cowboy' lobbing six against
the certainly less than remotely mighty Boo-hoo Blues,
Kelly's team. Later we caught the replay:
'Dick,' I told him, 'you know how to shake your head
very very well.
        Then, after scrubbing up a touch
we hit a turn, hoping the music wouldn't be
all that ooh-ahh-woo-wah 'Magical Mystery Tour' routine
which may as well be Lester Lanin. Some was some wasn't,
but one I loved. 'You ever heard Chuck Berry?'
I asked Joanne (someone to look at more than twice,
or twenty twice) who teaches further down The Valley.
She knows what she likes and wants us to meet again.
Again! I'll ink-in that!

　　　　　　　Right now though,
one more deadshit Pom has just been caught Marsh,
bowled Lillee.
　　　　　　And all night long I've discovered me
a theme song: 'My Ding-a-ling'.

Rhapsodies

　　　　Syd nudged:
'I'm after a tax-haven, I just bought another
laundromat.' For he can begin a conversation
where all others end: everything an afterthought,
nudging. 'Being in the land business now,
I know what situation the total Australian land
market's in. Fellas, how's the women?'
　　　　Dick, Karl and I took Syd to the cricket.
Dick sat smiling under his large zinced nose;
Karl bewailed the yahoos of Bay Twelve;
Syd wanted to know about Joanne:
'How's the little woman eh? What's she like,
does she go?'
　　　　Dick snorted and Karl berated
'Really! The man's in love!'
　　　　　　　　　　　So Syd got coy
and Syd got drunk, dropping an ice-cube down the back
of a young woman's shorts. Who snarled
'Hey, can't you drop something hotter?'
　　　　He may have blanched but kept on nudging:
for going home he was rhapsodic: 'Gee that one
was nice, she's got a beautiful bone structure.'
　　　　'Shut up about today's goddess and her
flaming beautiful bone structure!'
　　　　　　　　　　　　　'Hey fellas, I've this idea . . .'
'What d'ya want, a bromide?'
　　　　'No seriously, I've taken clients to the Corroboree Rex.
Let's go, they've a clinker bar and little darlings.'
　　　　'What y' flog' em? Six inches of bone-structured sausage?'
　　　　Syd returned to The Valley: 'Sites you know . . .

gee this is a beautiful country, a lucky country,
so much land; if only we had as much stray talent
as land heh heh heh . . .'
  Oh nghyh nghyh nghyh nghyh nghyh!
  And Dick said Jeez Lins I need a beer;
I'm after a laundromat, just bought another tax-haven.'

Jane

  . . . and still women find me out to tell me things.
  Like Jane, running to my car
one afternoon in Lutwyche Street:
'Can I see you now?'
     'Sure.'
       She didn't
do much talking for a time, but went
straight into tears.
      It was September,
the month I hoped the Cowboy would truly fire,
the month you start counting those weeks
to HSC; and get to measure kids by letters:
Jane was a B, perhaps a very good B,
'Stretch' was an A heading a D (she had days
and days), Wally would plod into C and be thrilled.
  Jane was telling me of Max, her Ag Science boyfriend:
'Look it's silly isn't it: here I am eighteen
and thinking of an engagement? And crying?'
  'Mmm. People over eighteen never cry?'
  She smiled: 'Look, nothing's really wrong. I love him,
but do I? Want to go to Monash. Funny,
I really enjoy studying. Think I've only started it.
Sir . . .'
  'Oh please, don't call me sir.'
       'Sorry,
these exams, you'll say I'll pass, and I will it's just
I wanted you to say it. And yes I know you would . . .
You won't think I'm crazy will you sir?'
  I could leave *Sir* for now but never *Crazy*.

Crazy? Jane you think you're confused but please
you aren't the first. Yet I couldn't say *That*,
couldn't say how Joanne and I were, what,
having altercations, Dick was out screwing anything
with tits and legs except Lexie, his latest,
and how this friend in Melbourne still went on about
this cousin of mine he'd met, once, four years before.
That all my years in the bush
had been great times, sure, but we were changing:
that love and bitching, activism and piss-fartin' round
only piled on the uncertainties.
Jane, I thought, the entire world that passes itself
for adult acts like kids younger than you:
from next year it's regression all the way.
Cry? You'd cry *Chrissakes grow up!* at half the things
we do. You Year Twelves are so bloody old.
  I considered this Max, some Young Farmer probably,
National Party deadshit, a more superior cocky;
oh well breeding counts in these parts and Jane,
the dentist's daughter, could add the 'tone':
plenty to say, but not trying to froth over you,
and yes great little tits.
      Even most Friday nights
she wouldn't be found twiddling coasters in some
bistro bar, she'd be studying something,
waiting for Max.
     '... you'd like him, he's into
more than animals and crops.' Then Jane smiled:
'Ohh not like that, but well ...'
  If only Joanne hadn't been so tetchy,
if only Dick and Lex were, at least, speaking,
we might have her round, with Max, to Kelly Country;
but got-to-keep-in-well-with-the-locals:
for them nothing beats the mighty balance:
him her him her him her.
      Jane said: 'All that crying, all that raving,
I'm a bit embarrassed.'
    'It's September,
know the feeling.'
    'Sir ...'

Then we paused, chorused 'Don't call me sir!'
and laughed.

A Credit to us all

  Since Syd left I've never been to the showgrounds
but, as the Americans are leaving, there's this
civic reception and here we are: me, Joanne, Dick,
a few more, and, on a visit, Karl.
        'Hi fellas!'
Enter Syd's cousin, the laundromat czar and
'Guess you know a by-election's in the air?'
(We know, he's told, what the air contains.)
'No doubt you won't be voting my way but I'm
your friendly Liberal candidate and future member ...'
(As if the seat's some dealership, a franchise.)
It may as well be. This end of The Valley
there's hardly any party, *our* party; well there is
and we the teachers are it. 'Say,' we're taunted,
'am I to run this race alone? Mates, mates,
give us some competition!'
       It's worse than
any Age of Snedden now, it's the age
of everything to follow: the gloating (his)
the backpedalling (ours) the age to ask ourselves
Slippery? Is he caked in Vaseline or what?
Oh for any victory! Something tonight to one day tell the kids
*And then we had him! For once
his great escape just wasn't on.*
  Later, at the pub, it's him again.
  'So what's your service club?' asks Dick.
'Kiwanis?'
    'Nah mate.'
      'Apex?'
        'Try again.'
'Jaycees?'
    'Mate almost there ...'
        'Rotary!'

'Mate the very thing!'
    'Mate,' mutters Karl. 'Mate. Mate. Mate.'
    We spend all evening tossing this frisbee
of a word. There he goes:
The Honourable Member for Mate, Mr Mate ...
Mr Mate out the door and into Lutwyche Street
with Karl, the craziest of grins slapped across his face
pursuing with a breathless 'Mate mate,
I thrive on fights. Come election day I'm your man and
you are on!'

    'The dirt,' seethes Dick,
'there must be someone with the dirt!'
    'There's none,' says Karl,
'and there will be none. He's not rootin' somebody
under age, CIA funds are not behind his
wretched laundromat, and if he spends Saturday nights
stoned off his tit well guess who does the same?
The only dirt, alas, is that he's just another dumb
small business cunt. He's grrreat! I love him!'
    Yeah Syd's cousin yeah will shit it in;
and yet there is a big *And yet* ...
no-one likes him. Oh we adore the little prick
but *his* mob: the cockies, ladies' auxiliaries, those
who suffered him at school, know if this triumph's
a formality, a duty, there needs to be a lesson with it:
which we, Karl and his friends, our party
will supply.
    And Karl, a bearded industrial advocate
masquerading as 'Nearly one of youse' is sure
exotic this end of The Valley; but it's a by-election,
a candidate can chance himself, the amateurs
don't need those bounds which face the pros;
Karl can open his mouth and really mean
'These are great towns ... you are fun people ...
I'm not the one about to cop a fright, I'm the one
enjoying myself.'
    Oh how Karl loves to work a room

of women. And he might be kidding any bloke
how the Tigers are set to job the mighty Saints when,
mid-sentence, even the Shire President is dumped
just so Karl can stride across to meet
even the most impossible of females.
Sheilaiser? Sex fiend? A credit to us all?
He is and apparently he is not. Though
when Karl told Dot 'Nothing happens, really . . .
unless it does . . .' she never believed it.

  Election day I drive Karl booth-to-booth.
'No, Lins,' he laughs, 'I'm not doing this for Barb.
How is she though?'
       Weekly, daily, you still don't
remind yourself about The Little Goer
do you? Barb, Karl, is as married as you
are not. Know how old her kid is now?
And if I have the charity to think Roger Heath
is just 'difficult' at times and nothing more,
it's nothing more than you can be:
you with your picture throughout the country now:
the man who swung the bush a seismic
fifteen per cent, the harbinger, the real victor,
the party's ascending star, someone who can even
momentarily rid the Rotarian that's just stumbled
over the line of any hint of smugness.
  So that, when the poll's declared, Mate MP is
'. . . serious . . . humbled, humbled . . . serious. But you,'
he informs anyone who's around to listen,
'you are going to get the best. And, when I say you
I truly mean The Valley, all The Valley.'
         And guess what?
I near-believe him, find I even want to trust him,
trust him at least as much as I am trusting Karl.
Just listen to what he's saying, my friend
who doesn't know how now's the time to turn professional:
'Well done, mate. Must return and use that
laundromat. Meet you in Spring Street.
I'm heading for a safer seat!'

Work and live

  So I told Joanne 'The old man may've got himself kids enough
and finally finished that unending extension,
but all along here's what we've been hearing
*I am certainly I am. Right now no-one else
is standing on this spot. I have conquered time and space!*
Who else would want to?
      All along
the family just kept fracturing; and nobody knows,
nobody is meant to. It's what families are
unless they aren't. Wasn't there a time
when all he had to do was get up at a barbecue,
sing "Abdullah Bulbul Amir" and hardly prove
much else? Dents in the fridge,
holes in the wall and *Outa my way, someone's
about to learn!* He's proved a lot now,
and not what he set out to prove.
And the rest. *Sure* he'll admit
*my salesman brother sells, but how could he sell
anything worthwhile? And with a wife*
the old man harps *A wife who has to return, return
to nursing.* (Yeah, the rest of us hardly dare to think,
ten-to-four, three days a week as if as if . . .)'.
  And 'Sorry,' I also tell Joanne,
'you better believe this too:
I just want to live, work and live,
on an oil rig.'
     Nothing too personal
she took it too personal. We split.

In the staff room: an epilogue

  In the staff room,
just before I left, I read this article,
designed to puff up and out the national chest
it tells us how-we-like-to-see-our-boys.
  Example: Craig Stubbs (my contemporary,

small-scale motelier, late of Real Livin' Toyota)
seems to have borrowed just enough
to buy this radio chain. *Heck gee wow*
Craig will tell anyone who wants to keep on
reading *Phew fellas! Pretty close eh?! This one's
a battler but.*
        Sure shows,
battling to keep his name out of the papers.
   (Right now, over at the Tech,
my ex battles to *Oh yawn!*
teach one more fifteen-year-old to read.)
   But Craig's insistent:
he's committed to *A fair day's work for a fair day's pay.*
It's just that he's the one who will decide
what's fair and, even better, fairer game.
   What a generation ascends!
It seems our latest gagman/deejay/songmine
is that same (let's be charitable) opportunist who,
his grandma unavailable,
tried to root his best friend's girl: my sister Dot.
   Well today, Aussie-all-over,
the man is famous!
               Someone I met at a conference once
had been at school with Mr Digby Gibb:
a circus even then: fatboy with generator,
out for your balls.

Radio Chook Raffle (i)

SCENE: SOME VENUE

    ...what's it called this dump?
Watch out Gibbo, you'll end up sprawled on y' rump.
This mob: the customers, your clientele,
want the only tale in town: how it all started to gel,
how, in that talent quest, playing the chook, you won;
and after, being patted, 'Brilliant, son,'
some agent breathed (calling you Dear),
'Gibbo's what this place requires ... sign here!'
    So whilst *Boffins baffle and conmen snaffle*
              Give that Aussie boy his jaffle
              Yanks their hotdogs, wogs, falafel
              You're with Radio Chook Raffle
Blaaaak!
    And, as reputation starts to blossom,
every day until the Gibbo possum's
stirred in my town, my town refuses to start.
    The morning's highlight is to guest some tart
as our 'Bitch for Brekky'.
What dog was that day's: Maureen? Laura? Becky?
Whoever, she deserves no *Thank you ma'am*.
'You idiot!' I scream, giving the phone a slam.
'You idiot!' And thought nothing more.
Yet, through the day and beyond, a guffaw
was mounting till *You idiot!*
echoed Aussie-wide: a nation getting giddy, hot
for their premium, A-grade, top shelf
Gibbo-boy, chock with all the *Blaaaak!* of himself.
    Yet, if playing chooks might earn an MBE
one day, imagine this sold-out MCG
with, since nothing beats the crassest,
ready everyone ... *You idiot!* howled by the masses.
    The last time I felt approaching this alive
was revvin' my FJ up some deadshit's drive.

(What was *his* problem? What the tut-tut-tut?
It's just Gibbo, don't you love the mutt?)
  End of part one. Here's part two, so attend.
  For every fella there'll be a dickhead friend.
At uni and beyond mine was Twev.
Poor dumb Twev: so in need of a rev.
Well, there we were: a couple of half-pissed nerds,
'Let's form ourselves.' I floated (in as many words)
'a ratpack: I'll be Frankie, you can play Dino.'
(Veritas sure was somewhere in that vino,
for a friend need never strip down to the nuddy
to tell another straight *You are my buddy*.)
  Put it another way: all things
were equal with us: the small things
or those to need more than a touch of straining.
  Like once, when he'd to miss on cricket training
I was delighted, so it should be with blokes,
to drive his girlfriend, Dottie, to her folks'.
And oh the dumb games you find you play in cars!
For more than some signal pulsing out of Mars,
more than the *Beepbeepbeep* of the mere feeler,
Gibbo's getting attracted to this sheila
and *Stop me!* his car is telling him. He stops it;
then with one question left, he pops it.
  Oh what a fury! And then what repercussions!
You'd think I had defected to the Russians!
And, though I was tanked-up-and-over the gills
next time I met with Twev: boy what a clash of wills!
Sure I'd played some joke on what's'ername . . .
'And,' I countered. 'Twev wouldn't do the same?
Gibbo should be rewarded, for his taste.
But knowing you both has proved one utter waste.
Excuse me Twevor, it isn't that we screwed!'
  Then (you'll love this) I rushed outside, and spewed!

Part 6

Barb, Roger, Sam	The Heaths
Shane, Claire, Vivienne, Phil	Barb's brothers and sisters
Lindsay	Barb's cousin
Karl, Neil	Barb's lovers
Mirella, Ken, Helen	Barb and Neil's workmates
The Poet	Claire's boyfriend
Benny, Liz	Neil's friends
Neil's Parents	
Neil's Brother	
Naomi	Neil's one-time girlfriend
Fat Donald	Naomi's father
Leo	Benny's friend
Ray, Chrissie	Roger's acquaintances
Daryl, Sophie	Karl's friends
Charley	Roger's psychiatrist

LOVELIFE (I)

BARB

(i) In the Mallee

     After we surprised ourselves with Sam, the folks
for our good or theirs, kept on with urgings to
Give this your best shot kids as if we ever had the time
to figure out what our best shot was. Then I could only feel
what I'd been told or read: the necessity of
just getting to know someone, wanting to ask
Don't know what we were hoping for, do you?
Love? Well it needn't be that and procreation ditto.
Sex? It's not mere 'sex' and as for fucking well of course
but not for everyone and hardly all the time.
Intimacy? But so much else is, whilst 'intercourse' sounds
mere textbook. For all our terminology, slangy and evasive,
I once knew a woman who'd never accept much more than
Ooh-ahh-ooh-ahh. Then there's my favourite 'the unnamable',
but imagine asking your partner (and that's another stupid term)
How about a touch of the old unnameable? No doubt
there is a language where one word reins in the lot;
or better, if none satisfy, make your own
Ooh-ahh-ooh-ahh.
     After our first full year together,
Roger's first one teaching, we lived in the Mallee. Any dawn
you could watch the day start building.
We often parked at a scrubby rise, waiting for the light to accrue;
Sam, an excellent sleeper in his bassinet;
our sneakers crunching softly around to the bonnet,
where we leant back, smoking (not dope in those days
that's how far back it was, with us still recently married
and him that intense and lean boy I hardly knew).
With luck by seven, I'd be back in bed, reading,
whilst Roger took his yoga mat into our garage.
We rented a dull-yellow railway cottage on, you could describe,

the edge of town; but then the whole place seemed the edge:
of a desert that hurtled up to Darwin, of what I felt
was possible, life each morning as the sun tracked out
of the night and Sam kept sleeping.
                              Or, lazier times,
roused by the Vinelander (Rog might grunt then doze on)
I'd remain awake, waiting. By ten-thirty, with garble
wafting from the school's PA, followed by its *pingpingpingping*.
I'd try to accept that a community so devoted to the fold unfold
and fold of growing ever needed a recess bell, or recess,
or the absurd back fences finishing their yards. It was then
I drove, out to our scrub again, parked and wrote back
to those I thought still mattered: tell all of this
serious business I had undertaken, of my considerate husband
walking to work if ever I need the car.
                              A rug was spread,
Sam played with his toys. Our sky was never that mottled ceiling,
a city sky, but the earth's flag slung out in whatever colours
it chose, as if to announce that this and its beyond
was the total-all worth caring for. Then, shrugging to myself,
I'd think of those trappings to sustain this young mother-and-wife:
bikini snaps a friend took only weeks before Sam,
contraceptive pamphlets, appliances Mum no longer needed.

   As day expanded the sky kept emptying, filling with clouds,
the scrub and earth hummed noisier.
                              In those months till
Sam arrived I knew Mum was near-waiting to approve, but Rog,
was almost born to be a son-in-law.
Not exactly a glutton for kids but families are a business
and I was her junior partner, opening the branch office.
'Get a phone,' she demanded. Of course we get a phone on,
but Rog heard of a dodgy booth: Melbourne for a local call,
and what we wished turned easier: to be left as long as
we needed, enjoying our somewhere else.

      I could've joined his sixth form Politics class
(he almost could) not much else to join. Sundays
I aright see the Mighty Bulls press-gang him into some bush shack
for Holy Hour: noon till stumps on recommended grappa,
carting him back like a toddler. I cancelled the evening,
he'd run it off by Wednesday, when we might stroll that dusk

beside the Renewal Centre, hearing the pastor and his flock,
all their *Je-sus-Je-sus-Je-sus.*
                         Innocence is ignorance dressed
for those who don't particularly care.
                         Recall that first time
parents never knew *Anything at all?*
                         Ignorance is fluff:
an endless container haul of compressed fluff.
    My faith, or whatever I had to have faith in,
wasn't *Let's try it this way* a sequence of novelty positions,
novelty assumptions.
                    Know what God is? Look at the sky:
to contemplate its banner of rearranging cloud is near
blasphemous.
    Or what sex is (if indeed it's 'sex')?
                              Or love?
    And where's that cloud before the last one?
Moved to be another in another's sky?
                         I should drive
into the Mallee once more, look up and know nothing.
    There would be worse to stay naive about.

(ii) In Surrey Hills

    If these were their patterns I'd patterns of my own.
    How did I learn lies were a necessity?
    Because my husband never lied and someone had to?
Because my brother Phil and sister Vivienne often stayed
with us, demanding they be observed, heard, admired?
(Because my brother Shane and sister Claire demanded that
their judgements get a notice?)
Because, if these were their patterns: wanting to find out/
needing to know; the rage and all the enjoyment in it/
the order and all the enjoyment in that,
I too had patterns I wanted followed through.

With room enough to be messy, rooms enough
for plenty to stay over, we'd bought an old and airy place
just half an hour from Mum's. We were home in Melbourne
(Roger teaching at a tech) and in that house,
once Phil arrived and Vivienne, mating time at the Heath-
Price zoo never seemed like ceasing.
                        Sunday lunch time
one or both might stagger back to 'Where have *you* been?'
blinking at the world with their latest friend.
    On Saturday afternoons, if they weren't around
and Sam was playing next door or at Mum's,
Rog would call me Barbski, not expecting, simply hoping,
my pants would just evaporate.
                      And then
(you may know the way) every few months or so,
plain-fucked-out he and I caved in on each other:
and Rog confessed how, though all our Mallee exile
had fired him for studies again, at twenty-seven
he intended more than a touch more raging.
New fashions had begun: he semi-punked his hair,
wore an ear stud on weekends, went out with Phil
and mates of his.
           And
if these were their patterns I'd patterns of my own.
 How did I learn lies were a necessity?
     Phil was lovable, for a pig:
the sort who appealed enough for any girl to say
'Yeah Phil Price sure . . . sure Phil Price . . . just
anyone but me.'
              Some nights, or rather early mornings,
I'd hear him bring home whoever this one was
demanding: 'Well are you or aren't you?
And if you aren't why not?' No woman
really held his interest; he hardly had any.
     Phil's friends, meanwhile, were getting into bed
with Vivienne ('She'll try to stay away from trouble,'
my husband asked, 'won't she?'). Well some of her nights
finished up that way. And yep, she was a big girl,
though not that big: just the kind of kid
who runs away from Mum because she

Can't live with the bitch! but really loves her.
    So guess where Vivienne lands?
Some place where there's someone keeping an eye
on things but who understands when she's told
Yeah, I'd this half a year of real stupid raging ...
someone to hear you say *I wonder what it's like
you know you know with* that *boy?*

    I had become a public servant.
    One afternoon a boss from The Department
took me back to his place.
    'My wife's a buyer
with Myer. That sounds good doesn't it?
Oh yes she's interstate, you guessed it, buying.'
    So who's this woman he thinks he's wanting?
Me I suppose. And why's she into all this kind
of thing as if it were the first time?
What useless necessity diverts me this occasion?
Being Barb Heath, the wife who tells herself
No, Roger and I aren't Ratshit period *not yet,
not half but* still the woman knows
if these were patterns I'd patterns of my own.
    And this man this boss did nothing, nothing
but ask 'So Barb, tell me about yourself.'
    Well I gave us Price-kids:
me Shane Claire Phillip Vivienne,
and talked and talked about my son. Sam Heath?
Who's he to worry over? And if the boy's temper
meant something, the charm still followed,
smiles all round for the ongoing novelty of
Sam at creche, Sam at kinder, Sam starting school.
No-one we knew were having children yet,
and some weekends he'd stay at Mum's, play with kids
out there. Or Phil might take him to the footy,
or Vivienne to the pictures.
    'Sometimes Rog and I
have holidays apart, we have to ...'
    And if I was

fond of saying *'It' and his studies* or
'It' and his plans this boss ought to know my import,
surely, there in his apartment. (He'd a big head,
and kept me building the tension word by word.)
    'So this,' he asked, 'is how we are defined?
Well Barb, you're here because I like you.
And yes the missus, he exists . . . as a front.
I'm even more safe than you must be. Queer if you like.
Well Barb, tea?'
                How'd I learn lies were a necessity?
That moment springing the boss's weird duplicity?
    Vivienne (I almost told this man the truth
but didn't) Vivienne had based herself at Claire's,
but well there were these problems:
'I love her,' Claire kept telling me, 'I do,
but you will have to tackle her.'
Claire lived by herself now and though there was
this boyfriend someplace, was overweight
and heading jealous.
                Shane still lived at home,
hoping to still become a sports star,
tutting his judgements on Vivienne and Phil,
about their lack of 'future'.
                We were still
that much of a family; too much at times.
. . . *I'd patterns of my own . . . lies were a necessity.*
    'Every family has some idiot' Claire was saying,
'to make themselves ashamed. You tell us Phil,
how I'm to tell my friends *Sure it's great
to have this small-time dealer brother . . .
but one who's dumb enough to cop
offensive behaviour?*
                Vivienne said:
'Never done anything dumb, Claire?'
                          And,
since Claire knew, we all knew, just how dumb
Vivienne had been (being any kind of user
makes for a mighty weapon) she was daring
any of us to bring her into it:
if Phil was stupid so was she and weren't

we all: it was a Price necessity.
    But 'You're a dickhead, Phil,'
Shane took over, 'a pest. Glad those cops enjoyed
seeing your backside? You ever thought
what Dad, what Mum and all your siblings
must've felt?'
            'Siblings, Shane,' sneered Phil,
'is the most pretentious word I have ever heard.
But, since it's getting rolled into view by you,
I'm sure it must mean something.
I'm sure it's bound to last.'
            After Shane left with Claire
Phil really had an audience: 'The old man
shows more interest in next door's dog
than anyone of us: unless it's Number One
Yer my boy, son, yer my son, boy.
Here, have a pat of Blue . . . Yer a good fella Shane,
yer a good dog, Bllew!'
Then roaring out of his *Huh yeah whatever* mode
'As if it was me brought on Dad's heart attack:
putting him out to pasture in some minor marina,
that one-star yacht club bar!'
            'No-one traces
the attack to you,' Rog told him,
'this is what did in Dad: being dumb enough
to think Craig Stubbs' Real Livin' Toyota
 could whip each dealership east of
Middleborough Road. And they did. Just not
with him around.'
          'All right,' Phil tried,
sure he hadn't helped, 'from now on I'm I'm I'm
growing up! I'll I'll I'll be a public servant!'
    And, being one myself I reckoned how
he wouldn't last an hour.
if there were patterns he'd patterns of his own;
learning, as we all had, lies were a necessity.
    'Okay: I'll join the army!'
                 'If they take you.'
(Vivienne knew her brother.) 'And if you quit dealing,
get a haircut, stay off the grog

and shed your mates. Most girls like uniforms but.'
'Leaf, mull, buddha, heads 'n' hash,'
sighed Phil, 'what a captive market!'

❧

    And this was Roger's pattern:
he would go out, he would return.
Enrolled in his course, teaching at some tech,
weekends were made to rage the sweat out,
down at The Ballroom.
                    And lies I knew were never his necessity.
Life without him?
I could imagine explaining to Mum
Of course I never will be out of it, really.
It's just this space that I deserve
lies elsewhere.
Not long before
I'd this acquaintance, ready to get married
who, for a few months, ended up with every man
she ever wanted, and some she didn't.
Was her boyfriend doing much the same? She didn't care,
and didn't care who knew.
                    Sometime,
with Rog, it had to happen. But this way?
We are in our living room: I'm staring at
the row of Phil's fraying LP covers: my husband's
being straight about it: he's about to see, no,
is seeing someone else: a girl a woman he'd met
at The Ballroom. To gauge what it'll be like.

    Things may happen like this or never happen
like this, but not so strangely it would be
accommodated. *I'll make sure of your pattern, or,*
confirm a better, a much better, one of my own.
And when it happens I won't be the one to tell.
When it happens really well I know it must be like
shoplifting really well, how later you are telling you:
Wow that's extraordinary! It won't happen again will it?
    Oh but Roger Roger
whatever became of Just don't tell me . . .
that unspoken pact we had? Don't say it never existed!

(iii) In North Caulfield

    Knowing his money well Karl had been able to buy,
in some cul de sac off Hawthorn Road 'It's little more
than half a house, Federation stuff, a few rungs up
from a dump . . .'
    So, what was appropriate body language to announce
*We haven't much time have we, Karl. Show us please
the dump* standing in Uncle Dave's extension
(an early evening get-together, family and friends)
me with this nervy smile and him with a tongue
just creeping up between his lips: dark curly hair,
solid nose and bustly charm.
                       One day
I might understand the appeal; now there was just this:
another not-utterly-detached male, but still one
you could leave when the time arrived, a man
to whom 'commitment' just might mean
not fucking over my life.
                      Remarkable eh?
   'So, Roger . . .' Karl inquired, needing to give
the event some order.
                      Roger was in Sydney where we'd move
towards the end of summer: him, me and our son.
He had this scholarship, he was up there sussing things,
the waiting was worth it.
                  I filled in more:
how in that year we returned from the bush
I joined the PS, how one of my sisters and
one of my brothers propped with us in Surrey Hills,
how my husband studied a bit, a lot.
   Well Karl just looked.
   'Circus Heath,' I let him know, 'is upping stakes
again. I'm about to make myself new friends
and entertain those that Roger does, *if* Roger does.'
   Though wasn't Karl bored with all this Roger-chat?
(Roger's wife was.) No?
                  No. Karl continued looking.
And, this evening, I didn't care much where the spouse was,
what the spouse was doing.

Lindsay was back from overseas
(that's why we were at his parents') and, a few hours before,
Lindsay's mate Karl, Karl-the-bunyip, had told me
'I remember, you're cousin Barb. You married Heathy,
right? That was quick!'
'No quicker, Karl, than it was for us . . .
real swept-off-my-feet stuff.'
Later I'd tell him:
'Soon as someone asked me *You'll stay committed won't you,
Barb?* someone else was answering
Yes of course Barb will stay committed!
And Karl had to understand how us Heaths lived:
of course our business was ours, but mine
needn't be Roger's. Right Karl?
That time, at Uncle Dave's
(where, it seemed, I'd met half the men in my world)
trying to give a fair-enough assessment of my husband:
'Well,' I had to laugh, 'you know Roger . . .'
He didn't really.
Karl had friends, Roger had friends; they intersected.
Then Karl told me: 'No-one I know *minds* Heathy.
There's friends that are his, friends that are mine . . .'
(they'd a conversation once, about the weather? /politics? /
footy? /tick where applicable then forget same).
Karl loved being blunt and, if I was to love him,
I was to love him blunt. You had to.
At his place
(breezing a hand between us) he insisted
'Oh you do all this to him . . . and you would do it
to me: fuck me, fuck the next guy!'
Oh come on!
Karl was different!
Yeah? He was a man,
Heath was a man, how different?
Knowing him better every minute now
(feeling intrigued that there were many ways to go
and one of them would choose us) I told him
'Been swept away twice. Loved it the first time:
just getting to know Roger for a few months, right?
The second time? I'm still living it: this marriage,

all the being committed. And yes I am a lot, most hours,
most days.'
        And had there been others? Like him,
'like Karl?
        And if there were must I leap up, run out
and never see him?
        Unlikely.
        No, no
(I was strong with this one): 'Betray Roger? Betray it all?
It isn't betrayal as such and he has nothing
to do with it.'
        Well what was it, what wasn't it?
        Today I need tell no-one but myself *Just this man
just this once*. For I had a say in something for once,
that's what it was!
        And well we tried a few times,
for something, a few times to understand
I wasn't set to betray myself, except, and only except,
I needed him those hours, those days: Karl,
Karl-the-bunyip.
        In his underpants.
        And me in mine
(ridiculous by now) who's saying:
'You ever try to think about all those friends of yours
and the sex they're having or not and you do or rather you don't
unless you do and you think of nothing else do you?'
        As he hears me, me almost out of my underpants,
I'm thinking *Can't help myself and won't.
Why? Frankly Karl I don't need help with this*
(even if it's my own help) any more than with those others.
        He was mine. He was saying
'Barb, if I don't get you walking out of here right now,
I'll start loving you. Then where'll we be?'
        'Both in love?'
        Looking at each other we hugged, then shut our eyes.
He squeezed me tighter, whispered something back,
which might have been *That's it*.
        What was?
        'Well, an orgasm,
if you could call it that . . . I'm hot,' Karl laughed,

'I feel a clown and, Mrs Heath, I require a shower. We both do.'

It was the first time, there were re-runs; he was detached enough, he was almost available.

LOVELIFE (II)

VIVIENNE, OR SEEING OTHER PEOPLE/CLAIRE AND CLAIRE'S POET /THE PHIL PRICE LIMERICKS

(i) Vivienne, or seeing other people

     I'd three months being almost tranced. People think they think
it's dangerous. For timid muddlers shit's that easy, it must be safe:
just to hear Hi *man* beside you with a fairly-
familiar voice wanting to ask *Haven't heard* . . . or something, sure,
they'll pay you back.
                After my second month thought I better tell
a counsellor: think I'm getting away with it: the trappings
might be grubby, they hardly qualify for *bad*. Couldn't take
my hedging though. Don't need to exist on *no, but* . . . Look:
Roger won't drink often, so when he gets wiped-out
that's complete. But what's complete for h-freaks? A friend was
working places: one night for icing sugar, her next and last
for Drano; someone, I heard, injected his eye with Marmite.
You like your near-trance, sure, though not so much as when
you've come out of it.
            My brother Phil might take me to
The Ballroom: Jo-Jo Zep, Paul Kelly and the Dots. I'll never forget how
Phil dances, you should've seen it! And after, hoping to bring
someone home to Barb's, we might arrive together (Phil and me
and Barb from who knew where). 'Here come the predators!' we teased
each other. 'Where've *you* been?' She didn't know how far I'd gone
past all she'd ever wanted to. Or so I thought.
               Went to this party:
Roger, Phil, my boyfriend, me. 'Ever try this?' and Phil's hanky,
drenched in amyl, clasped onto my nose; your heart becomes
a locomotive, even dying mightn't be all that bad like this.
Then, bouncing down again, who was Roger with? She knows him
and you just don't touch another girl, or let her, quite like *that*
unless . . . you prick Rog, you fuckin' bastard prick! I barged

across, slopped cider in his face and punched and punched
till all he did was hold me.
       Next day Barb said how
she and him saw other people. Couldn't believe it till I
believed it.
 'You mean you *knew?*' I asked.
         'Know something,' she replied,
'and maybe Roger does.'
      She had one (a friend, boyfriend, lover) too?
Who? Who?
     But all I said was (thinking of her friends)
'Bet I know who he is.' Bet I didn't. 'Well who do you *love?*'
   'Dickhead,' Barb calmed me, 'needn't be anyone.'
Okay was he nice? Yes he was nice; and that closed it.
 You go on dope you get off dope. Phil took me places and
I met some guys. Sniffed amyl once, hit Roger once. Barb was
fucking who? Those days it was the way things went like that.

(ii) Claire and Claire's Poet

 That's my sister Vivienne, I took it.
         She pointed to
a black-and-white enlargement on her wall
where a handsome (was she younger?) girl just stared.
On a low table by the mattress-bed were brooches,
South-East Asian trinkets, half an incense stick
an oral contraceptive pack and *Mansfield Park.*
 *Jong's had the gong! I'm going back
to when they really lived and really loved.
Last year, after I turned depressive, I OD'd
on Georgette Heyer. That was fun. Scrambled eggs?*
   Always with cinnamon and honey, we sat, ate
under her picture: the fierce and vulnerable sister.
 *I needed a haircut, a new pair of overalls,
a bubble bath. Something to snap-out a girl.
If you've really the mood, of course, little beats
good old s.e.x., but well I wasn't, not then.*
     One wouldn't say a thing; today she'd seemed to cope

with a stoned, post-ejaculation 'Hearts of Oak':
'We a-always are ready, /Steady, boys, steady . . .'
 Took some street level Carlton cocaine once,
beats me, Poet. Piss weak as they said
it would be. I'd this dealer friend'.
 Oh what imperial recesses of the psyche
marched into my beefy-booming 'Hearts of Oak'?
Under the sister's Kitchener stare
were we to think of England,
imagining all those pale and skinny grots
whilst we made our love on a warming Sunday afternoon
in autumn (all their frigging and sodding)?
 I've been this cost clerk ten months now
Don't aim to be indispensable, but it pays the rent
and it buys the food. Mind some Emmylou Harris?
No, Bonnie Raitt. Soon you'll understand why.
 Was I into ELO? No I wasn't into ELO and
nor was she. We may've drunk Evian and I lay back
looking into that tight, sad face in the photo.
 Vivvie's all right now, but boy she can
extend her family! We all can.
You're a poet: write about this one:
there's this big girl, thinks her body's a dump.
Well I could've done with some shedding then (still can)
but built like Bessie Smith I wanted to look
like Bonnie Raitt (if I were a bloke
she'd be my kind of woman.) Anyway,
I was a virgin, Poet.
    Virginity, I told her,
is even more a state of mind than we could ever
dare consider.
   Two virginities? Well, I lost them both,
together. One afternoon this guy I knew came round,
no-one was at home so I made him tea; or tried to.
Within five minutes we're looking at each other
eye-to-eye; we kiss and then I'm propositioned.
Cut to forty minutes on and I'm still saying
Jesus I'm glad that happened . . . was it, I'm asked, a long time
between, well . . . Better, he got told, my first . . .
First? Poor man sounded so bewildered. But wasn't I

twenty-two? And why? *Because, the easiest because,
I told him, no-one's asked me. And then
I started on about this figure: mine,
with all those et ceteras a big girl has.
And Poet, you better remember this it's wonderful:
Figure? he says, no you haven't much of a figure,
Claire. Who needs a figure? You've a great body,
a great body to fuck, adding that I'd a mind
to go with it. That afternoon I wasn't interested much
in 'mind.' A great body to fuck!
It's what he said, Jesus Poet I'll never forget that!
Just to be treated like something sexy for once;
and though I didn't know it quite
I'd been waiting years to hear that. I felt
so powerful. Soon we were at it all again.*

    That's a wonderful story.
I didn't love her and I wish I had.

(iii) The Phil Price limericks
for Tom Ball

1

Here's one for your textbooks and manuals
From y' Belgraves, y' Black Rocks, y' Banyules:
    This raw livin' ocker
    (A suburban Joe Cocker)
With his carcass preserved in Jack Daniels.

At twenty, and long out of school,
My rebellion, I worked it to rule:
    More likely than not
    In some sheila's cot;
With the rest of my day playing pool.

My first joint was like a spring cleaning
(Combined with a strong dose of weaning)
    For I howled 'This is *my* dance,

Vocational guidance!
I now know that life has a meaning!

Just sniff and you'll know what the scent is,
Sign the lease and pay what the rent is!'
      In its unending bender
      The counter-agenda
Took young Phil as their latest apprentice.

Some tearaway straight out of 'Neighbours'
Might've rattled riskier sabres,
      But the life that I led
      As this dealer and head
Seemed the ultimate laid back in labours.

2
With her temper part sunny, part shady,
I'd this girlfriend, Colleen O'Grady.
      And with little rehearsin'
      Here's the uncensored version
Of what I might tell the old lady:

All chances of marriage are nil, Ma.
(Though it helps that Colleen's on the pill, Ma.)
      Sure with fine hash to zap us
      We fuck like the clappers!
But I'll never play Fred to her Wilma!

3
When some hyperheads moved in and stayed,
And giggled for weeks, I was made.
      No umms and no errs
      From these dope connoisseurs
With the best words I'd get in the trade:

'For a drug that can turn on the svelte,
This sure gives the neurones a belt.'
      But temper all rumours,
      I'd advise my consumers,
Sure I've sold, but I wouldn't say dealt.

Though it's hardly like running The Lido
Please appreciate this as my credo:
    For a pragmatic fellow,
    Whose business is mellow,
You better believe that I need dough.'

So calling all Kylies 'n' Jasons!
I've advice if you're into negations:
    Hail fellow, well met,
    Phil can't hack regret,
Try it once: see the end of his patience.

For no matter how good the do-gooder
Don't tell him next day *Gee we shoulda*.
    And thus I'd appeal
    To the hippy genteel,
With their preference for Nepalese Buddha.

4
I was raised in a hard-nosed yet wry way,
By a family *Doin' it my way*
    (Not much to perturb ya
    In outer suburbia)
A mile or two up from the highway.

Now there may've been wealthier climes,
Like Toorak with its Baillieus and Symes,
    But all deals came up aces
    In this best of all places,
In the best of all possible times.

So when Fortune meets Dad he's assessed
And installed, pretty much, as her guest.
    Whole streets dip their lids
    To his wife and five kids.
Few North Ringwood lives seem as blessed.

For this dyed-in-the-wool Liberal voter
Ran a branch of Real Livin' Toyota.
    Would've swum in the Styx

For that company's pricks.
Pay dues? Why not triple his quota!

Well he may know what conjugal love is,
But in corporate terms count him a novice;
    Dad's no Arvi Parbo,
    But one Friday arvo
They invite him to drinks at head office.

First this heart-to-heart veered, then it tacked.
How'd they speak? Well they more likely quacked.
    With their buzz-word 'retrench'
    Came this mealy-mouthed stench:
Since none had the guts to say 'sacked'.

Then as hookers hear cost-cutting johns
(Like the Pies when they've lost to the Dons)
    An increasingly bolden
    'Ummm . . . our handshake's not golden . . .
So glad you've a preference for bronze.'

Being loyal can't come within cooee
Of such hypocritical phooey.
    So Dad slept and drank,
    And fished at Cape Schank.

5
It was then that my life did a U-ee.

It's his seventh night straight on the hops,
And your hero is tanked to the chops.
    Fee fi fo and fum
    Well he's baring his bum
To a coupla off-duty cops.

Now they raised us no hint of a hoot
This double act Smart Arse 'n' Brute,
    With their civil, sarcastic,
    'Your backside's fantastic . . .
Care if we open the boot?'

You know cops: who can tell how they sussed it?
Still Phil's not the bunny that's flustered.
    'Cause ha bloody ha,
    It isn't my car.
And some other prick's getting busted.

Whilst I stammered 'But but but but but . . .'
My Dad had collapsed in a *Phut!*
    Sobbing 'Exquisite! How nice!
    A son who does brown eyes!
My favourite has turned out a mutt!'

He'd a certain municipal clout,
Whose muscle lay hardly in doubt,
    But like pies on a pie night
    Even patience turns finite,
And the old man quit bailing me out.

By Tuesday I still had the shakes,
With the usual elephants, snakes;
    More dickhead than criminal
    (Though with sympathy minimal)
And them is (you'll gather) the breaks.

You can almost give thanks to the saviour
For the warning the magistrate gave ya.
    But it's not so appealing
    With a mate up for dealing
Whilst you cop offensive behaviour.

If I fancied myself quite a martyr,
I was shunned like a twelve-year-old farter.
    They get pretty dicey
    Relations with Pricey:
Don't you know, he's persona non grata.

At a party, if they needed proof
I'd over-played acting the goof,
    Being there at my peril

(Ex-mates had turned feral)
I yelled, climbing onto the roof:

'I'm a fraud in all shade of yellers,
With the von Dänikens and the Gellers!
    No wonder you're sulkin',
    My stash in his Falcon!
But trust us again . . . will ya . . . fellas?

Ahh suck on your Winfield or Camel,
Since you're adult you're male and you're mammal.
    But why get the hots
    For a half-dozen pots
When there's acid, there's coke and there's amyl?

I'm from Hicksville? Well you're twice as hicker.
 If I'm thick you're decidedly thicker:
    All primed round a keg
    Like a cartoon by Weg,
Pie-eyed and gulping down liquor!'

6
Though I'm not into small poppy lopping
I had glimpsed this here vista unstopping:
    Its ridges and valleys
    Were quiz nights, car rallies,
The odd barbecue and wife-swapping.

And some post coital *Gee Phil yer grouse*
May not rate in the mainstream of vows;
    But at my most beery
    Came this domino theory:
She's your girlfriend,
               fiancé
                      and spouse.

After that there's the future I'm facin':
With our two kids Melissa 'n' Jayson.
    Though we've done the hard yards

There's divorce on the cards;
Either that or we move to The Basin.

And if dealing can bring in some bucks,
As vocation it's hardly deluxe.
    With less grams than you think
      One can end in the clink.
That's bloody hard work. And it sucks!

After living with ulcers and stealth
(If you still ask *What kudos? What wealth?*)
    My advice to young dealers,
      Be they fellas or sheilas,
Is please remain true to yourself.

Just see your way through any quarrel
With a straight bat like Benaud or Worrell.
    And down-play heroics,
      Like dinky-di stoics.
Now I bet you're expecting a moral.

7
Well it's give up the bong and carafe,
Or finish like Sylvia Plath.
    You saw me quit whoring
      (Even sex became boring)
I dried out, and then joined the RAAF!

Lovelife (III)

Barb and Neil (i)

(1) Auctioneering

    They went north: he started his doctorate,
she got a transfer.
        Some mornings Roger would
awake calling her 'Barbski', which hardly meant too many things
(only one in fact).
        And, some evenings over dinner,
she'd be telling him and Sam office names:
there was Mrs E the trolley lady, and Helen Griffin,
Mirella Rapasada, Ken Hamilton, Neil Spencer ...
    Hardly attending, Roger was used to hearing Barbski
and whatever she'd to tell him.
        But later,
with Sam in bed: 'I tell you Rog,
the system leaks, that office gets so slack
so fuckin' slack ... somebody's going to take the place
right to the cleaners and beyond.
They probably have.'

        Then she heard about
the departmental cricket club: how it had auctioned off
a stripper. There'd been complaints of course,
but *Sweethearts that's her job* they'd been rejected.
Chantelle, you'd to understand, rather loved the work.
    Barb knew her husband,
his reaction didn't surprise: 'You know I've tried
at being one-to-one, you know *that*.
But an auction?!'
        In their garden, when she told him,
Roger spat then, wheeling round to her:

'But don't ask *How could "it" happen,
in the twentieth century, now?* This "auction" proves "it".'

&

    And here came something more to prove 'it':
their radio was ranting 'We've brekky time with Gibbo-goonery!
Over on the Gladesville there's this pile-up!
This pile-up with jam! So munch that muesli,
Sydneysiders! It'll get us movin'!'
Gagmaster, silly-bugger, guest-spotter, emerging icon,
telling the town 'How could Melbourne,
Melbourne of all places, contain Gibbo?
He'll be everywhere!'
                      It seemed as if
Gibbo had followed the Heaths, as if the four of them
had asked this of their futures: *anywhere, anywhere but home.*

&

    Karl of course had known Gibbo; even more
Karl had known Barb. Hadn't she been told:
*You better get to Sydney quick or else
I'll love you more?* Putting aside
one last night to visit him (Roger was bush with his
let's-call-her friend, Sam was with Barb's parents)
they were in the shower: Karl washing away Barb,
Barb washing away Karl, when she heard
Or else I'll love you more; this from her life's
most detachable man.
                      She headed off at two,
arriving back as Viv and Phil did, stoned
from The Ballroom, shedding that weight of what
their folks expected, though still acting like real Prices:
being cheeky (some would call it flirting)
getting liked oh yes getting liked.
                          Making friends
propelled you as a Price. And now, at the Department,
there was vacant-faced Neil whose very freckles
might almost make him one of them.

                    'Wouldn't you think;
he got asked 'wouldn't you think they'd *some* amount
of honour, the cricket mob?' Her husband had.
Roger was very honest. 'The auction?' Barb elaborated.
Had Neil heard? Most days she saw Lumpy from registry,
the auctioneer, and the winner Fritzy the Kraut.
    Neil scoffed, knowing the club as, every way
you bothered with it *Sick enough*.
Like most women, Barb, he wanted to explain
yet didn't, you're fortunate, hardly knowing
even the start of it. One afternoon,
needing a lift to where he lived
(just the inner west) his ride contained four senior clerks.
In the car's midwinter fug they'd continual talk:
just sex, sex. '. . . for your benefit son . . .'
advised the goanna beside him, 'this is the real world . . .'
how the MC was heading troppo *'Look at that cunt!*
Look at that cunt!' and then went truly troppo:
'Hands off, hands off all *merchandise!'*
    No Neil wouldn't tell Barb that.
Instead, late one Friday he talked of Kim,
his oldest (though by now his most distant) friend:
Lacy, this ex-drug lord somewhere in half a dozen
South-East Asian countries. Well it's how Spacey
big-noted himself, when really, for a while,
he'd just produced the local greenery.
    One of Barb's brothers had been similar:
'. . . and you know how they can really throw the book
at some kids? Well Phil was missed by *that!*'
(she quickly brushed her hands.) 'That much!
Then he joined the RAAF.'

                        Sydney, and back home,
Roger would get folk over (she would make them friends).
It might be her turn to try it, with Neil say,
Neil and his girlfriend? (A Carmel was mentioned,
once. Or had it been a Libby?)
                        But no,

she'd keep him for work. Hadn't he told her
*There's one word for this department and the word
is 'sus'?*
      She recalled the not-quite ambiguity
of Lumpy tripping into Mirella, grabbing her tits
as they fell; then, since he'd hardly meant it
Much like that of course, his giggling apologies.
      It was enough that, had she told Rog,
he would have cared (as he had about the auction).
But by October (another year set to unwind)
here at the Price branch office, the Heaths,
Barb knew those words she would cry
if she needed to: '... still hardly done much ... and these',
she'd itemise, 'are what I am now ... a sad eclectic list
which somehow makes me':
– 'Sam my son';
– the hand-me-overs from her mother and aunt;
– still getting caught most fortnights (despite her salary)
– the attendant small betrayals of marriage
(even those a wife was meant to enjoy)
and over-arching these
– the need to be *Such a good scout
suitable for any home or workplace.*
      Whilst her husband, pursuing what required pursuing,
evolved into Dr Heath. (For there were things which worked,
things which didn't.)
      'It!' she started calling him again
(to herself, even, if an occasion asked, to friends)
'it! and his bit!'
      There was this woman once (Barb knew
this as a woman's style of business, for yes
it was a business) this woman once who'd had
a year's shoplifting binge. Perfected it.
Never got discovered.
      It pleased Barb
to call that an adventure, knowing that some system
wrote it off.

(II) **Oh what a night it was!**

This is just imaginary she told herself for months
(months she never stopped imagining).
                                        It happened best
driving to the Department, arriving dosed in Gibbo-toons:
'The tracks of my tears', the bitter-sweet ambiguity of
'Eye-level', or, auditioning for 'art', that folksy-mod,
pop-classic theme from 'Rush'. Easy listenin' at
its easiest, playing footsies with Gibbo:
DJ/comedian/singer-songwriter/a personality
chock o'th' lad himself.
                        Yet too stupid, wasn't it,
even to imagine 'an embezzlement'. Wasn't it? Wrong:
The Department was almost asking you to try. Wrong again:
to succeed.
            If this imagination's torment had to cease
only two signatures were required,
one of which would be hers.
                            (In October
here's what Barb was dreaming: it's Melbourne and,
bar for her and Roger marching past the town hall,
Swanston Street is empty; on a review stand, parents:
hers, his; but there's no time to salute: the children
have to run: past the cathedral, the station, over the river
and down St Kilda Road: no cars, no trams, no one, only them.)

&

By October she was eliminating office staff:
Ken, who got stoned and blabbed;
Mirella, who was twenty-four, engaged and lived at home;
Helen, who with her vet husband,
was rich enough.
                And, though it was still imagined,
only imagined, that left *him* didn't it? Neil,
who thought the cricket club as *sick enough,*
detached, quite prepared to leave the place.
                                            One counter meal,
during overtime, she told about her families: the Heaths

(Roger and Sam, Roger's thesis, his workload)
and the rest of them in Melbourne, the Prices.
                                        The Heaths
still owned a house back there but here '... we rent'.
Perhaps she sounded bitter?
                        Neil mentioned how he lived
with Benny, this gay guy.
                'Eh?' asked Barb.
        Lived *with?* Okay lived *at* . . .
                        Benny counselled young men
who didn't know exactly what they were:
a pilot program.
                She listened, to an extent.
        Did Neil really know how slack the office was?
        Sure he did: a name, an address, a bank account,
a form, two signatures, knowing where the form,
its duplicate and triplicate, would finish,
how to make certain they never existed;
sure he did.
                They couldn't do it?
                                Oh yes they could.
Like some B-side from 'The Kim Lacy Experience'
wasn't it? One day Neil might prowl Singapore
and all points north just to find Spacey and tell
*Don't know exactly what you do but, simple as putting
a dish in the oven, I did it too.*
        You passed a form across asking *Sign this?*
meaning *We're doing it!;* then waited till a cheque
arrived; next day you cashed it, splitting the cash.

        The evening the form went out
their lift had stuck; they used the stairwell.
Following her, and seeing her turn to smile, he knew
how swift her heart was running,
how they had to kiss, how hard, long and shared
the kiss would be; and how it wouldn't be enough,
this life in the stairwell.
                'Won't be in tomorrow,'

Neil was telling her.
     We've done it!
she wanted to confess *If this keeps up
my pants will be wringing* and laughed that laugh,
that overlaughed laugh which told them
Well, we can do it again. But better.
       Right then
in the stairwell who was Roger? That boyfriend
she first met at Dot's reception/her husband at his desk
researching?
    Oh she could feel (feel ridiculous)
for Roger (even more for herself); since no-one moved
away from us Heaths, and it sure helped to imagine
telling him *Guess what? Soon we'll be one grand richer.*
(Guess what? Think I'm getting another boyfriend,
might even get a second husband.)
        That night
she felt so potent: knowing what she'd to do:
go home and demand, sweetly, but demand *Please Roger
fuck me tonight, you know which way I like it* that *way,
fuck me.*

     ะ

  It was a conspiracy? It was.
Therefore, Barb knew she trusted Neil:
even to telling him anything she wanted.
So how about *Back home there's still this man
I really like. His name's Karl?* Not that one, yet.
Not quite yet.

     ะ

    They'd chosen a bank.
  When one of her brothers (outer suburban
dealer-tearaway Philip George Price)
had lost his licence, he'd left it lying around
at Barb and Roger's.
      'Want to be Phil?'
she asked. 'Good thing they don't have photos, yet:

you're nothing like him.'
                        And, as if
her maiden name was saved for such a moment,
from those months before she married Roger,
Barb showed this old ID.
    Neil's address would be their address
and, bank clerks believing them, Mr and Mrs Price
opened their account.
                        'Roger isn't to know?' he asked.
(Isn't, doesn't, couldn't, won't. Given to lectures, Roger.)
'And yet'. . . he'd women, other women, back home,
right?'
    Oh yes
Came out straight and told her. (Much the way,
Neil thought, that you are telling me.)
'But we were younger. My husband's very honest.'

                      ❧

    Well everyone's been younger, Neil construed,
we can't have been much else. (Still,
if that's how she wanted her spouse . . .) But really,
had this man cornered so much of
the honesty trade; and if he had was he
much better for it?
                      Why, just to step outside
the *very honest* to do something truly dodgy, once
and he thought of those stronger, finer citizens
such antibodies helped to build.
The Shire had been full of them:
Spacey, the few times he went straight;
Frenchy, in non-fuckwit mode;
Toby; if he'd survived; Monica, Louise (even Liz he guessed)
everyone he'd bothered with had, in their way,
'experimented'. Yes even rabbity-fatuous Chrissie
(hadn't she married The Frenchman?).
    Well, and Neil was smiling, the Donellans might be
married, but hardly as the Heaths are;
and soon, he liked to guess, he'd join the Heaths.

                      ❧

A fortnight on they signed another form;
a fortnight after that with Philip Price *(their* Philip Price)
richer than he'd ever been, they stood
in their stairwell. He gave her share across;
they kissed.
    Can't bear he wanted to confess
being in the same room as you
(and that's how great it is). But here in the stairwell
let's look at each other.
      They did, each look telling each
I want to be thanked the best way I need to be thanked
the only way.
     Entering the photocopy room
she tried to joke *I've only seen you clothed*
and, if the words gagged, it felt so easy now
to step from your pants (as he was stepping from his)
to bend over the photocopier with the lights off.
  Then, Neil set to move into her:
'What if Mirella,' Barb was gasping, 'Mirella or Helen!'
  'Shut up,' he laughed, 'shut up and have me.'
              'Soon . . .'
(to tell a man *Not quite yet* made it even better)
'Soon . . . no-one will ever be in charge of you-and-me'.
(No use thinking *This is sus Neil, marvellous*
but sus they'd six weeks accommodating *sus*
didn't they deserve something even sweeter?
Didn't they now? Yes didn't they now!
'And we are doing this and everything for us!'
  Moving to love him Barb called Neil *My darling*
(name better words!).
  For it was their theft, their theft alone.

        *

  At Ken the office head's alternative Christmas party
there had been, was and would be a mighty lot
to smoke.
    When he arrived Neil went straight
to Barb.
'Try this,' she suggested, 'try this and feel

ridiculous. I had to I just had to.'
                              Not yet.
He needed to stop something.
No-one knew how each of them was fifteen hundred richer
than a month before, and how he'd seen all evidence
evaporate. Which of course was fine except
'. . . I'm not quite made for it. Can't be Philip Price
much longer. Let's close his account.
Let's stop everything next fortnight?'
                                Barb, too, was certain:
'Let's stop now . . .' (knowing what had to stop,
what would, what wouldn't and what had merely started:
living had living had living had).
                       Then,
in the middle of the kitchen,
whilst all present were doubtless watching,
she drew up some smoke and kissed it into him,
as Helen Griffin's silly voice kept saying
'Look at those two look at those two.'

    Watch out: next year sometime they could make
the departmental magazine: with all those social-clubbers
mugging it at some dinner dance (overloaded grins,
arms flapping around each other, movin' it on
the reception centre floor) now being told
what they'd known for months *Oh what a night it was!*

    But whatever propelled Ken's mull
Barb felt too happy. Surely it was enough
that Neil had ranged from useful to wonderful
(the lot and the lot again) that they'd made, yes *made*
their money?
                It surely wasn't.
                              Or you could celebrate
We've done the system! except *System?*
There hardly was one.
          Her brain in overdrive kept flicking:
the money; Roger; Neil; rich enough/dumb enough
Helen Griffin urging the world to watch;
the hand-me-over charity that went, still went,
with being the eldest Price kid; rental properties;
the money; and all its risks; Neil.

And I am something
you must have had back home with Roger and Sam
for dinner her stomach was announcing.
      Oh no you're not she told the stomach
Neil and I made all this cash like that!
and now I love him and now I have to go
outside.
      Since little else remained
except to run into the backyard
(trying not to make a further fool of yourself)
go behind a shed or something and,
discreetly as you might be capable,
vomit *Oh what a night it was!*

(III) Christmas in The Shire

      Past mid-December Roger took their son to Melbourne,
left him with Barb's parents, flew to Tassie with friends,
went bushwalking.
      Barb would wait until New Year
to join her families.
      Neil was bemused
Even if I shouldn't judge them this way
those Heaths are fractured aren't they . . . yeah, fractured
but intriguing.
      Barb and he would part, they knew,
on New Year's Day; whilst, till Christmas,
their purgatory continued: being in the office with
each other, being at home without:
some of Neil's hours devoted to avoiding her,
there were some, probably the same, she wasn't to leave
his sight.
      Then, having nowhere for her Christmas,
Neil invited Barb down to The Shire.
      'My father, Pa,
will want to engage . . . to engage.' (Hear half of what
was being said, then order in that corps of facts
she was to believe.) 'Ma, my mother, shouldn't be

as limited. Well not as much as *him'* . . . Neil
couldn't finish it: if only he could introduce his friend
to someone else's parents. 'Oh, and my brother wears
a stovepipe beard. His wife's a schoolmarm. They've two
apprentice thems. The four will have worshipped.'
                                          It was late
on Christmas Eve, settling into their conversation's trance
they talked past midnight on the phone:
Barb (never mind the Heaths) about the Prices:
Shane the footballer, Claire the fat girl, Viv the troubled kid,
though hardly Phil, Phil the young dealer whom Neil,
by now, knew too well: helped to make them both a trifle richer,
hadn't he? Not that this Phil knew it (or knowing, cared).
    So when would Neil pick up Barb:
eleven, eleven-thirty?
                        She knew her place was too untidy
to have him there (her place? why not her life?).
They met around the corner, at the milkbar.

    Half a block away they parked.
Ambrose Avenue was full: anyone who'd ever left
the street must have headed back that morning
and, from the other direction, always the other direction,
came brother Richard, Olwyn the wife, Rex and Pamela
their children.
                Then, as Neil waved, a rushing surged
beside them, and from behind a neighbour's fence
came *Krrack!* the anger of a sleek dog
enveloping *Krrack!* again, again, jolting them.
Her perfume rose from Barb: too rich, he felt,
for noon on Christmas Day.
                            Through the barking,
in her instant fug of Aquamarine, Barb held Neil.
Richard and family on the footpath, the parents inside:
she'd never meet them again, would she?
Wasn't this just an office affair turning
holiday romance?

But such a life it had!
Why certainly: a life that, given the chance,
would goose-step over everybody in her world.
Well, if one day it needed to be killed
(and it would) Neil and her better be the killers.
They had a week to New Year's, then she'd fly
to Melbourne, prepare herself for Roger's return,
recommence loving *him*.
She knew such steps (they had happened
before, they would again) of her ludicrous square dance
Take a new partner ev'ry summer
Make sure he's no codger
Last year Karl this year Neil
Then it's back to Roger.

❧

Mr Spencer wanted things discussed: 'Say this,'
he was demanding, 'this salt cellar stands for . . .'
(Clive Lloyd/The House of Reps/Jesus Christ)
'and that pepper shaker . . .' (Greg Chappell/the Senate/Buddha).
With Pa there was a law for everyone.
The law for Christmas was he'd call Barb 'Toots'
Come over here and charm us, Toots: intrigue us,
get us baying for more (and 'us', she guessed,
meant him).
Then Ma came courting too:
this new friend of Neil's: make her one of the family,
Christmas, surely, was meant to be like that.
And had Barb met Liz, for example, Monica,
Louise or Ray? Kim Lacy? Too-clever Master Lacy.
'Hardly clever enough,' put in Pa, 'bankrupt
isn't he?' No not now, not in Singapore.
'Lacy!' The father shook his head.
Yeah, Neil guessed,
that's how The Shire saw them
(if indeed The Shire saw them): con-artist and his dumb mate.
And Barb knew *We'll always be their kids* knew she'd get
along with Ma and Pa like she did with Auntie Wynne
and Uncle Dave: the folks, the oldies, the almost

former generation hovering where the slow wind-up
commences the fast wind-down.
        A takeover threatened:
like chess pieces Richard moved the salt and pepper
(The Windies were pummelling our spinners/
The Reps were still initiating money bills/
Guess whose birthday it was!).
       'Please,' asked his wife,
'it's Christmas.'
    'Captivate us, Toots,' asked Pa.
 Richard, head-tilting, mumbled out:
'Come into the living room, I have to talk.'
 Just surveying the scene? Be your brother's guest.
 Through the glass doors, still at the dining table,
Barb charmed the oldies, the sister-in-law, the kids.
 'She's married,' Richard guessed (Neil wasn't certain
how) 'your friend is married . . .' (Guess on!)
'Do you think . . .' (Yes I do think, Richard . . .)
'You should parade this?'
      His hands
made waves towards the noise: by now
she'd got them giggling.
     'Doing what?
Christmas with the folks and you lot?'
        'Yes, with them,
our parents: they won't approve you know.'
 Right now they approved and all Neil cared about
was now.
   'Yes, she's married:
she's Barb Heath née something, the planet's most
suburban girl, and by next week Pa 'n' Ma
might ask themselves *Say, whatever happened to Toots?*
and *Yes, whatever happened to Neil's nice friend?*'
 Richard sighed his *Do it your way*
sigh: he couldn't stop concocting Neil's life
as one unending wayout surf club dance
featuring (so Neil imagined) Kim Lacy and The Wrong Crowd
Ray Donellan and The French Letters
Louise O'Connor and The Love Children
Toby Nicholson and The Overdosers

Liz, Monica and every other weirdo-groover
I've ever known go-going into infinity
plus, today, almost direct from North Ringwood,
Victoria, Australia:
Barb Heath and The Phantom Spouse!
     Twenty-nine going on seventy-nine,
the younger son of a younger son of a younger son,
keeping things not-merely-tidy, Richard
tutted back: loving you to know
just how unpompous he could truly be
Send myself up? Sure I send myself up!
and '. . . yes,' he'd confessed a few hours back,
'we have worshipped, we have attended kirk.
Today is Christmas, tell me if it's not.
People like us really exist, you know.'
     How could Neil explain his brother's
moral pique, not to mention guesswork? That needed
too much elaboration: all the family behind the family
(let Barb do that with hers).

                                    ಌ

                  'Well!'
Out in Ambrose Avenue he was just too proud:
'Weren't you a hit!' Could she repeat the act?
'I mean I won't be visiting *your* family, *your* friends.'
Yet he wished to add;
                       Neil had this plan:
certain (how might he explain them?)
long term acquaintances (which sounded more pompous
than even Richard might attempt) held at-homes
(yes they'd done it often this couple the Donellans)
at Christmas: joints if they'd the makings,
one-time Shire identities in attendance,
people he'd told her about: faces-to-names stuff:
Liz, his famous Liz, for one.
     My friends must meet nothing urged him more
Liz and Barb must meet. Unless it was to announce
*Liz this is Barb we work together recently we did
our department out of three grand oh yes and she's*

this Roger's wife and as recently (like last week
yesterday tonight) we've been up to here in sex!
Everywhere!

☙

  A compact man with patchy post-pubescent beard
(who, she'd been warned, might rave about his sex life,
to a point) Ray set out the evening's music:
'"Desire" for connoisseurs of craft, "Silk Degrees" for you plebs
and the missus; "Sousa Marches" when we want you
to leave.'
    'Don't worry, Neil,' Barb reassured,
'I'll cruise on automatic, I can accommodate old friends.'
  And all their Shire-talk:
'Like you don't know me I'm Chrissie . . . Ray Donellan's wife?
Won't say GoGo 'n' me have never had our disagreements
but he's Ray's friend really.'
       And her husband explaining how
Spacey was in Asia now yeah yeah yeah
ever the bullshitter: becoming so he'd like the world to,
please, consider him one of Orchard Road's dead-set largest
gemstone traders. 'Spacey,' Ray elaborated,
'was GoGo's friend at school, the best.'
   Liz asked Neil: 'She your girlfriend?'
   Oh what a wonderful question, let's be taken aback!
'My girlfriend? Barb? For the moment, yes.'
   Getting nowhere on that 'Would you believe,'
Liz veered, 'this morning Louise phoned us
from Melbourne. Asked after you, Monica, nobody else.
She's meeting people . . .'
        And Monica? In Italy
trying to juggle '. . . (I shouldn't tell you this) two lovers:
one him one her oh wow!'
      For years now,
playing the young raunchy hausfrau, Liz sure knew
what Liz liked; plenty though still dazzled:
Oh, oh, oh my god my best friend into all that.
Well I would hardly try but umm gee
not one but two, wonder what it's like?

'Bob would . . .' she let Neil hear, 'Bob would . . . umm
yeah I wonder what?'
      And some years on
Two? Neil might be saying *Two? You should've asked Barb.*
Hardly tonight; to spoil the fantasy that here
was something set to continue.
        'She's so nice,'
Liz had to tell him, 'Barb might well be one of us.
Hope it's working out.' (For the moment, yes.)
'Remember,' came the confession, 'how I tried
to pair you with Naomi? That did me
with pairing off. I grew up.'
        True, though she was still
that warm inquisitive Liz. No need to demand
Well, how's the love life? Just suggest *Let's gossip
about you!* and ask *Ever see Carmel? Still know Libby?
Whatever happened to Leanne?*
      (Besides,
they all knew limits when they heard them.
'Congratulations!' Chrissie ambushed Neil, halfway through
his six months of Leanne. 'Congratulations!
You're in a long-term relationship!')

        Christmas
had to conclude. Would Barb be staying the night?
Maybe, maybe not; her mother might, somehow, call again.
For a few hours she would go back to his place though.
    Neil reassessed the Donellan's party
(well hardly party): 'It's always great meeting Liz,
and I'm glad you did. Otherwise, Darling,
why'd we go?'
   Darling!

(IV) Kidstuff

 Did Neil watch Gibbo, listen to Gibbo,
worship Gibbo like all Australians seemed to be doing?

(The line was down: there'd be no deviating now:
this merrymaking benchmark demanded it: we would
enjoy ourselves!)
     Did Barb know the 'fourteen' joke?
Fourteen: the best age for a Gibbo groupie;
either that or the best IQ: get 'em young or
get 'em dumb, but get 'em for Gibbo!
  (Donellan loving *This true genius, Go-mate*
rated him next to Dylan. Gibbo split the Prices:
Phil, for example never got enough; Shane though . . .
well Shane was straight. No, just difficult,
just different)
     'And Roger?' Neil asked.
(Near to the only time he'd ever ask
about the man, the air between him and Barb
seemed to tighten.) 'Roger?'
         'Gibbo?'
Whether at her husband, her friend or the comedian
Barb was laughing. Roger reckoned he was 'Off the dial'!
  Which was enough. Close the Roger file.
  Neil could only ask about the other man so often.
And the often was over. Even the lover-wife knew that.
Oh it was a poor way to be true of course
(a few would say it wasn't even that) and yet,
though Roger Heath would never know, honesty could,
at least, commence; who knew, now, where it
would finish.
    And Barb told how, once,
Gibbo (who'd been Trevor's friend, best friend,
or said he was) had propositioned cousin Dot,
that is Trevor's girlfriend,
now his wife. Did Neil get that?
        'Just.
Next time supply a flow chart.'

        ∾

      Ken, Helen,
Mirella, most of the Department,
were thankfully on leave. In that hiatus

before New Year Neil and Barb padded the corridors,
earning appearance money. The building could've been theirs;
time surely was: plenty of hours to confess
Can't take my hands off you sort of thing;
then leave together to play house and shag stupid.
    Which stopped when Benny flew in.

    He always had a New Year's Eve and,
Neil wanting his friend entranced, Barb would meet him.
    Then, into early January Roger would complete
Tasmania.
    And, trying to forget (for a time
doing this task well) Barb would tell her husband what she'd
done:
Oh this 'n' that this 'n' that.
    In Melbourne, at her parents',
No Roger, she wished to tell her husband,
there's still the three of us: you, me and our son.
Oh I sat about at work, not doing much, just talking,
you wouldn't believe this, about Gibbo. Gibbo 'n' stuff.
This 'n' that.
    Well, for an afternoon.

    Neil would mention Libby,
would mention Carmel, what Libby liked and how,
and also Carmel.
    'This is the first time . . .' Barb believed,
'since . . .' (you were to fill in any other time)
'that ordinary folk like us . . .' ('Ahh!
Have me on!') 'no really, can talk about it, sex,
all of it without embarrassment.'
    And Neil supposed so.
    She mentioned Karl: how, last summer
(and this was next to shameless)
she'd visit him and get back really late,
when her sister Viv and Phil (Neil remembered Phil)

were arriving home.
             Rog was still seeing someone else
those days: wasn't meant to be this way
yet it happened: one night he had the car,
the next it was hers. And here were Viv 'n' Phil
not quite certain what was happening.
Well Phil was certain and it amused him.
He'd come to stay, Barb thought, just to view
proceedings.
         That was one ridiculous summer
and Karl was such a good, sad man, really,
but tough.
         Neil explained how Benny, too,
was good and tough, but hardly sad.
Who didn't care for silly people much, and they'd
been silly. 'Only with the money, mind,
and I won't tell him *that*. You and me and this
though, Benny'll get it, Benny'll understand.'

   (The money had gone quickly.
Spending hurled it into the past, so much of the past
Neil may've been with Kim, raiding Fat Donald's
and how many years ago was that?)

   Benny was utterly un-Shire of course,
never meeting any of that crowd, although
Neil could imagine: Benny ignoring Chrissie
and The Frenchman, finding Liz a bore,
Monica of some interest, and hating Kim.

   Benny would love Louise:
who was as good as he was.
             And Barb would charm him.

   'I am,' she was told by Benny at
his party, 'one almighty restless bugger ...
and believe me that has helped your friend.'
   Whilst Neil had Libby-or-Carmel round
for mutual admiration, Benny would head out,
eyes peeled for M'sieur Right True Happiness
Freundschaft something quite cute recently poured

into a pair of jeans. He'd even had
a recipe: take one largish, easily-proportioned gent
with pepper-and-salt hair, lower him onto a Vespa
and send said gent scooting across town.
  And, since for Benny
scooting started Thursday evening (and might extend
Your place? / mine? /why not right here?
into Monday morning) Libby-or-Carmel could be
installed for days.
    Yet Neil-as-home-body
kept suffering: it was Benny's house,
shouldn't there be *Right things?*
  The landlord never thought twice:
why should Mon Vieux apologise?
From two young men on hormone overload
what did we expect? Just
Keep the home fires burning till this boy comes home.
  Now though there was Barb and this,
he thought, this is one charmer-dame and *I*
he could imagine explaining simply for her
I am for no dame. Well he'd tried,
after a fashion, once, for a while, so there:
and now, this New Year's Eve,
he was charming Barb.
    I will believe in it, Neil
he'd love to say *for your sake I'll believe,*
knowing it still has time. But scoundrel you
and Barb the charmer will have been together soon,
one day, for . . . pluck-a-figure: six months?
And love time sure ain't real time; Barb time isn't
Libby-or-Carmel time. Think about it:
six months, three months, one month, now:
mightn't it be, somehow, time to decide?
Until then though let Benny play mine host
to the Neil-and-Barb closet.
    'That's right,'
he told her,' closet. Everyone's in some kinda closet.
Poofs,' he elaborated, 'just label their closet
The Closet!'
  Some times, some places,

life has to be a qualified existence
(*Like yours is now* he wished to say).
And Benny told her how
In South Australia I was born/(heave away haul away)
numerous Adelaidean gels were squired abroad
by Benny Hull. All breeding the species now
(and fine daughters, sisters, wives and mothers)
they'd once aided this most exquisite ruse:
you'd someone by (even on) your arm
(Jane or Joan) and then (it was this easy)
a man need only glance or nod or smile
(didn't Masons require handshakes?)
and you'd find yourself saying 'Just a minute,
Jan/Joanne) this party/opening/reception
can do without moi: I've just met a friend
I've never seen before.'
     It would be oh!
a wonderland!
    Like hell.
       When the police
employed themselves to chuck you in the Torrens
Benny split. He knew no greater perverts:
Aussie all over so many cops and former cops
were justifying something to themselves:
how, really, that man (whose name they
remembered/whose name they'd forgotten)
had actually asked, yes he had,
to be cornered, bashed, fucked-over, fucked and
even killed. Now how could they deny him *that*?

    Bennie had a new friend; her name was Barb,
Barb Heath. 'You and him,' he waved across
at Neil 'are kidstuff. Keep it that way.'

(v) Last summer's man

      She followed her son to her folks and,
after a week, called Karl, getting invited round.
To try again? No, not this time, she knew
as he greeted her: knew there were more women
in the world than merely married ones. Shown through
the same half-house as a year ago,
they went out of its lazy cool into the warm
mid-afternoon.
      With crisp couch, elderly fruit trees,
and a dead fence, Karl's backyard was besieged
by cicadas. On a white, cast-iron table
sat glasses, a jug of water with, floating in it,
lemon slices, ice.
      Suggesting she sit he told her of someone,
recently met *Who takes up most of my time*
whilst *Top that* a smile was asking.
    Of course she would, though it had to happen
slowly: there'd be Neil to unravel, The Department,
the money, Christmas and Roger's return.
Though she'd tried removing Neil from her mind
there wasn't much success. Until now no-one had been told:
but since Karl had always enjoyed her,
and, well there was last summer . . .
      So,
what should she do: nothing? Something?
The lot? Indeed what was the lot?
Karl felt intrigued: was this a yearly
summer stunt (some families taking to Rosebud,
others to Lorne or Merimbula, the Heaths to affairs)?
Mightn't their marriage be (though really should
he judge) a tiny fucked?
      'Well then,' he asked,
'you're going back to both your men?
You'll have to walk out on one of them, one day,
unless he does it first . . .'
      Karl had turned smug,
and knew he had, smug to the point of torment:
with his black curls rising abruptly from his forehead;

the proud substantial nose; his shirt, white
and open-necked, Israeli-style;
the first of his chest hairs; a little sweat.
  Last summer had been an unkind one:
getting to truly like a woman then *Three bloody times!*
his champion My Lord Performance proving a mere
court jester: punchlines mistimed or worse
hardly punchlines at all. Now last summer's man
was pleasing himself, he was repeating
'You'll have to, one day.'
      'I know ...
I don't know ... not now ... not yet ...'
  She sat before him, nattering, still growing up.
(But weren't we all ...) No rather, Karl saw, stuck,
stuck at your year zero, that day you married
Roger Heath.
      He'd have never thought this possible,
twelve months back, but The Little Goer bored Karl.
Well this is what I've escaped he mused; and lied:
'My friend is coming over soon, you'll have to go.'

LOVELIFE (IV)

BARB AND NEIL (II)

The imperfect is our paradise.
Note that, in this bitterness, delight, Since the imperfect is so hot in us,
Lies in flawed words and stubborn sounds.

Wallace Stevens, 'The Poems of Our Climate'

... I am myself indifferent honest, but yet I could accuse me of such things that it were better my mother had not borne me: I am very proud, revengeful, ambitious; with more offences at my beck than I have thoughts to put them in, imagination to give them shape or time to act them. What should such fellows as I do crawling between earth and heaven? We are arrant knaves all; believe none of us ...

William Shakespeare, *Hamlet, Prince of Denmark*

What of soul was left, I wonder, when the kissing had to stop?

Robert Browning, 'A Toccata of Galuppi's'

suite /swēt/ *n.* **1** *a set if rooms for one person's or family's use or for a particular purpose.* **2** *a set of furniture of the same design.* **3** *Music a set of instrumental compositions to be played in succession — a set of pieces from an opera or musical arranged as one instrumental work.* **4** *a group of people in attendance on a monarch or other person of high rank.* — ORIGIN C 17 : *from Fr. from Anglo-Norman Fr.* siwte *(see* **SUIT***)*

The Concise Oxford Dictionary of Current English
(Tenth Edition)

Living at Benny's

    A friend of Benny's (a onetime flame of Neil's)
had introduced them.
                    With somewhere to stay and someone to stay
they suited each other
and liked each other.
    Benny had been in admission mode:
'First up I'm gay. And I trust you're not.
My idea of bliss domestique has little to do
with jiggy-jigs. I must be *must be* unencumbered by
the day after day after day of it.
And even if the antenna's primed for Mr Premium-
true-romance, Monday through Friday I'm pure stoic;
come Friday evening though a breach is made,
moral decline continues. Would you mind seeing some
strange young man in boxer briefs or less
raiding our fridge for Saturday brunch ... whoever would?'
    Most of Sydney Benny might suppose.
    Neil thought it wasn't tolerance so much
as detachment: to live at Benny's might be
like living with a Liberal voter; like home
(and all that teen-Bohemia back in The Shire
returned to him: theatre groups and surf club dances,
church folk nights and later, closer to town,
Oh help us! poetry readings). He thought of friends:
the self-proclaimed sex maniac Dylan freak,
the bullshitting grow-your-own dealer,
the charmingly arrogant poet-playwright junkie:
straw mates yet wonderful with it.
And hadn't he tried living with
that married hippy couple? After them
he could live with anything, anywhere.
    Certain things were plain and certain things were easy.
When Benny said *Really, isn't it in their eyes?*
I could hardly look into a woman's eyes
the way I look into a man's you turned
one eight oh degrees to think Naomi/Libby/Carmel,
made a few adjustments and understood.
    That was it: not what went exactly where

(if indeed it did) or didn't.
If living at Benny's required detachment
that's how this man survived.
(At least till Mrs Heath arrived.)
'Good,' Benny said, 'it's settled then.'

Walking away

What goes around goes where it wants to,
and stops.
When Barb was away The Department
started to tighten.
And the audit nabbed Mirella,
Mirella and what must've been the last of
a six-figure sum, that would've gone where
it always wanted to go: through her fiancé,
straight to his bookies.
And this would be
the simplest, plainest thing Neil ever saw:
Mirella, a dumpy, olive, former public servant
walking through the carpark, between a man
and a woman, then getting driven away.
Simple, plain.
Like Philip George Price, benefit recipient,
who, just before Christmas (feeling a little better/
getting some work now/deciding to go abroad)
had closed his bank account and, smart man,
evaporated. Though too smart that you couldn't
forget him for a while: kind of like
an office spook for Neil, with the office loudmouth,
office head, office dickhead, office embezzlement
and office affair, part of the surrounds.
It was the silliest job Neil ever had,
in the silliest place he would ever know;
and the more he thought of Barb the more
she saved it; but the silliest it remained.
How hideous:
to look down from your window and see

little fat Mirella being carted away.
         Philip Price
or *I told you there is* no Philip Price!
Neil gave notice.
      Conscientious enough,
he would be, to some commensurate degree, missed.

❧

 It is easy,
if you aren't asleep at dawn,
to drive six or eight suburbs away,
across the south end of the city and
pretend you're checking out Chez Heath.
 These were the shops they'd met outside
a month before and, around two corners,
a steep small hill; halfway down,
inside a long, thin, kidney-coloured house,
the three Heaths would soon be reunited.
 Dawn was over,
yet who was about but Neil, pausing for
a minute?
    Only a man walking down his drive
towards the gate. Roger. (Not one of her brothers,
surely?) Roger Heath.
     My heart! My heart!
Neil knew, *is turning worse than ever it does with her.*
 In white T-shirt,
tracksuit pants: sandals, slighter than Neil,
a trim red beard, the man was shrugging
to himself, working his shoulders round in exercise.
 And Neil knew more:
there'd be no better, greater moment of obsession:
what else could you think, you say, but
*I fuck your wife, I love her, and this moment
this* right now *is so much part of her life too.
And guess what Roger Heath you will never know.
And even if I love, which I do,
maybe this moment's something even better.*

Holding his morning paper Heath
turned his back to the street, shrugged
some more and, like Mirella walking away,
returned inside.

Some evaporation!

When Roger returned with Sam to Sydney
Barb stayed at her mother's, saw Lindsay,
Dot, Vivienne and old school friends. Avoided Karl,
she hoped forever.
And even if she tried
shelving thoughts of Neil (he wasn't Roger
that was obvious) at least he was hardly Karl;
Karl who charmed, delighted and, hedging,
let you take a certain charge until,
switching over from back pedal, commenced
to turn you into a specimen.
It had been great
performing with Karl in front of everyone
and nobody seeing a thing, but after that
who could you trust to tell? One day
only Neil?
All that summer
Barb craved Neil's comforting detachment
(him comforting her about them, what a recipe!);
just to hear him say *Yes we did it Barb*
but no-one's getting caught, it was November last,
 that name we chose has just evaporated
(it was December last and one more raunchy office fling).
And where'd the money go? Wherever you'd like it to:
isn't it just like sex, love, water: afterwards
it joins just money (just sex/love/water)
and then disperses. Let's rule through that one:
ta-taa photocopying room, oo-roo alternative
Christmas party, bye-bye Philip George Price.
We did it and we'll never do it again.

Neil's gone, they told her, and Mirella.
What together?
             Hardly, the scandal wasn't
that absurd.
          'You were too much for him,'
Helen Griffin said. 'Your mate's quit but;
and Mirella was caught ripping off the government.
Not that they're related but would you believe . . .
Mirella? There'll be some time of sorts
for her to do but she might escape the worst
of it.'
     (What could save Mirella?
Well a lot: she was dumb, her boyfriend
was a prick and, being duped, she was
doubtless very scared and very sorry. Even better
she'd this big family to do the looking after.)
     During lunch Barb called Benny's,
and someone *Just the builder* said
'Neil . . . that's right he's helping me. I sent him out
to buy us something.'
             She didn't leave a name
with Just the builder. But to ambush Neil
she would drive tonight to Annandale and,
if he was out, would make friends with Benny.

     There was some film, Neil was seeing it,
and Barb at Benny's door was blushing:
'I wanted to surprise him he's quit work
I'm not exactly worried but why?
What do you think?'
             (Ask yourself
she ordered herself.)
             'Oh Barb come in come in!'
The big man loved her being there: come in and
'Oh Barb I am impressed!' become his friend!

After the movie, outside the Valhalla,
Neil asked himself 'How old *are* they?'
He felt like a headmaster watching this student couple
strolling with their baby in a pusher
down Glebe Point Road.
                        How old? Same as the Heaths
had been when Toby Nicholson was two years dead,
Spacey had been near bankrupt twice,
and The Frenchman had started telling all these
lucky kids, the teenagers, his students,
how it would really be like: life after school:
like now, like watching these young parents
and thinking that's how they must've been,
Barb and that man in his drive.
    It was such an easy vision:
for no obsession Neil had (there'd not
been many, really) was this fine-tuned:
an intelligent girl-next-door who likes sex
confronts convention, stupidity, all the odds.
    Well this rabbit-here (Neil was near
to tapping himself) is a sucker for that!

    Back home Benny was heard
entrancing someone: and the galloped modulations
of his friend's performance urged Neil
down the side and in through the extension.
    Sliding the door back you decide
to put the kettle on: well there it went,
this much of your life, over the road
and back how many years, floating off, evaporating.
    Some evaporation!
    For Barb Heath was behind him asking,
demanding 'Say, aren't you going to say hello?'

Oh dear!

    Barb called Benny: wanting to meet him.
When they did she asked 'Seeing Neil too much, aren't I?
For his good, mine, my family's and anyone else
the gods of love rope in, aren't I?'
    Since, for the situation,
Benny was a near-to-perfect man
to hear the truth, she wanted to tell him Roger's tale:
that other truth her lover had
few concerns about. For Neil was scared?
No. Uncaring? Not quite:
just content to simmer down whatever fuss
was to accrue. Since he had to be
this-kind-of-ruthless: no-one, Neil vowed,
should ever be hurt.
    When Barb told Benny this
he wanted to roll his eyes and sigh:
just sigh and cry *There's little more lonely
than one who'd love to help but can't.*
    Exactly.
    And never should.
    So what's your addiction Benny,
Barb, Neil, anyone?
    And yes he knew
what his addiction was: *Everyone.*
I am hooked on everyone!
    And you tried not being some busy-
body: you tried telling her
*First off and only off I'm interested in
you Barb, not all this mess . . .*
Except he was; Benny-on-edge was primed
for plenty more.
    Barb was saying
'Roger had these girlfriends, see,
well one at least . . .' And they all went off to
dance venues: him, the girl, one of Barb's brothers,
and once, one of her sisters.
    Something, most likely everything,
was keeping the Heaths together, and someone,

Benny was catching on, someone was set to be
abandoned: who wouldn't be this Roger.
 Barb was continuing about her husband:
what she allowed him; all she'd done, was doing
and would do for Roger.
 And what she had allowed herself.
Call this selfish but back home
there's been someone else, this someone great
with all that necessary touch of the prick:
which he, Karl, had to have, which taught her heaps.
Down there for the summer
she'd gone round to his place, told of Neil.
And still she wanted to stay!
Karl of course had someone else now
and she couldn't. So why'd she want to?
It felt bad and she felt good.
Did Benny understand?
      'Oh dear yes!'
Most weekends he did: getting abandoned,
seduced and abandoned (or else doing the same).
But then he always was expecting this.
'So how's a large man on his Vespa
do it? It's never easy,' he replied to Barb,
'and yet of course it is: just avoid the clones,
the clones, anyone but the clones.'
      (But orright
if you think it's desperate-enough time
just pull alongside with the silly puttputtputt
of your machine to counterpoint
*Hellohellohello heading moi way? Well just follow
moi. Saysaysay now we look a tiny closer
I remember youyouyou: all very seduction
and abandonment wasn't it, and won't it be again . . .*)
 Neil, Barb and Roger were epic;
Neil, Barb and Roger were stupid. But epic and stupid
was hardly the start of it. Oh dear yes!
 'And now there's Neil . . .' Barb kept confessing,
(knowing she'd love to test Benny with
*Some days, some weeks, when I don't see him
he still just ploughs me*)

'and Neil is getting permanent . . .'
                              Oh dear!

Teachers

    Roger had met another woman, his first in Sydney.
    And hardly for the sex alone, and surely not even
for romance, they became adept at being together,
going out.
        Going out: at its most banal
you could just sit on adjacent playground swings
and chat; or, driving down the coast,
hit a stretch of ocean no-one else had found
that evening. They went to a motel once, and
(Roger knew this would appeal to Barb)
left because the heating didn't work.
    If all this was nearly anonymous/hardly
going places, they still liked each other and,
given such restraints, given whatever it was,
their friendship seemed devoid of tack, and worked.
    In its way everything held fair:
Barb, he sensed, was seeing someone now;
ever since he'd met his wife she may have;
but her boys were always stored some place
that he (or anyone else he hoped) would never know.
If it had a lot to do with love (Roger's for her,
hers in return) you weren't exactly meant
to bother why: weren't they, after all, surviving?
Wouldn't everything else just end?
        Back at his girlfriend's
her husband sat around and waited:
one of two would-be swingers: she with her mousey
acquiescence, and he heading hyper with getting the action
propelled.
    No-one would know they'd ever met,
the three of them, how Roger had been supposed,
it was suggested, to fuck her, in front of him.
And how, for a while, something like that

seemed quite likely.
    They were teachers:
silly, suburban, but tragic with it: and Roger knew enough
to imagine him telling some staffroom mates,
over their instant coffee and tea bag tea *Err Saturday?*
Saturday nights? Well we have/had a visitor/visitors . . .
part confession, part conspiracy with himself, part
wishfulfilment-on-the-spot, all innocuous.
    Roger wanted to close with this couple,
any couple, but she kept phoning him:
so they went out again to see some band
whilst her husband sat at home, thought of schoolgirls
and pulled himself.
        She liked to rock 'n' roll
and keeping up with the alternate press.
So thanks for the show, would he like this paper
to read? Or this one? This one?
    And a few got left behind in Roger's car.

A planet of Prices

    Recently Barb had made a play at the domestic:
come on by and mend his socks? beat up some eggs?
    No, he recoiled, come on by and find yourself
in bed, go out for films or dinner, flirt with Benny,
girlfriend stuff.
        One night the girlfriend
brought round some family snaps (not Rog and Sam
though): her sisters and her brothers.
    Phil in his RAAF gear was somewhere
in Malaysia, he had a Chinese girl.
Barb moved him on.
            '. . . and this one's Shane, our footballer.
'Yes,' she was proud admitting, 'Shane, after a solid wait,
is in the big time now.' A team was named,
had Neil heard of them?
        Even in Sydney, yes.
'You *have?*' Barb cooed in mock surprise,

'their colours, then.' (He got the colours wrong.)
'Well give us what they're called .. .'
                              The Demons?
Bulldogs? Witchettygrubs? were all that he recalled
and brother Shane wasn't one of *them*.
     When he went to Melbourne, though, Neil could
catch him play: then add to that Real Livin' Toyota,
Mitcham, where her dad had worked, Holy Redeemer,
North Ringwood, where she'd been married;
call it odd but neither were spooked by the suburbs:
Blackburn where the other Prices lived/Surrey Hills
where she and Rog still owned a place:
much like The Shire weren't they? Australia.
     '. . . and that was Claire and this is Vivienne.'
     With a certain joky satisfaction Neil sighed:
'There won't be any quiz to follow? No?'
Well well, there he had it: the near-to-entire
Heath ménage.
               'Heath? The Heaths?' She loved
that one! They were its, whatsits, Roger-the-hubby's,
whilst Barbara, Philip, Shane, Claire and Vivienne
were the *Prices,* and 'Neil,' she tried to chide,
'you should've known that!' (Known, even better, how
Barb had two families: her own: Roger and Sam,
and the Prices: Mum, Dad and everything else:
for then there were the rellies: Uncle Dave, Auntie Wynne,
Cousin Lins, Cousin Dot, Cousin The Man in the Moon . . .
and Neil visioned an entire planet of Prices:
which had to be stopped if not for eternity
at least for the evening.)
     As much as any 'seduction'
it was the veering which engulfed him:
every time they met they veered:
from first-hand, scalpel-fine passion,
to third-hand domestic banalities
(now she was telling how Thelma Heath
That's Roger's mum broke her leg).
     No, never spooked exactly,
but in this near, too-familiar freakshow,
a threshold would arrive; and being patient

with the being patient-with-it
was, Neil assumed, his limit. No less captivating,
no more gruesome, than other families he'd observed
(or had been observed for him)
these Prices and these Heaths were as two long
intricately plaited cords which knotted into
Barb, Roger and their son: so sinewy, so tight,
the more each pulled the stronger the hold:
the greater their contortion.
       How she needed
not merely what-families-gave but families themselves:
why stop at two when a third was here:
Neil and Benny, her Annandale odd bods.
 And if that builder ever thought
Neil not queer but simply weird to live at Benny's,
oh no oh no oh no that was nothing, nothing
but a start of things.
      For, Benny aside,
Neil despised nobody less than Heath,
the man in his drive.
     Barb
I've seen your place Neil had always meant to tell
and I've seen Roger. I've seen Roger.
That man is not my enemy.

The endless boyfriend

 'No, no,' Benny was insistent, 'the mousey one.
Who was the mousey midwife?'
        'Lib?' replied Neil,
trying to conclude the game.
         'Don't hedge, don't hedge . . .'
Benny knew his Lib, Lib taught something, it wasn't Lib.
 'Not embarrassed, Neil?' asked Barb.
 When Benny set out a march-past of old, mislaid affairs,
Neil only got embarrassed by the tack.
 Okay: Lib wasn't tack.
She was sweet.

They'd met in 'group'.
                        'Carmel!'
                                        'All right Carmel then.'
    'Caaar-mel,' teased his friend, 'Barb,
you should've heard them! I've been cruising, see,
with little around and no reward:
the rain's shut down all the beats, most bars look
mega-packed, my Vespa's hardly any ark
and as for two of every kind . . . well I was sad . . .'
(and Neil echoed *Sad!* '. . . but do my friendly duty
creeping in. *Entertain* had been mentioned earlier
and, through the frosted glass our fireplace and
all its blaze seemed prehistoric. Why not?
It's back-to-basics week with Flintstone here.
What were Wilma's favourite tunes for such events?
Monteverdi? Mantovani?
                        Barb turned uncontained:
'Scheherezade!'
                '*Smart dame it was, smart dame it was,
gets any heart worth thumping, thumping. Oh Barb
Paaam p'paam p'p'p'paam p'pum pum!* Oh Barbara!
All the world should try it!'
    Sitting in the extension,
smoking something out of The Shire Neil had acquired,
what else, Barb wondered, made her this carefree?
verged so near perfect?

                            ❧

    Some days she'd take an even longer time for lunch
and meet her friend, let Benny tell how lonely enough
he was for Master Right; let Benny hear more about Roger,
even more the silly destination she was arriving at: Neil;
how, even after Naomi, Lib, Carmel, another one, another one
and Barb Heath, he still woke to the next new day of living
as the endless boyfriend.

                            ❧

After a while Benny didn't need to know,
there was enough of him to guess: the Heath pattern
was this kind of pattern now: every morning
you would wave across at your spouse;
and Roger, doubtless preparing a lecture,
if not at you then through you to everyone
in the world.
        And all this grid
made Roger feel these were the subtlest of days!
Really!
        Banging around you might slam one door
only to swing another open; then,
falling over themselves, enter the lovemakers!
        And Barb thought how she, Roger and Neil
must be the world's most stupid people,
well correction call them tragic but then
everybody might be.
        She guessed the tyranny
choice would prove: for if Neil (or Roger)
would have to do the waiting she, Barb,
would have to do the choosing.
Why didn't she leave Neil?
(Why didn't she leave Roger just as much?)
Because she didn't have to, need to, yet.
        But any day now (like yesterday)
she'd get Neil overload too much,
like yesterday, last week and every fuckin' second
since they'd met.
        And, since Neil could always
walk himself into a realer, though never a truer,
world, why couldn't she open any number of doors,
and simply push him?
        Because.
For months now Barb had been treating herself
to a trust: where was the threat in big bad
Benny Hull? Benny who'd never exactly gone the way
of all those over-hearty bachelor uncles/
sad mean fathers/husbands who, never quite sure
what the matter was, sought understanding from
those they'd never met before and hardly would again;

who one day found themselves announcing
I didn't think anyone I knew would really understand.
    What wonderful polygamy:
Rog to set up houses/Neil for passion/Benny
who you knew would really understand.
        Yeah yeah yeah on Planet Who-knew-where!
        And some men are just too safe!
Leaving Neil there'd be no more Benny.

Catholics for friends (iii)

        Every few years Neil would meet with Liz at the Pacific Inn
for a *Lovelife how's the lovelife?* rev session. Later
Bob would arrive, taking him into the public bar
for a round of pool or snooker; Neil never knowing
the difference (or even if there was one).
                                Abalone diving,
oil rig supervision, Bob, Man Incorporated,
had his plans, hadn't Neil any?
                          Oh yeah,
making sure a certain Barbara Heath stayed
in his address book.
                  'No!' Liz had near-boiled,
'she isn't *married?*' Nice as Barb was
(and Liz had hoped one day they might be friends)
she would set Neil on the trail to nowhere
absolutely. Didn't anybody have the gift of
getting on just one-to-one like she and Bob had?
    For Liz and Neil would itemise their friends:
the brawl and make-up parade which was
the Donellans; or Monica: men trouble but loving it;
and Louise: men trouble but hating it.
Then the evening slowed and they had to put on hold
exotica like Kim Lacy or Hannah Little:
the careers carved out and money made.
    'Don't want to be a finger-wagger,'
Liz told her spouse, 'but that friend of GoGo's,
remember her? She's married.'

Which would, thought Bob, give Neil more, much more,
than something to do: half his luck
and double the fun!

☙

'I've always had these Catholics for friends . . .' Barb got told
(with Benny away the two of them playing house
semi-adult style: *Twelve hours to unfold
over your loved one, naked, gee that'd be grouse* . . .)
When she arrived he always turned dumbo
for a minute; then it was time to climb those rungs
of passion, pause for a near-eternity and topple off.
Later, after their post-coital mumbo-jumbo
has spiralled back into some sense (talk about speaking in tongues!)
Neil started telling about those days when,
taking a shine to/attempting to be gentle with the Mary
Immaculate girls . . . no,
there were other ways to put it:
unconfirmed ideas had been refined from memories, right?
And Barb having opinions (pretty good ones) well tonight
he'd like a few delivered: balanced non-judgemental.
'One party, Liz's engagement, I got Lacy in:
bringing with him our first taste of the universal
green stuff. So, down the back a few of us go . . .'
Every kid has to *Go down the back* sometimes,
thought Barb, you never stop being one unless
you do. First time she'd met Roger that's what
they had done.
But the shutters were always up
on Mr Heath for Neil, who told her how
'That dope hit us with a rather pleasant gale
and so we sang a bit, we sang a lot and soon
Naomi, this kid who was with us, Naomi
and I were pashing on. It was so comforting to know
she liked me and "sex" (if I thought of it,
and that night I was able to think of many,
many things) "sex" could be, quite strangely,
put on hold . . .'
And later: '. . . from what certain people

were to say I was guilt-struck; telling me she had
never been the same since I dumped her. *Dumped* her?
She'd been dumped *For me!*

❧

    If friends arrived, to Naomi's dismay
this might parade: her folks at play:
Leila the harpie versus boyo Donald:
her 'Please don't please . . .' / his 'It's just the geegees,
Mum.' And coming into the straight
her husband would turn the race call louder.
    He never punted. So, after correct weights
and dividends, he could spread himself
hosting the charm hour: hailing boys as 'Whiskers'
and where lay the harm inspecting girls
from top to tit to toe and return:
each dolly the primest flowchart of delights.
      'Once I arrived at meal time (his).
There he was tuckin' in the bib, his grunts
ending in what sounded like *Th' lotta youse.*
Then, looking up he saw me:
"Oh we've a guest, Neil isn't it?"
turning delirious with the adjustment.
Exit Naomi.
You know it's serious when you're sixteen
and Mummy still permits dindin demands,
all his *Chow means now!*

❧

    Something had happened, of course something had,
and what Neil hardly wished to know. Soon enough
though, Liz discovered the lot and he got told.
'Naomi wasn't too bright at times,
call it naive or young and yes maybe us big kids
(Kim, Louise, Chrissie, Ray, me) scared her
in our way. And so she had to tell her mum:
about this stuff, this grass, how weird it was.
And Mum didn't really understand. Mums rarely do.'

(He thought of Leila:
ramrod back, head tilted to the sky,
poised to spring one more bleak truth
onto a fellow shopper. The Red Queen? Perhaps;
though better, Neil considered, the dowager option:
Mary of Teck, Chiang Ching.
Certainly given her terms she was sane,
prove otherwise and the whole planet needed committing;
only mad as the next man: her spouse.)
  But things got worse, worse
than mere 'drugs'. And he entered, Fat Donald,
the breadwinner.
  'Into heavy petting,' her father challenged.
'Isn't he?' (And *he* meant me!) 'Well isn't he?'
  'Neil doesn't keep big pets!' Naomi howled,
plodding through the adult euphemism
minefield. 'But yes he might . . .'
  Soon enough she would wind her way through
communes, ashrams; live with a member of some rock group,
then another one: was belted about the first time
though, Liz had heard, the next time wasn't.
No Neil would tell himself *I couldn't have saved Naomi
or supervised her future* . . .

  But taken a stand? Yes, even now
he'd love to take a stand, even now his imagination
craved this confrontation: GoGo Spencer
and his truest enemy: Shire identity/community leader
Fat Donald: the newsagent as nemesis.
How he envisaged it! With hearts seething into rage mode
the men would climb from their cars:
all the speculation and all the attendant dead-end
flirtation for facts, ceasing.
      Now! Neil believed
was toe-to-toe time, that split second to out-stare
the man and hence, win. (You always did in dreams.)
  And yes, Neil understood
such parody, hate as mere hobby, an artefact.

Why? Because nothing happened!
    When her father, like some middle-aged headbutter,
approached him nose-to-nose, all the melodrama needed
to topple it into farce was one long sloppy kiss,
or better, Neil's husky sotto voce *Not this close Darls,
I hardly know you.*
    '... and there I'd been,
never quite knowing whether I wanted to get into,
correction beyond, Naomi's pants (well I had
and I hadn't) and I didn't. More flux than fucks,
that's adolescence. But wouldn't it have been great,
just great, to drop what remained of any manners
and softly demand *Who says, Fatso?*
But I just ran ... ran from Naomi howling
Fink! at her father, from her father puffing more
Rotarian clichés, ran till I hit the party
we were headed for, and got drunk stinking drunk!
I had done nothing done nothing done nothing!
Should've been a hitman ... pow!'

                  ॐ

   'A hitman,' Barb reminded, 'wouldn't have known
Fat Donald. Why not have hired that dealer friend of yours?
All places have them.'
    'Lacy?
He might've hired me one or said he would.
The old Space had contacts but,
they were his strength. Who made enemies when friends
were that much easier to run? So many wires
led from Kim: always with something attached:
the bait or the baited and most likely both.
Yet all, I'm sure, he really wanted were rumours
and a reputation; though when required
he'd be noticed: played a flashy guitar
charmingly enough: must've thought himself José Feliciano
for a day: but no time to wallow in the mire
for Kim baby. One week he became our local Fagin,
getting two twelve-year-olds to raid this row of shops:
and here lay the best of it all: this was our generation

doing it, nobody else's: everyone knew and no-one
told or did a thing. Even the Deputy Headmaster's son
(through all our suburbs who more approached
Prince Charles?) even he believed in the raid.
This was a job some kid simply had to do,
the most natural event in The Shire. Well,
Fat Donald's shop was first: and that turning
a success Spacey played for percentage:
with his little gang ahead they were disbanded,
and he came to school with kudos and bagsful
of the proceeds: fags by the cartons, girlie mags and,
for any stray intellectual, the passing paperback . . .'

Now imagine this, and almost feel sorry for
the newsagent: you have been a disher not a taker;
you have been humiliated and you can all but trace
where your humiliation started:
The Shire's forthcoming attraction,
either that one or somebody like him.
And so you wait for years. You must, you want to.
    But no, thought Neil,
just because I was a friend of Kim's, once,
and was around when Naomi thought she got stoned,
no-one condemns a newsagent for *that*.
    Okay GoGo, he rejoined, conjure this
If I can't love my little girl my way no-one else will.
Not that Fat Donald was (how went the euphemism?)
interfering?
        No? Well simply imagine what fits
C'mon Naomi, let's keep our secrets secret.
You tell anyone anything then everything stops.
Don't you like these silly games of Pop's?
    With a decades-old suburban docu-soap
for data, what else could Neil do but imagine and
imagine hard?
            There was no inventing
the last time he saw Fat Donald though:
with *You rat fink!* (Naomi's breathless cheep

of support) he'd learnt her father's latest lesson:
how to degrade well-intentioned mutts:
just barrel' em down the drive and out with your Michelin Man guts:
'... wanted to tell you this ahh'uh'ahh Neil, you're
            ahh'uh'ahh a creep!'
        But incest? Too dramatic, surely?
        Neil, Naomi and her father were just one more of those
groups, clans, families, recurrent freakshows,
each one proving its predecessors right/wrong/it hardly mattered:
Frenchy, Spacey and GoGo, Liz, Monica, Chrissie and Louise/
the Spencers/the Prices/the Heaths/
Neil, Barb and Benny /Neil, Barb and Roger ...

        What thrills better than a successful revenge?
        What is more pathetic than a botched one?
        Relax, Barb counselled, you'll never meet the man again.
Why frisk deadshits for even their time of day?
Secrets and all Fatso had long ago waddled away.
        And yet it seemed so fragile,
what such men might be hiding.
        And yet in any stand-off were one of them
to blink he would be Neil and 'Get real,' he started to ask.
'Incest? Who'd ever believe such gothic excess?'
(Get real? He knew of little realer.)
        But even putting out certain feelers
to Naomi or her mother ('Don't wish to pry exactly,
but years back ...') seemed callous, presumptuous,
cancel that, impossible.
        Well then, with no conventional fuss
his kind of debt would have to be collected Neil's way:
next time he sussed out Liz he'd tell,
ask, discuss, till, with all pieces slotted right,
she could sweep in Monica, Chrissie and Louise
with *Now you mention it* ...
and *I always suspected something though what exactly* ...
and *Her dreadful father yes if course* ...
        Okay: what was known were suspicions,
mere dreams of evidence (that and being half-dazzled

by the thought of incest, or the next worst thing).
But even if this is just gossip and rumour Neil sensed
he would have to justify *it's what I want it to be.
Please consider what you've heard, that's all.*
   Then, with such a germ at large,
he could retire all thoughts of the man.

☙

   Well something might come of it
(Neil knew Barb felt him shivering)
come of it so this was understood:
as you needed love you needed hate:
one inspiring, irrational enemy, your hallmark
of evil to consume.
(But after all this time . . . *Fat Donald?*)

Winter

   Winter, early Sunday, the year's stillest hour
(who else would be available enough either to dispute
 or share the claim?).
                   Someone is leaving again,
those few extra upbeats balancing her life and his
tell *This is still a comedy we'll end it right.*
   Who could, Neil wonders, own the street but us
and a few more lovers or drunks, watching nights
like ours snap shut with the dawn.
   Barb opens her car, stands by it. On the floor
a newspaper near-invites him '. . . what's this junk?'
to snatch up '. . . a rockpaper? You into rockpapers?
Roadrunner?' He knows she's not but still loves
asking this; what she's 'into', if you like,
is juggling emotions: husband/lover/thoughts
of Roger's one-time lover; *Roadrunner* she'll
accommodate, Barb has to.
   'It must've come with Roger's friend,'
her voice clips back, 'he gave her the flick.'

　　　　And Barb giving him this space
Neil wants it breached: 'Ahh . . .' he plays with
'Ahh . . . so I've this erstwhile colleague then?'
Risking enough one second he retreats the next:
'Forget that. You're leaving, leaving is addictive
and nothing stretches more than wanting you gone,
but only to return.'
　　　　　　　　　Maybe by noon
this will sound excessive but call it romance,
infatuation, even a match of *Top this*.
Why hunt for excuses now? Besides
there's other words and 'You darling,'
she replies, 'I do want more of this but I'd prefer
the lot. Hardly wish to be anyone else, but with you
I go so beyond myself who am I becoming?
Almost hate returning to you but I have to.'
　　　　Yes she has to (she's going home now) yes
she has to.
　　　　　　　And love? Does Neil want to leave Barb
with still more love? They know it. They are tired
of it. No, better this gesture of passion:
he'll risk words you couldn't forget:
'Come back. Meet me soon. Swallow me up.'

Benny and Leo/Benny and Barb

　　　'There's three types of faggots,'
Leo would say, 'there's three types of everyone:
mouldbreakers, clones, goodguys.'
　　　　Cicadas' husks, very early autumn leaves
and fathers hosing . . . sure you could carve it,
paint it, make it an opera, a ballet, an opera-ballet,
not though if you were these languid if intense young men
curled to spring Jack-in-a-box *Boo!* out of
the City of Churches.
　　　Yet, for a few hours of false perfection,
Adelaide was always one long late summer afternoon,
with a sundeck shaded in vines,

an Archiv Corelli or a Nonesuch Carissimi,
and just-this-side-of-a desert tang
about the air. Days for Leo Pengilly and Benny Hull
to swan (or even swim) about in backyard pools,
days to find where boundaries might extend,
days when you had to trust the law
stopped at your bedroom door.
       Outside
everything was still so quiet, call it silent:
which hardly helped when folk like you
were being bashed or worse; who cared with categories then?
Some nights these tarty old boys
might be around, protecting you (if not from themselves)
but first Benny left, then Leo; Leo, who,
making up for his Largs Bay shabby gentility,
misplaced himself to Melbourne, and now rough-traded
through the contact press or worse.
All an exercise in ignoring the great void,
Benny announced to himself but, never allowing
judgement to interfere with friendship, kept mum.
  It was just part of the Pengilly reinvention:
lapsed High Anglican priest, lapsed tobacconist,
public servant (twice), teacher, painter
(when he bothered); in cowboy hat, dragon tattoo
and face Byzantine yet bemused, Leo the legend
(Leo the would-be polymath:
who thought he'd get through his one Russian exam
on acid, and didn't): turning thirty-five
Leo the partygiver.
      Had Neil been to Melbourne? No?
Then gird yourself for life in Leoland:
where beneath the huge Doré steel engravings,
in near-to-lotus pose; between bongwater gurgles,
Leo's lady, the Lady M, murmured her husky asides.
  In all its parody, anarchy and silly innocence,
its clumsy dictatorship of taste: nurturing, delighting,
whatever flat 4 number 9 is, thought Benny,
little tops it: call it family.

                 ಶ

'... we drive down Friday, return Monday.
It may be stupid but must be done. What,
hasn't Neil told you yet?'
                          'Benny,' she was crying,
'it gets too much. Nobody knows and yet I'm sure
everyone does. He'll be hurt, but since we met
haven't we both been building up for hurt?
I'm sure Roger wants it over. You ever lived
with anybody, Benny?'
                     Not so much yet,
not that it succeeded, mattered.
   Well he had to understand how now,
without much of a plan, 'Neil can go
and I can't, Benny, can't. And worse
I'd never ask him to stay for one weekend
when, anyhow, I won't leave the house.
I want, I just want, to imagine where he is,
what he could be doing. And now I can't,
not when he's in Melbourne.
                           There he was,
drifting along from Naomis to Libbys to Carmels,
when up looms this ambiguous Mr and Mrs Roger Heath,
with all that's backing them and binding them,
all that's trying to rip them and complete them;
then up looms love and there he is, there we are:
saying all the great sexy things ...'

Karl at Leo's

        ... tell you about the husbands though.
The first one I ignored: we'd mates in common
so I had to; the next amused, bored;
then I started loathing. Neither was a friend:
I may know the man involved (may? I did!)
but they're off limits, friends.
                           Back then though
(it's only months ago) when I still specialised
in wives (and Benny you must guess

there's little in the world like *Her* the wife)
back then last year I knew this dyke,
Kate, a mate, a drinking mate who said
'I know why you have all these faggot friends, Karl
... you are one prime opportunist: no competition.'
    Come off it Kate,
if Leo wants to know as many people as he can
(and so do I) and if he's no designs
on this here bunny ... take 'er away, Leo!
    But Kate of course was near to right
except *Why the wives? Why* in all
the glorious hell they are, the wives?
I'm not so ruthless but if someone
– whom I hardly want to know –
has a wife, a girl, and she's available
(or even isn't at times)
there's little less brings out the bastard,
makes me feel the activist, that politician
I thought I'd like to be.
                    But an opportunist?
Would sometimes that I were!
                          For pick 'em!
    I'd a mate and he'd a cousin: eighteen
or so, a little goer.
                Sure I was flying out;
and sure the cousin had started seeing
someone else who wouldn't last, I hoped,
but did; flying out to London and beyond
forever. Six months on when I return
the little goer's married, and they've gone bush.
    I shrug that off and just increase
my activism: finish another degree,
run for parliament, lose; but meet
more women (not wives, not girlfriends,
merely women).
                And yet, that little goer ...
my mate her cousin teases me and always
keeps me tabbed. For I recalled
so many things (not merely face and tits and bum,
anyone with taste remembers them)

but Benny such cheek she had, such
pleasant cheek! So now and again I would
still imagine Barb giving lip, the sweetest lip;
even to that husband.
    And then, one afternoon years on,
at a function I'm alone and so's
the little goer. No Benny I'm not ruthless
right away, but something starts and starts
for weeks.
    Oh but pick 'em!
This time she's the one who's flying out:
she and the husband and, by now,
I'm liking her, truly I am liking her . . .
    Just a few months back
I was all politics and wives:
an activist who helped claw back a marginal,
I was set for my reward:
a pre-selection in a near-to-safe.
All I had to do was wait, do nothing
absolutely stupid; carry myself tall
(but not too tall).
    It's such a precision instrument, the ego.
    And any world has ways of getting
what that world expects. Well guess
who never knew this, never remotely
knew this?
    It was set to be a wonderful summer:
I'd found a couple to amuse me:
Daryl and Soph,
hippy law students: all the proper issues,
all the correct feelings.
    And Daryl,
eased out of the law, set up a gourmet-grub-to-go:
each evening in their communal lounge
trestles sagged in the joy of Dazza's quiche-o-rama.
    Soph had large, cold, almond eyes;
Soph had lips too thin even to pout;
but *Look at me world!* Sophie would demand
just by shaking out her ringlets.
But at least she didn't giggle: not once: giggling

was *his* domain.
                        So I'd survey what seemed like
pallet loads of quiche and, hoping to get
their bleeding hearts bleeding even more
Plurry good tucker boss
I bunged on the abo.
                        And Daryl, Dazza,
the mighty Daz, just giggled.
                                    'Come on,'
I wailed within, 'come on quichemaker,
haven't you any real convictions?'
        . . . you know why I like Leo, Benny?
Because he isn't weak, because he doesn't giggle,
because, never kidding he's a rebel,
he really does rebel; because if poofters
rarely hit they still are tough, they have to be,
because he knows there's more beyond Leo;
because he won't condemn anything that isn't
merely fad . . .
                    and I was getting to like her,
really enjoy the way Sophie arrived
and where she was headed:
if her old man was a top shelf QC, Dazza's
was what? A pharmacist? I got to know
she thought that way, got to know how sick
she was playing the hippy wife;
she wanted to be a lawyer, quick.
        So, whilst Daryl and simply all their friends
travel up the coast, trailing all these
rock group tours of summer, she stays back
doing extra courses. When they're over
(and Daryl it seems is stuck with The Niddries
in Townsville) Sophie, sick of waiting for him,
waiting for just one man, doesn't.
                                    Well,
if she's an opportunist I'm an opportunist
and if, sometimes past, each loathed the other,
surely we could try a bit of liking?
        But Benny, all I knew was, soon,
the quichemaker's heading home and he'll want

to be where I have been.
                    Oh how
I could strut myself about with her those weeks,
oh how when she was coming over every atom
of this body honed itself.
            Was this heading love? Some opportunist!
            'Darling,' Sophie says,
'Darling there's little we can do and nothing
I can yet.' Then, for a moment, panic arrives:
'But don't ever tell, don't ever tell!'
            And now I'm floundering: floundering cool
but floundering: me who once mistook her for
some air-brain erstwhile hippy,
me, I'm so well into enjoying her (want her
enjoying me). But silly prick, I should've known
she'd be my mark two little goer.
            And guess who's back in town?
Bullseye! Barb! Who visits me.
Let's make this life of mine real dumb
I almost tempt myself but *Calm boy calm*
I urge *Every wife that enters here*
can't just be yours.
                    Indeed they can't.
Whilst she's telling about her latest boyfriend
I order my eyes apart and swallow every yawn:
next please!
                Next indeed. The king o' the quiche
is next.
            . . . if we finished anything we finished off
each other rolling into the middle of their street
and back into the gutter: where I bit him.
            One more husband, one more wife,
one more wife who wouldn't leave him, yet
(for *don't ever tell* meant in effect *I* want to tell).
They'd been tiring me.
                    Bored I almost had
the gall to *Look Dazza-chum / buddy / my man / my boy /*
ol' son, let me pat your back,
knead your shoulder, look my rival dead
in his eye: Sophie's told you hasn't she?

And I'll admit that was a silly thing to do,
but it was summer, you were away . . .
and I don't blame her but doesn't she overdo
things, right?
    Instead
I would drop by with *More tucker, boss?*
   All giggles, though, had ceased.
   I tried to modify his name,
but after Daz and Dazza something didn't gel
with Dazzo.
     He just wouldn't say a thing.
Who did though?
      There was a time
when somebody might've taken the dive
and tele-movie style propose *Let's forgive*
and all be grown-ups, grown-ups together.
Except one afternoon as I climbed their steps
Daryl jumps me, gurgling in his rage
'We hate you Karl we hate you!'
   No cops were called.
Someone (the QC?) simply rang head office:
a standard-bearer in a near-to-safe
prowled married women, bit their spouses.
  'Karl,' someone with a certain sympathy observed,
'if you must play up, get elected first.'
   And what could be my one rejoinder?
That man, comrades, made quiche, nothing
but quiche . . .
     You're right though, Benny:
if it hadn't happened I wouldn't have
got the knowledge. Put it down as knowledge
then.
    Knowledge, learning, waiting, avoiding wives? Why not?

A flexible honour

   And Barb thought how
'open' or whatever word had fashion,
she surely didn't intend to fall in love:
now *that* would derail too much; too bad
it had to happen. Then she thought
of certain times back home, the times of his
'flirtations', a word so twee it begged
you add *And the rest!* Every so often
Rog had gone out, primed for it,
just as she had; though here lay the exception:
later he always told her.
   That he was 'difficult' helped:
after putting up with Roger Heath
who wouldn't begrudge his spouse an 'interlude'
however brief, that signalled something of 'cheek',
of 'escapade'.
     Yet still
she had her loyalty: that kind in which
no-one else was ever meant to judge him.
After a friend, an approximate friend, blurted
Rog sure is a bargain . . . a hard bargain
she wasn't even approximate.
       Okay,
so Barb had never total honour: well
hers was a flexible honour, one to tell
I've been invited to dinner or
There's this film / this play / this opening or
I'll be out tonight with work friends.
A truth which succeeded till her husband
allowed his wife to know some things
were understood.

      ✿

   And yet,
that she and Rog could be apart for months,
and the man she'd been loving less than a year
had gone away for a week, leaving her so dis-

attached ... now this was too much loving.
    And no matter how settled down they were
becoming, trancing each other, Neil was from out there:
an ambassador.
                    Barb thought of Melbourne:
all the places she couldn't quite imagine him.
She'd loved the idea of planning an itinerary
(as if there would be time to do a Heath/
Price pilgrimage! as if he'd want to):
her old schools, her son's old schools,
Dot or Lins to track down, Auntie Wynne to visit:
and why not check on Real Livin' Toyota?
    At The Department 'Bongman' Hamilton
still asked after 'Mensa' Spencer.
    'When are we going to meet your hubby?'
Helen Griffin demanded. 'When are we going
to get a peek at Roger?'

🙶

    'Well this one's been who?'
Rog had smiled a bit. 'Who?'
    Little here was three-dimensional
(like *Why?* or *What exactly is it?*)
but a bland, a sober *Who?*
That's all he demanded: truth of the simplest kind.
    Was it a crisis?
    Yes, but hadn't the Heaths
been born and nurtured in crisis?
    'Neil.' Barb would admit.
'Just Neil. Just a name.'
    She would be coming back to Roger.
    They were from tribes who huddled in.
    They understood each other.

🙶

    At least Barb had a friend in Benny,
she trusted him, trusted herself with him,
so back from Melbourne Benny got told

(knowing perhaps she shouldn't but someone
had to share, to understand): 'He's got to know:
*Neil, you must find someone else, don't call
for months. Neil, please . . .'*

    And Benny volunteered to ride through town
that night to check on his new beloved, Wal.

∂

    A few months on the word was out:
'Big Government' was over: departments like The Department
were consolidating, acknowledging the finite.
                                           And,
before the merger, the time arrived for 'Bongman' Hamilton
to institute the grand reunion and farewell.
    'Gee Neil, since you left the place just hasn't . . .'
'Been the same mate?'
                        'All the old gang . . .'
'Miss me mate?'
                 'Barb Heath mate?
For a time eh, you 'n' Barb got on real thick.
Still see her mate? Not likely?
We're threatening her to bring the husband eh?
Everyone's expected. Even Mirella mate?'
    No, there'd hardly be Mirella; who anyway
was pregnant. 'She must've wet her daks,'
Bongman drawled, 'each time she knew
another cheque was going out. Gaol mate?'
    Nahh. If she missed it by an inch
she missed it by a mile eh?
Neil didn't have to be in mensa mate
to know the gods were with that girl:
went to a pretty good school for one and,
even better, hadn't she the ultimate chick excuse
My boyfriend made me do it!?
    Where would the function be? Not somewhere
down The Shire: The Oceana Room? Pacifica Receptions?
    Nah. A local watering hole eh. But reasonable:
plenty of chick appeal. Nothing too rough mate.

∂

And Roger asked:
would he be there, her one-time wonderboy,
this faces-to-names-time, this now, this once?

          ઠ

    Barb phoned Neil and said
'Roger of course, you'd never know him
would you?'
                That man coming down his drive
one January morning who stretched a bit
and then returned inside? No Neil didn't think so,
didn't want to sound *that* ludicrous.
    But how he loved the ludicrous!
    'If I were gay I'd take Benny,
if Liz weren't married I'd have her for my escort.
I'll be a fool to go and so will Roger;
you'll be a fool to take him there and
have me there.' *Yes ludicrous with everyone
cancelling everyone and foolishness as norm,
as leveller . . . let's go!*
'Oh and 'what's he know?'
                        'Your name.'

          ઠ

    Neil and Roger looked each other's way just once:
when owning all the space between, their eyes lined up.
Part betrayal/part sport, only lovers look
like that. *What you receive and share I receive and share.
Who'll blink first? You. Let him be you!*
    And the line stayed taut,
long enough for every thought of Neil, of Roger,
to scuttle out, pause, send itself and return.
*Does she look at you the way I've seen her?
Even to think she might admits that soon
for me or you or her all this will cease.*
    Another second (was it even that?)
approached and galloped by.

       My heart's a losing coach
Man up! *it rasps* Man up!
*But this game having been so rehearsed, even before
I heard of you, here we are and* Man up! Man up!
what else am I doing?

      ❧

  Later, when she needed someone,
who else remained but Roger? No,
not even Benny but Roger:
who never accepted the psyche much
— thought of it as merely a 'sealed-in section' —
who'd still believed she hadn't any secrets now.
  *I just make love to Rog when we need to.
Then I try suspending the lot.*
  As she moved to sleep beside him,
Barb felt his fingers roll from her shoulders
and on, to below her thighs.
       'Now it's over Barb?'
 'I've already phoned him, seen him,
already told him.'
     Yes it was. Yes she'd try.

Benny, watching or Blow it up!

  So the hiatus over, during Benny's lunch next day
Barb had called him. Benny was such a solid friend,
she wanted to say thanks and although they hadn't seen
each other really much she hoped to meet him one day.
  That night Neil truly, bluntly said
'She won't be coming round, not here, not for a while.
Barb has officially returned to Rog.'
  Nothing becoming nothing quite like a tossed aside
Benny just wanted to ask his friends
(Carlo the drama coach, Mark the activist,
Leo the soul mate, Wal the increasingly beloved):
Our carry-ons aren't their carry-ons are they?

Are they? Constantly they were!
For gay, straight, or the Plutonian on Pluto
why was everybody so full of bittersweet bravado?
Gonna get myself through all this mess just watch me
might be worthy of some latter-day sampler,
but not much more.
                      By the next night Benny got
so sad he craved that charge which flesh, mere flesh,
can give. So off he'd Vespa'd. Soon, not yet,
he would be true to Wal.
                    Soon, not yet,
Neil might quit being so inanely stoic. Until then
the flurry of it!
     Benny would recall (better he couldn't forget) Karl,
that appalling man in Melbourne, everything about him saying
I'm confident about trying to be confident
and believe me, please, it works!
                        The initial power
that man must've had with women, the power
Barb must've loved! Why didn't he just start
a suburban gigolo agency: Housewives' Choice?
     Heigh ho! If someone had to supply the empathy
why not this would-be bachelor uncle
watching it all unfold, hearing an improving tale's
latest moral update *I promise I'll try being honest,*
modern but honest.
               Karl, though, was too much for Benny:
he clung, he jarred; where'd Leo find such friends?
Where he found you and you found everyone, Bennyboy: in the world!

     As over eighty were expected they had arrived at Leo's early.
     'So, before we're swamped,' came the host's
avuncular request, 'tell me about yourself . . .
where you've been, Neil, what you've done.'
     And, giving him a joint, Leo heard of Spacey,
Frenchy, Liz, Louise, Naomi, Barb, her husband
Rog and Benny.
                Oh my! Oh wow!

Such self-effacement hadn't been impressive
but 'Leo, Leo,' Benny later urged, 'flex your tolerance!
Neil's girl is otherwise engaged, otherwise attached,
and he knows where it's heading. If he's a sook
he's a justified sook, and everyone involved is sweet,
good, civilised, including me. I don't care what's repressed
and don't care why. I only know I feel for them:
when Barb goes, as she will, I lose her too.
I can't say *Let it weigh on them!*
I'm in love with life, all life, too much.'
    Yes it sounded wrong, Olympian but nonsense,
to invoke *I am above it all. My life controls itself.*
And even if it seemed it did, this big 'this'
got in the way: The Benny Hull Fuckathon:
the sweet agony of a fine considerate man
who can't help cruising.
                  Neil had said
'Really I envy you, you and your cruising:
no obligations: just a new lover every time.'
    'Mmm yes well wait till you are busted, bashed
or worse, my lad,' advised Benjamin Arthur Tregear Hull,
counsellor, libertarian, sex maniac, friend.
    ... *and given the rest of your life as one of these*
he really didn't have to ask *What would you rather,
hey?* Friend! Friend! Friend!

    Their dishes done Neil still had his sleeves rolled.
Mmm, Benny thought, *Gene Kelly or a dentist?*
(With those arms, those teeth, his air at once of vigour,
precision and clean living Gene Kelly *was* a dentist!)
    And Barb having scuttled back to whatsisface six weeks before,
Neil was this public servant (ex) turned handyman,
moping his way through the Benny extension.
    A firm if tender talking to! That's what he deserved!
And if Benny were to deliver such presumption,
he'd start, as always, with an anecdote
        *Who hasn't amused themselves on yesterday's lovers?
    I do perpetually.*

But though the past accelerates Where's he go?
We did that? *memories keep swooping your libido*
like cyclones!
        Someone we adored still circles above us as
Hi! *we gaze up* What is tu obviously after?
Spiral on down. Did moi hear 'Head'?
Ahh not today well maybe yes, yes, yes! *(Till y' both dead,*
in the footnote sense if course.)
        Don't drag her
back, you mustn't Neil: merely to make up numbers
for one more final-night-together,
and then the next and then another next. No matter
how many of those sambas, tangos, rhumbas
you hoofed together . . .
        Benny might start with this,
but knew he couldn't; talking about 'head' though, that's where
all of this would stay: inside his.
And, as for the psyche . . . *Bugger the psyche!*
What your friend does not require is a sprig o' jargon,
fresh from the shrink. Just distract him,
distract him!
        And Benny tried: 'Let me tell you more
about my latest: Wal's an infuriating slut,
but Neil I can never wait until our next time.
Who needs saints? Benny's captivated . . .'
    Distract him! Distract him!
    Though he'd never admit aloud Benny was very fond
of Neil and, right now, in this kitchen after washing up,
such an affection demanded that he stay looking onto,
looking after, his friend. *You'll continue, you both prevail*
this look announced.
        'Somehow,' Benny found himself advising,
'somehow tonight, forever, Barb will always love you.'
(Have I said *that?* he asked himself.
Oh what an agony aunt!)
        'Sure,' Neil nodded,
'I believe it, I have to . . . simply because, though right now
I hate her, I must believe in what's occurred. I must.
But Benny . . . this is . . . this is . . .'
and, unwinding, his voice spiralled out into a sob
which rose into a scream of 'Ghastly! Blow it up!'

Neil: three unsent letters

    Dear Benny . . . you won't find my feet stuck out of your oven.
Nor ever again catch me blathered in my idiotic
pity (ranting in our very own demotic
only you could really understand).
                        For above 'n'
beyond us lie such worlds of lovin'
(aerial, terrestrial, aquatic:
hunt everywhere and everywhere's erotic)
and we aren't alas (and not alas) born to govern
where our too too fickle fancies take us:
tracksuit or tux, g-string or skirt;
hermit, spouse, cruiser; women, men,
or bits of both; there's a something makes us
what we've always wished to be; and where the joy-or-hurt
was sent, who cares: the joy-or-hurt arrives! Eh, Ben?

    Dear Liz . . . it's hardly our lot to stoke and restoke the fire
of anybody's past. But go on, try Liz,
surely you return to keep tabs on The Shire
sometimes? Not that much?
                        Okay, let's start again: Hi Liz!
Remember when we, almost courtesy cousins,
would take aim at every sook, bore, bullshitter, skite,
and how sometimes (one night
or two they still seem in the dozens)
we hooned our suburbs butchering the hits of the day:
'With a Girl Like You', 'The Dedicated Follower of Fashion';
when all was growly, smashin',
ripper, beauty, wunderbar, olé!
    Now, I'm advised, we've marginally matured. Yup:
The Shire met the Rest-of-the-World, and we grew up.
    But ahh Liz ahh. Why wouldn't you
quit all your well-intentioned blurting:
'*Barb!* Neil *Barb!* Couldn't you . . . couldn't you?'
    And yet I've never felt more proud, more certain,
than when announcing 'Liz and I are mates.

Everyone loves her.'
            (Or those times, like dogs
in excess mange, we serenaded our double dates
by covering The Kinks, The Troggs.)
    There's little need now to mask
if I would rather a lover or a friend;
oh gimme right away a friend to ask
'Don't want to be a sticky-beak but after The End
now what?'
            Now what, Liz? Just another instalment
of rediscovering what hitting-the-wall meant.

    . . . conjure this indulgence: you lease a passing Saab
or Volvo simply to pirouette-out where a freeway's
daemon (at one-fifty, two hundred ks)
urges *Now!*
    Yet it was never like that, eh Barb?
Even when your stark, plain loving
had frozen and you just couldn't be back,
it still was love.
    What else saves us from unending flak
of nothing? (And I was afraid of *Nothing*:
for then *We* wouldn't exist!)
            Out of one trance
he pads into the next. Not sensing how that clogged, unlikely
spouting which passes for his psyche
has banked with enough romance,
tears paused then toppled.
            Our final scene sees this cast-
of-one sob out infatuation's final taps.
Drying to a lined, drained face perhaps.
He's creased, he's bleached, but rational at last!

MATEYS

'Rog!' hailed Ray as if he really knew him;
Roger waved. What else was done?
                              There seemed
a protestant mustiness with Ray, echoes of
Christian Science's lapsed fringes, say, the Adventists,
any near acceptable faith. Mormons? Well hardly the Mormons;
besides, all was guesswork.
              'Roger Heath, my wife Chris Donellan,' Ray announced;
a little tubby, slightly florid, stroking his
patchy beard, competent at sighing *well* . . .
'Well then Rog, thought we'd like to meet again,
see Chrissie eh?'
              Then he expanded:
how even couples get stale, acquire new needs,
how relationships work when they must, the what-it-takes
to 'mellow on out and swing'.
So Chrissie was launched.
Not quite.
              'Ray you're making us fools, believe me Rog
this man never uses words like that. Did he?
This afternoon?'
              'Roger's from Melbourne.'
Her husband beamed.
              'Melbourne? I hear it's nice.'
False start, Chrissie, would he fall for that? Try again.
Like Ray did: 'He's another chalkie.'
                              'I was.'
'We all are,' Chrissie laughed, 'but Ray's almost
a drama consultant. You're let out Fridays then?'
       'My wife works, we've a kid, I've been studying
all year . . .' these facts and implications
setting his bounds: don't apologise, but never forget.
       That morning Ray had phoned: 'Rog? The name is Ray . . .
never thought we'd call?' A salesman, trying
to be tasteful he'd faltered over-pat:
'Umm, like to meet?'

                              Like to? Roger thought,
in this game yes no and maybe haven't a chance.
'After lunch?'
                 'After lunch?' Ray turned on
a hearty shock. 'Heck, why not after lunch!'
       This bar was named. With near-remembered tunes
as if they were the air itself, mock mahogany,
sporting prints, was this a soapie set? It only
lacked a passing cleavage and Ray sucking
through his teeth *Getta loada that!* Not yet.
       '. . . tacky but quiet,' his verdict ticked approval.
'See that bar attendant?' Head to the side he
bobbed it slightly. 'One night . . .' but let his story glide,
'I'll tell you soon . . .' Blinking he straightened up.
'Well.' Again came 'Well.' Then 'Just me so far,
Chrissie sends her love, she's out with friends,
but this snap's her.' Was Roger frowning? 'Relax.
She's not a kid. Like me she's twenty-nine,
most fellas love her, Chrissie's great.'
                          'There've
been others?'
              'A few, guys we've met . . .'
Did Ray's head indicate the bar attendant?
'An ad or two . . .'

```
       Hey! Fellas! My Lady Would Love
             Meeting You!
       And We'd Love You To Meet My Lady!
```

'. . .women?' Ray asked himself, 'We're working on it.
You like porn? I'm partial but Chrissie . . .' Smiling or pouting
he shook his head. 'It's still fun but.
We all get nice 'n' stoned, see what happens,
put on some Dylan . . .' sounding as if they had them
back for cocoa.
                Dylan? Music to swing by?
'Dylan?' Roger blurted.
               'Bob Dylan,' Ray shot

an agitated stare. 'You must like Dylan . . .' moving
into reverie gear 'everybody does . . .' Knowing though
he'd played too much of one line, another got produced:
their flat rented for the water views 'We're still saving . . .'
and when these facts had the new friend relaxed,
serving the record collection 'Even the problematic ones
Self Portrait! Nashville Skyline!' But at his best
recounting, *Chris 'n' me,* about their past, if not
present, life. 'When we were kids we worked
vacations, me in footwear, she in kidswear.
During our breaks we had great gropes . . .'
Good at summing up Ray was better or worse
at presumption. 'Like yours mine's caught onto
Women's Lib . . .' or 'Tough when you're young and a kid
comes marching out.'
      If he never appealed, the curious
always left with a restrained fascination,
since there was Chrissie, and Chrissie was
willing to do *that?* and what exactly
that was might be discovered, same bar,
later today.
    After they got married Ray
would catch her, late at dinner parties:
'Mark my words . . .' sounding like her mother,
'behind each great man there's a good woman.'
You hardly heard that now. When Chrissie got
real out of it she just re-flogged
'There's something quite hateful with you Ray,
near demonic.' So she believed this?
It hardly changed that almost-love sending
him to work, for quickly ripening Angela, or Gary
whose not quite adult charm might swing him,
well, any way you wanted. Dylan, Chrissie, the kids,
nothing else was Ray and what he loved. Dope,
having guys around, drama classes, these
supplied mere venue.
     Roped in that afternoon by Ray's
'Ever watched your wife . . . like to see mine?'
Matey, Roger mused, even to consider Barb and
Wonderboy is dangerous enough. That one's outabounds

isn't it, not playing it am I?
    Chrissie kept talking: 'I want to meet his kids,
at that age ohh . . .' her hands were clenching
and her face grinned hard; here was something to love.
'They've got so much and hardly know . . .
it's wasted . . .' The cue hung,
Roger and Chrissie chorusing 'On the young!'
    'Chris!' Ray started taking charge, warning
'Chrissie . . .' but warning what?
                        'One day,' she looked
to Roger, 'One Saturday morning, I'll drive out west
just to imagine: he could be Gary and he
could be Mario and isn't she that yummy yummy Angela?
It must be!'
         'You coming back?' Ray was staying
organised. 'I'll go ahead, set up the place.
Chris wants to know you. Going home with Roger, Hon?'
His brain flicking up any amount of half-
remembered Dylan, Roger drove her.
    'Does he understand I couldn't give
a flying fuck for Maggie's farm?'
                    'Nod
when required. He won't suspect.'
    Clouds had washed these suburbs but, clearing,
their sky looked beautifully naked. Under that big fat moon
everything shone like it.
        'He won't try to speak
or sing like you-know-who?'
            'Would have
once, but no, Ray's growing up.'
                'Yeah?'
    Dylan freak, fuck freak, Roger saw how
it had to work: you started edgy if diffident,
but ended obsessed and were at all times serious.
If you must name it something name it,
he supposed, sex, though who'd ever thought
to question *how ridiculous!* and leave off
(or continue)? Roger perhaps when needing
to be pressed, certainly tonight, but hardly Chrissie,
never Ray. If this was all creed to him that man,

Roger started to see, was its evangelist.

And what was the altar of his entrancement but
Chrissie-with-men, so much alive!

'Look,'
Ray would whisper to himself, 'look at her, my woman
loves it, she's so loving it and I am right,'
he knew, eyes blinking quick, strong, 'so totally right.
Who says this won't turn mainstream, if another year's
Help Me Make It Through The Night
won't be sung about us and no-one will laugh then
cause we'll be so appreciated, pure M.O.R.'
But ages before, Dylan would have understood,
his was always the next adventure,
that something nobody else tried contemplating.

How long would this repertoire remain?
Roger might ask. It couldn't stop for Ray was real,
realer than even Dylan. 'They're so straight to weird
and back again, leave,' Roger repeated, 'leave the Donellans.'
Though with the thought of Chrissie, like her jeans,
T-shirt and sneakers, easy, no doubt and comfortable,
why not, like the others, risk it?
If occasions demanded a briefest rescue
Roger would oblige.

She kept telling things.
When he was younger this friend was called
each time Ray scored, asking him to tote' em up:
*ninety-six, ninety-seven, eight, nine, hundred,
one fucking hundred matey!* '. . . or every time he
liked to think he scored and may as well.
Then we met, Ray really started scoring,
the phone calls stopped. Much later the friend told me.
Ray doesn't know. Guessing what's in his head?
Guessing how much? You are for one.
Bothered being part of his imagination, Roger?'

'Can't stop it Chrissie.'

She could rescue herself of course.
*One evening soon Ray would just suggest
something to do but, but . . .*
'Sorry Darling,' *(he'd still be Darling)* 'can't.
Going out tonight with Rog.'

      'Raging with Rog? Sure Hon.'
(And she'd be Hon.) '... Well how was Rog, old Roger eh?
enjoy yourself?'
     'But really Chris, he'd love to see you
scoring Dylan, right?'
       'Stop here?' she asked.
It was a playground. '... my playground. Whenever he gets
too bad I come out here, try being a kid again. Dylan?
You're right, not hard to guess.' Her swing kept lunging
higher till it wobbled itself, jolted down and smoothed
up again.
   'I want to see you,' Roger told her,
'won't come in tonight though.'
       'Sure. Your wife
go out?'
   Go out? With a term so extra-twee
what was left but 'Barb's seeing someone, Wonderboy.
Don't know what's occurring. Not worth wishing
the fuck I did though. We won't split. Can't.'
She climbed off the swing, his mind kept re-
arranging the game. 'There must be a pay-out, one day,
couples are like that.'
     'And you might do the paying?'
He thanked Chrissie's neat concern, but
'Then, of course I fight.'
      The glib was her forte
and she seemed shocked.
      He sighed 'That Ray, he's
certainly a Dylan freak.'
      She gave a simpler reply:
'The world is full of them. Where'd you meet?
I'm curious as ever. The ad?'
      A word Ray used
that afternoon seemed the best: 'Just floating.'
  'Oh floating.'
     Into her driveway their words became
near interchangeable volleys and returns.
  'You smoke?'
    'It makes me tense, I drink.'
  'You don't smoke?'

                'Barb does.'
                        'You don't trust us?
Ray's not *that* weird. Dylan has a line somewhere ...
Dylan has a line for every day.'
                                'I'm sure he has.'
        'It's all in Dylan.'
                        'I'm sure it is.'
        'Wonder what he'd make of us and this?'
as if their lives and how they spent them were
just the next door wall she waved towards.
'It's funny I suppose but in its way this,
this might be love? Dylan would see that.'
                                        'Love?'
        Oh yes it was, it was, she graded the powers:
first 'Ray lets me ...' then 'He wants me to ...
sometimes I must ... it can be fun though ... because,
because I care, that's why!' And, since she was excited
'I love him but it's the twentieth century Roger!'
Every breathy sound of Chrissie's clamour cheeped
out like a rodent's. 'You know how many friends,
real friends, he has? Sometimes it's Ray 'n' Dylan
versus the world, then even Dylan fails.
This'll sound trite, call it pop psych, but Rog
it was his childhood.'
                        He knew the rest,
how it would be unspoken *Help me love him,
Ray's not a happy man, he hates so much. But yet ...*
and this *but yet* was Roger, Roger and all
the guys.
                If not tonight she would see his body, soon,
though it was his eyes Chrissie wanted first,
probably the most: just that little scared she hoped,
like each first time that really mattered;
how it could be the best yet, by looking at them,
into and through them; only then would this lean,
angular man be required, on hands and knees,
panting for her, with Ray emerging from anywhere,
close by screaming 'Now, I want her now matey, now!'
his cries turning all three such wonderful monsters.
        'Love to meet you soon Rog. Go to a pub, see a band.'

She grabbed his arm.
　　　　　　　　　Roger asked 'What's he doing?'
'Now?'
　　　'Yes.'
　　　　　　'Thinking of us.'
　　　　　　　　　　　　'Sure and a bit more,
I bet ... you certainly have a quiet street.'
　　　　　　　　　　　　　　　　Chrissie liked it but
'Don't like the quiet ... any first meeting gets you nervy ...'
wanting to keep talking, she wanted to hear him talk,
wanted to ask 'What's Ray been telling?'
　　　'Not that much,' Roger decided dead-pan.
　　　　　　　　　　　　　　　　　　'But what?
tell me what.'
　　　　　　'He said you don't believe in underwear,
you never wear them.'
　　　　　　　　　'Ray said *that*? What ...'
she sounded dazed, 'a con-line what a fabulous
con-line ...' But not too dazed' *That?*
You made it up?' He wouldn't answer. '*That?*'
Still wouldn't. Chrissie sighed 'You're bitter Rog,
but cold and bitter. Still, I like you ...' Her eyes were closed.
'Roger,' she shook her head, 'There's been so many deadshits.
You know where he gets them? Two one night,
Bernie 'n' Jack and they were ancient. I'm not sick
of all this but, please, don't be another deadshit,
be different. Let's go out soon, get to know
each other, a pub, a band. I have the gear,
roll some logs, you'll fly ...'
　　　　　　　　　　'Sorry I only drink.'
　　　'Drink then, champers, the very best. And you can
call me something very special: Kitten.'
　　　　　　　　　　　　　　　　'Kitten?'
　　'Yes Kitten or something.' Her eyes closed again,
starting to repeat his name as if it might melt in
with Kitten.
　　　　　　Roger/Rog never sounded sillier and
'I'm needed,' he understood, 'These clowns need me!
They need me!'

LOVELIFE (V)

ROGER, OR OF LOVE AND ITS ANGER

for Phyllis Webb

And yet I shall have to do something.
Ah, the key of our life, that passes all wards, opens all locks,
Is not I will, but I must. I must, — I must, — and I do it.
ARTHUR HUGH CLOUGH, 'Amours de Voyage'

1 Chez Charley

Who hasn't seized on that urge to dump it
and snarl *Mop this, Charley, disinfect the stink?*
But Charley's hardly m' darling, he's m' shrink.
Likeable enough, the man's not one to trumpet
symptoms, causes and cures (nostrums for what life
is or isn't); as I am less than a dead-set cert
psychotic with overabundant traumas to blurt
upon Dr Charles Bell FRANZCP. Were I some housewife
(to be charitable, older style) trying to rid
herself of what she's become, I might cross-refer
to such tableaux as nappies soaking in their trough,
toast staling on its breadboard.
                      Well whacko-the-did!
For Roger has to hang his jacket of despair
upon the hook of what, mmm? Just nothing and the lot.

2 This

'Our marriage,' Charley hears, 'seemed as nurtured, caressed,
as . . .' I consider *or so I thought* but shirk
cueing it in. 'The thing, dammit, worked!'

'How come, then,' he asks, 'after such a harvest
you're left with the pips, the pith, the rind?'
    No question is newer, no question seems older.
For a reward I tell him how I told her
what facts I wanted known. Time then to rewind:
why'd this occur: the this of 'this' and the 'this' of *'this'*.
After such close-ups therapy zooms back and pans
out to a declaration. 'Oh little equals that nearly-
enough sober passion I have for her ... anything amiss?'
my slow smile baits.
             And 'Roger' the man's
guard-dropping, 'Roger! Come off it! Really!'

3   Grammar lesson

    It was about then I sensed him: Neil.
(Of course the name came later.)
And meantime, coining verbs (to partially-hate-her/
to even-forgive-him) I began feel-
ing how, now, better and better I knew my wife. Funny,
the items that were realigned till, whatever got purged
bloomed into an exhilaration as each suspicion surged
into my next new verb; e.g. to be-taken-for-the-bunny-
I-never-thought-I-was. Except I was; whilst the inanity
of being-somewhat-jealous got dumped in with the hoi-polloi.
After that power of Roger! Barbara! Neil! what would verbs
prove? Yet, though I'd done with them my vanity
released into another: to Wonderboy;
and I knew she had a lover, was a lover, was in love.

4   The Wonderboy Variations

    Though someone never met, never seen,
allow us, still, to improvise our bit
*Rag and Barb and who ... what, please, should come between
this three of us?*
             Fold dovetailing fold, here's the fit:
if someone's leaving, someone's taking over

and when I'm luke-warm you'll be undoubted hot.
Then, after test-running sarcasm, lover,
I sighed, here we are and not,
Wonderboy, my three-dimensional shadow!
(See how we weave, how we duck and feign!)
  Barb and I ate out. And given an hour to toy
round with the kari laksa, mee goreng, gado gado:
'He's who? Who?'
       'Neil. Just Neil. Just a name.'
And just-a-names just help eh, Wonderboy?

5 Sorry

  Roger's tears were dammed. There are those myths
that knit us into families and he, trying
to invent a further few, saw no per cent in crying;
only this need: to step back from the Heaths
in their marriage, its warp and weft,
and behold!
     After a dose of them's-the-breaks
(them's ideals shedding like eczema flakes)
he took himself to a whorehouse, but left.
Its intros, amusingly percussive,
offsetting the lingerie: *I'm Lee-Ann I'm Jess*
I'm Chelsea I'm Starr.
      Cows moo, ducks quack
and 'Sorry,' was heard from Rog, 'never enough of a spiv."
  And later, when nerved to scan the contact press,
what hit him more, its tragedy or tack?

6 Roger and Ray

  'Chrissie's adventurous, don't tell her but. Floating
are we? She's nice, says I'm a bit of a hack
in the cot, but honest.' (It hardly seemed gloating,
they'd hunt out floaters, bring them back:
Honey meet The World; World, Hon.) 'Ever watched
yours at it? Mine?' His eyebrows raised:

'No mate?' sighing, proposition botched.
    'That's novel,' I offered, passing it for praise
that he misheard.
                'You're *writing?*'
                          I smiled.
'Possibly' as good a line to help intrigue
my present lot (or his or hers).
                      Wouldn't douse
that afternoon in Chrissie, though seeing him beguiled
so by the world and his wife, next time, in league
with curiosity perhaps, I'd check it, meet the spouse.

7   Roger and Chrissie (I)

    I saw them as my kinda couple-
you-meet-on-holidays (there seemed no-one else);
Ray's motives ringing more bells
than a cathedral. Sarcastic? I was doubled
over. Like *Douches, a User's Guide* or *Where to Graze
in L.A.* we were magazine fodder,
and 'open' or otherwise I tried to prod her,
tenderly, out of marriage.
                Some days
we drove somewhere, sat, kissed,
exchanging similar enough plots: how a whim
can bloom into commitment. Then, as her throat unloaded
sobs, I held that darting-mousey face: 'Chris, Chris,'
(turning shrink/director/coach) 'stop doing this for him!'
    The wailing would ease; softly under my hands she exploded.

8   Roger and Chrissie (II)

    We're still *us* with added rider *just*
and if this mightn't be exactly love
it's believable. (Hoping to be a cut above
hypocrisy, our motto's not 'Fidelity or Bust'.)
Then, since she says how fine tip top okay
Chrissie's feeling, to stymie potential pouting

we hit a film: Americans are shouting,
always have been. (Though Rog and Barb and Ray
and Chris seem little better than the soaps tut tut.)
    In last night's dream *us* with our red setter
just jogged some forgettable foreshore, and indeed
what fantasies aren't as disposable?
                                But, big but, 'Roger,' her eyes still
say (no eyes say it better)
'I need you, need you, need you, need . . .'

9 Eyes

    After Barb's spillage of his name and history
made me know I could feel second-best,
and since I'd been quite enough a guest
at my proposed defeat, I saw no mystery
to solve. Just hunt that parallel which fits.
This day's been either some outer screaming carn!
I thought, *or with her contained response, pavane-
like. And I'm thankful, given both, it's
how she tells her truth.*
                       But Barbara's eyes
were shut. 'You had her candid,'
the lids informed (near enough to bricks
commandeering window space) 'accept how such a prize
she's had to be.'
                    Events hedging a mean, a standard,
let's focus said pavane upon domestics.

10 Games

    Believing *this still works* we waved
off any love; learning to redeploy
such passion left, we iced it. All faults caved
in, accommodating whoever. (Wonderboy
say, what was his name, his name:
Waldemar . . . Boris . . . Ahmed . . . Chuck?
It gets to be a game beyond mere game.

You rove, okay, just keep me in the ruck.)
Or my turn: Chrissie: three wooden brooches
chorus-lining a lapel, pragmatic smart
and pleasantly abrupt, lean hips
tatted with butterflies. Each lover coaches
for the next. Beyond mere game lies art.
These are the ways you have relationships.

11   Fifteen minutes

    Thinking to go out I shaved
and, so used to the sound any shower
makes slapping onto her, never gave
it my mind: one more quarter hour
of marriage, except, taking this punt
she stepped over the bath, flicked her
eyes my way. What did we want?
Something neither could predict or
didn't have to.
              Another near-defunct
affair was closing.
                  Frame some rules because,
Charley, there must be rules. One-through-ten
tonight were concertina'd thus: don't get
used to your lover (whatever he was).
    Looked as if she needed me again.

12   The Heaths (I)

    We met at a wedding minus my *and friend,*
(this mate's sister who'd snaffled out a virus)
with a requisite summer evening to fire us
into kissing. At that age, when the means and end
seem one, you'd think I'd try for more; instead
we merely pashed. Next night I took her out
and given a week it never looked in doubt
we'd find ourselves, somehow, in a bed.
    Barb still tells what each other wore

as if, from then, she was in training
for the nostalgia. And though my cast's wider (the result's
most of my life) it's premised on this necessary lore:
we made the other happy; little needed explaining;
nothing seemed difficult.

13 The Heaths (II)

     Love for that age has neither rules nor regs;
the intimate was there to be seized
for nothing was less infinite. Being so pleased
at becoming us, we would (with her grade six legs,
my hardly-any pecs)
giftwrap the normal, dump the exotic back on its pallet.
Blunt as filigree, delicate as a mallet,
that's the charm of dear old s.e.x.
Which I sort of *got* one day.
                    So I kissed her
by my car (proposing a rendezvous,
a continuation) ever on our slight alert
for the arrival of friends, her folks, a sister.
     That summer all we had to do it seems,
was lift her skirt.

14 The Heaths (III)

     The question was its answer; with 'Yes,' a parent asking
'but what can you *know?*'
                      And tempted to say
the alpha and omega of s.f.a.
I surely shrugged, all the time basking
in that sweet reflected shock of *living together.*
Though two youngsters tipped into a vat
of compromised excess, we'd hardly considered *that*
and would agree to, well, whatever:
circles dotting your 'i's and 't's crossed with swirls,
invite the planet!
                As I coached my teeth

to tighten through some glass-charged MC lurch-
ing forth his *Ladies an' gentlemen boys and girls
beupstandingplease . . . meet Mr and Mrs Heath!*
'. . .we'll do it,' said her mother, 'at the church.'

15   The Heaths (IV)

     Sprung in a diary or a panel van
there's little kids prefer to getting caught
(unless of course it's nothing of the sort,
which wasn't us). *After* we made Sam,
or given our dilemma found we had,
I started a wordsearch. The night
he arrived it stopped: perfect? correct? No, *right*.
That Barb and Rog became Mum and Dad
seemed as simple, plain. And call it *Straight pride*
but there, for preference, went the closets
we'd never need. Or consider how lucky
we still are. *But for preference* I could've joined that tide
of men who sweep on north (glands cooking up deposits
of Oz) for plenty South-East Asian fucky-fucky.

16   The Heaths (V)

     So a friend might return and, in an aside,
tell of some girl from Denmark or Illinois.
Which gave Barb the breach: 'But you're a good boy!'
    I loved and won't forget the one-time child bride
raising her eyebrows to send our guest flailing-
free: 'We toured a bit . . . I'd hardly call us lovers.'
     'What, just one, Andy? Surely there were others!'
(As if on our behalf she was saying
Well, we're adults now.)
               And, as he volleyed the taunting
'More? Of course there were!' Andy's reserve bent
to her cheek, her charm.
              'And okay what,' I joined our tease,
'gives in those bars?'

Though if the theme's jaunty-
enough (near to a decade old) here's today's variant:
There weren't others. Just him, that one, Neil, please . . .

17   Grit (I)

Strange, though my pain has melded into top shelf
restraint, its message stays this elemental:
*I know where you've been . . . gonna tell myself
on you . . .* Yet if the game's that parental
who then's the parent? Together
with everyone we'd devised this clomp-clomp
choreography: one special pas de whoever.
If that's how adults dance bring back the stomp,
I say or said, still sufficiently ill awe
of what is possible, with no desire to identikit
me as some martinet, addict, abuser.
But oh, when did the grit arrive, that flaw
which, although I hardly knew it
then, was steadily turning me loser?

18   Grit (II)

It won't square with ladies but getting decked
is a compliment; if you can hit and be hit
so can he. When fighting implies a certain respect
why thump your loathed one? (It's better far to spit.)
Wonderboy deserved neither. If hardly innocent
his acts were love-fuelled.
                         As if direct from the shit of battle
I wished I could've signalled this opponent
*You 'n' Barb . . . d'd'dit dardardar d'd'dit
don't send reinforcements just rest my fears
and tell me why*
                 But exit all thought of puttin' up y' dooks,
to day's far more a case of this: combs raised and fighting fit,
two more chaunticleers

strut respective barnyards (mine, Wonderchook's)
pecking into their wondergrit.

19 Roger's dream

    ... and the grit was love, love or her need/
my want, which doubtless approximated.
So, had he that just-enough ardour to free her,
briefly, from our growing up? Me, I never hated
any two the less, though the tears wept
were milked by Barb Heath and her boy scout,
and for years I've conjured, though hardly slept
through, Roger's dream.
                      Whilst the household's out
a man passes into my home: he's no thief,
hardly touches a thing, but *These are their books*
he notes, *they've made their beds like this.*
    We'll never meet so what could be the brief
of any shadowboxed defence, when violence is for sooks
and only my want informs me he exists?

20 Anger

    So maybe she needed him, but to fall
once, then fall for the falling so it would gel
into obsession, now that's betrayal
and I am confessing Charley: to tell, re-tell
of love and its anger: the flame, how we fan it
to a blaze. Risking small chaos, smaller harm,
he'll seize his pain, seek to inform the planet
a full paradesworth: that's the charm
of an angry man. What's better breached
than despair? Where's passion better lodged
than with, let's say it, truth? When a rage is spilt
rehearsals still wait to get preached.
(Barb, I wanted to ask her, we've dodged
our fears enough, let's have them killed.)

21 Love

      But hate is never the risk love is; and I will love.
      There are those, who, sliced to the quick-of-it/
shying from the thick-of-it,
demand (not even the odd kid glove)
nothing but the barge pole option. They're allowed.
My life has just one law: somehow I must
keep this faith: she took me and I, her: on trust;
till we more than lashed that braying crowd
predicting our demise: we made this: our family and its home.
It has to have been love: what else frees you from errors
you're meant to commit? Oh my wife might sling me cheek
(and I tolerate this as I always will the foam
of Barb) but she knows I'll never get conned by the terrors
of failure: seduced by their bravado and mystique.

22 React!

      An open marriage? An open sesame
on those bones in mine, yours, anyone's attic?
Ever accommodating (didn't need to impress me
but Neil had) and ever pragmatic
(want someone else? then he's that someone else!)
I mapped him through her:
whether they danced on asphalt or eggshells,
mock-honeymooned in Eden or a sewer,
I could attune, wait, as 'React!' Barb simmered,
'Fuck you Rog, react!'
                      Well some men
cry, some men laugh, some put it in writing
and I can't forgive but could forget, since the winner's
moi! But if all happens, as all happened, again:
tell them Charley, as I told her, he's fighting.

23 'How Affairs Succeed'

     For no-one reads an article or book
to think yes, that's the way to run it.
At least I don't. Those reasons some *Cosmo*-hack
gives in 'How Affairs Succeed'? We'd all begun it,
whatever *it* was, generations before.
The early-to-mid-twenties of this family man
slotted into an inevitable mosaic, sure;
but Barb liked me. She never, per se, planned
to share another's words breath body farewell-kisses:
which seemed the silliest events on earth,
at the time. For me simple *going at it*
wasn't simple. I'd other ways to please the missus
if not excite her. Don't try them? Then you're not worth
that pinch of proverbial. No, something better mattered.

24 The moon of your marriage

Yet, she's seeing someone. Doesn't need a barrage
of love-bites to be hit, for one more crater
to pock the moon of your marriage.
Oh you always hear from clever men, years later,
what they would do: stay very single, forget
if any kids were ever hatched.
     But Barb, I and Sam lived what we had, for *that?*
Pragmatics are too passionate. Try it detached,
you still need to conceive (italics/
capital H) *Him*. Enough contenders bound
from the blocks, most you'll never meet (the price
of a good imagination). This issue, the smart alecs
know, requires a more soluble state. They pound
the problem (yes, you have one) with advice.

25 Man-to-man

     So when friends mind your business it's an art
to wear their blunt moralising:

Man-to-man Rog, you married a tart.
A skill, sure, like Barb disguising
not *Him* but her despair: the hocus-pocus
affairs need to continue. (Or love, who knows?)
      I'd get myself asleep hardly rousing notice
at the hour she might return, stoned I suppose.
By spring Barb seemed caged to the haywire pulley
of infatuation. Near Christmas she came clanging
back: their trysts, assignations, dates
had closed. And I'd the future: enough to sense *bully-*
the-lot-if-it: sharing her round, hanging
out for what's thought martyrdom, by mates.

26   The Heaths (VI)

      Since most times we'd adjust. Those nights I'd end
on some past-the-heel edge of the city:
or her quotation marks round 'catching up', 'friend'
(fugues that curled out and back to routine).
                              Self-pity?
Less happier men can't tell themselves
She's fucking this guy it doesn't matter much
because I say this someone else
is only lucky now ... (He was as clutched
to what us kids, for we were kids, believed;
and that was passing.) ... *with all their perks*
of love a highly probable grand finale
approaches. .
      So much for those ghosted entries heaved
into *Open Marriage: How It Works.*
I never over-dupe myself on books, Charley.

Part 7

GEOFF CATTERMOLE .... ANGLO-CATHOLIC PRIEST
BESS CATTERMOLE .... HIS WIFE
LEO PENGILLY .... FORMER COLLEAGUE OF GEOFF'S,
                                                    NOW PAINTING
M .... LEO'S GIRLFRIEND

NON IN SPATIA SED IN MUNERIBUS CAPITUS

for Anni Cleary

The Argument

Melbourne, the early eighties. Geoff Cattermole, an Anglo-Catholic Priest, and his wife Bess, an agnostic social worker, are invited to the thirty-fifth birthday party of Geoff's former colleague, Leo Pengilly. Having left the priesthood to become an artist, Leo now lives with his girlfriend M in the world of St Kilda's bohemian bonhomie. During the course of the evening many strange people arrive and a cross-section of mind-altering substances are taken.

&

Geoff has a wife now, in fact he'll have Bess always;
they've got two offspring, which he considers plenty
for a fulfilling family nowadays.
His wine is fortified, his toothpaste pepperminty.
Taoists his flock boasts, Maoists, greenies, gays
(whilst only one parishoner in twenty
could be remotely termed a redneck zombie).
Cords are Geoff's trousers and his van's a Kombi.

Their daughter's Stella (they baulked at Alana
when, hearing this name, his mother cried out 'Eeek'!).
Bess reads Christina Stead and Helen Garner.
They go for walks beside Merri Creek.
Geoff has friends from Cooktown to Kiwana,
and corresponds with them not twice a week
exactly: that might be overdoing it
(temper your pace or else you'll end up ruing it).

But imagine a kind of pride that's always branded
'trouble' (as if some deity with a knack
for mischievous malevolence had commanded

'Thou shalt forever row against the flak!').
Bess has that certain pride: which landed
her, luckily, where it did. Eight years back,
whilst young adults were pairing all the quicker,
she leapfrogged the lot and snared her vicar.

And, whilst the chains of conformity keep clinking,
Bess a true-born one-agin-the-many,
is oblivious to what her peers are thinking.
Peers? It seems unlikely she has any.
'Words may be cheap but worse their value's sinking,
opinions now get flogged at two-a-penny,'
thinks she whose hallmark's never to be had
by latest bargains from The House of Fad.

Life after this one? Bess seems hardly frightened:
she figured long ago at Sunday school
God might exist and then She mightn't.
Mere blind faith? This woman's no such fool.
It only serves to get her hackles heightened.
But how she loves to blurt her golden rule:
'See here you useless bunch of no-good jerks
my life's devotion's doing decent works!'

With four-square flair (like some symphony of Haydn's)
that's the Bess way to run a drop-in centre:
with few demands and almost no contrivance
(only the bigots and the ignorant resent her)
here's some examples of this woman's guidance:
strategies to neuter your tormentor/
suggestions to each abused and spaced-out waif
they try some subjects at their local TAFE.

    Her family's modern, has fluid gender roles
(none of the clout, a lot of the caress)
whilst (like a bottle washed up in the shoals)
their message to the world is nothing less:
'Thanks for calling, we're the Cattermoles:
Geoffrey, Stella, Alister and Bess.
So be you oldie, middle-aged or teen,
leave your voice upon our phone machine.'

But coming home to all such well-meant dirging
(parish pump enough through which to churn)
who wouldn't give their messages a purging?
Well, tonight, here's one call he'll return:
a voice, precise if mellow, which keeps urging
'Tune up your fiddles, we've a Rome to burn!
I see a blaze where now there's but a glimmer!'
   Leo Pengilly's inviting them to dinner.

   Lithe if languid, with a trim austere beard,
part animated icon and part satyr,
nothing in Leo you remotely feared.
Who didn't love his oratory and chatter?
Though evangelicals found him rather weird
(masses rarely equate with low church clatter)
for it must've galled when, to say the least,
an artist manque appeared as their parish priest.

   A number's left, he's omitted an address.
   'I bet you any pound, mark, franc or guilder'
(though Geoff's excitement wilts when it meets Bess)
'Leo's living somewhere in St Kilda . . .'
   Which could, to his wife, be the bottom of Loch Ness;
the thought as you might gauge, has hardly thrilled her.
But, though there's sighs at whatever he's proposing,
she'll tag along upon the night that's chosen.

She often does. A martyr's mission (hers)
includes church fetes, dutch auctions, crazy whists;
plus Geoffrey's centrefold parishioners
(chosen for these imaginary trysts:
a harmless diversion since such a petition errs
towards restraint; and who's been, even, kissed?).
Yet, to herself, Bess has often said,
lying in wait upon their marriage bed:

'Espoused saint I'll tell you *Where's the diff.*
as I lie, loins quivering, ungird,
Bess I hear *be with you in a jiff.*

Yet whilst my stew's waiting to get stirred
you play a well-strummed auto-erotic riff
courtesy, if that's indeed the word,
of Messrs Hefner and Cuccione.
(Some crave their playmates? I'd prefer their money!)'

    It's a bit extreme to gawk at a firm high bust
(rehearsing another round of gimme/lemme)
but it's overplayed to term this simply 'lust'
as some would wish it and demand; since many
a shapely leg and pretty face you'd trust
to be as much God's handiwork as any.
    With half his mind on Raquel, Bo and Farrah,
Geoff glides his Kombi Van across the Yarra.

    Now imagine (though this parallel hardly fits)
Punt Road a (not quite) occidental Ginza,
and, thinking they're Lauda, Mansell, from the pits
the Saturday traffic zooms southward into Windsor;
their radio's ablaze with Sixties Hits:
'Hey Jude', 'MacArthur Park', 'Needles and Pins-a'.
(Music to do your wheelies, drop your U-ees,
from the days of Marlboro Men and poor dead Louies).

    Green is the colour to give a driver balm;
and green it is when they speed through The Junction.
    But Bess keeps sighing. So, faced with wifely qualm,
Geoff turns paternal, without the least compunction.
Parking, he murmurs: 'Calm please calm.
We really should enjoy Pengilly's function.
A pleasing thoroughfare this Foster Street.
And here are tips to cause us no retreat:

'pretend you're a Chappell going into bat . . .
it won't be like the nude scene out of *Hair*.
Still if disaster's sensed well that is that . . .'
    But his face starts sparkling for, taking whatever air,
Leo saunters the driveway to his flat
admitting, through a pleased if vacant stare,
that he who's greeting Geoffrey like a brother
is influenced by some drug or another.

non in spatia sed in muneribus capitus

'Cattermole!'
             'Pengilly!
                     'Geoffrey!'
                              'Leo!
Meet Bess my wife.'
                 And there's a bow: 'Enchanted!
Tonight should prove *Furioso e con brio,*
and though till now the evening's merely cantered
we're sure, by dawn, to sweat ourselves some B.O.'
    Bantering on like hosts have always bantered
(and certain his bonhomie's witty, supple)
Leo's pleased to usher in the couple.

    'Joie de vivre requires no special pleadings:
it's total war and you are General Patton,
it's Wimbledon and you head the seedings,
so think of those hatches we're not required to batten.
And read these passwords for tonight's proceedings
above the door there, conjured up in Latin.
Study them well, may no phrase prove more apter
to grace a verse, a poem or a chapter!'

    [Which they do now. Okay you reader guys
(no-hopers, nannies, notaries and nerds,
the wonderful, the wicked and the wise)
to see who are the wheys and who the curds
I'll institute this quiz without a prize.
Let's hear from those who can translate these words.
So be you man, hermaphrodite or female
drop us a line or contact me by e-mail.]

    Geoffrey grins as he reads the motto
(its calligraphy quite exceeding par)
and whilst he's no antipodean Giotto
or any kind of brushwork superstar,
Leo's talent, like third division lotto,
is a small yet pleasing prize. Thus far,
however, few guests have hardly flipped
at this pithy phrase set in a gothic script.

But where is Leo's dinner? Well that's altered:
a party's ragin' and its swing is full.
The beer is Cooper's, the whisky's double malted
(there's a pile of grass they term 'the Isle of Mull')
With each new guest our host turns more exalted,
he won't permit a solitary lull.
Since, being one to no way underpin it, he
has enlisted nearly all this town's humanity.

But Mrs Cattermole's lips it seems are pursed.
Well, sweeping this guest into his bacchanalia
Leo terms her 'Good Queen Bess'. He wasn't the first.
So? One word tonight is banished and it's 'failure'.
Since this is Operation Fred Nile Do Your Worst
time: we've a world to gain; well okay Australia;
with zeal of a Loyola, patience of a Gandhi
underpinning our modus operandi.

As this his six-and-thirtieth year commences,
Leo feels like a bowler verging on a hat-trick:
'Now if you think my guests have lost their senses,
are with the fairies, holed up in some attic,
they're decent folk though, Capricorns to Cancers
and return. And here's our best: M, the enigmatic.'
His girlfriend who, wrapped in a sarong,
says 'Pleased to meet you, like to share a bong?'

Bess declines the joys of getting addled
and who can blame her? Geoffrey goes the plunge
(his brain goes backstroke before it's doggone paddled).
But here as elsewhere history takes its lunge:
tonight throughout the world a cusp is straddled:
the past is hippy and the future's grunge.
But how can we know that with Leo slaving
over a hot party? He continues raving:

'I met archangels once, whilst on some acid,
and, to their boss I hollered Howdy Gabes!
This creature grinned, his handshake wasn't flaccid:

since Jacob was Jakes and Abraham was Abes
he'd heard much worse and took it very placid:
"Out of the mouths of near-enough-to-babes!"
were strange words to, in greeting, give me,
or else they were a way of coping with me.'

And now from every footpath, laneway, road,
the muscle-bunnies have commenced their entry;
each hoping to be the subject of an ode,
a Billy Joe for someone's Bobbie Gentry,
their self-obsessions stalled on overload
(a pity Leo can't afford a sentry).
Yet if their torsos probably are glistening,
they sound banal and nobody is listening.

Though we feel (what biceps! pecs!) a trifle humbled,
embarrassed by our last attempt at gym:
all pain no gain, we merely strained and stumbled,
our strict regime proving only whim.
Vanity, vanity! How our ambitions tumbled!
    Then Leo, staring, sighs 'Regardez him!'
propelling his friend about to view a young man.
    This muscle-bound, tanned, decidedly well-hung man

(he sports suspenders, hair tinged with puce highlighter)
has equipment sheathed in low-slung leather jocks.
    'My!' exclaims Leo. 'They'll hardly get much tighter:
The things chaps do to shovel off their rocks!
Looks like, Geoff, we're in for an all-nighter,
so stay for breakfast: bagels, cream cheese, lox.'
    'But it's the sabbath, father, we'd be peppered
with that scorn reserved for a somewhat errant shepherd.

'Oh there's little limp in any of *these* wrists.
And, for the secular, they're sure red-blooded.
The things you see! That man's just kissed
a man!' And Geoff imagines being tut-tutted
to by an outer outer-suburban evangelist,
mealy-mouthing far worse than Elmer Fudd did.
Whatever Geoff once joined it ain't the wowsers
(though doubts if anyone will drop their trousers).

But the interrogations get the curlier:
'It may be me but Cattermole don't you think
this year's boys seem to be getting girlier?'
is followed up, you guessed it, by a wink.
   Had Geoff and Bess arrived a trifle earlier
they'd have caught the plonk and plunk and plink
of koto music. Now games of *Hello sailors!*
are sound-tracked by Bob Marley and his Wailers.

[But to accommodate this party's tones,
nuances, shadings, one sound stands supreme.
Bel canto? Be-bop? Robeson's mighty groans?
Well it isn't Lully and it isn't Cream.
Ladies and Gentleman . . . the Rolling Stones!
They've sung The Earth from Chile round to Cheam!
   So here's to Mick and to his partner, Keith
(whose prospects 'round this time were rather brief).

And to their rivals from some decades back:
John, Paul, George and Richard nicknamed Ringo.
Who caused upheavals equal to the sack
of ancient Rome, they certainly did by jingo!
But I must get *The Lovemakers* back on track,
for few, I fear, can understand this lingo;
nor rhymes which getting Wearnier and Wearnier
could give the English language quite a hernia.]

   So for respite from drug-crazed hippy lechers,
and, as if engaged on some research,
the Cattermoles are viewing Leo's sketches.
This gives the night a pleasing kind of lurch:
fuelled by a brace of generous you-betchas
(for unlike their holy, mother church,
parish priests have little in their coffers
and knowing this too well) Leo offers

'A portrait, Geoffrey, Bess, to be done gratis,
as of now it seems like a good idea.
I have a dream: it's to become an artist,

with cash and a reputation by next year
Which may not, I grant you, sound the smartest,
but wait till Public Taste gets into gear.'
    As a joint is passed from a lad with rippling sinews
Leo smiles, takes a drag, continues:

'Now here's an observation worth the weighing:
art's been a longtime consort to the cloth.'
(Take it from Leo, he knows what he's saying.)
'Fras This 'n' That and whatsisname Van Gogh,
knew how to get wowserdom a-braying;
just grab your phone and check with a fine arts prof
how the Uffizi, Hermitage and Prado
are crammed with many a priestly desperado.

Another joint? It hardly could get crazier
than putting on a pair of boxing togs
to go a round with Ali or with Frazier.
This place is heading to the best of dogs.
(Throw in the Kiwis then it's Australasia.)
So ratchet your inhibitions down some cogs.
As moral decline carves in a further notch
shelve the soul: this year's for the crotch!

Back in those days of the Twist, Watusi, Fug,
I figured sex much more than making babies:
a quite refreshing option to have dug
and not the form of intellectual scabies
which still takes coupling for a kind of bug
like influenza, cholera, or rabies.
And so to hell with what's or what's not fashion,
I only feel these bounds placed on my passion!

And I could write this as a twelve-bar blues
with singers to perform it, if I knew some.'
(Leo's confessions have shortened Bess's fuse,
though he's just absurd and not remotely gruesome.)
'I find,' he says, 'often that I muse
whenever I meet a cute, milksoppy twosome:
You mean your passion's hardly more than cerebral?
And no-one minds? Well I think that's terrible!'

A migraine's feigned, the two of them leave early.
But Bess will drive and deal with navigation.
Geoff's not in the doghouse, it isn't that she's surly
(he knows her well and discounts pre-menstruation)
or how his wife can't be remotely girly.
But it won't be just spousal imagination
recalling for years how the missus groaned:
'Father Cattermole, don't you know you're stoned?!'

A bit abashed, though this side of ashamed,
to make amends, to show Bess he's still her man,
let's play some records! And the music's named:
John Coltrane? Or why not Lazar Berman?
Then Cattermole wilts (he, so rightly famed
for booming forth a mighty powerful sermon):
'Forgive me please if this sounds like tripe
but, I suppose, Leo's not your type?'

'Geoff, good lord, my tolerance spans the prism!
Sexual preference, socio-economic;
from Gellibrand to Kooyong via Chisholm.'
Bess rebounding her force seems supersonic
to accommodate any fetish, ism:
Mensa members with the sub-moronic,
round and flat-earthers, dries or damps or wets,
plus devotees of funny cigarettes.

'There's only hypocrisy which I find so grubby!
And that's not just some malignant elf!'
      'Tolerance, tolerance. Aye there's the rub.' He
muses in soft measures his spiritual health
snake-oil cure-all. To anyone (bar a hubby
quoting the Bard essentially to himself)
her complaint seems obvious as a girder
but, Bess understands, he hasn't heard her.

'Goodwife, m' dear,' he gently lectures, smatter-
ing metaphors unworthy of a priest:
'the bread of living's going to stay as batter

unless our planet's artists give it yeast . . .
okay okay then, see it all one platter:
the fast a merest flipside to the feast.
Lent, therefore, will put us in recess.
But after Holy Week we'll have them over . . . Bess?'

 As in the tale of Toad Hall's Mr Toad
home they go the drivers and the drived:
up Brunswick Street towards St George's Road,
in North Fitzroy midnight has arrived.
Tomorrow: work for Geoff (a pleasant load:
he's not about to get his parish tithed).
Kick out the cat, let's pull down the awning.
God's in his/her heaven. The vicar's yawning.

 Bess loves him but since Alister was born
their passion's flickered. Well she'll have to wear it.
If centrefolds are erotica not porn,
and *Playboy's* bought for literary merit,
and some nights she will stay awake till dawn,
there's always her Henry James with which to bear it.
 How true how true *Amor vincit omnia*
has yet to be a charm against insomnia . . .

Part 8

SOPHIE	LAWYER
CROSS QC	HER FATHER
ADRIAN	HER BROTHER
CHRISTIAN	HER BOYFRIEND
DARYL	HER HUSBAND
KARL	HER LOVER
KARL'S FRIEND	DEALER
KEVIN	IN REMAND

Sophie

197–

    Towards the end of school
I asked a friend 'Wouldn't you love to bring your mother home
someone truly vile, someone you'd been with
half an hour before? And stand there,
glowing?'
        My friend said 'No' and
'What are you running on?'
    Should I have answered:
'No-one hits a girl quite like a mother hits her?'
or 'I mean, when you're sixteen and a mother hits you?'?
    Need we talk about it: a family in collapse,
our better schools, the house at Lorne, careers
and career changes, everyone in love with the guilt?
    Whatever they used to write novels about,
isn't there something more important around?

Ades

    When I was with Karl he wanted to know
all about my family, said he was
a family junkie.
        He'd heard of Dad, of Dad
and Adrian.
        When he's nineteen someone at
his club announces 'Ades, you're nothing but
a sports star.'
        Adrian is a dog
and this is his bowl.
    Does Karl know how Adrian
does crazy things with crazy women?
He will soon: halfway through our next party
my brother's off with some ridiculous nurse,
first to the Lorne house, then right along

the Great Ocean Road.
>   These are the times, this is what they are.

Trophy

>   When I'm eighteen and a waitress,
Christian often arrives at Pizza X.
Looking at me he's looked at in return.
(Though when I mention him it's all prefaced with
'Well, apart from the bodyshirt . . .')
>   Then he says 'When we're out together
don't bend over too much. Have to hold back
the hordes, won't I?'
>   Am I to think he means it?
Christian means a lot of things.
He does karate proud and as for Zen
reckons he understands it.
>   He loves the way my ringlets have been done
and thinks he 'gets' me.
>   Aren't I Sophie the trophy?
>   He'll have to do.

Black belt

>   That January I walk out on mother
and go to Christian's unit.
>   I study law.
>   Thursdays and Fridays, though, he drops me off
at Pizza X.
>   He's eight years older.
He doesn't drink and one night
I am drunk enough to tell him
'Loosen that black belt, Christian!'
>   So I am hit.
>   He's sorry
but at times he'll hit again,

thinking in his arrogance I can be trusted,
trusted enough to stay.
                    Girlfriend and cash,
he'll leave both lying around;
deserving one another they leave together.

Boyfriend

   If Christian ever finds me
Daryl won't save me from Christian.
Yet I have Daryl now. He has a pretty cowlick.
His father wants him as a solicitor.
He'll try, although he'd rather be a chef,
at least. All the time he laughs.

A regular

   We try living in the hills,
and then attempt communal houses
closer to town.
                    In one place a regular
is Karl: eight years older than us
with his deep, black beard.
   He says things like
'Too yuppie to be hippy, too hippy to be yuppie ...
meet the Podes!'
                    I am not a Pode,
my husband is: Daryl Pode, chemist's son from
Templestowe, Ivanhoe Grammar old boy.
   But our household meets the Podes:
who have suspended law to try out for
'Gourmet Grub to Go', their catering game.
   When Karl calls Daryl 'Commander Quiche',
I like it though I shouldn't.
I'm laughing but I can't stand Karl.
And I am not a Pode.

Lawyers

    I had summer classes but Daryl was ecstatic:
he, the household and some mates were following
Eddie and The Niddries' 'Eating the Hand that Feeds You'
national tour.
              'Good,' I was encouraging, 'good . . .'
being on Pode overload: Daryl's cowlick,
Daryl's giggle, Daryl whom Sophie married
to make sure she was well away from Christian.
    Karl didn't go. He'd phone though.
    'For starters, Karl,' since I had to trump him,
'even quiche takes a vacation.'
    Then I'm asked to 'Name your subjects, Soph.'
Since he's a lawyer, too, and wants to help.

The course

    I had been living for my summer course
(what I expected would happen)
but Karl, who loved announcing
'Meet the Podes, quiche-masters to the universe!'
Karl would soon be telling the obvious:
'Right now it's you and me, Soph.'
He was thirty, single, set on proving his way
as one of the very few ways.
              It wasn't love
and there was too much of it.
I'd never liked him and here he was
getting me obsessed (if through my summer course).
    'All this,' Karl confessed
by the second week, 'brings out the bitch in you
and the bastard in me.'
              'Thanks,' I had to say.

Dealer

    There'd been an even simpler of proposals:
a friend of Karl's had hashblocks, cheap.
He brought the dealer round.
                      And the man's talk
was rice trail talk: Asia, drugs and women.
I bought the stuff and got him out.
    'So where'd you get your hideous friend?'
I asked to no reply except . . .
    'Brings out Soph the schoolmarm does he?'
    'You're the one attempting show-and-tell,'
Karl was told.
            Which didn't faze him.
'Sophie, anyone can grow, sell to mates, share
around, but at his level nice guys needn't exactly
deal.'
        How did he know? Karl didn't.
I was hearing guesswork. Oh yeah?
'Well he's no more my friend than my accountant is.
You and everyone are so naive.'
                    'But, I mean,
The Rice Trail, Karl?'
                Then he turned hard:
'Does it alter the stone? If he had the slightest,
further notch of class, if he'd yabbered one word less,
if he wasn't some cabbie with this loud
Hawaiian shirt, you wouldn't have
that hash. In her head there's still the thrill,
that special Sophie thrill of slumming things.
So get that LLB of yours, and then defend him!'
    Here's what happened every second evening:
Karl turned up, we argued, then got stoned
and fucked.
        Why did I need so much of it?
Any of it?

The case

    It may mean little now,
but remember the Kent case? I was five or six
when Dad became a national identity,
defending a copkiller right to the gallows.
    When I was seven or eight
he'd left the Bar and gone to the Corporation.
    When I was eighteen we both had left
my mother; four years later Daryl was my husband
(everybody tolerated Daryl Pode) but Karl,
Karl Gold was my lover.
    And other than rolling with Daryl into the gutter
the only worthwhile thing Karl seemed to do
for me was this: after I'd named
where my father worked and said I was sorry
'Need you apologise!?' Karl exploded.
'Since after what was done to him
(and you mustn't defend your Kents the way he did)
he had to work some place.'
    Soon Karl was even more enchanted
with the idea of Cross QC, telling me
'It was an election year,' as if that part of the legend
wasn't known, 'hanging helped to keep
certain pricks in power. Your old man couldn't stand
their pace? Neither would I.'
                     Had Karl read the case?
That Kent was a killer, total.
                     Karl shrugged.
                            'Would you,'
I asked, 'give up all that you believed ... for a killer?'
    The trick, he told me, was not to believe in
very much at all, which is what an activist,
his kind of activist, did.
    Sure I'd have taken him to Dad except
Dad rarely was in Melbourne now,
and Karl was not my husband.

Wife-man

    When I inform him
'You never listen much to women, do you?'
Karl tells me he hasn't done much else.
When all of them are married, how couldn't he,
being a wife-man: 'If you're a wife then
I'm your man.'
                We are in bed.
He rolls me onto my stomach.
And I'm saying what I have to say:
'Just a little gentler, Karl. Make it better
than last time. Love us a bit.'

Wife-man (continued)

    Then Karl starts crying, actually crying,
knowing he is making it a mystery and how,
for me, all mysteries are made for solving;
so he tells me about the last wife
(how the husband was like Daryl, not a friend, really)
and how it never worked the way
it's working now.

Great-and-ratshit

    It was the summer
everyone discovered some deadshit 'using'.
At a friend's place I saw a letter lying about.
The letter started 'I'm using again.'
    But my time wasn't deadshit time.
I would have two months of summer course
overlaid with half as much again of Karl.
    When they returned, Daryl and the household,
we held our biggest party:
where Karl kept calling him 'Dazza'.

  Adrian arrived, took up with
a toke or ten, and ran off with the nurse.
When he was gone a week his club,
keeping it out of the press, nearly sacked him.
  That year the media would re-name him
'Mr Magic': meaning great-and-ratshit-together,
since they were the words he used about the nurse,
needing to feel good about himself.
        Like I do.
With Daryl home I am hating Karl.
Yet when he arrives I still follow him:
all over our big house.
      My husband's taunted.
My husband doesn't know he's being taunted.
Karl asks 'Hey, Commander, still slavin' over
the hot quiche?'
     Daryl asks me
'What's wrong Soph?'
       I can't stand that wimpery
passing for a spouse, and confess.

Gutter

  Words are going to help, words like
It only happened twice, I was lonely,
Karl was helping me, he's hardly our friend,
it couldn't happen again.
      Words until
one autumn afternoon in our front yard
he starts outstaring Karl.
       But it's only when
Karl advises 'Ah! Ah! Hold firm Commander Quiche!
Hold firm!' my husband jumps him.
From our path out they wrestle
into the road, then back to the gutter,
where Karl bites Daryl.

Grandma

    Daryl, delighting in his ignorance,
embarrasses me.
               When a household member
puts on some Bessie Smith
my husband hasn't got the brains or taste
to wait and find out who she was.
For him a name's enough.
    'Who's that?' he giggles, 'Patti Smith's grandma?'
He's the grandma!
               The household's
sighing hard.
          Leave him!

Deal

    'Go on,' Karl had dared,
'find out what it's like: get yourself a dealer
and defend him.'
             And in a year
I may've had a degree in law, but this career
in a damn lot less. Defence? No
I just worked for someone defending the best.
    And when I went out to remand
no use in asking *Okay, just don't tell me
about it, right? This* one was going to anyway,
right?
      'I flogged the Grange Hermitage of grass,
once. Dealer? Now I merely work for one.'
He'll also tell:
'Them narcs hunting their movers 'n' shakers:
all they get's us shufflers 'n' wobblers.'
    He's the big boy of some small-town
carpet salesman for whom
'The present seems fairly dumb . . .' but yeah
you should've seen his dumber past.
    And then he adds:

'Except, maybe most cops/all cops, someone
has to do it, Sophie. And that's my motto:
the dealers deal, the judges judge, that guy who draws
the funnies keeps drawing them; even your old man
must do whatever he does . . .'
    And now he'll say:
'Not me now but not horse.'

The bench

    He was dreadful. (Can't anybody see how dreadful?)
So this is what happened: sent out to Pentridge
I'm to meet him, right? Kevin, sullen yet cocky,
innocent till proven, and he may have his past
but Kevin needs a chance and wants to prove
that chance; the interview room is chilly yet
his jacket comes off; he's laying it on the bench.

Book Two

Money and Nothing

Part 9

Gibbo .... radio personality
Mr A aka The Alien .... aka The Baron aka
                                    The Kid: taxidriver

Leo ⎫
M   ⎬ .... his friends
Jack ⎭

Kevin Joy ⎫
Kim Lacy
Cap'n Midnight
The Jeweller
Jungle Jim
The Human   ⎬ .... of the Joy Boys
Harper   Drug Syndicate
Jasmine
Mick
Pattty
Lisa ⎭

Bernie Millar .... deadshit
A New Zealand shearer
Porn .... bargirl
Chrissie .... teacher's aide; Kim's girl
Sophie .... lawyer; Kevin's girl
Morgan QC .... barrister
Craig Stubbs .... businessman
Johnee Kwok .... hit man
Basil .... Kevin's brother

Radio Chook Raffle (II)

Unless a new princess arrives by nine
Gibbo's returning to the frog he's always
told he is so anyone please say yes
tonight Gibbo you could be lucky
enough to stay until even
the day after *Good-morning good-*
morning good-morning time we light up
our smokes-in-the-shower cause
it's Radio Chook Raffle *Stanko 'ere moite*
'day mate Stanko eh? don't tell me you're
B'beep b'beep a homo sssssapien? *Good-*
morning good-morning good-morning good-
morning good-morningahhhh I beg your
pardon why would I promise you a
rose or any other form of
garden? got our weather DeeDee Co-host?
Twenty-five the bureau says but hotting up
and Gibbo you know me no pork pies
unlike my mate and extra special guest
the King of the West Craigo Stubbs
deals-a-plenty Stubbsy?
Bigger 'n' better Gibbo
like surprises Craigo?
Name a man who doesn't matey
Well catch DeeDee in her Chook Raffle
T-shirt turn on the hose and boy
does she have whoppers 'cause
anytime *B'beep b'beep* is nipple time?
did he say chocolate ripple time?
yes he said that yes he said that
Good-morningahhhh

On the Rice Trail: Mr A Cruises North

Why have such scores of lovely, gifted girls
    Married impossible men?
                    Robert Graves, 'A Slice of Wedding Cake'

I've seen the devil of violence, and the devil of greed, and the devil of hot desire; but, by all the stars! these were strong, lusty, red-eyed devils, that swayed and drove men — men, I tell you. But as I stood on this hillside, I foresaw that in the blinding sunshine of that land I would become acquainted with a flabby, pretending, weak-eyed devil of a rapacious and pitiless folly.
                    Joseph Conrad, *Heart of Darkness*

Yessum good morningahhhh! Gibbo you silly prick.
Here he was back at his old mum's,
that fibro cottage in Ashwood where,
after all night in a cab, you just went into your room,
caught a touch more Gibbo, stoked a chillum or five,
spun out, read up on facts and,
until late afternoon, crashed out. Then, maybe,
made yourself around to M and Leo's.

    Why were all these men cruising with
good women?
            Where had he first met M? Brisbane?
If that was the town what had he, she and anyone
at all been doing there? Mullmixing? Chillumstoking?
    'Cruising?' M had once suggested,
calling it straight-as-that! Like M always did.
How he loved that lady, any lady who could announce
Shut up, pack the bong, light 'n' pass it!

If only he could have truly cruised with M;
if only he could have cruised with that good woman
Terri, Terri the hooker, who wanted to cruise,
sure, but not with him.
  How that girl loved hearing about Goa
'n' Lanka 'n' Chiang Mai! But, once she quit
the game and got off speed, he only saw her cruising on
to a big house in Patterson Lakes,
or rather some dull prick who owned it.
  Besides, how's a working girl heading twenty-five
and jangling off her tit quit speed?
        And speed
was a man, a very bad man. Terri would
no more quit *Him* than M would quit Leo:
her very fine man who had to be respected;
her very fine man who had to be protected:
for although Leo knew a bit, thought at times
and enjoyed just about the lot, Leo never believed
what you were telling him. Leo wasn't meant to.
        Oh well,
just bring 'em over blocks of the darkest hash
and let what really happens, the facts,
stay hidden with him.
    Jack was as close as they'd get
to the facts and Leo had made it pretty plain:
Jack wasn't to be seen again.

  There's that moment you walk in somewhere and it's you
telling you *I know it! I know this place!*
Well at 4/9 he did: this was the pro's flat:
the pro's where, that summer, hardly out of short pants,
late of the stormwater drains, he'd been The Kid,
their mascot: yeah, them: Desley, she was always great,
and Iris, the other one.
    'Hey Jack,' he told him,
when Jack was back working in Melbourne again,
'I've these friends, never guess where they're living:
where I met you …'

                    (Where he'd met
that deadshit Bernie Millar, and learnt what to do
whenever you copped the over-matey hard word.)
          He never thought *I've just the friends for you!*
but with anyone welcome at 4/9
why shouldn't his very latest meet his oldest?
          Why? 'Sorry,' Leo told him soon enough,
'but that Jack's just another seedy opportunist.
You brought him once and once passed.
But twice is much too often.'
                              That phial of amyl
proved okay, and even talking a bit too much
to M, but listening to Jack elaborate
'I can get you, and I mean this, anything:
think of it and think on it: anything ...'
you knew you could never explain to Leo
*There's those who'll defer to Jack and won't
to anyone else. But he heads nothing,
and he runs nothing: like you he knows people
and people meet.*

&

          Taking a night off driving
just to be with friends at 4/9
(Benny might be down from Sydney,
or Karl the lawyer, almost a dozen more)
there he'd be: grilling 'em and drilling 'em
('Well!' sighed Leo, 'if this is paranoia,
it's good-natured paranoia!'):
who was stuffing his economy and why;
who (and even more why) was stuffing our economy;
how two times, two times (coming home from
Chiang Mai first then Lanka) two times
he'd cruised his hash right past the armies
of The Man: there may be a third
but never the unlucky fourth!
                    Leo of course
could put a stop to even *that!*:

'Be a good lad and please help Lady M
to grind some mull.'

&

    Crashing at Mum's,
crashing at Leo's, cruising Melbourne, cruising
the rice trail, pick-ups, deliveries, and listening
to passengers, working it out, it-all-out:
sometimes he just wanted to say
Leo, M, anyone who'll possibly attend:
you don't know, you are never to know,
but outside here there's so much evil now.
I need this place, this 4/9,
for just like those old times it's even better
than Mum's.
    Y' see, this is what The Man has
and I have not: only that gift to say
'You 'n' you empty your pockets!'
'You 'n' you bend over fast!'
'You 'n' you right in the slammer!'
   But what a gift!

&

    People met all right.
Last night, after not so many months, Cap'n Midnight
climbed into the cab: yeah The Cap'n:
if all Port Phillip Bay were smack
hey, wouldn't he be one old sea-dog!
And if the very least you could do with
all the Cap'n Midnights was to loathe 'em,
there had to be an admiration for that nerve
announcing *Now now now's the time: fantasy*
stops being fantasy! (Or the utter truth behind
The Jeweller laughing to his mates *If we last that long . . .*
which had to mean *If we live tonight ho ho . . .*
Now *he* was one who knew the truest winners
had to be those who, when finally shot out of this world,
would still remain: a full dead grin, gleaming back

So, you think you've won, eh? Scarier than living.)
  Well last evening, driving Cap'n Midnight,
The Cap'n got around to figure then to finger him.
'Taxes?' he spruiked. 'Don't say you're paying taxes?
Hey, Mr A! The Man? Getting too greedy is he?
Then try *our* bank.' (He named his bank.) 'The ultimate
non-bank.' Everyone used non-banks now. Why?
Since today everything is almost legal,
non-banks made 'em even legaler.
'Don't you get it Mr A?' Then, since his trip
was turning the Cap'n Midnight Riddle Hour
'When is a bank not quite a bank
but even better? When it's a non-bank!'
  Yes, everybody non-banked now:
a broad platter of professions and institutions:
Americans of course and even The Man himself . . .
  Taking so much of Cap'n Midnight,
unsolicited financial adviser, hectoring from behind
(as if he was being truly chauffeured) you had to
turn on your radio.
    Gibbo was on your radio:
Gibbo was never off it now.
     'You ever hear,'
Cap'n Midnight asked 'anyone like him, like Gibbo?
No-one in Aussie is better than ol' Gibbo eh?'
(That clown must've been on something eh . . .
even over the air couldn't you almost hear him
sweatin' it?) 'Bet you Gibbo banks
the non-bank way, hey, hey, Mr A?'
  Yessum, last night it was unproductive
to sneer back *What's this 'Mr A', Cap'n Midnight?*
Instead he just suffered it, demanding:
'These non-bankers, who are these non-bankers?'
  War heroes turned Christians turned businessmen.
'. . . imagine a Guns-for-Jesus acumen
that makes *You* rich and face it, Mr A,
your kinda dealing wasn't designed for riches.
How many runs you done?' The Cap'n asked.
  'None for anyone, two for myself: hash blocks,
smokin' material.'

'Well face this too:
you're hardly even a cog in *our* machine ...'
                                    But Mr A
didn't mind *Hardly even that*. Yessum, it suited him.
Whose side was he on? His own.
For no-one else was. No-one else could ever be.
And if one day he might be the man for
the man for the man for the job, he could play at that.
    'Debts 'n' taxes? Debts 'n' taxes!' Cap'n Midnight
was onto a refrain which had to end 'Mr A,
we can take over all your debts and taxes.
You see,' he grooved into an explanation,
'there's our merchandise and there's our paperwork.
Well,' he proposed, 'the latter, if you want,
is Mr A's. Treat yourself by taking it north
to Lacy. Kim runs the classiest of acts,
he will reward you. Kimbo ...' Cap'n Midnight paused.
'Kim Lacy? Lacy commences things,
then gives it all, all of us, a cover.'
    Aussie total should've known the rumours:
like how when Kim Lacy and Kevin Joy were
just beginning, some idiot amateurs thought they'd raid
these new boys. Then, seeing how much there truly was,
they swallowed sharp, apologised and left.
    Lacy, you gathered, had been a someone once.
('Yeah,' Kim would sigh, 'a someone else:
The Shire Free Press Young Businessman of the Year!')
He certainly was a someone now:
exporter, importer, wholesaler, retailer, not quite
the Emperor of Patpong Road (yet). What are you,
Lacy?
    All of the above then add some more;
never a client but.

                    ও

            He'll be tall this Lacy:
Dennis Lillee mo and tinted glasses,
who puts out he owns (part owns) a bar,
adding he's '... into gemstones ...' (since someone

has to fit this self-effacing combination).
Though on the phone he presumes and leads with
'Mr A?'
  This requires a pause: 'What's with this
Mr A?'
  And Lacy, believing his charm
is built on every word that can be mastered
is bounding back, explaining: 'The Cap'n told me how how
you're okay his very words were *Mate mate
he's Mr A-one the best* and so you're Mr A and hi hi!'
  You shouldn't mind the fawning
and you don't, but Lacy sounds preposterous.
Still, he's why you're in town, can tell you anything:
'Mr A come over, we'll treat you like the king
you are.'
  'Soon, maybe, but all I need right now's
a shave, a shower and a chillum to stoke.
Yessum and a nap maybe.'
  Then meet Kim tonight
'. . . at my place Crazy Horse!'

  A tuktuk's hailed.
There's some Kiwi shearer sharing it,
and all he talks about is *Yellow cunt.*
I bin waitin' months f' this.
  As someone could be
disgusted (and that's their business) so someone else
will be bemused, another blasé;
if they don't understand they should:
how the worst is constantly available: its limits
are never to be reached.
  The shearer knows
Crazy Horse, cobber, and The Horse is prime!
That and The Fucfuc.'
  Then,
after disposing of all the passports, US dollars,
traveller's cheques, it's time we got acquainted
with mine host: him and everyone.

Something, you guess, happened to Lacy, once,
something amazing/maybe remarkable/probably respectable/
certainly desperate. With all his
Who doesn't want to be liked?
Lacy has that kind of charm you know
turns sour. Weak? No just banal;
and we're in for an hour of trying a touch
too hard, of being told who's just right
for Mr A.
   'This here's Porn ...'
         'Here's what?'
 'Here's Porn ...' who also has a brother up the road ...
 But Mr A's not so taken with brothers, brother,
well not tonight, nor ladies neither;
though that time will arrive.
       Till then
Porn listens, he pays her to, knowing
unless she turns wildcat, she always will.
One day soon of course she'll ask
'You take me to Aussie Mr A?' and
'My brother also?' and 'What do Aussie have?'
 Aussie have the lot!
       That night though
she just takes him some place to smoke,
to smoke for starters, and getting excited he explodes
but *Never mind that!* sweetly.
      Returning, Lacy joins them:
and here's the news: Jack is going Asian:
'... heading north to manage the drinks part
of my bar.' Then Lacy asks him
'You know Bernie Millar then?'
       He does.
 Well Bernie's over at The Fucfuc. The whatwhat?
 'My other place. Need an introduction?'
 By now it seems obligatory to answer
in something like a code
(even if it's merely for yourself):
'Bern's been like an uncle to me. For decades.'
        A re-
introduction?

'Don't bother, I'm not into uncles.'
'Mr A, you come back?' asks Porn.
Yes he'll come back, though this is what
he'd rather hear: *'Go on, tell us, in one word . . . why?'*
So he could admit *'Porn I'm in all this for just
one word, pleasure!'*
        It's heading four, he hasn't truly slept
in thirty-six hours.
      Your friend, they say,
is leaving.
   'My *friend*?'
        It's the Kiwi:
he's blown-out stoned-total and suggesting
'next time we share a tuktuk to The Fucfuc.
hey cob, hey?'
   Yeah!

                ත

   Next afternoon Lacy starts proposing things:
seeing you he tries a little bow,
pretends he's flustered, starts speaking fast.
'Mr A we we could use you more eh Mr A?
Then you could use the bank. And now there's Porn.
Like her don't we? Y' see,
we've this silly fat kid, little more than
a schoolgirl really, who's flying back for us.
If things stuff up we have to mind her.
We have to mind her anyway.'
   It's within a fortnight. Think on it.
   And within these weeks he thinks all right:
of Porn. You couldn't do much else:
for this isn't a case of 'liking' now, they're cruising!
They wake to it, see out the day and need we
mention the nights: sometimes he just has to
roll her over, other times Porn plants herself on top
and won't get off.
        The shearer's still abroad.
Don't tell the cobbers back in En Zed
but over at The Fucfuc he's discovered

(rediscovered?) fellas. But that'll pass.
This is dream country.
      And you are stoned.
Seems now you're always stoned.
You're writing letters and you love *that*.
   Dear Leo/M
   and all at 4/9 . . .
      there's us and there's them;
there's me and there's The Man.
Guess what but, if any life ever had a plan
this shmuck's got his. Her name? No I won't reveal
her name.
   I've got this job though: it'll be a steal
what I'm to do . . . just hop on a plane, fly,
land and wave this little fat chick byebyes.
   Did you know that The Man is cranking
up his wheels for me? Tell you where I'm banking
one day.
   Am I taking care?
Up to a point who isn't, yeah,
but beyond that, nup . . .

      ❧

     He ripped it up.

      ❧

  Kevin Joy and his Joy Boys:
Lacy, Cap'n Midnight, The Jeweller,
with all their legends, loonies, bitplayers, backup staff,
were, really, just the world;
with those like Jack, like him: shitkickers anon,
the support who just got paid by those who came into
very very recent mounds of cash. *You there*
in that Hawaiian shirt, even though it's mid-July,
y' see this parcel? Take it to Brighton/ to Coburg/
to Werribee/ take it to where it belongs!
      Delivering,
even driving, for these people, you just walked through

a mirror, turned around, looked back at The Man
and waved.
           Kevin Joy had done that all the time,
and Kevin Joy was no loonie, yet.
No, he was still a legend.
                  That last occasion
he was declared not guilty (and for an hour
just had to be alone) guess the cab he caught,
guess who drove the great man round.
                              Yessum,
drove but hardly met him. Sorry,
I've done nothing, know no-one and just
drive taxis: sometimes I hand over packages
and get to know . . . everyone!
                        (Knock knock.

  Who's there?
           Don't ask who ask what.
                          Well what?
  Y' pile o' rock.)
              And you might hope to avoid them
but they were business and knowing yourself as that much better
you felt great.
          Once,
when he'd to drive a load of all that scum
over to The Jeweller's *Since I'm the fuckin' rich man*
sang Cap'n Midnight, fanatic for The Niddries' Greatest Hits
That scene is gonna change today!
          Yeah, Cap'n Midnight, richman who already had:
wasn't that almost the time he threw half a carrybagfull
onto a bed in Elwood, stared at Jas 'n' Mick
right into their irises and announced:
'No-one sucks quite like junkies, so suck,
suck hard and move it!'
                   But, by then,
all the Joy Boys had made enough to cause
(even better afford) such gestures, such rumours, such legends.

And very soon, alias whoever-he-was,
not merely workin', but flyin', spyin' and who knows
dyin' for these rich men
Mr A would be up in *Business* yep
in *Business*! earning his smoothest ever ten g:
hardly a twelve-gauge Winchester but riding shotgun
on Patty the overweight dropout.
  And, with a few choice blocks hidden
on himself, once he'd made it past The Man
this time, that was it: no more runs.

       ❧

  'But yessum, everything is shrinking', he told no-one,
'everything is shrinking: even friendship,
particularly friendship, and all this sure ain't
friendship.'
     Everything *was* shrinking; except love though,
for the world had to be advised on that one:
'Yeah, that one, love: for I have found somebody,
somebody I can cruise with. This lady's looking after me
like she'll not look after any Kiwi shearer.'
  No Kiwi shearer, no Bernie Millar,
no men anywhere on the planet
would ever give this girl the kind of firm
sweet lovin' Mr A knows his Porn deserves!
  Oh Mr A! Who is kidding Mr A!
Soon you'll be heading home,
on Patty's first run, as chaperone.
And that's long past taking The Cap'n on one of his
midnight rambles, now isn't it?
If your Porn and all her love is good enough
she'll wait, she'll have to. Take your hash blocks
right away, this final time, and run.
All else is poison!
    Yes he knew
Kim Lacy/Cap'n Midnight/Kevin joy
your mob is far too big for me.
Join you one day, I'll be joining death the next.
(Or I could make an even swifter dash

to the scaffold, and tell the cops.)
Wanna shotgun Kimbo Lacy? he didn't ask
anyone but himself *Well try the shearer,*
try that dumb shearer; then have him sweat out
a few choice small runs to make him think
Oh wow I did that?! *Next*
let him try the merchandise (he will have
anyway, that's what goes into legends)
and then, rounding off the pattern, the lady.
Very soon that Kiwi's gonna need the lady.
      For, over a decade now, all along the rice trail,
you'd hear this chant developing
One woman, mate, just gotta meet one good woman.
Then I clean up my act.
      In these desperate nowadays even Kim Lacy
mouthed something like it (though how cleaner
could that act become: wasn't his the purest?).
Just one woman, one good woman, man.
Then we streamline, we rationalise and we expand!

      Well soon Lacy would have to: for The Man
had deigned to meet The Yellow Man
(only the best now bought The Yellow Man);
and together with The Richman all three,
nothing was surer '. . . are gonna come down
on us, the hash block small-timer shmucks,
hard! Hard! Hard! Get out!'
he ordered himself, 'Mr A get out!'

Nothing But Thunder

for Steve Anker

Could great men thunder
As Jove himself does, Jove would never be quiet.
For every pelting petty officer
Would use his heaven for thunder,
Nothing but thunder. Merciful Heaven
Thou rather, with thy sharp and sulphurous bolt,
Splits the unwedgeable and gnarled oak
Than the soft myrtle. But man, proud man,
Dress'd in a little brief authority,
Most ignorant of what he's most assured,
His glassy essence, like an angry ape,
Plays such fantastic tricks before high heaven
As make the angels weep; who with our spleens
Would all themselves laugh mortal.

WILLIAM SHAKESPEARE, *Measure for Measure*

But the best

of all is heroin. One day.
One day you'll own a big house.

JOHN FORBES, 'Drugs'

    But you've always had that touch of the flirt, eh Chrissie?
Bet you have.
    Bet there never was a time you
weren't one. So. That's settled. Why kiss me? Why try?
Just to prove things? We're quite at ease right here:
you've got Kim, I'll have Soph and we can defer
any of your adolescent thrills.
    Yeah? Me, I'm happy wondering
what exactly were those pills before the last lot

since tonight, tonight, it all seems clearer than it ever was.
Notice how I'm saying words I've heard and known
but hardly ever used? You might. Till then let's make that
lesson one on me: it's as if the pills supply a fuse
set on burning back. And strange how soon, you take
an afternoon for some, people find vacation friends,
and, being Kim's girl now, well, makes you one of us.
Besides, I said these pills keep fusing back: like to a bomb
marked *confession* lying under my mind, say in some cartoon,
set to explode. And all tonight's that clear.
                                            Y' know,
wasn't the sunset gross? Almost chemical?
I glowed naked, sweat teeming away in the dusk.
After a shower I dressed and, standing on my balcony
glanced at the floodlit pool, saw nothing.
                                        Dreams stopped.
'Boss!' One of the wogs looked up waving. 'Hey!
Mister Kevin Joy!' Or whatever name I'd given the resort.
He pointed out this bar, just stood there, grinning,
waiting his reward: a squat pharmaceutical tube
with a tip inside. 'Mister Kev! You still number one!'
and the night heard 'Thankyou. Thankyou. Thankyou,' till,
as it ended, I turned inside, gulped another
and descended.
              Anxious? Sure I chewed a nail yet, really,
feeling fine. Kimbo was smiling, he'd you at the bar,
like, look at this one here, Kev. We laughed you laughed
all was A-one. The wog band posed c 'n' w,
their lightweight serenades turning even lighter, and his luck
was, well, working as ever. Up north deals got dealt
and he'd met this bonus: a friendly Aussie girl.
I saw you rub his legs. Sex or just affection:
who'd even guess? Kimbo logs up lots of ladies
so maybe discrimination's been at times erratic?
Some chicks don't know when it's quits? But
I see he likes you heaps and, if not for keeps,
trust Uncle Kev: It's a help this end of the gemstone trade.
      Oh, and hadn't you bounced over Asia for weeks,
pricks like pogo-sticks, and mmmm? How'd you
phrase it? *Only thirty once Kev* . . .

Oh divorced . . . a teacher's aide . . . The tropics,
liquor, dope, cocks, even fannies, how potent Chrissie, and
if you've spent time with other guys, haven't these days
with Kim turned real trumps? If his hair recedes,
the teeth cave in, he slumps, so what? What's required
he gives, what's lent gets returned. You'd months ticking
barbarian after dull barbarian off the list since
your divorce, and now we see that heady spacey calm
just being with him entails.
       I did. What was it
without him? Peddling leaf in foil to kids.
  Woman I lived with dabbled but, and that's important.
Turned to use, that's important too, any extra-
cash just pumped away. Droughts were even worse:
stoned-out on tequila for Chrissake, and
you could ask why bother with this useless bitch,
who just shot up to make some Jew-boy richer?
You could ask that, I did, so we visited her dealer
me 'n' a mate and, soon, I met Kim.
        How'd I meet Soph?
You simply trust that jokers you've never known
can get you bailed, how if others fail the Morgans
can succeed. There's no choice, the fucker has to.
Funny sort of trust. I don't know anyone
and my cash just floats away. I'm Santa Claus!
Trust him? Yes.
     This was no case where the judge snores,
even doodles in the dust, the jury plays gropies.
This could only be my stripes, diploma, my three-gong award.
Jeez you looked a goner Kev. Sorry wrong guy.
And a whole damned planet set to split apart.
  'You seem,' his voice flowed out sleek, par
for the job, 'a loner Kevin? I'm not mistaken?'
  Correct. He knew I couldn't beat him, had to join him.
  Want to meet him? I can give one
unforgettable reference. Dirt? There'll be no dirt.
When Chrissie's sober we've a nice girl. She
only wants to flirt, only wants to suffer nights
like this and men like me for cash and Kim
and what would she love more?

                              Morgan loved
his tones, just relished teasing me to tough it:
he knew who suffered: 'Won't defend dealers,
Mister Joy. Addicts, sure. Understand?' We'd read
the papers. We knew. Knew how any shit-heap of ideals
tapers away the more you're offered. Four yachts now
float with his name.
                    As Kim floats with yours.
No use pining for some half-stoned teacher
you've divorced, or bothering with the ocker-hordes
of Asia. You needed someone, enter Kim and all
the smorgasbord reduced itself to this:
to make it now! or just break off before it
even starts. Which won't work. What beats the might
of what you want? And nothing feels better than
a night of *Gimme gimme take it take it* right
past a tropical dawn.
                      But think of a chilled, wet
annexe in remand. The least it needed was manners:
I took my jacket off, laid it on a bench.
                                           Who's this?
she blinked. But you give what you can
in such a place. 'Thanks . . . I'm Sophie Cross.
I'm with your solicitors . . .' Piling on the fidgets,
apprehensive, perhaps scared, and I know she caught
the damp stench they tried to excuse as plumbing.
Supposed to be October. I shrugged as this
slow, cracked heater tried numbing the room.
Had to talk, clear the muggy tension.
What's the tale, Kevin? Why you here?
      '. . . I've liked people, that's not clever. This time?
Trusting the wrong bastards. Remember,'
she got informed, 'I'm needing help. That's
what you give Miss Cross, why I hire you lot.
Lectures are for the cops and then I don't listen.
You listen. I've sold grass before who hasn't,
it's not me now but. Not horse. Smoked dope?'
She had and sweat grew a damp fuzz over
her top lip. 'Well this is different Sophie. Not in it.
Never.'

           Were we playing? She thought I was.
I thought she thought I was. She thought I thought
she thought I was and yet, name any more
appropriate game, or better one, for a first time.
Guess we were scared, Soph with her class
and me my class-of-a-kind; (class enough to risk
and make her mine when later I'd be hers.
We hadn't even touched.) With narcs mad for my scalp,
remember we're just smaller stuff, I needed anyone,
just like some dag botting smokes outside a third-
rate youth club dance. Why sacrifice a swell
organisation poised to roll, for just a few
questionable grams, two junkies drying out,
and fate? Next time I gave my hand, we shook,
not scared now, nervous but, and fifteen years in the can
apart, my case seemed almost passé. But then
our routine was stopping all the *I employ you work*
it never had. Her hands were moist. Each day
till she arrived I'd get headaches added to wanting her,
needing to want her, for Chrissie, just
to count her mine would complete me!
                                            Yeah?
But who'd ever blunder into loving Kevin Joy?
And why risk giving myself those daily/nightly
friskings of doubt? Sweet bitch bound me in options.
I was Sophie-crazed by now, sure, but
was it even worthwhile showing this?
Talk of hedging your bets, then, cadging
one of her Kents she touched my arm.
'Don't fret.'
         Oh yeah?
                  'Don't fret Kevin. He's a whiz . . .'
She snapped into work whilst I stared out
twitching like a lizard.
                        Those places make you imagine.
Shaving, like, I'd catch my Joy Boys file round me
for the group shot. Or, awake by three, I'd lie
whilst the sun got nearer gibbering myself awake:
what happens when everyone left in the mirror goes
and I'm the only broker? And get up pale,

poker-faced, a headache growing, advising:
*Kevin, don't doubt it, this game's beyond even love
or money, without it you might as well be some
joker running his used car yard. Not any clown imports!*
    I'd never felt this deliberate, I need a pause,
to borrow hours that wouldn't be her. An affair?
Couldn't that brim me up with fears. Kill me
risking it? Like you Sophie's a good girl.
Good girls fuck the best. They love it. For keeps.
    And tonight all my will we/ won't we
lies resolved. She flies in tomorrow.
                             Want to deal?
Simple. Go to any Hicksville, look round for a drinking-mate,
ask quietly. Careful, only dags are caught. You
want to be found! Had a *Playboy* once:
you imagine this stir: thought I'd make some friends,
be a two-bob-a-peek entrepreneur. You can't.
There's a boy pushing smut! Cops got told,
and the school pumped out its giant taskforce.
Dumb buggers, dumber Kevin, they were after
freebees! Whole town wanted to blow! Me?
I just smiled back: what's that?
If you have something they need, you work.
Not easy, dealing, just simple. And stunts
which end, end. That night saw me peeling page
after page, watching them flap into the ocean.
Bye-bye Miss March 1963, you'd keep,
somewhere. I wasn't getting into no slanging match,
like, on any rock group's North Coast tour I'd hang
outside the youth club's dance with those other dags.
Well? Who needs the collective will
of a few hundred fat virgins caked in Clearasil?
We weren't known and wanted nothing.
Take any Sydney street who'd notice me?
That's an easy salvation dags learn well:
the anonymous pull the best stunts. Sometimes.
    We learn but. All my old man did was nod.
I opened the door and sat beside him.
'You're an idiot Kevin,' and Howard drove on
through the streets of Lawrence muttering.

I saw a smart-arse wave. Piss off, I blushed. Some kid
whose Dad we knew, anyway he turned to every prick
in town. We both squirmed. All the red-hot respect
that Howard craved puffed off in embarrassment:
knew the headmaster from lodge, see. And 'Kevin Joy,'
this toad announced, 'wants to say a few words
to the assembly.' But then he had to. Sorry school,
won't happen again. Nup. Not bad for a dag,
trying to be like something out of Carter Brown.
(We'd wagged it, see. Brought a girl back for something
planned if unspecified. Stupid headmaster arrived.
'Sorry Sir. It's me mates. They locked her in this wardrobe.')
Well, I surprised them, see. Apologising becomes me, all things
do if they're needed.
                        But he won't hurry. Why should he?
The boy who has to say sorry gets called to the dais,
rising to crown himself king of the dags, and he doesn't
stand before Lawrence High School now, but this
champagne march past, magnum after magnum,
whilst slater bugs, the norm, kids in uniform,
stared up. I left that year, not knowing how
I'd seen the future: what would be mine:
house, boat, houseboat, cars, girls, Soph and champagne
no-one drank but me. Then, though, I'd only one ambition:
to quietly state *No, never fuckin' again*. What else?
Marry, hit the piss and attempt another generation
of carpet salesmen? A mate 'n' me left and Lawrence
never got a chance to cry *Poooor buuggah!* Chrissie,
you try kissing any hometown bye-byes with this
block of farts. Nearly died with the pleasure.
                                     Why look
so pained? Tampon packets might lie strewn through
your place: such bravado hides nothing. Aren't we
so respectable? Want to slum it? Expect
the barest manners. Can't tell why I'm talking still
except those pills perhaps; except your heading para,
have great little tits and, given a day or two,
these raves can end: this tourist junk you wear
will get replaced. We're used to sprucing girls as
stenographer, nursing sister, teacher's aide. But yet

its more than *used*: all of us love the gall, daring
and that warm cash coming back home, just to roost
on respect. We disappoint no-one. We serve all clients,
often before ourselves: a market so delighted
to love us, have us love them. If, say, I owned
Carlton and United I'd be Sir Kev. Great but shove it,
Chrissie, for where'd be the love? And what is it?
Why to know you love is love, and better:
to reach for more than the lot. I'm not
another bearded teacher *Just cultivating* backyard stuff,
who freaks each time a chopper flaps above him.
    See, everything was turning special:
I was getting this place up north, a wide,
white, isolated monster being carved out of a headland,
you have to arrive by tunnel. I needed to think
how and what and who to fill it: the show
was moving: contradictions, fabrications Morgan proved
just that, simple disappearances. Time then
for all those remaining Joy charms to get reactivated.
How I loved 'n' hated it, laughed when found out
giving: 'So where you live Sophie?' for a line.
                                         Me?'
    'Yeah you.'
              'I'm never at home, get me at work.
South Yarra. An apartment.'
                       She smiled, all choices
narrowed and we heard the other breathing. Give me a week
I'd visit her.
             'Not guilty.' The foreman marked it plain,
plain as Soph gasping 'Kevin! We won!' She couldn't embarrass me,
this was the girl I wanted. You can't love that much
and me I only love winners. So, like beginners again,
we were stalking ourselves. In less than a week,
but quicker and quicker, I'd shed my forged cover
of cool, totting up, grass, perfume, dinners, whatever
she'd want, clothing, trips to Paris. And couldn't I
feel the rest. What shot up my spine and down?
Over in the hotel's plushest suite the boys would see
our party on track. Me, I needed to pause,
for Chrissake all risks had been mine and always were.

How could this Sophie woman even attempt being
capital B Bad? She'd see it that way and, yes,
she'd love to try but how could her reputation
ever bruise except that it'd be mine? The world
believes nice girls, they have nothing to lose. Could I
believe enough to stake myself with her, with Soph?
  Jim is propping by this mound of oyster shells, see,
scooping caviar whilst all our party eyed us:
Soph 'n' me. 'So?' says Jim. 'It's their fix.'
They get nix, 'cause that night nothing scared me
more, you know, than her: Morgan patting the ringlets
like she was his pup. You'd all keep: we'd tried them,
they'd tried us. They'd delivered, we'd delivered. Below,
another town, a market, relaxed. Nothing at all
was wrong and this was class. A tax adviser
had to leave. 'Great party, Kev.' 'Take care matey . . .'
Vast ranks of them would hurtle on down
if someone really probed, or, say, tried to begin it.
How come? There is no 'crime' and we are partners in it.
  Three well-known merchant bankers get farewelled,
then Kim sidles up with cigars. 'The lawyer-bird,'
he murmurs, 'she's got you on the brain.'
Ho ho funny place for a brain but right, 'cause she
looked at me then laughed as if *Oh, oh, shot you Kevin Joy
bang! with my dark round eyes!* Well well surprise
surprise: wasn't it time to get ambushed by class?
Not quite yet. Morgan stood aside, munching party pies.
Kim bragged: 'Wasn't I correct? He's like you Kev,
the best.' Reputations never did harm:
X slaps on the charm, Y splats the prosecution
like a sumo wrestler, Z snow-jobs the juries;
and, as with some tart whose talent's in blow-jobs,
you pay for the mouth.
      Oh I'd been calm,
till the verdict but then I needed to cut everything,
almost wanting to sweet-talk any narc. Go on why not.
What's your line: Kevin Joy sux? Haven't I,
courtesy of a judge and jury, the greatest of credentials.
Not guilty? Yet dazed (and almost near amazed
by my remaining market), I'd left the court, to be alone.

(We're raking it off the surface, there's that much,
Chrissie, and sometimes even that much can wait.)
Real making it started tomorrow, I erased yesterday
and strolled to what's its names, Henry Buck's,
ordered a suit.
                    Jim snapped me with this Dom Perignon,
Smile you happy bastard smile. I couldn't, I was unnerved
that night, needing someone, anyone, to keep Soph occupied,
or else I'd simply slide on in and it would be it.
        Hold on but: 'Hey señor you fuckin' marvel!'
My brother Basil offered her boss a toke, but neither smoke,
and so he giggled something like:
'Planning to toss the odd run too. Keep you on side?'
And later: 'So we've cooked up beeg money, señor?'
But Basil's always excused, I would anyone approaching
blood, kin, relations, whatever way you tag it,
providing they don't grass, 'cause even if he's an alkie,
no doubt a faggot (you'd hate him) Basil's jibber-
jabber is open slather on deadshits. It's Daffy Duck
for a brother, all another language, he's my real
live deadshit detector, right? Why'd I want more?
I don't because he's never been bought. 'You find this,'
he scoffed to Morgan, 'worthwhile? Look, look
who's king of the shitheap: me brother Kev. On yer Kev!'
I watched Morgan sipping, staying his balance, smirking
through all the piss Basil held and *Bud-deeee!*
the endless black power salutes, as if ho ho young man . . .
well ho ho Morgan lick the nipper's boots, even the odd
flock of vultures got to sell themselves, even dags
want somehow to be accepted, checked over, vetted
just clean enough, to cop all those predictable hints.
        I don't get blasé mind. I open my eyes real wide
to suck the info in *Huh? Y' don't say? Really mate?
Taa. Won't forget it.* Aren't there times when it's best
to bite the lip, nod and catch the advice they palm
across? Of course it's best, like: next time obey
the eleventh commandment Kev, *Don't get caught.*
                                    Weren't they
there to amuse, help me pronounce the champagne brands?
That party turned to this glorious shunting yard:

anyone of use on either dope or a retainer,
my dreams, proposals, orders, turning themselves to the truth,
this wad of lawyers soaking up the dregs they lived off,
loving it, for just one night never getting enough of
the Joy Boys: voyeurs over a life they needn't explain or,
after their tolerance leached into tomorrow morning,
not have to concern them again.
                         But not Soph.
I hadn't been so scared-to-slices as when her body brushed
that ever-so-slightly by, wrapping me round in chills,
hoping tonight he couldn't imagine such the sweetest bitch
in creation murmur him aside like:
Y' great Kevin. Let's meet again? Please?
Till, as its tide could hardly consider stopping
love would sink them into its glitzed forever.
Love? Oh Kev-in, only sucks contemplate that
in the script. Keep telling yourself no matter how
top shelf this one is, she's potent. Keep the trousers zipped,
all the available steps between you both were danced
in remand. You'll chance what for what?
Wardrobes of snappy businesswomen's suits can't fool me.
She's crazy, ten times fuckin' wilder than you ever were.
        Then, a few days on, I glanced through a phone book:
found I was just waiting to con myself.
It named this smallish block of flats I thought
I recognised. Sweet small events had
blown my cover: those odd beautiful occasions.
In court, say, she writes him notes. Notes?
For Kev that's bullion from the tip, find better,
God or the world got ordered. They didn't 'cause
she cared, I flipped, and a future was on, even
the present was over.
                    He's catching his cab in a heatwave
this man with an enormous bouquet of roses.
What more is needed to snap *pffft* at the past?
Someone helped: the foyer was unchecked: I must've ignored
the intercom: and can't recall any of the lift-ride up.
Say Chrissie, with that look you gave, think I'm
a sucker? Those few seconds outside her door were spent
feeling my heart pummel each rule of organisation

I'd ever set. But she was different: I knew it:
almost fearing (and yet near daring) her to package me
prime cut, blue ribbon, take me back to your mother.
Who or what taught Miss Sophie Cross to blush, recover
and coo 'Roses! Well, aren't you a darling!'
Camberwell Church of England Girls Grammar School?
How long was I to be sent mad-and-a-half just waiting
to kneel, tongue her clit, see what followed,
as if I wasn't aware, hearing how Soph was:
'Crazy for you Kevin.' Still, there was time to think,
like how does class screw, real class. With heartbeats
refusing to take up her slack and Soph at her bathroom
saying like how she'd be back; (and now I know that sweet routine
by rote), then smiling she returned, split and I
entered for we were, and Chrissie you got to hear this,
lovemakers. Lovemakers, nothing less.
And more: getting told how much she
missed me, that unhinged enough, turned me too mute
to reply but I knew, then, if other women existed
I was tamed if ever Soph said so, making me feel, well,
ashamed if you like, I'd contemplated Rent-a-Root back
in remand. Tarts bored me. That week, concealing little,
those dogs the Joy-birds got the shove-along,
with one real lady-lady ripening for the rage, you think
I'd ever page Dial-a-Date, just to sop that extra cash
I'd gotten around to spend?
Don't shit me! Don't play me further games of let's pretend,
please use a few brains and imagine, Chrissie, how we were
blessed by the gods of love, Cupid and his gang!

    Yes gods. Oh he exists. I saw him tonight. That wog
who signalled Kim's return. For love dope cash friends,
there's little between them. A god, a wog?
I was satisfied. He made me happy as Kim can
you could and as always Soph wraps me in,
get this one, joy! If fucking alone were love,
and even I've gotten round to learn it isn't,
but imagine if it was, we'd always want to
double-the-lot. We're all so wired to get-get-getting.
No wonder sucks need more, no wonder they still fall
for stunts like that stupid mock flirting you've done

since we met. Just by wanting it love can be smack.
Don't I know what the world needs now, Mister Bacharach!
People want and I'm their kind of cupid. What wouldn't begin
were I to have Kaiser Stuhl, Carlton and United,
the Dom Perignon stunt? *Arise Sir Kev, gobble your oysters,
keep these pearls, unfurl your coat of arms, and my!
what a smart matching silk shirt and tie you're sporting.*
But since Kimbo and me and yes you now are importing
love first, and profit only later, I tell you
that makes for real danger. They're frightened.
    Like I was. This could be love, real love. I knew it,
could never demand it. Orders were over and minus them
what was I? Soph had to tell quick:
some crim to notch up for a whim,
or the one man to scream for: imagine the narcs, say,
bursting in halfway through screwing *I'm his lawyer:
what in the hell y' think y' doing?* Giving her all for him
him him! And that him, me! Could it be that?
Oh understand how someone really loved me,
Kev the dag, and it was to be all dreams, if only
for a night: deals, money, would never drag me awake.
And better than dreams were the eyes screaming out
Yes Kevin yes and, would you believe, maybe I was
horrified? As if whatever gods were operating knew
even I cried for someone and had set me with a lady
brave or crazed enough to chuck her lot,
like only good girls can when they're in love.
    Like Chrissie will for Kimbo, not of course,
for some maniac dag she thinks is sitting opposite. I've
caught to that, but you, you were waved on hours back:
it's been like talking to my legs. When you're sober you might
get that one. *Hello legs. Quite soon you'll stroll
through customs, be climbing into a cab . . .*
But hasn't the drum been given, now, how many times?
Point one: even if you're bustin' to piss, got a headache,
relax. I've said the facts, what narcs, cops and judges
are with us. How many? About the world at times,
although I'm middling. Funny how I don't own a freight
terminal, a trucking firm. The Joy Boys big?
We're big enough to buy off those who think we are.

Just middling but: I'm no corporate bastard,
not for them the tense crazed delight
of a crushing. They've football teams to buy,
chat shows to appear on. Why bother skiting over
some arsehole journo you had slugged,
even sacked, who's been tagged your 'judge of the month'?
Know these men, Chrissie? Real men?
Real men never see the stuff.
Like: what's this heroin really like then?
Something in bags on the six o'clock news.
Their grandkids will be moving ks by laser beams.

    Jim but, was anxious. Soph was excessive! It wasn't
that he'd never mixed with class, he never wanted to.
Old Kimbo you can guess just lay down and floated
into the charm. 'Kev's lawyer-bird's an asset,
makes him almost respectable.' Not our dumb wog but.
Didn't want to see. Poor shrink who tries frisking
your skull. What's this overweight Tongan without me?
Look here Jungle Jim she's hardly a risk, she's not on smack,
she's a lawyer. Get it? Stick with the gee-gees,
you're backing the wrong-un this time.
Had to be kept on but. Propping the back of the boys are always
legmen, gamblers. He bores me? But the whole game
almost can and I was stale enough at times to vow
retirement. Tomorrow. Tomorrow, sure, the next time.

    Out on the tan track my head was swampy with ideas:
gelling slowly into schemes. Next time, sure.
But Soph 'n' me changed gears: relaxing into parties,
wine, coke, sleep, each other.

                      One Saturday
she drove me to her old school fair: my tête-à-tête
with class. Class? Couldn't I buy out the lot? And spent
a second, even less, seeing my retirement. One more run say?
Imagine: wiping the frigging slate. To what?
There must be a next deal and a next. That's all.
Why join those mutts just wanting to exist? I need
to live, to feel myself curl round and into every
part of fate. Men, her friends? husbands of her friends?
semi-pissed, approached, trying to hold the booze through lunch.
I clutched my plastic cup, tried looking I belonged

to whatever they were, even if my skull
was gonged with headaches. 'Course I stayed:
you choose to stay with Sophie Cross, parade
her arm through yours: spuds with sour cream,
lamb on the spit, wog food, who wouldn't send
their kids to such a place?
      'Coming back?'
One of her brothers was it? He drove me, dealing facts:
some famous quack lived here ... the Minister for that
lives there, pleased he poked the air, men like him
want things like that known. When you following, Soph?
Without you I've this flair for s.f.a., and I stood,
blank as any Asian, helping the brother bury me
in small talk: 'Meet Kevin. With him a spade's
a regular spade.'
     'Hi, she thinks I'm direct ...'
Know what I do fellas? '... mainly gemstones, bits
of developing ...'
     Hands lay resting over my shoulders.
'Always our shout here, Kevin, what'll it be?'
  Rich kids, lucky kids on smack making suckers of their folks?
Don't wince, you made a guess. Clever Chrissie. Clever Chrissie
does her run, a few days pass, their luck's notched up again,
best game in town: once it hits the blood it
and everything bad just vanishes.
      No, that day it wasn't hard
being a dag, one more anonymous rich dag.
Not enough gel for a stockbroker but all right,
this skinny tanned joker with crazy grey-blue
Paul Newman eyes, he'll do. He sleeps, shits, eats
and sleeps again. Never seen a living thing that
won't die. Something will start in space, and we'll turn
as cold 'n' dry as Mars. But don't get told different:
I'll even love her beyond Pluto. *Heard about this crim
and his nice girl, fellas?* Get this: after Soph suggested
I insure my prick with Lloyd's she stripped and I
covered her in fifties, took polaroids. *Like to see
some snaps, fellas?*

  They let me hang in there. *Kevin?
Seems a kind of quiet type.* Not much to say, that's why,

till her little sister wants a crack at the Joy magic,
starts to flirt. You know what's best girl? Go wait
in your folks' laundry, we won't leave till the place
tastes almost too thick of steam, detergent, us and cash,
your address book packed, praying to get smacked.
Who knows what any kid-sister does, given enough
of what she wants and promised more? True, not anyone
can pull these stunts and, hijacked by headaches
I couldn't. That day. Wouldn't you rather dreams?
Dreams that are working or dreams that have even
arrived?
        But then give you five minutes, say,
and isn't Chrissie's one-time husband always reoccurring?
Ray always says . . . Aren't former fucks a most professional
obsession? Or present ones since I should talk.
I can wince just like you: at the mention of
Ray's mighty sense of humour for the tenth time.
        Later, with Kimbo off to bed, the flirting getting nowhere,
our bar lining up another round and, no, you didn't need
them mixed, neat was enough, later it's Ray this Ray that,
screaming for all the room, 'How dare you think I'm drunk!'
No, if you say so and, once again, your marriage gets recycled.
Ray's history, there's only Kim now, sweetheart.
Know why you're joining him? We've money, love, the future.
Pension off the past, why remain there? When whacked
do you always mention this Ray this genius Dylan-freak teacher?
        Fed-up being someone's ex, with a life of bit parts . . .
We've an upcoming feature starring, simply, you.
Any Joy-bird will vouch how it's easy bringing a case
to customs, brace yourself just like the Valium allows.
Relax. On two grand plus a month that underwear
shuffling narc is one of ours. Near the city this friend
will pace a flat. His phone rings, pacing ends for the day,
with each question answering itself: yes!
Our game's on hold, the pack has been shuffled and cut,
the dice are poised to roll, he hangs up and the call
unfolds like some huge and magic cum:
the deaf hear, the dumb speak, on, on, just like a religion,
miracles et cetera, person after person, happier and happier.
        And aren't you pleading till you're numb with this

I've been respectable, I'm still nice. Anyone is
if that's how they want it. Nobody's nicer. Scout's honour.
But here, north, things are different. Simple. On a visit
you met someone to amaze your friends: yourself.
Asia provides all a nice girl needs to escape caddying
for genius egos, to fend off sugar-daddying.
As Chrissie bummed Thailand, Malaysia with Kimbo
all her answers bloomed: you're a goner for thrills,
forever primed to blossom out in shudders. You didn't exclaim:
Drugs eh? That's a buzz! You merely looked it and why not.
Tonight all covers just floated away: easy when we're
both stoned-drunk, short of keeling to the floor, of course,
of course, you're not that pissed. Kev's a ready bunny.
Chrissie wants his ear, any ear. Still worried over
all that money owed to your sainted Ray? Just wait:
smack kills off any debt, magic always does,
or love if there's enough of it.
                        But listen.
What's that? Beyond the wog-band packing their gear,
those few remaining couples chatting up. What?
No need to wonder. Nothing but thunder. Just that. Listen
and imagine if our dusk had sent its own storm warning,
ever felt safer? Couldn't you drink on through till dawn
merely to view the resort blunder back for breakfast?
I'll let you upstairs soon, want to stay raving but?
Let's pretend we can tell anything, let's say you're some
lady cop. I'd buy you . . . There but. That noise again. Thunder!
It's almost a friend. Can't you imagine galaxies where that's
a warning? Not in mine: it's an order, lightning follows:
and, since you or anyone can be as bought as smack
(or thunder) can't I calculate the where when how why
of anybody?
                    Let me tell you how The Human started
bloating till he rose. Some fucker hadn't weighed
him down. Gases grew and up it bobbed, floating
the harbour like shit. Grassing moves both ways.
Harper, this cop I knew, traced Operation Overdrive
to him. I survive by juggling payments, attempting
to keep the remainder tidy. Why just exist but?
I had to thrive and The Human needed to go.

It all freaked me: weren't we kind of friends? Yes
but hardly colleagues. What was he? A pest. Why?
Only because he'd stuffed it and had to grass.
      Anything's a drug: a run, a hit, a kill. Life by nerve-ends:
'cause after that first you may never want to try another
but all the rest gets easier. Guess what?
We're just doing a job and nothing happens.
Facts stick, if indeed they're facts, only if you're careless.
Who'd want that? You can get more 'n' more.
Something is to be done. You'll do it. Like facts
your first run just happens. It's no huge step
taking on this. You're protected. The right people know,
know I'm very generous that, like tonight, the night before
and the night before, any night's on me.
                                      Soph but,
she's different, let's talk of Soph then. No? Kimbo? Later?
If our guest wants it. Same for the lady, waiter.
Huh? Don't call you *that*? *Lady*? Oh well,
blame the pills, blame whatever Chrissie's latest little
fad is. And don't you want to be so extra-good?
Though why all your confessions must keep on with their
same reminder: I mean we know it now, who needs
Ray's got himself a little lady . . . Michelle 'n' I
we really get on. Woman, where you from?
Just couldn't believe hearing *Anyway, what's money?*
The reason you're trying to con me to accept *I'm this hippy,*
well kinda.
      Maybe cash is shit, you've needed it.
Needed to let Ray bail you out the times
you're going broke. I know the score: girl drinks,
still can't forget him, screaming at the bar boo hoo,
boo hoo, you'd clutch at anything, clutch like
Ray's got himself a little lady now. She a dwarf?
    Don't pout. Only trying to joke. You'll know if I'm not.
     The Human didn't. Talking about him wasn't I?
Had to leave, going to dob us, cops poised to once more
bust him. Like, who'd ever trust him?
He'd been big, fat-gutted slime, always picking up the tab
to buy some friends. He used and that's important
'cause he was a wreck, though it never depended

on junk but, the excuse was him, it's just about everyone's.
Shrinks try weaving us into something they think
is just this little bit unique: fat chance.
So here's Harper barging in at four a.m. bust style.
'Human's floating. What fucker did you hire? Stay sweet.
Without me Kev, you'd be floating too. Up shit creek.'
Pleasant bloke, Harper, though he can't get out any more
than you: simple: why should he leave us? Why would you?
Still wondering where the famous buck stops? Doesn't.
Nobody's straight. It's only their price hasn't been
arrived at. It always will. With cops, junkies,
we only know one dance. Like I said fat chance.
Who hated The Human? Half Sydney. The other lay
indifferent, covered in two words *Drop it*.
But for a day I went walking, just that, ground
into a half trance. Why were we that thick? How?
Harper got his slice and I got out.
    Back in Melbourne, uncertain, not enough of a local.
So? I knew of another tale: once upon a time see,
there's this north coast yokel hits Sydney,
becomes a legend. Needs to stop just grassing safe jobs, see.
Meets Kimbo. And next, you could almost plan
within a year this young guy receives how-
many-grand a month, watching respect and
self-respect grow with every deal.
    He's back in Melbourne but. Stuck with the biggest but.
Grassing. Like Jasmin 'n' Mick, two friends, a.k.a.
Lara 'n' Max, nice folks real nice folks
were passing lies for facts, for cash for dope: shame,
whatever the names they'd given. Either them lifting the lid,
or Patty the courier kid, out of school, whooosh, straight
on the game. Interstate someone needed to help: today,
not tomorrow and I'd prefer last week.
    We'll call him Bill. Ninety grand straight to your account,
Bill, c.o.d. each cassette. 'Cause we suspected them,
Jaz 'n' Mick but jeez. Put it this way, ever hear yourself
getting bad-mouthed to the narcs? The mouth dries,
the guts drop and Chrissie that's just what people are:
you've always known it. They'd blown it, sure, but all
their bad-mouthing and lies turned them to shark bait

when it stopped. Not even bait now.
'This about does us, eh Kev?' as he curled
onto her. Tough luck Mick. Checkmate, mate.
Look: he never tried acting the hero and I admire it,
admire their drying off programs, stuffing down the 'done.
You ever put a feeler out for smack? Please don't.
It's nothing, real nothing. I liked them once. They weren't using
then. Try losing y'self on something you can control,
Kimbo say, 'cause when the end arrived
they hadn't. There was no Kimbo. They just glittered
for a while.
         Or I'll say what I said to Lisa:
'There might be excitement, sure. Try forgetting it.
The glam's peripheral. Our world is bordered by
one word: organisation. Have I to slam each syllable
till it sticks? *Look they're nar-cot-ics. Ill-eg-al.*
I could love them like the inevitable garden parties
they're not, but they're not.'
         Think after barking,
long enough, something clicks? So what she just
wouldn't understand you must: without orders one more
pinhead rushes in, little's questioned, nothing's answered. Like
just another fad she's picked from one more client:
imitation battery cells, more bells than a cathedral.
'Please . . .' you know how it goes, 'We'll have a great time.
Love you Kev. Please this once . . .' till, and imagine this,
she would do anything. You're game as Lisa,
right? Wanna drop Kev's strides? Go on, meet the leaning tower of Pisa.
No? 'Course Lisa could flinch like that. 'Not tonight.
Please mate. Headache. I want out.' Knew she did.
      And knew like her the lot had always returned,
driven by just this: they needed to be in it.
Why give Lisa the benefit of some half-cooked-up
conscience? If indeed it was? And yet,
why bother snarling further orders? She lived in
a free world? Why mention just how small this free world was?
And some things were necessities for Lisa:
their steady beat held on: in any day she'd almost
break her neck, or anyone's, just to return and help.
Lisa, I told you, would do anything.

So even, I thought, her judgement might be working.
'Kev ... this chick ... something to snort?' Heh heh.
How'd I suspect? Within a week cops are attempting
to quiz me. Or, like, she hadn't dreamt of a takeover
had she? There'd been orders to check, cash was down
on Lisa now. And where is she? Somewhere, I think
on forged papers. I've been told, I want to forget and
I mean to say, Lisa had her orders but Lisa wouldn't obey.
She flew but. Helped Morgan, Soph and me to stuff them.
 'So maybe,' Jim got told, 'the gods exist.
Haven't we beaten 'n' joined them?' The breakfast lay
just brimming, still letting me enough to shout:
'I'm free, I've won, I've Soph, just want to keep winning
and the whole bloody world is opening up!
A planet dies waiting to be filled. Kimbo!' I telegraphed,
'fly down and celebrate. I'm out and heading north.'
 So, when I arrive he has you:
just like we've had so many: comfy: one more yacht,
another mortgage, disappearing debts and, since
my freedom props so much I'm needed out and
needed total. My generosity gets gorged like bait?
Fine. Who else could feed them, dress them my way?
Joy-birds should look just as Lisa did:
so straight a narc might blush to think ... a cop
couldn't even let her stop.
      We'll wipe your debts, keep you
a very comfy Chrissie, but remember my clear
and necessary orders. Better, know them. And try,
please try not getting this pissed again. You can stand?
Let's go up. I've some Berocca in my suite.
You'll need them.

HOLDING THE DRUG CZAR'S HAND

(Prologue) Kevin

    This is how he liked to think it started,
how, that summer day he moved in on all the class
which Sophie was (as if she hadn't done some
moving, round him and round him, of her own).
    But out of his cab and into the foyer,
past where an attendant should've been,
movin', movin' (at the pace his heart's been
clattering for days) whilst *her* heart,
with him there holding the roses,
is set he hopes, trusts, knows to be derailed.
*And even if he guesses one of us sure is on
with somebody so wrong . . . though who? Well,
being a busy man Kevin will never figure out that,
so . . . 'Watch it', some little bird tweets, 'watch it.
Just a word might surely botch it.'
You are telling me; my heart's on notice;
and here's the lift: thanks Mr Otis.
This week I've had to order, beg
my head for peace, needing to renege
all I believed till now, scrub my mind raw.
But it's evening, Saturday. Walking to your door
something's on. Can't tell what. To ditch
it and find one sweeter, wilder bitch?
given all lives possible, no-one would.
Even if she's ten times crazier than I could
ever be, why bother thinking 'Turn back mutt'?
For just one night, tonight, find better but.*

(1) Kevin

    But? Back north again:
today he's trusting no-one . . . and if last night

there'd been pills and Chrissie, well now
this afternoon, knowing that since he's faltered
once, he might again: that there are some things
whose control never will be his ...
And right they were just these minor strutters,
and right, right merest pussy-men,
but right, right, right he sortov owed them
and a month back, needing to make their lives
a little major they ripped off Kevin Joy:
two Aussies and two locals: real bigfellas,
who somehow guessed someone hadn't
prepared himself enough. If only Kevin
hadn't been so stoned, if only he'd the sense,
the nerve, to check; but by the time he thought
he should've there Kevin was: no cash,
no dope, past midnight near a drain
that stank of shit and echoed of frogs.
  Good revenge will wait, he knows a better kind:
make yourself Emperor Kev and set up a deal
that history has to applaud: your final and
your finest.
    And now, hoping this deal
is slotting in, having an hour or so to waste
till Kim returns with Sophie, till they
and Chrissie gather (so Kevin can
flowchart the run, fine-tuning
its junctions) his trust-list gets compiled:
those he'll never feel like trusting
even now, those who, for starters, deserve
this certain 'feeling' Kevin has; not Kimbo
surely, nor Soph surely surely,
but, back south, Cap'n Midnight, The Jeweller,
and even dumb ol' Jungle Jim plus half
(no make that all) the New South Wales Police ...
And these are friends, these are still alive!
Quite careless making such friends, but a man can
always learn, improve.
      Like, there's this someone
you arrange to meet in some bar,
where you'll recognise something in each other

as the chat grows with all the volleying chant
of the weirdest folk dance *You get/ I move?*
I get/ You move? No no no!
We *get and* we *move!*
                        Soon,
Kevin was going to move somewhere . . .
and stay there . . . and if movin's just
one-leg-after-another stuff to you, squarehead,
please understand: how much motion
can any kind of importer/dealer/distributor take?

(II) Kim, Sophie, Kevin, Chrissie

It was noon when, with Kevin still asleep,
Kim came out to meet the plane: walking tallish,
walking lavish (if just this side of silly)
for you were meant to notice, though admire
the tinted prescription shades, his cowboy hat:
silly, yeah, but easy-with-it:
still the Joy Boy's energy, charm and everything
except their brains.
                    Brains belonged with Kevin:
a reasonable divvy of nature's spoils until,
last month, ego-fat through living on these brains alone,
stoned on some thing some place, dealing away . . .
well Kevin the boss (which everyone assumed
he was) Kevin got ripped off and ripped off big!
('Let's rephrase it,' Cap'n Midnight had leant
across to Sophie, 'we all were'.')
        That, though, was their trade: the movin' trade:
one moment you might be heading the UN,
the next you couldn't even run a village store.
        They should've guessed that by the time
she knocked Kevin's door and breathless entered
Chrissie was hardly movin' keen: but it was late,
far too late to pike.
                    'Ohhh fellas, I dunno . . .'
she tried telling Kevin, Kim and Sophie,

'I'm just a happy amateur that shouldn't?
Sure but sure but could I do it?
Look if anything happens I'll plead, can I,
like I was fucked in the head? Partly?'
    No, they told her, no
that was your hangover speaking. Everything was
set-oh: why up in Business someone would
ride shotgun.
    That afternoon,
in Kevin's suite, caught in the *no/yes/maybe* tides
of Chrissie's indecision, Joy and Lacy
had stoned themselves again: most likely
on stupidity: Kevin lay down,
closed his eyes and snored; Kim still pleaded
Do it Chrissie Chrissie do it.
    Whilst the girl herself, propping her arguments
with half-remembered middle-period Dylan
got around to (would it be *Yes!?*) Yes!
The whiz-bangest moment in her life.

(III) Sophie, Kim

    Now was to be recompense hour/
making-sure-we're-never-played-for-mugs-again
time. And Sophie had jetted into this:
grooming some cretin she couldn't even dream of
how not to stuff this or any run
(as if there'd be another).
    Sure if Chrissie did it
(the run) she wouldn't (stuff things): is what
she told them ... but would she do it?
    'How'd we get her?' Sophie had to ask
and, getting Kim aside heard how the two had
recognised each other.
    'And what's she know?'
    'Err nix. Nought. Zero. That's what I told her
Soph. Said I was in the gemstone business.
Which I am. That Aussie big bucks, which

there are, were backing me 'n' my mate
Kevin. How we part-owned a place someplace.
She was a fuck: this holiday fuck
who follows me back ... and ho ho ho Kevin thinks,
here's just another courier in tow.
Well, we have one now. Listen,
her ex, Soph, he was once this mate
of mine? There were three of us: him, me,
this other kid?'
                  How could such a rattle-on
as this clear any air? He might be trying,
trying fast, but his words were just some
big 'n' clunky Valiant, chugalugging down
a nightmare freeway, and all he wanted
now was getting off it, onto Pacific Drive
and home to Frenchy, GoGo and The Shire.
('Say Soph, did you know I ran, I *owned*
this chain of clothing stores?')
                      Soph? Was Soph
set to cop such outer suburban nostalgia?
No more than she was copping Chrissie, right?
      'Okay okay, well Kevin had this wand once ...'
(Kim had veered again, but she allowed him.)
'The day we met that wand was waved
and we were movin': Joy and Lacy
two of the best we really were:
I arranged, Kevin carried through ... or
something like it!'
                Sure Sophie understood
such magic: but Kevin magic now
was bad magic, danger magic: hey presto
this here's what he'd conjured: Chrissie,
novice runner to the max, some Dylan's freak's
ex-wife.

(IV) Kim, Chrissie

    Then it all, saw Kim,
was spiralling down to her:
Frenchy's woman, Frenchy Donellan's one 'n' only;
The Shire and now the Joy Boy's finest:
eager helper, eager pleaser, eager lover.
    'Came all this far to find me a fella
or two ... and I met *You!*' She'd been
a trifle rapt. 'Up north in what's it called
that town? When I saw you once? Or thought
I saw you? And then the next time
was I certain? There you were there you were
there you were ...'
               Sounding nostalgic
about what he knew had been this time
last week, 'Kim?' her voice moused-up,
'Hey Kim Lacy? Aren't you the ol' Spacey,
Mr Kim Lacy? From The Shire? It's me,
remember Chrissie? Ray Donellan's ex?'

(V) Kevin, Chrissie

    After it started thataway
Kim brought her back to meet the business mate.
    'Then this,' asked Kevin, 'is your hippy phase?'
    Her what? Oh give this girl a break, well
why not, kinda?
         'Accept,' returned Kevin,
'any phase you like.'
              Taa and Chrissie would.
    And take as many risks.
                If they came by
she'd take them.
         Kimbo then, was he
a risk?
    Well Kim was one-sweet-guy. Perhaps
there was a risk in that?

'No world,' she heard,
'was ever run by one-sweet-guys.'
  Well but, she's enough of the rest.
         And Kevin
liked that: 'Sure friend you have.'
        Her friend?
Her friend? He'd a lot of nerve!
Did Kev like Dylan?
  'Ray my ex,' Chrissie had to tell him,
'gets *that* depressed by Dylan.
He loves him though. Some nights after school
he'll roll another log, get pretty down and
I mean down, put Dylan on again. *Chris*
he'll say *he makes me that depressed*. So?
Why keep him on? Then he gets annoyed:
fuck Dylan this fuck Dylan that;
so *I'll* get upset and want it off.
You're not taking Dylan off? Are you?
Small games . . .'
      And that's how it was,
their last months, just small games.
Ray was clever mind, still made her laugh.
And Chrissie had this letter:
did Kevin want to read it? If so
get her drinkies! Get her drinkies!
  He got them, but dismissed the letter,
said she'd this touch of the flirt,
and hired the woman.

(VI) Sophie

  One summer evening back in Melbourne
Sophie had walked past a pub scene
(and pub scenes were hardly her scene)
where this girl (early twenties, heavy enough)
was moving through the tables
to collect . . . let's say a door prize
from the lead guitar (there was little adventure,

never had been) just one-of-a-group,
not even their token moll, only somebody
who might spread her legs to see how things
occurred this time, and trust they might be
worth it. *Oh why not*
Sophie could almost see that little shrug
Oh why not: something has to happen . . .
   Which meant, to anyone knowing people
Sophie's way: she's hired!
       But,
not even for herself, let alone for
these new friends of hers, here was Chrissie-
at-Thirty still thinking she was doing
her bit for counter-culture. That must've been
one long long holiday: no doubt she'd need
another.

(VII) Sophie, Kevin

   Kevin did.
   Anytime, last night, just after dusk
she reckoned, a few choice pills had got dissolved
in Kevin's bloodstream: by now each internal organ
was coated in the stuff.
       He wanted to appear
so much awake for her (and really wished
he could) 'Yet even at this hour,' he offered,
'I could do with one more solid snooze.
Sorry Soph. I sat at the bar until whenever
grooming this one mad Aussie bitch of Kim's
you see we're trying to recruit.
Sorry Soph.'
     Back home
he never apologised; he wasn't back home though;
and since last night had been a potent one
much of his life needed to be retrieved,
coordinated: like his wellbeing, like
most of his senses, but mainly his ruthless,

sardonic gift of judging what to win
and how to win it.
    And such a recovery,
she guessed, would never happen now:
he had become what all his Joy Boys
were predicting: doing pills 'n' powders
the boss had lost it: inside that brain
each hour was cocktail hour; every day
was varnished by such slow evenings
of liquor, which slid into and beyond
his guts, like mellow lava.
    Kevin
(might as well be nice about it: try being easy
with the man) *that was your pirouette
on centre stage, it's been well done but, well,
it's done. Just hunt out the twilight home
for one-time dealers: settle down then soak yourself
in decades and decades of Joy-life:
you have forty years starting from . . .
now!*

  She enjoyed her wit, knew how it sounded
quite concerned. But knowing he'd hear everything
and listen to nothing, she'd hardly say it.

(VIII) Sophie, Morgan

  Sophie was in this, too much the woman was;
and knew no better way to prosper and survive
than *too much*. Back home,
for a few lunchtimes, sprucing up
The Friday Club, she would move around
the tables: adjusting the barristers' ties,
combing away any cowlicks, always ready
to do it again.
    'You live,' Morgan QC had told her,
'live in that world where it's so much harder
for girls (whatever the *it* and *so much* was)
where Sophie mustn't display the smarts

that often: out there
were a lot of rather dumb men,
and she was being mentioned.
                              So,
came the advice, lower your sights
for merely half a year, take aim,
breathe in a bit, and marry one.
            Oh yeah? Well, some day she might again;
till then there was Kevin. And now,
if she wanted him (she knew it) Kim:
amusing, considerate, though great company
for a time, if weak. And like Kevin,
a trashmale.
            If she had a feeling
for this sub-species, Ms Cross would never get
too sentimental over facts.
                              Yet,
Know what it is/was with Kevin?
She had to ask herself. *I've never asked
'Why am I doing this?'*
                        She'd never been
truer to herself, felt more special.
      'Joy,' Morgan let her know, 'Joy's a peanut.'
      Kevin had met the family though: the brothers, the sister,
mum, a few school chums, spouses
where applicable, the daily help.
      'Poor Joy . . . how'd the drug czar cope?'
      'Pretty mute, but he was liked.'
                                    'Gemstones,'
thought the barrister, 'developments . . .' The peanut, sure,
had little actual use, still and all
Kevin Joy was a simple, amazing man.
      She sighed and wondered how this man
might finish.
            'Charred bones on a Thai beach?'
predicted Morgan.
                  'Who, mate,' his protégé reminded,
'employs you.'
            And didn't Morgan know it.
'Mmmm,' he nodded '. . . and Joy isn't guilty.

Hardly has been, might've, but he isn't.
Might've been a rock star, or a rock melon, a quack
or a quark . . . might've been guilty.'
    Let her be reminded what he almost told the jury
Not only has my client done *nothing,*
believe what you're told enough the man
will disappear, for Kevin Joy, ladies and
gentlemen, is nothing. All that so-called evidence
was surely someone's dream; make it yours as well.
Look at my client one last time, now close your eyes . . .
Ready? Open them! There! You'll never see that face again.
Joy's gone.

(IX) Kevin, Sophie

    He wasn't yet.
   'Legit.' After he woke up and took her out
Kevin said 'Legit. We might turn legit.'
    This much into his life what else did Kevin know,
she asked, but illegit? Kim at least
had, once, tried something else.
    No no no you-may-not-believe-it-but over there,
by the Straits of Malacca,
at the crossroads to ev'rywhere,
Joy 'n' Lacy were gemstone traders; and now,
having met an Aussie who really owns stuff
(sportsman's friend Craig Stubbs: motelier,
car sales guru) Kevin and Kimbo were investing in
a bar or two (Crazy Horse for starters,
followed by The FucFuc.)
                A gladhander squarehead,
prowling life for diversity and South-East Asian
boltholes, Stubbsy had all the glib sincerity
of a voice-over *For sheer*
real livin' there's little beats getting out to meet
y' fellow man and giving it a go!
    So he did/Kevin did.
Like Sophie, Stubbs could highlight

hidden strengths and virtues.
      No Soph?
 'Kevin, we all have something to cough up, spit out,
sometimes. And each of us gets caught, sometimes.
I could be very much Miss Kiss-and-tell …'
 Which hardly fazed him:
'Depends who does the kissing then. Know what?
I've never bought you.'
     'Bet you could've.'
         'Could've sure,
but you'd be one improbable whore.'
       Even better
was this: she's never seen any of their stuff
 Call me bored, Kevin often confessed
and even now it didn't seem she would
 get up to breakfast, a shave and a shower
Kevin, and Kim, possessed a few simple abilities
 then drive to squash or a workout, a sauna or a steam
to improvise, negotiate in codes, run up phone bills
 spa, massage or sex or both, check the accounts
 buy Soph something, wait
demand loyalty, wait
 dinner with the fellas, all done fellas?
get paid for the above
 taa for a lovely day
and invest it.
    Sophie thought of people using
the cliché *coalface* and knew she'd given up
too much to let it crumble.
     Here was where
you got life lived, where you imagined this Chrissie
arriving in Sydney, and how,
one blink later, an officious bull dyke
of a narc has run up Chrissie's first and not so last
all-over body search.
     'Who's shotgun Kevin?'
         'Patty.'
 'And who is Patty?'
     'Soph …'
       'Who is Patty?'

'Patty-the-kid.'
It was wonderful to wince,
his Joy Boys had been shaved back to this:
Patty-the-kid and Chrissie.
                      'Lose her Kevin.
You're trusting *that*? Pension her, poison her but
imagine this: she never existed. If Chrissie stays,
I'm off.'
        'How'd your reputation ever bruise?
The world believes nice girls, what they
ever lose?'
        'We are hearing things.'
          'Who are we and what are we hearing?'
      'The Cap'n, The Jeweller, me, others.'
                      'Hearing Soph?
I've been hearing all my life
Clean up Kevin, wipe y' frigging slate
and for what? To join those mutts just trusting
they exist?'
          'Think of zero. Now zero times it.
That's your Chrissie.'
                  'Okay I'll speak with Kim.'
    'And Kim's the boss? What is Kevin on?
Kim isn't one more user poncing through Asia,
but a dodgy gemstone trader with a penchant
for stupid women; and this one is prime
*Hi Australia, you mightn't know this but Kim
(he's my boyfriend) well Kim's this real live
drug dealer, isn't that amazing, for guess who . . .
Kevin Joy and the Joy Boys!*
We are hearing things.'
                'What?'
'Just lose her.'
            'Hearing what?'
                    'Or I quit.'
'What? What?'

(X) Sophie

>One last run, one and a last
>of what it's always taken, one and a last
>of anything to turn us straight.
>How'd that raucous disco ditty go
>I will survive/ I will survive?
>   If that's
>the way it sounded then that will be
>the hymn, the creed, the prayer.
>For little is so total scary as Kev
>the wannabe legit.
>   Unless it's
>Hi I'm Chrissie, Sophie right? You don't know Ray
>but Kim he might've told you, I'm his ex?
>He's into Dylan, Ray?
>   Oo-hooo, Kevin! If you
>can pick investments like you pick couriers
>we'll be in hock by morning tea.

(XI) Sophie, Kim: the proposal

So they were going straight?
Oh yes they were, they were and had to.
   'We have the money,' Kim got advised,
'or at least money that leads to money . . .'
and consultancies and partnerships (even,
when Sophie's imagination over-reached itself,
a merchant bank). 'We are going to be
so useful (and, even better, get paid for it)
nothing more will ever matter.'
   Surrounding them were nations
getting beyond the development stage,
and out there so many fabulous puzzles were waiting,
just waiting to be solved. And these two,
former barrister's groupie/ one-time
clothing store hotshot, were set to solve them:
Sophie Cross/Kim Lacy: middle persons.

She thought of 'Big Boy',
'Fido', 'Jumbo', 'Ding Dong' and half
a dozen other well placed Filipinos
with silly nicknames (and these
were merely starters) all itching to commence
joint-venture projects.
                    Who with?
Why take this Stubbs for one:
Toyota whiz-kid, sportsman manqué, the ideal
developer for the developing world:
ungrubbed by any dealing 'n' using.
                    And then
she thought of Kevin: who led onto The Jeweller/
Cap'n Midnight/Jungle Jim and
(almost worse than even barristers) all their
dreary cohort.
            'Sure, I've done a bit too ...'
Kim was telling her 'users but, can't stand 'em ...
well it's illegal and that is how it should be.
Yet look, one day we might be dealing with
another galaxy, and feeling great about it.
Until then guess what? Right now
there's just one world to live and work in.
Kevin and me and all the boys
we had no other choice, what other market
was available?'
          Trying to lull her
with quasi-cosmic claptrap,
Kim was speculatin' fine:
fine as he had back in those Shire days,
GoGo for his straight man.
      But Sophie, nothing like Go-mate,
was chafing. *You catch this hour?*
She wanted to demand *This minute, second?*
You better Kim because it's right now
and from right now it's time we started ...
time when she wanted *it* not merely legit
but legit and so much a bit, her bit.
       Well Sophie snapped: 'So I arrive to find
all rumours true: smoked, sniffed or swallowed

the only thing Kevin doesn't use he flogs,
what he doesn't flog gets hijacked;
when he's ripped off (it may be once
but in our game that means always more)
guess what? We're all ripped off!
Jungle Jim needs it stopped;
Cap'n Midnight wants it stopped;
and The Jeweller, well The Jeweller tells me
Clean him up Soph, clean him up
or clean him out' . . . Monitoring Lacy's nods
she moved in: 'And what of you?
How clean is Kim?'
                            'Scrubbed,' he vowed,
'from today scrubbed raw.'
    Hardly much of a promise,
a Lacy promise, yet it might hold her still;
they weren't to know yet: in a weak man
and a desperate woman mightn't there be
strength, such strength as no-one could suspect?
For you needn't be strong to give such a strength,
to find or make it in another. Kevin, once,
had shown Sophie that (shown her, though,
how you could overdose on anything).
    Ahh well, as Morgan always told her,
caveat narcoticor.
    After the paranoia of his raucous colleague
Kim seemed quieter. A hippy quiet?
If Sophie had known his state
as merely stoned-enough, why yes. Hardly, she hoped,
loser quiet: for the game was arriving at this:
he hardly dealt exactly now: he, you might guess,
seemed almost a businessman; he'd even said
he knew Craig Stubbs. Near straight with contacts then,
after this run it had to be Kim:
Kim or quits.
    'Can't' Sophie asked 'Kevin understand
how any single white girl backpacking it
is, at best, a pest? We need a courier
sure, but not some half-whacked one-time
teacher's aide. How long has she been yours?'

His? Lacy hedged:
well growing up in Sydney in The Shire,
they had mutual friends, sure,
he's known her sortov, once, before.
Now but? Recently?
                    'Up north ...' expanded Kim,
'but you must know the plot Soph ...
how into this caf comes someone, someone
who has to be an Aussie; but better
an Aussie who looks familiar?
And so she's asked *Yeah aren't you ...
aren't you ... that's right Chrissie,
who married my mate Frenchy, swingin'
Frenchy D, world's greatest Dylanfreak?
Well she is she's Heeheehee Chrissie?
Ray Donellan's ex?* and telling how
We're still friends but and how
Ray, he'd really love to see you and
Yes Ray has another little lady now?'
        Which was nice, so nice,
it got Kim's heart clicking out of neutral.
Well Soph, they liked each other, had been
together, over a week now.
                    Sophie winced:
'And what are you and Kevin grooming her
to carry? A tub of margarine?
Right now you got a grand?
Well pay her off. Chrissie, from today
is clamming. Promise her another thousand
later, and promise her if anyone is told,
anything can happen. Who to? Why not
sweet ex's little lady? Anyone she cares about
we'll nominate.'

(XII) Sophie

This she demanded of her memory,
what had been the start of *this*?

Telling herself she'd to accept even more
of *this* before she got out of *this*.
One last run then, the big cleanser
setting them straight, so very straight.
Which had been done before though:
those times when, just looking into Kevin's eyes
everything you wanted lay there:
your share of love, evil, their good times
and their big times: the full boil.
But now, poor crim, hubris aside, what else
could he give again? Holding the drug czar's hand
Sophie had played at nursie-moll too long;
and if he'd taught her anything
he'd taught her how to finish people.
It wasn't she required just the infection
lanced, but someone who could drain
its breeding ground.

(XIII) **Kim, Sophie, Johnee**

    'Why not,' Kim was proposing, 'Johnee Kwok?'
Johnee who'd been draining round these parts
for many years.
        There'd be more for Soph
to know of course but for starters *Kwok!*
had the slap of somebody being attended to,
a near-to-silent *Snap!* which
had to happen.
        Though,
with that bland kind of remaining polite
which goes on behind steel-rimmed glasses
Johnee has no more a killer's face
than one anonymous Kevin Joy.
            Whilst
in a small sparse room with only
his long low bed Kwok just lives
with Kwok.
      No-one has to like him:

they just have to hire this man who's worth it.
    Well go on call him, he'll arrive,
meet anyone you find special enough to
nominate . . . and take them anywhere.
    ('Sheeet . . .' thinks Kim aloud to Sophie,
'now where'd I first meet Kevin?
Through Jack the Barman? The Americans?
A few mug users I'm very sorry now I knew?'
    'Ahh no you're not,' thinks Sophie
to herself. 'Kimbo's sitting here at this resort
diversifying business interests. There's just one mug
abroad in his life now, and that, alas
is Kevin!)
        You aren't to call all this a hit,
or an assassination, or even a job-well-done.
Client services? Mmm if Johnee lets you.
Just trust him, that's all, you needn't see
your special one again: that certainly is all.
    ('Do you know . . .' Kim is asking Sophie,
after they've loaded Chrissie with the smack,
telling her she'll do fine, 'Do you know
when and where and what was my first deal?
Soph?' he shudders 'Sophie?'
For she is crying. 'Look . . .'
Kim had this plan: 'Look, if we're ever asked,
not that we will be, let's say Kevin runs
a bar somewhere. He may as well.')

(XIV) Kevin, Johnee

    'Well Johnee well, simply like the old days.'
    'Kevin yes except, now, change gets itself
about so much, these *are* the old days.
But tell us Kevin, tell us about your old days.'
    'Well Johnee, once,
once I'd this mighty vat of dope . . .
but every freak in town was simply
too smacked-out to move it. So me,

good Doctor Joy, I was doing house calls!
     And Johnee this was the old days too:
I learnt a bit, got to meet the world.
And so I said to Jim *Me 'n' blacks, I know
what it's like* (and I do I do) *Who says?*
asks Jim and so I tell him *Kevin says!*
Well what? he asks *What do you really
understand?* He's told *I know about you blacks:
Maoris, Abos, anything Pacific, everything Asian.*
Well got him there! Reckon he agrees!
Y' see Johnee, I'm on the outer,
just like you guys ... and that I learnt
from a dumb black cunt named Jungle Jim.'
     And now, if it's permitted (and Kevin shall)
Kwok will pretend to take him dining;
at least until it's understood
there's not much of a meal. Johnee but
he's nice about it, wanting Kevin
out of the car, just to get their legs stretched:
which is normal, which is strange, and which
makes everything *Just about it then, right?*
     And like a victim Kevin needs a piss
and needs a laugh, and needs to know
which is arriving first. If betting could've helped
he would've bet on both:
but time forbids it: time belongs with Johnee Kwok's
employers, whoever they are: some place,
back there, hours from their quarry: the victors.
     Who aren't the scary ones: for Johnee
is apologising and *that* is scary:
'So sorry Kevin.'
               'Oh don't pity me,'
comes the minor-grade bravado,
'I've enjoyed myself ... I could've been
a carpet salesman ...' It's just
'Wouldn't mind a reason, Johnee.'
     Sorry, no reason. And, if such a tiny *why?* remains
(though merely to compound all those final
and much bigger *why?*s)
well life's mysterious isn't it? And,

as *I am* turns swiftly to *I was*,
this respected importer, fun-times lover
and occasional low-level grass
(yes even at this end of his life
a drug czar might tell someone anything
and everything) this quite Mr Big-enough
(who, at times like even now admits
enjoying himself) yes this Kevin Joy is ordered
not to struggle, just to kneel,
so that he might help out Johnee,
his friend, and other friends this once
by going out just *Snap!* That's right
Like that!
          So Kevin agrees. He hurries, too.
The Joy Boys might be globalising,
Sophie and Kim even turn legit.

SMALL-TIMING:
THE ALIEN RETURNS TO MELBOURNE

After burying the blocks and sticks at Mum's
he got himself a flat with tolerable neighbours:
i.e. he never saw them, and no he wasn't paranoid,
and no it wasn't just The Man, but yes by now
something had grappled him: The Alien knew
he'd never do another run: if you were a genius
or mug, sure, importing was for you:
otherwise find what you could get wholesale here,
and deal. He knew that time and chance
were setting him for a three-way pile-up
unless he stepped aside. Okay he would.
                                            At Leo's
someone had naively asked:
'Don't say you *smuggled* this?'
                                                Well what else?
But *smuggled*? '. . . let's say they never found it.
Someone has to bring the stuff in: that shmuck
is me; The Man just hasn't looked yet . . .'
      Though next time on the fourth run, that nearly-
always-never-lucky fourth, The Man just would;
and virtue re-doubled, carrying zero, The Alien
was set to let him: already he'd rehearsed the lines:
Got my name on your computer? I'm honoured.
Strip? I'd love to. And bend over Mister Man?
I'm your guest or, if you'd rather, host.
Empty my bags? I know no greater pleasure.
Answer the following? Certainly. But why not let's
condense my replies into three short words:
Me? Drugs? Never!
      Back on the cabs now, and dealing,
one of his house calls (three honey-cured buddhas
once a fortnight, thank you very very much)
contained a sensible, if cut 'n' dried
girl student, who worked her weekends at
some crisis centre. And, he understood,

whatever this job was, like driving or dealing
someone had to do it. Wouldn't he like
to call all this 'democracy'? Yes, but
because his customer was from *over there*,
and because her dealer was from *over here*,
truly they were never meant to meet, or meeting
talk much.
      'Soon,' the student got to know,
'I'm cruising north again . . . the rice trail . . .'
(Which was?) 'For a few months most years up there,'
he vaguely pointed, 'I get myself an Asian lady
and cruise: she looks after me, I look after her . . .'
      How could he ever understand the ideology
churning through this student, how from here on
at this Brunswick weatherboard he wouldn't be required.
Didn't he live that kind of life he thought
the-world-that-really-mattered (like
the student) wanted to see him live:
cheap dope and generous with it? Providing no-one
was hurt, providing, when necessary, you did
what had to be done in private, providing
as always you stayed out of trouble, whatever you
wanted to do, shouldn't it be done?
      And who got harmed?
Not his lovely lady Porn, not by this bunny.
Didn't the student know what gave the rice trail
its bad name? Those who sent away for
teenage Filipinos, pimped-'em or whacked-'em
pow! into a coma or worse.
That wasn't his style, shouldn't be anyone's: press him,
as the student should've, he'd volunteer for hangman.
      Being summer he was fond of arriving, yet again,
at 4/9, and staying there. One midday, rising early,
he commenced a letter back to Porn.
'Up north I've this lady, Porn:
now which reads better: Dear Porn
or Dearest Porn?'
      'How about,' Leo volunteered, 'not-quite-
exactly-inexpensive Porn?'
      But at 4/9 being with friends

Any of you will keep would never be inflicted;
and *Porn!* okay you had to laugh at *Porn!*
    Leo had once considered showing porn,
and did (well this friend of his from Dandenong
had said it was): a parade of antiseptic pre-ops,
though more like visitors from outer space:
two tits with added dick: looked at once
why bother again: they showed realer, worse,
at The Fucfuc, which, whacky-doo, he'd seen.
    But try telling the student *that*,
try telling her very much at all, poor student;
though he had liked her as he liked people:
enough; and if he'd never received as much
liking in return ... blame The Man, he after all
was available.
               Always available, always on call.
    For Lacy had arrived in town.
Yes, with contact lenses, an attempted hair transplant,
Lacy: who'd still be certain to say
Heh, heh, heh get it down 'n' boogie Mister A!
for if anyone was sure to be picked
a man of The Man Lacy was. Could he
be getting nastier? Oh yes and had to be avoided.
    But that evening at a hotel rank,
Kim with his latest lady just opened up and entered.
Staring from the rear vision: 'Now where to, Mister A?'
he asked, and answered: 'A quiet somewhere
that's never known the meaning of deceit,
of running out on mates, in short:
Monomeath Avenue, this town at its most respectable,
though we're relying on what Sophie says and, well,
this lady's biased. Darling, meet Mister A, some time ago
he 'n' me did heaps together: not the main game,
more of a fun-packed curtain-raiser. Now I am who
I am and Mister A is driving us around ...'
How could they contact Mister A? And Lacy hummed.
P'haps the yellow pages under Y for yellow or,
being charitable, D for deadshits.
So how could, where would Mister A be seen?
'... we might need another drive:

you owe me something fuck, so why not that?'
    And, with these words as muttered base-line,
The Alien recalled the last ones he'd heard
from Lacy . . . *one good woman, man.*
Then we streamline, we rationalise, and we expand!
Which seemed to have happened, though nowadays
streamlining meant helping anyone who wished to use, use,
and getting paid for your devotion.
    So how to announce all of tonight later?
How to arrive at 4/9 and expect them to believe
Hey Leo, everyone, guess who I drove out to
Canterbury? One of our leading . . . one of this country's
biggest . . . one of Australia's most successful . . .
Though no matter how many adjectives got shuffled
he only knew such judgements as banal;
besides, for all the bong-filled bonhomie
(the Gregorian chants, reggae and multiple-choice sex)
Leo was a kinda skypilot still: and the naive,
always getting something important wrong,
he'd need protecting. There'd be another part
of the truth to tell: *Last night I drove*
someone from up north; like you he's an old friend;
you can't meet him sorry.
                Besides,
wouldn't the businessman Lacy was
rather attend to Cap'n Midnight, The Jeweller,
like minds who settled things, made living even easier,
so that Kim and this friend in the back seat
were set to do *what time?* because there'd be
what crime? because here was all you needed knowing:
sweet slime was on the rise:
with a few more people and then a few more
set to slip on something no-one was supposed to.
Unless you wished for that kind of joyous anarchy
sweeping in with trouble, be careful,
always listen to whatever babbled from Lacy
(or anyone so special to The Man).
    Oh The Horse, Kim confirmed, was much the same
and yes The Fucfuc; though they were getting in
some silent partners.

Businessmen, the non-bank knew,
Some bignoter Kim had met in a bar.
                              And this, The Alien decided,
is what Lacy wants me to know:
look out for The Horse's partners,
ditto The Fucfuc's: they're silent as the universe
or death.
         But already he knew that:
there'd been news, via Jack, from Porn:
how Big-Aussie-Money was facelifting the street:
much more was getting expected, sometimes it scared
Porn and her brother. Could this nice Aussie,
her man, him, help?
                My Dearest Porn he wrote,
look after yourself and of course your brother . . .
Then he wondered how to add the rest,
since slime was oh so on the rise;
not even our special kind of Melbourne summer
would ever parch out The Man's slime:
there or here someone's gonna get their neck broke
please not you my darling Porn.
                              But he thinks too much,
he thinks he'll be accosted by a bright girl journo
whose opening remark is: *You're a man*
whose finger's on the pulse: so tell us:
what's driving Melbourne? And yessum he will tell:
like every other town: s.m.a.c.k.,
getting around to The Jeweller (if that would help)
or Cap'n Midnight and what remained of the Joy Boys.
But instead of journos he has only friends
to educate, and 'Do you realise that . . .' he'll start,
and 'Yes we realise that . . .' they'll cry
before the question's finished.
      'Well *don't* you realise . . .' (one)
nut doctors were after him: them and/or The Man
were set to stop his smokin' material;
(two) you give the local ayatollahs
the next few years and every Aussie lady
would be stuck in purdah; (three)
something was happening in Niugini:

tell him what and why it was spelt that way;
(four) you give him an hour in court,
in any court, and people would have to listen.
  'But till then,' interrupted M 'shuddup and pass
the bong.'
    'We'll have,' Leo then informed,
'a dearest couple coming here again tomorrow:
Father Geoff Cattermole and his goodwife Bess.
So please, this once, no catalogue of
South-East Asian blow-jobs . . .'
  And this request got answered with a smile,
an *ahh!* a *hah!* and a bleating
'Sure Leo sure. I'll be a good boy . . .'
Another skypilot did he say?
And a Mrs Pilot? What possibly was easier?
Hadn't he got on well with all of Leo's friends:
e.g. that Sydney nut doctor?
      And Leo curled his beard
as, from scepticism to disbelief an *errrrr*
unravelled its journey; try thinking the best
but all that you recalled was purest bloodsport:
Benny being greeted with *not another shrink!*
To imagine some terrier cross-breed, yapping this dignified
great dane into a corner was hardly difficult
(For The Alien hides so little and always has).
  He wishes to cruise and to cruise is
cruising light. All his shirts seem to be Hawaiian, though,
when cooler, a flak jacket may be added.
(Since he needs glasses they'll be hornrims.)
His voice scrapes like a used wire brush;
his love affair is with the word *individual*;
when Leo tells him *we're all individuals*
he tries understanding Leo and M
as soul mates, wishing M was his soul mate
(if M enjoys him, which she does, he'll hardly know it).
He wants to project himself as 'mean' but merely,
only, makes money and saves it; with Mr Taxman in pursuit
he talks about Swiss non-bank accounts (years on
someone starts to believe him: it'll take this long
to peel back the parodies from the paranoia,

the paranoia from the parodies.)
Oh, and another infatuation is trouble; he has strong ideas
on trouble or, in his cases, how to avoid it.
But he'll avoid too hard:
this thin, sandy-haired loner heading for worse-than-
the-slammer, about to become that most injured of
the most innocent he's always thought he was.
  And it was starting now:
with Lacy just wanting him to listen, to understand
how much Lacy had changed.
       For anyone like The Alien,
who saved his mouth for after hours,
most listening was fine. Though once a night, at least,
your opinion was required. Take that public servant
returning from his retirement party, last December:
behind his Santa beard, which obviously he'd just
got around to growing, this man was plastered;
and urgent for answers: dealers and what this driver
really thought about them.
With a blunt integrity (soured by more than that night's
alcohol) he was the kind who four-wheel-drives
the Simpson Desert, or thinks about it.
Let him be tested.
     '*Hard* drug-dealing?'
(Carting a stash and making sales needn't turn
everyone into some death merchant.)
'It's the hardies who have the protection, Mister,
not the little chaps.'
      Mister wasn't hearing:
with 'Mother, dance with me!' he grappled his wife;
with 'David, don't!' he got shuddered aside.
She wasn't very happy.
       Neither was their driver.
Few terms goaded him like *drug-dealer*:
it had the know-all satisfaction of being-in-
on-a-secret, everyone knew drugs; how a lot used,
a few dealt. Had they the time, sobriety, interest,
he could have shown these passengers where
The Jeweller, Cap'n Midnight, Jungle Jim, Kevin Joy,
lived, worked, had lived, had worked;

and beyond all them his friend Kim . . .
who now from the back seat
was accounting his changes and how good lovin'
had heaps to do with them.
So where did that public servant live?
With enough gall they could stride, Mormon-like,
to his door:
'Your local dealers sir, just in the area!'
  A wonderful thought, but Lacy was talking,
repeating and asking:
'Remember Kevin, Mister A?' (Mister A sure had . . .)
Well Kevin wanted Kim for a corpse, but Kevin
was a born novice. 'Know what's required Mister A?
Care and protection. It's all I need, all
I pay for; and this evening, driver,
right to here that's what you've given.'
        And passenger,
an unspoken reply held itself, *tomorrow, given a night
off cabs, a night off even the chance of Lacy,
I'll tag along to Leo's latest party, meet the crew,
and look out for ladies who just might cruise.*
Which wasn't exactly now.
       With the kind of confidence
that wanted to know *Notice anything different?*
Kim answered himself. And sensing *I've changed*
as a touch dramatic, a touch un-Lacy,
he permitted *evolve*, for Kim had certainly
evolved. Just as the game had:
people were looking after things: a run now,
was never quite what a run had been
and Lacy asked: 'Did you know that?'
  The car stops, he leans over,
breath and words pouring like a lover's:
'The change? Sure you can keep the change.
Still small-timing are we Mister A?'
Kim though could forget and would.
'That's right, forget; and almost forgive.
Even though you owe me, fuck.'
  Little use pretending you could avoid
the unlucky fourth.
      Just ask for him at The Horse.

Part 10

Hannah
Margie } .... public servants
Jo

Keith .... former public servant, Margie's ex
Benny ....friend of Hannah's

'THE FIRST THING WE DO, KILL ALL THE ECONOMISTS'

(SCENE: CANBERRA IN LATE AUTUMN)

(I)
    When a household's as finite as ours thought Hannah,
couldn't we arrange at least one group shot?
To the left: herself, chubby but hardly fleshy;
to the right: Jo, fleshy though not quite chubby;
with, for their centrepiece, Margie: to someone, once,
The Madonna With The Long Neck.
And though there was such a neck, of course,
try picturing any stray Our Lady with
short ginger hair and this broadcast of freckles:
you weren't to deify anyone that fetching, forget a woman
that original.

(II)
    Keith certainly hadn't.
Margie was at work when,
wearing his trademark greasy parka, he hitched in from Sydney.
Though never appealing much to Hannah, that day
she tried not levelling her sights too much towards
one more square-jawed loser; besides,
at their age, few women (Margie the least of them)
would get besotted with men whose slow,
over-adult voices exceeded any powers
of mimicry (though countless times they'd
attempted 'doing' Keith). Now preferring dress-ups
(and you weren't to call it drag)
she'd half-prepared a comic turn for Jo:
cloth cap to an angle, chin slanting up,
an eyebrow cocked and, to top all:
Bit ov orright eh Guv'nor?
    Keith made to smile, Hannah tugged on her braces.
'A tiny something ... for my friends ...'

she tried explaining 'should've trod the boards . . .
you know . . .' sounding more like a question,
he didn't know. 'Yes the boards . . .' she echoed
to her audience, feeling that here, with the Valium Kid,
she was safe, which was at least a plus.
He might cry a bit but
what else could happen?

(III)
      'One always says,' Jo had told her friends,
'that one should take one's guys in stages . . .'
Given the absence of a better creed
this seemed to mirror Margie's.
He'd flummoxed her at first but,
during that grad-trainee induction some years back,
who hadn't noticed Keith:
arriving at seminars in cowboy boots,
quoting what doubtless were Italian Marxists,
but never calling anybody *man*
whilst 'Bourgeois?' he asked, killing off the stupid word
with 'Well I am if you are . . .'
      A refugee from Sydney's evangelical underbelly
(the sister taught kinder, the parents
Baptist and retired, his beard checking in at nineteen)
but more than 'left' enough and cynically proud,
Keith seemed ideal to get *taken in stages.*
His suburb was named. So what was it like?
'Fibro,' got replied.
      'I've had this boy since
high school,' Margie said 'we've broken up . . .'
      Whatever his family believed it seemed almost
your duty to go and get caught doing something;
and he would've, if only there had been
anything suitable and worth the catching.
'Sure I believe in God,' Keith wished he
could say, 'but I hate him.'
This, he knew, was the worst crime:
being guilty of nothing, innocent of the same,
and once the major-est finito stopped,
and the even more major-est infinito commenced,

nothing would save you less.
Art was once suggested and trying to catalogue what art
had bloomed out of the shrivelled bush of faith
that might have been his, Keith reached George Beverley Shea.
Okay, to have been an LDS was doubtless worse;
he had no greater comfort: not as bad as the Mormons!
    Hearing Margie boo-hooing like Blondie
over a new hat, Keith told her he felt as useful as that
thin, cheery, white-collar family man: Dagwood,
another Baptist!
        Taken in stages? Yes well yes,
except that Margie chose an extra stage:
she left him.

(IV)   So what was passing itself as fate
had arranged Hannah's flex
just to make her flat-mate's ex
feel comfy enough.
        'Then we haven't heard the last
of the trickle-down effect?' she asked.
    It didn't seem so and Keith's time,
political economy's finest hour was, as he told it
exactly 'Upper than up . . .'
        'Then if I'm a martyr to fellas you're one too . . . ?'
    Keith shrugged:
'Someone else's romance with the self-interest ideal?'
and smiling a bit at her he left.

(V)   The man had been brilliant! No verdict seemed
more damning for between his soft-drug benders
and those outer circles of ministerial advice
Keith had mislaid Keith.
Someone might have herded him into
the next growth areas: consultancy, branch-stacking,
but sheer getting-by-with-people
precluded that. 'I'll never work again . . .'
he wanted to confess, but feared being challenged.
Somewhere the latest model MBAs

were getting launched and though 'the alternative'
hardly equated with him,
Keith commenced his next career:
hitching up and down the East Coast.

(VI)
  Given an hour and Jo was home,
home to Hannah complaining how
'The Economist was round this afternoon.'
  'You mean,' Jo who always qualified, qualified,
'The Political Economist', not knowing that the joke
had ceased over a year before. There wasn't much
to say to Hannah, and this seemed it; this and
'Were we at home?' near ignoring her
behind a *Cosmopolitan*: 'One-o-one things
to love in a man mmmmm let's see . . .'
The magazine, incongruous it could be felt
in an acting Nine '. . . brings out the receptionist in me . . .'
(More than you'd ever know, thought Hannah.)
'. . . *I have a Gumby cat,
her name is Jennyannydots* . . . so when's he coming back?'
Knowing this didn't need a reply
Jo had to continue with something:
'There'll be another big return,
surely but this weekend that's it, it *has* to be.'

(VII)
  Any weekend, Hannah thought, *that's it for Canberra,
this girl has to get to Sydney* . . . Where she'd eat
with Benny, her friend/carer/confidant
who'd escort her to the Star 'n' Garter's
old and young queen sing-along,
with The Silly Man, The Goonie Bird and her Benny,
very last of the boy sopranos, wanting a girl
just like the girl that married dear old dad,
still calling Or-strayl-ya home.
When *who else?* cared for Hannah
don't even mention fag-hagging:
*Look, if it weren't for something (I've forgotten what,
God presumably) I'd be a nun* . . . and home

they'd taxi, their voices' mingled rasp
advising creation: *So if y' wanna fuck y'self/
take a candle off the shelf/ship ahoy! Sailor boy!*

(VIII)
      Should've lived on her own, but when
she joined The Board it seemed like
flatmates or not much else. Could choose a commune,
but The Board would hardly approve of communes.
And set you up to be busted, communes did,
though early next morning someone friendly
(she usually worked at The Board)
arrived to clear your mess, post your bail.
Two hundred dollar fine but since you're a first offender,
no conviction posted, Miss Little.
Hannah, besides, was hardly commune partial:
you over-did only what you felt
needed over-doing, and she could tank-up
on requisite bohemiana at any Sunday craft mart.
Wasn't it enough merely to predict the crabs,
the blocked dunnies, those preposterous
imitation Neil Youngs who used to infect
only uni cafs but now, just like economists,
had spread throughout the planet?
                                      Economists!
Wouldn't it be better if you could only dream of them?
Sometimes it felt that all Canberra throbbed
with the group migraine of their collective indignity:
that theories should be sullied so, by humans
not perfect enough to want to let them work;
and shameless in such ignorance.
You don't believe in what we're letting you believe!
the economists wailed at Hannah, and
I only believe the earth deserves much better!
another intelligent young woman snapped in return.
She felt, sometimes, as if this god had decreed:
*There must be work for all these economists,
okay, let's create The Economy!* that and the sheer inevitable
of theories turning nostrums turning fad . . .

(IX)
    ... or men like Keith: one year second division bound,
the next: just another lumberjack-shirted
leftist droob; who arrives to find Canberra's
a music hall with moi, Hannah,
set to barnstorm him with Gilbert The Filbert
or Burlington Bertie; for if she's probably heartless
as any Baptist congregation, there's times
this girl's just gotta let down the hair.
    Though there were ways to pacify him
you'd never cheer up Keith:
you might run your tongue and lips over
his stubble, strip off the parka and the shirt,
look at the rib cage then listen to
the heart thump, but know that soon
you'd be seduced to hear the reprise
of all his other Political Economy reprises.
Oh taa but no taa.
When you're fattish, near thirty, haven't had
a guy in years, you still can be attached
to a single word, and that word's not *seduction*,
it's *dignity*.

(X)
    One day there'd be no more Keith or rather
those interested would catch these rumours:
the sessional work at some regional TAFE,
the eventual girlfriend with her bonsai cactus,
and how, each seven p.m., their brown rice
alternated with their lentils; good reasons all
to care and howl about his future, which she
didn't and wouldn't since even better reasons
informed her: there's this Keith you meet,
another that you think about and you'd be
hypocritical, Hannah, missing either.

(XI)
    Better that she entertain the friends.
    'Ready for the tang?' she'd ask them,
'ready for the vinegar? C'mon and laugh,

clownesses (we three destined for greater things)
laugh!' And her mode quick-changed
into the husky-intimate:
'Ladies, not neurotic enough?
How long, madame, since *you* were
meaningfully depressed? When *I* really
need a problem I choose . . . men!
Have I lived this long without you, fellas?
Oh how I miss your mess, inconsideration
and power! But know what I say?' and Hannah
screeched into her macro-pleb:
'Try as I may I've never 'ad
a decent chin-wag wiv me vibrata!'
    'I hardly can with a fella,' Jo's candour
interrupted.
        But the spruik was concluding
on its owner's terms and Hannah leapt
upon a chair and, like some Irish auctioneer,
poked the air:
'Get y'selves a man m' gels, today!'
                Life like this
should be a musical, Jo thought,
and Hannah a kind of ingénue's best friend,
her performances weren't unforgettable,
just unforgivable. Did men perform amongst
themselves like this? Doubtless most times no,
and no most women either. Do mates so overload
on mates that the only mate response was
to recycle *fair go* . . . *steady on* . . . *barley Charley*
and all those other clichés of restraint
that got the old man through the depression,
you name which war, his mum and missus?
    Keith would know, no he probably wouldn't.
For Keith was feminist.
            'A feminist man,'
Hannah groaned, 'is kosher pork.' For that hour
The Economist was out, he became The Sister.

(XII)
      With all the walk and whisper and look of living
why didn't they ask her, she'd write the book:
Farce and Melodrama: How to Play These Allied Manias.
For someone *that* advanced in arm-chancing
Hannah needed to believe in its limits and
wanted these limits known.

(XIII)
                          An example:
she had been a grad clerk in Recruitment
and the lift was carrying ten that morning
with slurring, lop-sided John, a registry c.a. four,
setting up Debbie or Kelly,
this kid with a cold sore:
'Love that cold sore, sweetheart.'
John stared into her face, down at her tits
and up again; his prelude was over.
'Say don't he love you anymore, eh darling,
isn't he speaking now?'
      Time, place and target were perfect
weren't they? The girl could only stay mute
whilst Hannah forced herself, once more,
to understand how this was a world
of Johns, of there-there imperfection.
But 'Just shuddup!' a man's voice (were it
Hannah!) was demanding 'why don't you
just shuddup?!' till with that crazed,
near-joyful men's anarchy
(she could admire if it didn't terrify)
here came his over-reaching:
'You're the only spastic I've ever felt like hitting!'
Never had time seemed so extended:
wars were piecemeal, cities founded on
so much less. Through Hannah's mind
all thoughts ran express: *This one's
the noble knight, that one's the evil dwarf:
oh it's brilliant oh it's hideous oh it's
noble and pathetic and it's too early for mythmaking.
Please, this morning, let's just play bureaucrats,*

please? The door opened at Recruitment.
She'd been off blokes for a while and
was enjoying it. No wonder.

(XIV)
    Oh men. Men. Menmenmen! But haven't we all
our brace of routines? When she'd reached Canberra
Hannah had *kick-start me* fine-tuned;
and Margie, near-sensing that her friend
understood how few truths succeed like
slapstick truths, would roll up their morning paper,
demanding 'So no-one looks less like Carly Simon?
No-one looks less like Ma Kettle!' and whack the *SMH*
onto their kitchen bench. 'You're you!'
    Okay then, she being Hannah,
would set herself for further male trouble
and *Ooh-la-la crème de la crème bon soir*
she, with her Two B Honours French, returned
to play that sucker-when-I-want-to-be
for any Jean-Paul straying through the ACT;
providing he wasn't an economist.
How could you talk to *them*
who'd said it all? (And their it was shit.)
Life, though, had undoubted grandeurs,
for economists. Didn't a grateful public
pay you to intone *trimming the fat*?
And Hannah's voice would plunge to that
testy, authoritative contralto
she didn't do badly. One day, of course,
there'd be no public servants, just economists,
but till then she'd her two careers:
at The Board of course and the other?
Well think of this near-to-unknown breakwater
set in the path of the New Right high tide.
So she imagined that? A woman had to do something.

(XV)
    Jo was asking:
'Can you imagine Margie trying to really tell
it's over? That last time he must've

got *a* hint, though men like him are made
to miss *the* hint,
'*I* always say.' (Jo whose only lack
was charity.)
            'As Friday night descends on Canberra . . .'
Hannah was moving into travelogue mode and,
to book in next weekend, Sydney was phoned.
    Sorry, came the soft cheeky sound of the homeminder,
Benny was o.s., well sudden was the word:
someone having got their friend a conference gig
he'd be away a month. '. . . and you're?
. . . oh Hannah! . . . yes, certainly, I've heard of *you*!'

(XVI)
    She wanted to get into bed and not think about
very much at all; but Margie came home,
Keith phoned, and Margie went out,
returning to tell them how he said he understood
and that he'd stay with friends in Queanbeyan;
for a reward she lent him her car.
    Well we're all single now, Hannah wished
to say; and how she loathed the man
and wasn't he fascinating. Great:
no more of this economist, he'd just wander away.
    And this is what she'd do:
to compensate for Benny's absence,
start to bushwalk; to celebrate Keith's departure,
continue tomorrow what jogging
she had done before.
            But even early Saturday
(the week at its most benign) hoons,
no let's really say it, *men* could emerge
from the mist, set to thump you, or worse.
Dumb hoons: Hannah had her whistle and
some neat lead piping.

Part 11

Carrie	NURSE
Adrian 'Mr Magic' Cross	FOOTBALLER, HER LOVER
Shane Price	FOOTBALLER
'Old Scotch' 'The Facilitator'	PARTYGIVERS
Amanda	MADAM
Bernie	PIMP
Gary	COP
Shannon	CALL GIRL
'Starfuck' Neil	CLIENTS
Wal	Carrie's friend
Benny	psychologist, Wal's friend
Barb Leo M	Benny's friends
Hannah	Benny and Wal's friend
Mason	her boyfriend

NIGHT JASMINE

Adrian!
              Here came Carrie in that short, pleated skirt
(she wore because, crazy and ripe with lots of fruit and flowers
it made you good to look at);
here came Carrie swinging up towards the host's house;
where, looking down, Adrian was smirking.
      She could hold a decent self-respect
and controlled that urge to cliché up
Oh fuck! Wouldn't you know it!
But teasing her to do exactly that,
here in the hills, among the banana farms,
on the verandah, lounging over like the place was his,
Adrian seemed set to announce *Yep Carrie*
this is the return of Mr Magic!
      Some man behind him, seeing them react,
cried 'Hey! Hey there Ades!
Do you two know each other?'
                              'Oh we do,'
the boss-of-the-moment smiled, still leaning over.
     'We certainly do,' Carrie tried not sighing;
Carrie in that skirt to love because
as she might've told herself months earlier
each time she tried it on *No matter the envy,*
the excitement that it causes, this skirt is great,
it's lucky: and tonight I needn't lift or
lower it for any man.
                 Yet up north
what could any nurse in transit do when,
after hunting all that money-and-men, the energy
just left you? Head further north for more?
Or move a little to the south,
and then recover?
      So in a place with a name like
'Pelican Waters', a unit was rented:
down along The Corso opposite the breakwater.
One long dull summer at the hospital,

that'd do Carrie!
               Then,
'You're somebody I met once back home right?'
In the health foods a woman
(a friend of a cousin? a cousin of a friend?)
recognised her: 'Melbourne wasn't it?
You must be new here, sorry but I'm stoned.'
She was no snob but in the hills was
where they lived: the woman and her husband.
'I'm in community radio, facilitating . . . doesn't that
sound silly? He helps people out: building domes
'n' stuff.' Some friends were staying over
this weekend and 'I'm no elitist but
if you haven't much to do . . . this town is
hardly made for meeting anyone but us.'
   Now there she was behind Adrian and
her husband: waving, apparently still stoned.
She put her arms around her man, hugged
and smiled.
           Why couldn't Carrie love like her,
just love a half/quarter/eighth of that?
But then why should answers arrive
tonight? It was late spring in a place that
always believes it was late spring,
and this evening was meant to dazzle like her skirt.
I love it! Nothing more need matter!
you and everyone were meant to cry.
   As the facilitator almost did:
'Carrie, that skirt must be you, for you look great!
But gee you hardly know us. Well this is us
and our friend Adrian. Come into the kitchen
and share our drug of choice, unless you have
your own.'
            If this wasn't that Gold Coast style of
get-to-know-us Carrie knew
who needed that?
               'You prick,' she smiled
at Adrian. 'We never were supposed to meet
like this. So what *is* this? Your pre-pre-season
Mr Magic?'

If Carrie cringed at this name
some journo gave him, and all Victorians used,
she sure enjoyed operating with it.
 'Mr Magic?' she'd throw at a fella.
'Oh yeah I know Mr Magic. Sure they've slapped
his face on products, maybe yours,
and the products sell. But I know him
better than that, better than you do.'
 Now Adrian was telling her
'We made the finals, just. Just wasn't
good enough.'
  As if she cared!
Even as a girl she never liked his team.
And he knew it.
  'Oh yes,' the host remembered,
'We've another couple coming: lawyers.
Just in case you two want to sue us.'
 'Couples?' Adrian rebounded. He smiled at Carrie:
'The women are on hold.'
  'Gee taa.'
 'Briefly but. I'm up here with a mate.'
His mate came back from jogging:
 'Always in training!' Adrian crowed,
like on their club's behalf. 'That's our Shane.
Although he won't pass up the weed
on holidays.'
  A private school lair
('Yes there's a few left') making his nickname
on and off the field, was Adrian obnoxious?
No more that he was charming.
 Just prior to dinner Carrie asked this Shane
how many games he'd played.
  'Around one fifty.'
 How come she'd never heard of him?
Mere ignorance?
  'Hardly Carrie. If I didn't play
I couldn't name you ten.'
  Lean and serious
Shane Price was someone else's type;
and even if she had the inclination

(which Carrie didn't) wasn't that the why
she'd left the Gold Coast? All men,
for a while, must be someone else's.
For just so long you trusted your stupidity
to trump that of stupider men. Then, of course,
it bored you.
                Adrian was telling her:
'And if you fear another footy loudmouth,
don't. This is what Shane-baby does:
sure he smokes 'n' drinks,
but he teaches, he turns up to training, he plays his
faultless non-show-pony game; pats kids on the head
and signs his name. Hardly headlines at the discos
do you Pricey? This Mr One-for-one
has a steady lady who really trusts him.
Right Shane?'
                If Adrian was envious, laying it on,
Carrie wanted it laid off, right off.
But ragging his mate soon tired him
and he announced how, back south, all dues
were set to be repaid.
                'Come the new year
we cut back on this stuff,'
(he waved towards the wine and mull)
'until, of its own accord, it just
drops off . . . then we turn heroes again!
Now though, not on a bread-wrapper,
nor even a bubble gum card,
we stand total flesh before you!'
    Carrie baulked: 'Oh Adrian!
Give us, give the world, a break!'
    It didn't move him: 'No, no really,
the further north we go the less
we're known. Which suits Shane and me.
We flew to Sydney and drove:
turning into investors checking over properties.'
      'He's speaking for himself,'
Shane said, 'I'm here just to meander . . .'
      'Meander' eh? Carrie enjoyed and understood
'meander'. A few months back,

locuming round the Gold Coast
(tucking in the geriatrics, only to know
they were all simply peeling away)
Carrie had to make a second life:
many nights meandering into the better bars
she heard herself breathe out
*Mmm sounds good enough . . . what else have you
in mind?*
  Oh being a nursing sister
was fun! You could advise the latest
condescending white-shoed hoon:
'I've just completed a twelve-hour shift.
At the award rate. During all this
somebody died.'
   And no poor hoon
would ever get more apologetic.
 'I can aim at so many sensibilities,'
Carrie knew and Carrie glowed,
'hitting that one and that one and that one!'
 Oh you could call all this amoral,
but only because, these days, what abroad
was moral?
  Soon though she knew
*I'll have something quite heroic to perform.
And I don't mean just lying back
letting the fella-world do anything.*
 Sometimes, after a decent deal,
someone from interstate might look for
company. Then Carrie would be company.
And you coped with such a roll-of-events:
the next day would be just that:
the next day.
   'From Melbourne eh?
So big fella who do we follow?
. . . well even you must've heard of Adrian
'Mr Magic' Cross. I'd an affair with Adrian:
right in the middle of this party we just left,
went on a holiday to Lorne and . . .
we'll leave it there at *and* . . . Magic?
Oh magic and stupidity. I'll only say that Carrie,

she's me, Carrie Larson, learnt things.
And not merely footy stars are so, so human
(you can almost hear them aching *Gee,
wish I could grow up!*).'
                    Later,
for a Carrie kind of fun, she might round on
her company: 'But please don't use
that phrase "the little boy within"
even as a joke.'
                    Much later she might tell him
'First off I knew his sister, Adrian's sister,
Sophie . . .' (who possessed, or thought she did,
the training manual for those with a certain power
and always in need of more:
requiring that witchcraft to let you say
*Look over there at that bitch that
dickhead who is she is he when and
how did they waltz in I want them out!*
For Sophie's rate was hardly the award).
          To tell these men all-that was only a diversion
though: soon enough Carrie knew she'd hear
'Gee small ladies always do it best!' And
'Oh Carrie, I'm not normally a tit man
but yours are turning me into a baby,
a giant baby that just wants love.'
         She's long since quit being too self-conscious
about *them* but why couldn't men say
something about her fine fair hair:
she was so proud of that!
         Some nights the phrases might turn stranger.
Someone once was wanting her to say, say
after him, 'I am a beautiful person I am
a beautiful person . . .' which Carrie did;
and though he hadn't love exactly,
this latest man from Melbourne wanted
to send her something (it seems they all did)
and, if unambiguous, money was crass,
the hour for that was either too early
or too late.
               There'd be little like 'rough treatment',

locuming round the Gold Coast
(tucking in the geriatrics, only to know
they were all simply peeling away)
Carrie had to make a second life:
many nights meandering into the better bars
she heard herself breathe out
*Mmm sounds good enough . . . what else have you
in mind?*
       Oh being a nursing sister
was fun! You could advise the latest
condescending white-shoed hoon:
'I've just completed a twelve-hour shift.
At the award rate. During all this
somebody died.'
       And no poor hoon
would ever get more apologetic.
   'I can aim at so many sensibilities,'
Carrie knew and Carrie glowed,
'hitting that one and that one and that one!'
      Oh you could call all this amoral,
but only because, these days, what abroad
was moral?
       Soon though she knew
*I'll have something quite heroic to perform.
And I don't mean just lying back
letting the fella-world do anything.*
      Sometimes, after a decent deal,
someone from interstate might look for
company. Then Carrie would be company.
And you coped with such a roll-of-events:
the next day would be just that:
the next day.
        'From Melbourne eh?
So big fella who do we follow?
. . . well even you must've heard of Adrian
'Mr Magic' Cross. I'd an affair with Adrian:
right in the middle of this party we just left,
went on a holiday to Lorne and . . .
we'll leave it there at *and . . .* Magic?
Oh magic and stupidity. I'll only say that Carrie,

she's me, Carrie Larson, learnt things.
And not merely footy stars are so, so human
(you can almost hear them aching *Gee,
wish I could grow up!*).'
      Later,
for a Carrie kind of fun, she might round on
her company: 'But please don't use
that phrase "the little boy within"
even as a joke.'
      Much later she might tell him
'First off I knew his sister, Adrian's sister,
Sophie …' (who possessed, or thought she did,
the training manual for those with a certain power
and always in need of more:
requiring that witchcraft to let you say
*Look over there at that bitch that
dickhead who is she is he when and
how did they waltz in I want them out!*
For Sophie's rate was hardly the award).
   To tell these men all-that was only a diversion
though: soon enough Carrie knew she'd hear
'Gee small ladies always do it best!' And
'Oh Carrie, I'm not normally a tit man
but yours are turning me into a baby,
a giant baby that just wants love.'
    She's long since quit being too self-conscious
about *them* but why couldn't men say
something about her fine fair hair:
she was so proud of that!
    Some nights the phrases might turn stranger.
Someone once was wanting her to say, say
after him, 'I am a beautiful person I am
a beautiful person …' which Carrie did;
and though he hadn't love exactly,
this latest man from Melbourne wanted
to send her something (it seems they all did)
and, if unambiguous, money was crass,
the hour for that was either too early
or too late.
     There'd be little like 'rough treatment',

nothing like Adrian's little big boy stupidities,
and though it all was games games games
(nothing was ever sent from Melbourne)
she never felt like spoiling games.

  Yet, after a game, one or both must leave.
Adrian would know that, even though he wouldn't know
the Carrie details: Georgie Chan the sweetie Asian doctor
who saw her through the torch singer phase,
or those half a dozen Melbourne men she met
those months she was the short dress gal
testing out Surfers and environs (though Mr Magic
they knew you!).
      Who cared about the theory?
Whenever it came to men and their chaos
all was practice for Carrie.
She lived for such times and 'Why bother?'
such times demanded.
        Then she'd think of that
half-generation of women before her own:
their voices rasped-to-useless from scotch
to tobacco or volleying far too many put-downs.
For which of them could ever sort out Mr Magic
and Sister Larson, let alone the past
few million years of men 'n' women claptrap?

  Oh you tried of course, like tonight
here at this table set for seven.

  'What brings you to nurse the Northern Rivers?'
the man from legal aid asked, he of the happily-
henna'd-fellow-lawyer lover.
        Men? The Gold Coast?
Carrie never had too much of an answer.

  Besides, the host was set to give a host speech:
'Being a scotch old boy I've never been
that much on the back foot. Still,
we have had our share of derroes and here
are two: Ades 'n' me . . .'

  How long was it since we've seen each other,
Carrie wondered, three years getting on to four?
God how I was stumbling then! But then even in this skirt
I stumble. They may not know it but

I can be so clumsy. Always have been.
    And if you went to such a school
or such a school (and during this time
you gathered how things worked,
how even if you didn't wish much stake
in proceedings they still could work for you)
it was just as easy to tell your men
'Oh Dad's a barrister.'
                        And some were even impressed.
    (Yes a barrister: and how he enjoyed making
all his Carrie-gags: 'She'll just end up a nurse,
you know. The halt and lame will love her.'
And who visiting Surfers wanted to know *that*?)
    Yet if hers had been a man's world
and ridiculous with it, she loved the performance
it gave her and allowed her.
Beneath the show something might exist;
though Carrie doubted that.
                        She doubted lots. Once,
hearing some Women's Studies postgraduate,
everything turned Minnie Mouse and the cartoon began:
after a daughter or two had finished the De Beauvoir/
the Friedan/the Greer, it lay about the kitchen till,
girding herself for all the fuss, Mum would
take-a-peek; next minute she'd
clamber into overalls, choof over to her CR group,
snap at the men-brigade *Get it y'self!*
    Well that was all folks, the cartoon was over.
Try telling the above to Larson QC,
charmer, old boy schemer, crusader for
the latest six-figure-per-annum underdog:
try telling his ex, girlfriends and certainly
his daughter.
                 It was time to distil this for the table:
to inform the party: 'You see, if Adrian's father
is an old money company counsel,
mine's more gritty, private school but gritty:
more often though just a two-bob sleaze.
Well Adrian was running away from his background,
I was hurtling from mine. And then

for a fortnight we collided.'
    We thought Carrie was poised to admit
let's break ourselves a few of the old rules,
make ourselves a few more of the new
and then demolish them as well.
                                The lawyer girlfriend
of the legal aid coordinator hadn't got it.
'What' she asked, 'you two were together?
Once?' And, whilst the woman dug in deeper:
'I didn't mean . . . I mean . . . well yes I did,
you haven't did you, you didn't have you?'
everybody moaned and, better, laughed
until 'Right right I get it
weeooooee I get it!'
    Now hadn't they been indulging!
('But these,' it was Shane, Shane the serious,
'these sure are indulgent times . . .')
With 'Don't Throw Stones'/ 'The Boys Light Up'/
'Business As Usual'/ 'Diamantina Cocktail',
Hunter reds and Mullumbimby heads, say,
who rostered this night as dinky-di
all-star Aussie?
                  Why their host,
the stockbroker's ex-hippy son of course.
So Carrie, knowing his worlds (yet not exactly
of them) asked about this place, how many rooms
it had. And, before dessert, she was taken touring:
two bath, six bed
(one doubling as study, one more as disused
dark room) kitchen, separate dining, separate lounge,
and, presenting themselves to the district,
their verandah.
    Adrian was back on the verandah,
proffering how, if this house
tucked in the hills here with the bananas
was just a mite too cute he could live here
one day, couldn't Carrie?
                      Oh yes,
that same way I might have a baby:
not with you, baby.

      Even so
these were the dreams of an everyday subscriber
to *Vogue Living*: the lattices, the caneware,
the off-white matching slacks and blouses,
the civilised dope 'n' drinking patterns.
  And the jasmine, this night jasmine:
there must've been plantations of the stuff:
you just went onto the verandah for a drenching
telling yourself *Wow! Glad I'm not allergic to that!*
She mentioned his sisters,
Sophie to be specific, that lawyer one,
the one she knew through friends:
censorious, an exploiter, everything Carrie never wished
to be. You could imagine Sophie
glancing at the skirt, mouthing something smug
and flouncing off.
      '(Oh the things you thought
people might say! Sometimes your brain just sent you
all-over-the-place!)
    Sophie was merchant banking. Asia mainly,
and Adrian ticked over half a dozen
new emerging economic forces. It went,
he told, this way: 'You give a certain
team of nations a name . . .'
        'Like Mr Magic?'
  'Right,' he had to agree, 'and then step back
to see the spin of things. Some people call that
economics . . .' But Soph?
Oh well there were fellas, there always was
with her.
    'Ahh yeah . . .' and, coming back from
all-over-the-place, Carrie half re-engaged herself,
'We all know Sophie.'
       But *All-over-the-place!*
That's what Adrian, dope and night jasmine
did for her. And yes, one day soon enough,
she might get herself a baby, easier than she'd
get a house like this; though not of course
by Adrian: even their particular portion of history
had limits.

       Men were to be
where she wanted men and here in his Joe Coolery
– what Tom Foolery! – was Adrian, still elaborating
on Adrian to the facilitator hostess,
to the henna'd lawyer (for if a man
talks about himself, doubtless some woman's
asked him to).
       By now the offsider, Shane,
who was nice but hardly Adrian,
had been delivered a migraine and was
absent.
         And if his very doggedness
had made her flirt too much at dinner
I know my limits Carrie should've told him.
*I trust these limits. Trust yours, Shane, and
lighten up boy, lighten up. I'm just flirtatious:
Ooo la ma'am I've been taking gentlemen
for turns in the garden since I was five!*
       She'd hardly been debutante-fodder,
was always known to come-in-from-the-side.
But . . . and now she imagined all these old girls
gaggin on *But . . . as a nurse?!*
Then, being them, they might calm
a touch *Ahh well, that makes it easier
to finish with a doctor . . .*
               Mmm yes a doctor:
once, heading midnight at Georgie Chan the registrar's
apartment, Carrie heard this wonderful sad song:
'You've Got Me Crying Again'. And then another
'These Foolish Things'.
            With little for her
better than the bittersweet, she should've been
a torch singer. She was hardly Miss Barracoota
at The Oaks: cheesing 'n' pouting for fun and
the women's pages under her wide white hat.
       Flirtatious? Ooh la and this much more
You want Adrian again don't you?
Knowing of course one day she'd be dumped again.
That was her, that was men, that was her
and men and that was decidedly Adrian.

  She made one thing certain though
I'm old enough to enjoy myself . . .
I only shot off the rails once,
after my sweetie Doctor Georgie returned home
to Penang and, yes, got me crying,
I overdid the tabbies as only a nurse
can overdo and finished up in cas.
  Attending a shrink came next:
Carrie, arriving straight from work
still dressed for the wards, would sit with
a dozen plus post-adolescents mad as she was,
talking about themselves or not.
  'I wasn't the dreariest,'
she would answer those who asked its worth.
'Sister Larson got her chuckles,
and gave them something to go on with.'
  Of course, much like tonight, you'd never mention
too much of the really wild stuff,
though she was almost set to ask,
You are down on this guy, right?
But looking up at him, right?
Right into his eyes, right?
Smiling as much as you can you
are in control and he is cra-zee. Well,
how should you really feel?
  Instead she hinted to the table
'Wouldn't it be great to get yourself
a fantasy, then ride it and ride it.'
  So 'Gunrunning' somebody said,
someone else 'Antarctica' and a third
had to ask 'Evangelism?'
    'When you do it,'
the lawyer-girlfriend offered,
'You'll all know you've done it.
Bet it involves sex, mine invariably have.
Once this lecturer of moi took moi
for a week away and well he took moi
and he took moi. Whenever you hear the words
Dunk Island think of moi. She's done worse times.'
  'Worse times,' the facilitator echoed.

'Three a.m. it's me again wouldn't you know
Old Scotch has put on "Silk Degrees". He always
puts on "Silk Degrees".' Daffy but kind
she asked 'Now where's your friend?'
        'Who? Oh him!'
(Carrie never thought of Adrian
like that). Gone to bed perhaps?
        You're too stoned,
she got told, and probably too drunk
to drive. Why not stay in their
big big silly house; they'd spare beds,
free toothpaste, towels, spare clothes and
she could shower.
                        Old Scotch yawned.
He had one enormous day ahead
of pure and simple bugger-all.
        He was a 'type'. Carrie was sick
of 'types': professionals turned hippy enough
turned semi-tradesmen; and sweetie Asian doctors;
and businessmen you wished you'd never met
even in the better Gold Coast bistros
(even if you couldn't stop remembering the sigh of
'Christ Carrie I'll never forget your tits!'):
and nursing sisters whoring about Surfers confessing
'Why do I like fucking you? Because it works!';
and nursing sisters recovering some self-control
slightly further south; and all those Mr Magics
she never loved, sometimes imagined, often
anticipated, but always remembered.
        She went to bed. Lay there
wanting to join in little more than this
(since, for the hour, it seemed everything):
the easy warmth, the easier cool:
knowing that at the base of these hills
surf never ceased arriving, just like the light
from all the stars; and the wind moving branches
of night jasmine, moving its hyper-scent
into her room, into all the rooms;
moving her *Fuck it fuck it fuck it*
to Adrian Cross.

Now who wouldn't be jiggered sodden
with this idea: how she'd arrive
wearing only what she wore
on nights like these: one damn nice body.
    (And hadn't much of the party
paired off already: only last month,
the lawyers had been too pleased to tell/
or the hosts: 'We've been at it for years!')
    Carrie was going to arrive with
just her body and feign
I couldn't sleep, the night jasmine
and feign and feign.
    Before she knew she was standing
she was standing, thinking
Better make it to the right room
knowing she couldn't apologise
*Gee pardon gee, I haven't arrived
for a threesome!*
            No need to worry:
Carrie sensed the room, sensed
and knew he wore as many clothes
as she did; knew he'd ask *So,
what took us this long, Carrie?*
    Near-asleep or not
no doubt he'd been primed for her
since dinner (since the past three years!)
    'Adrian. The night jasmine.
You smell it? I couldn't sleep.'
                    'Yeah?'
    Which all was going to be,
if Carrie wanted it, an adventure.
*Okay last time was silly . . . try it again? . . .
Why not?*
        No foolish things, no,
not even night jasmine, reminded her of him,
yet.

Making the world Revolve (i)

Carrie, Adrian

    When Carrie followed Adrian to Melbourne
her friends were aghast: 'She's not with him again?'
    Then one day, knowing it wouldn't last another half an hour,
she called him 'You wet fuck!' Which was stupid.
    Well he slapped her. Which was stupider.
And he knew it (apologies cascaded from Mr Magic)

knew he was losing his magic.
    Not that she'd tell Melbourne.
Footballers' sex lives? Nothing could be stupider.
Weren't they supposed to perform again and again and again?
    'But it's not the sex,' Carrie explained, 'it's our relationship, stupid.'
    So who was moving out? Adrian was. He had half an hour

and equivocated.
        'No, half an hour,
Carried was firm, 'tops.'
        If crying had a certain magic
so did cheap plonk. Drunk that night, just to be stupid
she went onto the balcony and yelled: 'You listening, Melbourne?
I wanna meet a man named Michael Finnegan! And begin again!'
    Sounding like she was back in crèche was anything stupider?

    Yes, staying with Adrian was stupider.
And screaming like that had taken thirty seconds, hardly half an hour,
and if Carrie was lucky it wouldn't happen again.
'Who needs Adrian and his meagre magic?'
she asked herself. 'Get out of Melbourne.
Get out of Melbourne, stupid.'

    A few months before it had been *Return to Melbourne, stupid.*
And, knowing she could always take that one step stupider,
Carrie imagined making it to the Brownlow, allowing all Melbourne
a perve at her cleavage for what seemed half an hour:

there's little magic like tit magic!
    Unless it was the non-magic of making the back page news again,

for Adrian, once again
had done something stupid,
and the headline told it all:
WHERE OH WHERE IS THE OLD MAGIC?
    Each week his game was getting stupider,
until last Saturday it took the coach less than half an hour
to bench him. (They were playing Melbourne,

a team not noted for its magic.)
                        If 'stupid'
was turning 'stupider' Carrie wasn't staying on for 'stupidest.' One more
    half an hour
of Melbourne would be too much. Soon she'd move again.

Amanda, Bernie, Gary

    When the industry sleazed and started running kids
(mainly Filipinos) cynicism took the inevitable upbeat:
it sidetracked them, Amanda knew, into the fatuous.
She should've guessed: after months of Bernie
(who'd flog his mum to any suburban cowboy)
why expect more from this king of the discount orgasm?

    True her colleagues sulked: attending to some John's orgasm
was no big deal; but kids, Filipino kids?
'Sick!' the verdict rang, 'every man's a cowboy!'
    Challenges though would send Amanda upbeat:
sixteen-year-olds were par for Uncle Bernie;
be outraged, sure, but any surprise seemed fatuous.

When all else had been covered you copped the fatuous,
any working girl knew that: it went with the orgasm.
    'So why not', she proposed, 'skim Bernie
of the best: staff, clients, and start our own?'
                                  They giggled like kids,

it sounded so Amanda: ambitious, cheeky, upbeat.
'There's just two things that make this world revolve or I'm a cowboy.'

But she needed muscle, and to have a cowboy
and Gary, her cop (was anyone less fatuous?)
came trumps. His response went upbeat:
the idea of selling the young for orgasm-
fodder made you vomit! If only for those kids,
then, him and a mate went and heavied Bernie.

'Fellas . . . really . . . am I like that?' cringed Bernie.
He'd never asked, the shudders continued, anyone to cowboy
round the Philippines collecting kids.
What was he taken for? A fatuous
'Jeez . . .' was sighed. It faded like an orgasm.
The smirking police kept turning that extra upbeat:

Good cop/bad . . . their routine flowed into a rhythm: upbeat/
down: 'Know how pathetic you are, Bernie?
Think you're some X-rated dead-cert orgasm-
machine? You're about as erotic as a singing cowboy.
So, when the tabloids go arse-over-tit fatuous
Dumb prick we'll say *only had one weakness: kids.*

*Nothing but kids. Well if they were his freeway to Orgasm-
ville ours are a touch more upbeat!'* Boy were their shrugs fatuous!
'And one thing's sure: you're not much of a cowboy, Bernie.'

Carrie, Amanda

She'd met Amanda through some of her father's friends
(the even more well-heeled, the racier). New to Sydney
the bars she'd seen were tack, couldn't give a flying fuck
for discos. *Discrimination* in a word was Carrie,
but when an intro was proposed (to the usual *broad
cross section of the influential* saying yes seemed simple.

Adrian, Melbourne, had had the gong, it was that simple.
At twenty-six with minimum commitments and most friends
scattered into marriage, other cities or abroad,
why not, the sun and salt-spray cocktail which is Sydney?
Why not, for once, that essential independent Carrie?
Wasn't Adrian, her last man, her last man? So what the fuck . . .

One more single nursing sister aching for a fuck
or its equivalent? You could say that but, in her simple
pleated skirt, neat-boned grey-eyed Carrie
was straight-out charm.
      'God's own city,' one of the old man's friends
explained, 'the devil's too. Everybody knows that Sydney
sprawls; how can't it though, being as broad

as democracy itself.'
     A voice arrived beside them: broad,
warm, thankfully feminine. Soon it said 'You had that *Fuck
I'm stuck with this one* look. Late spring in Sydney
all of us go like that.'
      Given a few hours it became so simple:
the afternoon was making them friends.
All that needed giving were names: 'Amanda.'
           'Carrie'.

   Given a few weekends of coffees, dinners, one saw Carrie
steady herself to plunge into the broad,
vigorous currents of knowing Amanda. Good friends,
though, were like that, having the strength to help you say *Fuck
it all, I'll tell!* Only Amanda hadn't secrets: just the simple
truth of how she ran a 'cathouse'. Surely the best in Sydney.

   '. . . I wandered into it. Get to know this town and Sydney
makes you plenty. I never recruit though, Carrie.
We've a plain ethos and my style is simple:
it's me who gets approached.'
        This braced the younger woman, her broad
vulgar cheek erupting 'Well then, what's the price of a fuck?'
(It seemed the least she could say, being, as they were, friends.)

Sure it could be added how one more broad raring to fuck
had hit Sydney; and her name was Carrie.
But friends, really, is anything that simple?

Amanda, Carrie

Amanda never trusted thin-lipped women
(part intuition, part something-from-a-book)
and bad teeth, too, only stood for trouble.
Her final test was looking them eye-to-eye.
This game she knew *gives so much choice,*
then everyone I choose will be the best.

Though she wanted little but the best
Carrie never had it much. And seeing some women
making luck their own she knew the choice
by now: to run your life by the book,
or follow those broken rules that come onto the ego's eye.
(There's something delicious falling in love with trouble.)

'Like to guess,' Amanda prompted, 'my biggest trouble?
Bo Derek clones! To be among our best
ten is no requirement. Know who'll catch the eye?
Girls like us: you-make-me-feel-like-a-natural-woman women.
We're halfway into any little black book
before we even start. It may seem like the fella's choice

at first, but worked at hard enough any choice
turns yours. This business is rewards, so take the trouble.'
And Carrie would, although Amanda's unwritten rulebook
bemused her with its *Good better best /*
never let it rest routine. Smart women were sexy women.
Appearances count. You were to trust the eye.

If Sydney seemed stacked with guys poised to eye
her off, it always would; and Carrie's choice
by now wasn't to choose. Last May she'd joined those women
lapping up articles like 'How to make men trouble

work for you'. How indeed. Most nights at best
she'd propped herself with records, wine cask, book

(nine hundred and fifty pages worth of book)
to see her through the winter. Though better eye-
strain than suckered by some conman at his 'best'
When she thought *that plain responsive guy, my choice,*
thanks me for all my taking trouble,
count me among those other luckier women.

    Given these best of dreams (this one's for the book,
and this the apple of my eye!) were hardly trouble,
she made her choice and joined Amanda's women.

Amanda, Shannon, Starfuck, Carrie

    Part common touch/part born to rule,
Amanda, though hardly known for screaming,
Could still be flinty as any lady ocker.
She called the feminist mainstream 'thought-
policewomen' and snapped whenever 'the game' was criticised:
        'They're at it again!'
    Yet once she commenced a trickle of tenderness

you sensed there must be those reserves of tenderness
going with the job: to rule
the roost meant you took the raps: again and yet again
the buck stopped with Amanda.
        Shannon wasn't exactly screaming
that afternoon, just crunching up her face with the thought
of Starfuck: this fat rich john, a, let's be honest, seedy ocker.

    But the boss turned upbeat: 'Even the most unlettered ocker
can at least attempt a morsel of tenderness
don't you think?'
    Yes, Carrie thought,
recalling a previous Amanda golden rule:

'If they have you screaming,
and they will, you'll see them again,'

    ... and they will, you'll see them again.
if this had reached the ears of any ocker
the poor man would've scrambled from this building, screaming.
    But oh those things you did to institute tenderness
and the little you were promised in return!
                                   Amanda, as a rule,
believed in considerate things, but even the nicest thought

remained a thought;
and she was heading towards pep-talk mode again.
    (With Starfuck about to arrive Carrie switched to the rule
of memory; she was eighteen, Max Merritt was still the thinking girl's ocker
and when he and The Meteors launched into 'Try a Little Tenderness'
the gig couldn't stop screaming).

    'There's one of you who get Starfuck screaming,'
Amanda announced, looking at Carrie.
                                   'Thanks,' she thought,
'but this is a girl who needs her tenderness
right now, today.' (For though she would go through with it again
the man was hardly Carrie's favourite ocker.)
    And even if there was one rule

alone (the rule of tenderness)
the thought of Starfuck almost sent her screaming
Not that ocker again!

Carrie, Neil, Amanda

    Here's how Carrie met Neil:
at the Penthouse she saw, admiring their harbour vistas,
a man: eyes, ears, hands, arms, legs, feet: two
of each. Why ask for more?
    It was Amanda, obviously of all women,
who joking asked 'Well, what you want, Mac?'

She seemed to know him. 'This is err Mac.'
   'It's Neil, Monica.'
               'Okay it's Neil.'
   Later, Carrie would tell him what women
kicked against: relationships with no more vistas
than the inside of a dunny. Need she say more?
'Though name a better number in the world than "two".

If it works, which isn't often, I find I'm finding myself.'
                                    'Me too.
Even the flasher in his trademark mac
deserves a 'love interest'. Who's yours, Kenneth More?'
   If he must know she'd a preference for Sam Neill;
then, giving their conversation unguessed-for vistas,
she asked 'What gives with women?

I'll tell what gives with women:
unless your melon-titted, twenty-two
and white-hot for a root, shut down all vistas!'
   Later she told of this truckie, less-than-fresh from his Mack,
who ordered Shannon *Go on and kneel,*
kneel bitch and suck that cock! An exaggeration? Well more-

or-less. Still, weren't men eternal Oliver Twists, always wanting more?
       He wasn't to let that pass: 'And women
don't?'
        It wouldn't be her last time sparring with Neil:
'Well Eva Braun didn't cause World War Two!'
   Carrie was more lethal than Mac
the Knife . . . and the vistas

she opened! Their sweep rivalled Vista-
vision; their humanism, Sir Thomas More:
'We offer class. Don't expect a Big Mac
when you dine at The Ritz. Though when it comes to women
some guys are thicker than a four-by-two.
There, on the floor, lay this muso, Neil,

too too out of it (I've seen the weirdest vistas)
honkin' 'n' screamin' *Gimme more, women!*
Who'd he think he was, Big Jay McNeally?

Neil's story

  So he'd tell her about Barb,
tell almost as much about Roger, the husband
and yes they'd a child, a son
   '... well here's my theory: since they never fought
guess what, nobody had won.
That's why their marriage was so much on the rocks.'

  Did Carrie feel this gelled?
       'It rocks,'
she admitted.
    He'd never known the younger Barb,
Neil wandered in long after Year One:
when she acquired her husband,
stockading a family behind their domestic fort.
  (And Neil imagined that 'support' his parents would give *their* son:

'Messing with somebody's wife: We're with you all the way, son!')
  After work they'd walk around The Rocks,
his daggy wit a bittersweet forte
under the circumstances: 'Speaking of spouses, Barbe
Bleu now there was a husband!'
He liked that. Made him feel a regular Don Juan.

Well an intellectual one.
  Caught in her awe of Roger (exemplary father, perfect son-in-law) '... little wonder,' Carrie observed, 'his wife would husband
any amount of guile to have you. These were her rocks
and she was getting them off!'
      Call it a truth (it was barbed
but certainly perceptive) and not the kind you fought

against.
  Looking Neil over Carrie fought
his indulgence: 'Oh,' she half-sneered 'you are a one!'
as *Barb, Barb, Barb, Barb*
Neil bleated. If he'd a touch of the sun
it was leavened with pinches of shit: a girl sure had rocks
in her head listening to this!

       'So the husband,'

Carrie asked, 'did she fuck the husband?
That's what wives are for.'
       He didn't know, it didn't matter, he'd fought
it through and, over many a Jim Beam on the rocks
was glad, 'Glad I'm out of that one!'
  It seemed kind of a natural law: there was a sun
but under it lay nothing new, not even him and Barb:

Breaking rocks in the hot sun
He'd fought the law and that law had won . . .
  (One day, perhaps, Carrie might meet Barb's husband.)

Carrie, Neil

  In bemusement she thought 'Smart girls
mightn't say "franger" but was ever a word
clumsier than "prophylactic"?'
       Watching him peel off his condom,
she almost became a detective. (Throughout the world, between
humanity's legs, a mutual psyche kept playing at *Well well well
what 'ave we 'ere?* always had, always would.)
       Her bourgeois

upbringing with its balance, detachment (what ultimate bourgeois
strengths!) went with the job. Their men required good girls
(good-enough being never enough) who were the well-
spring of Amanda's motto *Where only the best serve the best* whose in-a-
  word word
just had to be 'style': no time for floundering betwixt and between;
and no use considering *How plebeian, the condom.*

  It must've been simpler, Neil decided, when, like a condom,
a class label could encase everyone: upper, bourgeois,
working, and all them lumpen guys between.
  'So where,' he asked, 'do we place you girls?'
  'Honey we are the world,' she purred.

'Word?'
Neil had misheard.
Oh Carrie liked that: 'Yes, and it as well.'

Enjoying such banter they did it well
and had to: as if even language (yes, like your humble condom)
possessed its use-by date, and hardly any word
seemed safe. 'Yuppie' was overtaking 'bourgeois'
(at least for abuse) whilst 'chick', 'bird', 'sort' (though hardly 'working girl')
sounded thankfully redundant in that centuries-slow unfold and fold
between

one tongue and the next.
That day though was put *Just between
ourselves*. After she'd well-
versed him in those essentials for a modern girl's
night out: spare cash for cabs, tampons, the credit card, the condom,
he replied with his upcoming journey: it wasn't *that* bourgeois
his wanting to quit Australia, was it? And 'exile' seemed too strong a word

for a man who, wanting to keep his word,
would send her cards.
As ever she'd get paid, paid today to be
somewhere between
Neil's ex and the wide blue yonder.
Then 'Got you something,' she said.
(Still bourgeois
and predictable enough his face signalled *Well?*)
'I'd like to present . . . t'taa! Your final condom!'
She means it! his look indicated, *she means it!* Carrie would have to
tell the girls.

And this was his final word: she should know he despised that well-
trod fallacy: how between the desire and the enjoyment fell the condom.
Cautious, bourgeois Neil needed to please and protect (even be pleased
by/protected from) girls.

Carrie, Neil, Shannon, a German engineer, Amanda

  Though with Neil you could play at being kids
again; and somehow that gave Carrie a corner
for her self-esteem. (Being susceptible
to mere cash wasn't enough.)
         After watching Shannon fuck some beached
    whale
of a German engineer, 'Some might call that sex,'
she thought, 'I can't quite.' (Later, with a bemused mind,

she'd sought Amanda; who alas had larger working girl problems on
     her mind
that day.)
    Doubtless forgetful of his frau und kids
'*Eine* girl to votch?' Hans had demanded, 'Please next time fünf! sechs!'
The glutton!
     (Though if you turned the historical corner
back to those crinoline and whale-
boned day and nights, the game was worse.)
          She wasn't being naive but
   If being men-susceptible

means rather liking them at times, call me susceptible.
  Amanda never was that vulnerable. Often, her friend's mind-
set concerning her, she'd confide to Shannon: 'To promise a whale-
of-a-time is one thing, but Carrie kids
herself if it'll be more. Never paint yourself into a corner
As a substitute for any man's ex.'

  But given that sheer bartering side of sex,
if it seemed possible, pleasant enough, Carrie was susceptible.
  'Could you,' Neil had asked, 'go over to that corner,
put a hand on either wall and spread your legs? Do you mind?'
  Of course not and, as they moved together, like kids
adjusting for the first time, Carrie heard him wail.

  'That's okay,' she urged, 'keep spouting you gorgeous sperm whale
of a man!'
    She felt his heart-beats and later, as his sex

subsided, he, being wide-eyed, flushed, told her, 'Kids
never get it good as you can give.'
       And Carrie, susceptible
to seeing a man enjoy himself with her, agreed. 'Though mind
you,' her proviso came, 'when it's my turn for pussy-in-the-corner

just watch me!'
     'You're not,' asked Neil, 'about to corner
a fuck franchise for the whole of New South Wales?'
   Carrie couldn't stop giggling: she'd have to tell Amanda, the best
       mind
in their business.
      And sure it was liked, but that pragmatic afternoon sex
was just sex: it didn't sound so original. Some days the boss felt susceptible
only to the heart-strings side of it: e.g. street kids

standing on some corner at The Cross, flogging sex.
She might Save the Whale but Amanda was hardly slogan-susceptible.
'It's all child-minding, Carrie. Men are kids.'

Carrie, Wal, Benny

  So Carrie met men who kept her out of danger
Learning to cope with all their passionate gushing:
'I'll be back,' she constantly hears, 'don't worry about *that!*'
  At the hospital came different attempts at friendship:
the smile, the date, the fumbled pass. Sex might be a god,
but hadn't Carrie other things to value?

Why didn't most men believe *No* too had its value?
True the interns, registrars and specialists proved no moral danger,
but each tin god
with all their preposterous gushing
propositions, what were they after? Mere friendship?
Sister Larson knew just one way to tackle *that!*

A high-pitched delivery and confident *Howzat?*
would get these gentlemen walking (talk about value

for money!).
                But this is also the tale of Carrie's friendship
with Wal; and since he was gay go on ask her *Where's the danger?*
And no he wasn't just another gushing
queen.
      'Do you believe in God?'

she asked, once after work, not knowing why.
                        'Does God,'
her friend replied, 'believe in me?'
                       Who told him *that*?!
    No-one had, he'd made it up. And a blush came gushing
over the man.
            Wal, an orderly, knew his value
lay in the hospital's pecking order. Knew, too, the danger
to be found in cruising. But then he'd this great friendship

with Carrie brewing. And another one, more than a friendship
now. With Benny he didn't have to worry *What a stud! What a god!*
and, when self-esteem became involved there was no danger
in someone sniping 'You're seeing *that?*'
      Carrie understood: if little is ever value-
free (and so much of life has equal shares in biting and gushing)

'When I'm with Wal,' she knew, 'I feel like an oil well gushing.'
Did that describe their friendship?
'It does, it does. He knows my value,
I know his . . .'
                And it wasn't as if Cupid, the god
of love, had struck them pow! *Like that!*
Unless you truly fell for Wal you stayed away from danger

well away from danger.
                'Oh my god!'
cried Carrie, 'we like each other heaps. But there's little value in gushing.
This is more than a friendship!'
                    '. . . and that,' said Wal 'is *that*!'

Wal, Carrie, Benny

    He would phone her: 'Hello Angel.'
    Dearest friends by now, this wasn't some fantasy:
it had love and it had balance: Carrie's acid
to Wal's alkaline, her straight-till-something-better-arrives to his
                undiluted queer.
    One more Perth boy who had headed east
to make his life better than it had been, Wal was hiding from his thin-

walled, fibro shack of a childhood.
                        A tall, thin,
somewhat floppy rag doll of an angel
(whose hair – neither north nor west nor south nor east –
knew few directions) Wal was hardly a homoerotic fantasy.
    When he was younger Wal often felt a trifle peeky ('queer'
if you like). So back then Mum stocked up on the antacid.

        If only she could know how, on some beats, all you thought was
                Not another acid
test! Besides, Wal's patience with the cops was getting thin.
How many times did he have to ask and answer 'What me? Queer?
Now honestly sergeant, be an angel . . .'
Carrie could understand her friend wanting this fantasy
(if you could call it that) to end. So the time came to move east:

to that few square miles of approximate heaven just east
of Sydney's CBD.
                For months it felt like Oxford Street was
                  seen through a sheen of acid,
and it might've been, except this was no fantasy:
with all these exciting men (anything but thin
on the ground) life had turned decidedly real. *Even the devil was a*
                yummy angel
once. Strange, though, that having been lumbered with 'queer'

you were expected now to pride yourself as 'queer'.
Wal didn't know why and neither did Carrie.
                              One night a new man
        rode east

on his Vespa. Good to be with, making Wal laugh, 'I'm no angel . . .'
Benny confessed.
           A few evenings on Wal took acid
and Carrie didn't. Poor Wal. She'd to hug him, he was so thin-
blooded. They talked one fantasy

after another for hours. Carrie's fantasy?
It may've sounded banal, even queer
to some, but: 'Having the right man forever.'
                              There was a thin,
pale line starting its expansion in the east.
Wal was coming down from his acid.
Good. Carrie could get to sleep, to stop feeling like a guardian angel.

    And what music was her fantasy to wake to? Not the thin,
dated effects of acid rock but full-bodied Sinatra: 'East
of the Sun and West of the Moon'.
                          'Nighty night angel,' said Wal; not
            accurate exactly, but hardly queer.

Carrie, Wal

      Part ingénue/part flapper, Carrie could sing *Do do do
what you done done done before baby*
high steppin' in with top hat and tails, kisses,
trilling a quite passable do re mi;
in this, Wal's other world, with all its democracy of hugs,
she could ignore that malicious sneer *Getta life!*

For it was envy which fuelled the getta life
syndrome: if her men were where and when required . . . whacky doo
    There is a certain premium in hugs:
Carrie had often craved them like a baby,
But no use blubbering *Why me?*
Why the woman in the moon!
                          Then though came the kisses.

You could lose your brain with kisses.
And, once they'd evaporated, 'When will I really getta life?'
you asked. 'What went before was hardly *me:*
all that strangers in the night dooby dooby doo
taa ciao see ya round baby.'
   Wal always greeted his friends with hugs,

there was no other way, hugs
were a necessity.
     'But Carrie,' he confessed, 'the kisses!'
Oooooh baby!'
And Wal, OIC Operation Gettalife,
let forth a Flintstonian *Yabba dabba doo!*
What? Embarrassed? Who? Me?

   Wal's friends enjoyed Carrie. 'They know me,'
she felt proud to say, 'know me as safe.' (Though attempting anything
     but hugs
would find her up past the neck in deep doo-doo.)
And if you had to double-take men giving each other kisses
in today's world, well getta life,
get two!
   And if Wal sometimes was one big baby

thanks for the practice, one day she might produce a baby.
(Since there must be some dimension beyond *Me,
myself and I* name her a better way to getta life.)
  But would that be the final outcome of the hugs,
the total destination of the kisses?
For they could chill her, all the intricate dos

'n' don'ts of hugs 'n' kisses,
and the smug resignation of *It'll do me*
was never Carrie's way.
     'Getta life?' she asked no-one but herself.
    '... getta baby?'

GROUP PORTRAIT WITH BENNY AND WAL

for Phillip Siggins and Chris Wheat

(1) Wal

      That muggy Friday he stayed home preparing.
On Lunchtime Hits of Yesteryear they
played it (though not exactly yesteryear,
thought Wal), a soft light beat of this
smoothest instrumental turning him to hum
'Ma-cho/ma-cho/ man/I got to be/
a ma-cho man . . .'
                He smiled:
didn't Mark the Activist want them
banned for Chrissake, *banned?* who, never
explaining how, became like The Village People:
a novelty item, a party turn. 'Mock faggots!'
Mark would spit, 'head-dresses, hard hats,
who needs acts like *that?*' Well, half
the Sydney Wal knew and, besides,
weren't they more passé than gay, if
gay at all? He knew someone,
Wal knew he knew someone who'd slept
with the bikie or the injun chief, and
this someone was a girl and she
('You mean you're *not?*') was told
'Hell, none of us are, it's bullshit honey.'
      And now, this afternoon, a People number
was getting laundered out on strings,
synthesiser and horns, time-sharing with
Manuel and His Music of the Mountains.
Wal had to tell anyone.
                But Carrie was busy.
(he'd wait until tonight for her) whilst Benny would
sigh *oh yeah?* at never having heard it
first and Mark would use long words you
never knew and didn't want to.

Although, sometimes, The Activist amused him.
'Our service industries!' one rant got recalled,
'jean-shrinkers, moustache-trimmers, checked-
shirt importers . . .' Sure they could get me
grumpy if I had to, Wal replied;
he wasn't heard. Mark continued:
'How can you even start being *you*?'
    By taking a Sundrenched, a Sundrenched
Excursion of course, where he met Mark and
everyone or, rather, where Benny really got to know
this skinny woolly-headed man: clambering
balconies, bombing pools, crawling in jocks
down hotel corridors in Honolulu/
The Bay Area/ Vegas/ where-are-we-now?/
Disneyland till 'Tether that mutt-
on-the-loose,' a manager demanded,
'or you, the lot of you are out, deported!'
Tears crashed from Wal, and fucking it up
for Sundrenched, why shouldn't they?
'We've hardly met,' Benny volunteered,
'but trust me, I'll look after him.'
    A few years volunteering later Wal
knew where the balance stayed: trusting
his friend enough, he'd had to.
When you really liked someone, well you
needed to look into their eyes (or feel
that way) for hours. On their flight back
Wal knew he could, Benny had volunteered.
Who else was there? That bi guy back home,
someone on a train he wouldn't try
forgetting, and Carrie, his friend; gay, straight
or calathumpian everyone should have
a friend like her.
        Mum had summed up
Wal (too much she had); but now in their kitchen
in the lunchtime daylight, he forgot those things Mum had said:
'. . . not many brains, plenty of heart but . . .'
telling and retelling the world. Nights though
he'd hear these bats of words squealing
around him, never repeating them, come morning,

to anyone: you lived for morning when Mum
stayed back in the dark, Benny made
them tea and toast, and Carrie might call,
speedy already with something Wal might like.
The world deserved to have a Carrie each,
Benny even.
        Who, as Wal laughed, rang:
'Book an extra seat. It's Barb. Bye now.'
Barb? Or (one more American) *Bob*?
'Hey Barb,' he thought out loud. 'Hey Barb.'

(II) Benny, Barb

   'Barb!' and, knowing the so-pleased voice
beside her, she turned from the retrospective's
obligatory triptych, to Benny's 'Hey!'
him grinning like Yogi Bear. 'Still needing
The Big Hug?' The counsellor himself:
vigorous tracks half-circling his jowls,
that mini-savannah of pepper-and-
salt hair.
      Near hoisted by the man, Barb's memories
re-emerged: of his effervescence:
silly, seedy but always generous.
   'Not midday yet and we're not working?
Let's confess.'
         'Long service leave.'
   'Three hours worth of cancelled crazies.'
   Years since the last Big Hug she prepared
for further fruity bellows with
never-to-be-used rejoinders. *No, we weren't
'happy as sandboys'. Sorry Benny,
those days I was in debacle mode.*
Better she predict his inanity-coated wit.
     'This display,' Benny told her, 'feels like I'm in
some Saturday colour rag. They've done
this one? So much genius must
be fatuous and I'd say so, except,

it's what those dinkies want. Were you
arriving? Leaving?'
      Still can't
pick her age, he thought, *eighteen?*
Thirty-five? But still the same small
woman with the same round face,
who no doubt will always look as
enigmatic . . . and geared for clientele
or company, problem-solving or gossip,
'. . . y' wanna lunch?' A place was named
whilst Benny would drive her there and back
if necessary. His shout? Please don't refuse.
  She accepted; though lunch with him
might risk some Neil-talk:
his friend/ her last affair/ the big boo-hoo.
For it would seem too pragmatic:
to tell and hear how Neil had
finished painting the extension, had graduated
(courtesy of the Benny connection)
to more; how later he tried studying
(uncertain what); met this woman
(uncertain who); left her, went away.
Who said ex-lovers never knew the script?
She'd near-coached that one, now all
it had to be was true.
      Benny
phrases rushed back through their drive
and 'How's true happiness?' Barb asked.
Wal (she recalled the name) Wal was
vego now and heading vegan:
'Keeps bullying me to diet. *Try it,*
he pleads, *C'mon* and *for once* and
for me. Today's orders? Alfalfa mating
with beancurd. *Don't ask when will it end?*
It has. Here.' (At 'Good f' th' Goose
Gourmet Grub'.) 'Okay, so a client recommended it.'
And he breathed in 'Anyway . . .' breathed out,
reddening, 'now Neil, right? The latest?
You knew he'd left?' She hadn't. 'There's letters
but specifics? Y' actual destination?

La Paz, the tundra, any stray kibbutz?
Truth is he's on one now.'
      Was her
face relaxing? That smile, thought Benny
could charm half Oxford Street to bed
if not for jiggety-jigs then comfort,
companionship, the warmest of getting-
to-know-yous this side of
the two-backed beast. *And why not?*
his mind unwound, feeling even more
avuncular. *Poor Barb, she had it all*
but for a happier end.
     'Pleased he's away?'
asked Benny.
      'Don't want to appear quite pleased but
yes. There's still the fear we might meet,
like this, like anything. Only stuck with
memories now, the need to disguise
I loved him and to believe such lies.'
  Benny squinted: had to believe whatever
she was saying, the more so if it didn't, somehow,
tally.
  'Yes,' he agreed (to what he hardly knew)
'it's always lies. Me for example, some
ersatz Mister Natural?' He bit the sandwich,
swallowed, coughed and 'Agh!' he, gasping,
blinked, and coughed again, 'Not this black duck!'
  As he performed Benny knew sentiment
was bilging about his brain. But it felt good
and since it went like this,
he let it: *Fancy dropping Neil*
from Barb's All-stars, and still play
the world with, who was it? Rodney? Raymond?
Who of course, she'd never exactly left.
       Yet
why should Benny keep on
blushing? 'I'm hardly a daytime drunk,
and I can't eat big (if this is eating)
for tonight we dine!' His face grew hotter.
'Please, this evening, you have much on, Barb? Opera?

Macramé workshops? Leather bars?'
It sounded propositional? Might there
have been a time (very well once)
in the previous further adventures of
Benny Hull, closet straight?
'Why not make it eight at eight:
Wal et moi, Leo and M, Wal's friend,
the folks next door and, if she surprises
herself, *you*! A short notice is
the best notice, I tell all the girls.
And Wal's tits are hanging over our stove,
right now!'

(III) Carrie

     In the lift descending from The Penthouse
Carrie thought of Wal, loving him
in her way, no-one else's (how sometimes
he got too special). He could cook,
and he could jive (what men did today?)
yet on the phone this morning
he was uncontainable: 'Listen, listen,
fennel vinaigrette, sugar pea and
coriander soup, Byzantine millet pilaf,
apricot syllabub ...
and Leo's bringing his girlfriend M.
Yes M. The mysterious M.
Then there'll be our neighbours ...'
                              Carrie knew
of Leo hitting town for Mardi Gras
and big production-number rages:
might this week see less of Wal?
She recalled how, when she reached
their bar the afternoon they had turned
more than friends, she'd been crying:
'Motor Mouth says you're a root rat.
Well I hate bigots, they're always ignorant.
So wap! I slapped her in the mouth.'

Wal had looked queasy. Friends just never
hit on his account.
Smiling weakly he raised a tiny bottle,
and Carrie closed her eyes. She didn't,
he didn't, need another blow-me-up
and crash-me-down. She loved him
and he copped it. But worse than any
root rat Wal was pure danger:
to himself. 'Hate it Wal . . .
Amyl's a gorilla . . .' She snatched the phial
strode into the ladies and flushed it down.
'And *for* gorillas, honey. Come back and
share some lines I'm saving for your
birthday.' (Wal she saw didn't feel like
asking where or how she got it.)
Well, that evening, she'd throw on a blouse
and after eats he'd take her out
where girls were welcome. Where they
could jive!
        The lift door opened.
She'd showered four times today.
Carrie would go for coffee.

(IV) Leo, M

    Each year Benny did the round trip:
Adelaide for his folks, then east to Leo's;
last August taking him back for holidays.
As the freeway swept north, the Karelia Suite
commenced and buoyed by the intermezzo's
confidence, 'This music says one word,'
cried Leo, '*now*! and *now*! means fuckin' good!'
Glancing over to the trim torso and
Nebuchadnezzar profile this, the best
of the familiar, almost embarrassed Benny.
When escapades headed the agenda,
none improved on Leo; who,
ten days later, satisfied-plus,

calling himself Meinherr Overdone, returned to Melbourne.
  'What of the boyfriend?' M enquired.
  'Oh Benny's? For someone with little
to say, quite the nicest possible. Took me
raging: for two utterly bland nights.
He's from the west, escaping mother
and the power of prayer; somehow
he late-developed into an adult delinquent;
got saved when Benny cruised out
of some night on his Vespa,
I prosecute bullshit emblazoned
over a T-shirt.'
            Yet nothing preened
or pranced in Benny. 'Work ethic,
play ethic, sloth ethic,' he proclaimed,
'it's all life, and living, you must exceed!'
Coming back at two, one morning,
Leo found him nodding at a table
strewn with case-work, the house near-
drenched with Les Indes Gallantes swelling
from the speakers.
            I might request the same,
tonight, thought Leo, leaning over
a small balcony, six floors above the lane,
pipe smoke mixing into the warm damp.
Life was rising: and one of the city's
easier events, a TeeVee beat,
reassembled for the night to come.
    She saw him, and waving up blew kisses.
    'Hurry M,' Leo called behind,
'our local Terry Tinsel's blowing kisses.'
    Towel spiralling from her hair
M joined him; their new friend holding out both hands,
pouted a smile as if confessing *Two of youse?*
Well why not. Been there . . .
could do it all again. If not yet.
She recognised a car and waving *bye!*
climbed in; Leo murmuring 'Delighted!'
    Flying in today from Melbourne they
propped at Carlo's flat in their perfect city:

not merely the harbour flaunted,
even the laneways desired as well.
Wherever soapies locate, Carlo was
on location. The keys had waited
at the agent with a note:
    Dear Leo/M: eat out my fridge,
smoke my dope, check all locks,
twice at least, water the plants,
please. See you mid-week,
love 'n' regards. Carleau.

    Downstairs, outside the salerooms,
kids arrived: William Street changing into
night mode. By one a.m. when M returned
there'd still be the bulk of this doped-up honour guard:
hardly blowing Terry Tinsel kisses,
just stepping forward as rumour city's
final chorus for the night.

    Carlo had a friend who had a boyfriend
thugged last year. By whom?
Gossip traced itself to a euphemism
which unfolded into a nickname,
who employed people. Half a day
in Sydney and you always knew the rumours.

(v) **Barb**

    Flinty with eczema, self-sufficient,
Roger would get Sam away to school,
return to research. Shabby as only
'the alternative' allows (though with
the genteel overlay of his in-laws'
old appliances), the house was love enough:
he thrived on it.
    But that year,
so much for Barb turned better:
having met Neil (and keeping each other longer
than either would dare/dare predict)
she got to know his flatmate

'My flamboyant confidant,
the landlord who's not, quite.'
She never saw the Vespa,
putting through a night of Sydney showers
from bar to beat and back again,
but understood Benny hunting
'*That unending fix, true happiness*'.
Just as hers and Neil's collapsed, his
was revving: '. . . think I've found it:
the bunny's name is Wal and, well,
Wal's different. I like him
and the whole world better!'
As if he meant it all.
                    But soon
she had to slow the overload of Neil-love,
then cut completely, disappear,
and never meet Wal-bunny. Something
had to end as something had
to start.
          Tonight, with messages,
their son phoned in from a skating rink,
Roger arrived for something (dental floss?).
You could call him what the folks thought
as a *good man*; well yes, you could;
Barb hardly did though. Seeing her mirrored face,
framed by the bubble bath, she tried
concocting a pleasant if daggy come-on,
to anyone in the world; and thought
of risqué attempts at album covers,
their not-quite-intelligent glamour:
Carly Simon pouting in silks
or Ronstadt doe-eyed on roller-skates.
Or better, those two boys she'd seen once,
with a Ricky Lee Jones, on a train.
Call it a fantasy or the sweet bullshit
of pretend innocence/ mock experience.
But Barb just started to imagine . . .
anything she wanted; they were men
and men weren't conned these days,
or only those whose wives had, so simply,

fallen in love, elsewhere.
                    Ho hum went there,
got too involved, then came out
the other end of that one.
And how like Neil: to set out rules
to their game of fucking and honour:
'Rivals are so much myself,
how can I hate them?
Hate one and he stops being one.
Your...' and she remembered how
he cast for a word when only his rival's
name was adequate.
                    'Roger,' she supplied.
    (Her husband working something from
between his teeth rinsed and spat.)
        'Roger's an equal. Why envy equals?
Inferiors bring out *my* jealousy.'
                        Well
he hadn't known how couples
could dry off into the scrub of home-life:
work, meals, sleep.
The only certain way you love
with someone else was running it till all stopped
and you sent each other anywhere:
over the road, round the world, into outer space,
anywhere tonight bar Benny's
('See me as hausfrau, the apron
will be mere effect though')
featuring the re-run of his Yogi Bear bravado
and The Big Hug.
            Rog would pick up Sam,
Rog could tape something she might enjoy,
he might cook something for the next few days.
Whenever friends unleashed
a dog-pack of near demands:
leave/stop propping him/throw away
his name/do what's expected/
she knew that playing swap was only that:
new sets and costumes, new cast,
same play, same Barbara.

        Though *Ask me* she often thought
to tell Neil, *try getting me to leave,*
go real obsessed, plead me to leave them,
turn so crazed, and demand I stride out on the lot
for even if you smash this spell of ours
I've been seventeen again,
with all I've learnt since seventeen,
buoying me. Test me, try it, ask.
        He wouldn't and she never did; and
Barb lounging in her bath prepared
for Benny's. Was it three, four, five years?
Please don't itemise, she had to demand . . .
all right, but then (and we know *then*)
did I say that, hear that, do that?
What were we?
                Marshalling some wine,
a handbag, the taxi fare and return,
she was going out.

(VI) Mason, Hannah

        Australians, Mason thought:
those kids down the road Americans
felt they knew. Their quirks, though,
were addictive:
easy to pick up things they said,
and say them,
soon he might dream in Aussie,
sooner, need to decide:
here and Hannah/home and Hannah/
home and himself.
                He watched her,
naked in their mirror. She saw them, too:
Hannah and Mason, all part of
getting to like what you see.
Work and affection got her too comfortable,
putting it on round the bum:
not enough bushwalks now,

even less diet. I'm adequate-broad,
she thought, not talking *fat* but
my size *has* to impress. Tonight they'd have
other guests, a few of their fag hags, no doubt;
with quiet, compliant gentlemen-friends
for side dishes. Given this hour to prepare myself,
though, they haven't a chance.
  And wasn't next door a comfort?
Like this evening's *yoo-oo!*
Wal's Ada over the back fence,
so she as Elsie could *yoo-oo!* back.
If she hadn't seen them for days they'd
always be there and thanks, tonight,
they were: each Friday having to blast
out of her word cocoon:
the Policy Unit's working party.
  Sizing then deferring earrings,
etching then moulding her lips into
a cupid's bow, she knew Mason just
wanted to softly unclip the one, then
lick off the other, so Hannah played him:
'I wanna do roight by da bois . . .'
Well *he* never spoke like mock mafiosi.
'. . . Oh quit perving Mase, it's not on now,
we'd be all night. Go next door to Benny,
keep him amused. There'll be
an hour of this. I love it.'
Abrasive, if turning affectionate, like all
Australians who mattered, this
was their form of friendliness working the best:
  'Never bores you does it?'
  'Sex, Han?'
    'Yes. Sex.'
      'Never.'
  Four years back, after they were reunited,
all he seemed to hear was
one week's worth of crying and
a skull of songs:
I wanna go home lord how I wanna
go home. Till, darling,

she demanded, please make it fucking work . . .
and they went bush.
    You meet somebody trekking, that's
how it starts, when the fire's low,
the final toke's been sucked down,
flicked away, and a loud Aussie
wants to know you better, only if
till tomorrow. But something felt like lasting.
High in Idaho, a fantasy he was uncertain
existed, shaped into the future he was certain
would: part environmentalist, part
burlesque queen, or how he'd imagine them.
    Their January summer hurled him:
tears and songs evaporating, they bushwalked:
the tangy dry of dust and eucalyptus
igniting Mason: out there
he could signal his origins,
say something so American:
'A man *lives* this way . . .' would it matter?
    'A *man* eh?' Hannah snorted.
Won't say a thing . . .'
                         The sloppy versus the crass,
they stayed out of their tent one night
for her 'Starlight screwing . . . yum yum.
Let's end by baying at the moon.'
    Vulgarity fitted her and he loved it but
'Goddamm't Han. In the bush?'
                                     Still,
they tried her fantasy *Aaaaaooooo.*
    'Lord,' he sighed. 'You can fuck anywhere
in the world.'
                  Now who was being basic?
                                    Well Mason,
sometimes, but Hannah almost always,
even at her softest with phrases like
Turn off the light . . . there's no-one else . . .
Let's go into the dark; in one day
she could exasperate again: her speciality:
telling too much:
'I told them you were slow, considerate.'

'Benny and Wal aren't Masters and Johnson.
Next time you orgasm just run up a flag!'
(Sounding like one of them, like her)
                              But no,
these kids weren't *us*; and Mason still was *us*.

(VII) Benny, Carrie, Wal

    Better set for eight before the hash worked
and his mine-host routine succeeded,
too well (sometimes, when off-it,
the only way to cover the course
was galloping through the mania, paranoia,
inappropriate desire: catching quips, heaving gags,
sheer over-doing it).
              Not yet.
These were among the better set of minutes,
when the night was prepared
and your guests hadn't arrived:
time to indulge: a number/session X
of some longterm foreplay/even
a neat spa with the beloved.
    But the front door chimed and perky,
husky, Carrie was waiting: 'Sorry I'm first,'
near-shy to enter this early. 'How's Wal?'
    'Well I've just tackled a biscuit,
they're always prime.'
              'More going?'
    'Please, my guest. The boy's showering.'
    This time last year Wal had blundered,
in at four-ten, blotto; Benny sensing
a re-run of the Sundrenched days.
Luckily not. 'There's this girl at work.
You must meet Carrie. We've just done
Freddie's, for a treat. She served it up
to Motor Mouth this arvo,
saved me from the sack.' And Benny baulked;
no, he wouldn't ask why;

content to shudder at his friend
in the workplace. Yet was this Wal's style:
hocking his heart to some Sister Floosie?'
   And meeting her Benny knew:
some of Wal's heart was gone, a part, though,
that never had been his: part-falling
for the loyal, bittersweet cynic in the woman;
the nervous tongue licking over the pale
pink lippy. 'Boyfriends?' Benny asked him.
Many men liked Carrie. 'Girlfriends?'
When the novelty demanded.
   'You men are much more fascinating,'
Wal was told. 'The most fascinating persons,
though, are women. Guys . . .' she sighed,
'gays, patients, clients, those I won't
see again . . . beyond that point they're trouble.'
   They went to dinner.
They all went to dinner. Once,
when Wal had left the room, Carrie blazed:
'You're a lucky man, isn't Wal superb?'
Yes, well, there was good luck, bad luck
and Wal-luck. Some hours later, leaving them,
she modified: 'Sorry I got so presumptuous:
you're both lucky. Anyone who cares for Wal
must be worthwhile.'
Since nothing much too sayable remained,
that's where their friendship parked;
though after a dozen times (still somehow
shy with Benny) it was a friendship.
He went to her parties, she came to his.
At gift time gifts were given.
   Steam gushed from the bathroom as
'Getting clean sweetheart?' she opened it.
Wal, happily annoyed, shut her out.
   After he dressed a scenette was arranged:
Wal's voice: a campy mock-nag:
'Put on The Village People, Benny.'
Who stung back, over-avuncular through
the serving hatch, 'Later, Wally, later.'
   Wal told her of the easy-listening Macho-man:

'You didn't hear it?'
                        No, that afternoon
she was '. . . in the rooms. I left at five.
That was enough. Look sweetheart,'
an urgency was added,
'glad I'm here, someone has to know.
Why not you? There's a few things I'm hoping
happen. Want a secret?'
The question didn't need replying.
'First a baby, in a year, say,
go on the single mums', become a photographer,
moonlight a bit.'
                'Don't look at me!'
Though Wal seemed pleased. 'You'll need a dad.'
        'There might be one back home,'
she waved this on.

(VIII) Mason, Benny

        'Not intruding early?' Mason asked.
'I've been sent in.'
                'Hash biscuits . . .'
he heard mumbles, 'something's happening . . .'
which Benny felt he needed to explain.
        'Hash oil? One trip,' confided Mason,
you had to listen hard enough to, almost,
reassure *The walls aren't tapped, we're friends . . .
aren't we?* 'one trip, back home,
I got into another soul, only it was . . .'
his voice was dry and softly creaked:
'it was . . . it was a goldfish!
We stared each other into an eternity . . .'
        Well, time to slap his back and mate-
like ask, 'So, Mason, what's y' musical poison?'
        'Bit mellow, I'm afraid. Mitchell, Cooder,
Jackson Browne, Eagles.'
                        Hmmmmmellow?
Benny considered, positively post-autumnal!

>   Down from Mason's hair (a slowly thinning
> grey bouffant) he seemed to blend with
> whatever was available.
> No-one intruded less; so calm you wished
> he would; and so quiet, quiet as Dr Crippen:
> a thought so hideous Benny apologised.
>   'Yeah?' Mason blinked bewildered. 'Why?'
>   'Something I thought.' A chair was grasped.
> 'Please get Wal, I might be going mad, but only
> just for now. It was your goldfish . . .'
>   Something to trust, the chair was firm.
> If he could simply steady, Benny knew,
> these minutes (yes they were only minutes),
> were the merest nick in the night's corner,
> dust, briefly, in its eye:
> Mason as Crippen and needing to apologise.
> It all became a distraction that didn't distract,
> an anxiety feeding off itself, where panic was obligatory, a litany
> of what wouldn't happen:
> *I won't hit, or get hit,*
> *I won't die tonight, nobody will.*
> *What I need might be a walk, a drink,*
> *some air, somebody to arrive.*
>   'You seem to frown . . .' Mason purred
> in soft-American, Benny subsided:
> all that death, life and the paranoia between
> had distilled into a frown which *seemed*.
>   Opening a window he relaxed enough
> to set up Mason. 'Mason . . .
> your great and powerful fifty states
> of ongoing freakshow, the evangelists!
> the massacres! those drugs we'll never
> try approaching! when in doubt experiment!
> Why would you want to leave?'
>   'The bullshit.' Benny liked this.
> 'Or rather . . .'
>   'Yes?'
>   'I prefer your bullshit
> to ours.'
> 'Mason, you're noncommittal to that fault

it would be if tonight we had one.'
Benny loved his words, how they
could near-arrange themselves. 'Howzat!'
    Spreading his hands, Mason drooped his face;
yes, he was liked. 'Obliged,' humming with
the calmest twang, 'obliged.'

(IX) Barb

    Back home, last vacation,
minding her parents' place,
she'd wandered down to their yard as
sunrise started washing the neat sections
of 'natives'.
    When Barb saw him,
back-to-her, she needed Roger, who,
knowing someone was there, turned.
The dawn on his face thudded her into
a future: this light after hours
of sleepless warmth hinting how they'd grow:
how only death could end her accommodating
these mean icons of his thin love:
a parched approximate passion,
the desire to get-it-right.
How could this man ever believe she
might be hurt?
    He has a lover
she told a friend once, *I'm very hurt.*
So? Now? The lover didn't last as Neil hadn't.
    Barb waited, knowing soon she might
share something with this body facing her:
the concave cheeks, the slightest tick on
the upper lip; or, forgetting his face,
the nerve-ends, the nerve-ends through both
of them: love or its substitute.
    Birds sliced up available silence,
round the corner someone revved,
the morning coasted now as, bland and adequate,

they might have. What was her dividend?
And when?
         Much younger, after marriage
and their child, they'd snatch some bush dawns:
a kid-couple sharing cigarettes:
contained, trying to arrange the rules.
Some years on a few days started
with Neil, at Benny's;
buoyed by a chilly energy and off-hand cracks,
she'd leave in her car, she always would.
     And this was another sequel dawn:
back at her parents', standing with 'natives',
still needing desire, knowing how the future
never rewards, rewards were always now.
Being loved weren't you remade minute
after minute? Love could never live
in the future, it was always now:
that made it love. Yet she believed
in sunrise, how there were always more;
next time she wanted one, she'd
have to hold it, though; as if, somehow,
nobody in the world had, ever.
     'Damp enuf f' yez?' Correctly,
her cabbie wedged this evening in.
Useless to mull on how to superannuate
your marriage, or what exactly got divorced
when that happened: you were being driven
through a Sydney evening, to Annandale
and tonight's diversion, dinner at Benny's.

(x) Barb, Hannah, Benny, Leo, M

     The trees had spread, each year his home of
kidney-coloured bricks got better hidden.
     As Barb rang the bell (a woman,
hustling by, yelling her way inside)
Benny appeared. '. . . She's Hannah.'
                        Was it?

How easy, dull and doubtless next-door
neighbourly to shriek *Where are you Benny?
Wal?* Wanting to leave,
Barb's eyes were closed. What was being offered?
More of this fish-wife? Neil's renovations?
So much of Neil bar Neil? Photographs?
She winced, but was being introduced
to others who'd arrived behind her,
    'Like myself, Leo's Adelaidian . . .' Leo, who
tried to click his heels, then raising her hand
kissed it. '. . . And this is M, subtle bon vivant.'
    'Like Emma?'
                  'No like M. Like James Bond's boss?'
With soft slight laughter sprinkling from her,
Leo pointed to the headgear of his
slim, pale friend: '. . . the hers
of our ill-fated his 'n' hers cowboy hats.'
    M looked quiet, if not silent, but Leo
in the hall unwound: 'We've jetted up,
stashed our stuff at Carlo's, had some smokes,
taxied over here. Why here? Action round
these parts?'
    'Plenty in my head, I've just . . .'
Benny waited seconds to decide
some words, 'you find it.'

(XI) Barb, Benny, Leo

    'Wal seems a problem?' Barb was asked,
as Benny's smile concurred.
'Got a conspirator's looks: just wrap him in
a toga, place him by a pillar.
It's said he's shy with ladies, but look at
him 'n' Carrie . . .' (whose light, husky voice
drifted from their corner). 'Don't she smoulder?
The best girls always do. That voice alone
makes for something so sexy-sweet,
if I were straight, if I were female,

if I were anyone but I, Benny;
but don't be jealous, you've been praised,
Barb, boy have you been praised!
She's Wal's old mate, they've worked together.
Leo and M are up for Mardi Gras,
Hannah and Mason live next door,
I'm me and you're you. What's Carrie do?
Let's say she's been a nurse, still is.
I'll sit you with her . . .'
He turned bureaucratic:
'Wal will head the board, with,
on his left M, Mason, Hannah.
I face Wal with Leo, you and Carrie . . .'
And then, near-paranoid: 'But outside,
outside there's a heap of pricks tonight
and every night; so when I say eat, eat;
starting now let's be a little more intolerant.
You all turn towards me? Benny's off again?
Well, he's feeling good, perhaps too fuckin' good.
Name us your drug before the last one,
Benny: it was *glorious, glamorous,*
and that old stand-by amorous . . .
or put it another way, I'm not paranoid
but take me for a walk someone? Now?
Yes now. Sure I know it's din-dins . . .'
    'How far?' asked Leo.
    'The pub.'
        They went.
  'On nights like these,' Wal told the guests,
'you're not to worry. Paranoid? Who's paranoid?
Not Benny. They won't be long, just
plot/counterplot then back to plot again.'

(XI) Leo, Benny

    Leo came from the bar:
its tiles, its beer-paintings,
that incomprehensible rugby on the tube.

Wasn't it a winter sport? He let them play.
Sydney tonight seemed all body,
from the lush invisible drizzle to
the barman's mighty pecs.
Yet Benny was sighing:
'We walk out and drink but, you know,
it's Wal.'
                'True happiness?'
    I saved him, no happiness is truer;
my grand self-destructive holy fool
might be dead now. And one holy fool's
another village idiot, right?'
(Whatever such stoned insight meant,
tomorrow, Leo thought it good enough.)
'Had Kenny the Quack get him
his orderly's job, Wal thrives there,
it's where he 'n' Carrie met.' *Hmmm*, went Leo,
'Like her?' Benny asked.
                        'The hair's
amazing . . . why won't it float away?'
    'I *think* she's nice but y' sedentary poove
hasn't much to offer Carrie Fastlane.'
    'Jealous?'
                'Well *she* won't fuck him,
but when he grooves on out to Vaseline Valley,
some rabbit does.'
                'Getting jiggy-jigs? You?'
    'A few.' One could've had a few last night
and Leo knew this for an annual few,
at most, when a bed might be for company,
sometimes, but for sleep, certainly.
'. . . just a very king of the bric-a-brac,
mutterin' and motherin' round his
naughty boy and bone china. Any odd foray?'
Benny wouldn't answer himself. 'Leo.'
He stopped their walk and stared, doubtless
some hash-fuelled melodrama clutching him.
'Leo: we must be careful.'
                    'So they say.'
    'What you will do up here?'

                              'Smoke drugs,
chase ass, Christ Church St Laurence,
live-a-bit, but be as a friend of mine
would say, indifferent.'
                    'M?'
    'Some of the above.'
    'Come to Mark's tomorrow night.'
    Mark's, thought Leo, liberation strategies
and piano duets: 'Scaramouche'/ 'En Bateau'/
whoever needed 'Bats in the Belfry'?
'... that active activist?' he asked.
    'More celibate than active now – but,
as I told you once ...'
                    'Adelaide '68?'
    'The very place and time, you know
the line: restraint: just another form of sex life.'

(XIV) Wal

    Arriving back they caught the guests
suspending their concerns, turning towards Wal
and a story he was telling.
    'Wanna hear it too?' He smiled. 'Bet Benny does.
One cruising tale you haven't heard or told
or horror! don't appear in.
The Case of Cross-Dresser Dean, take two!
Now, in all those choreographies for
happily married men and others,
I met no more than three real shits,
whose stories we'll forget, mine have happier endings.
There was confusion? There's confusion
eating a pie, but little I couldn't accept
and try appreciating. Imagine this:
holed-up with young and frantic Dean
on Perth's discreetest beat, believe me
that's discretion. Straight? The straightest.
Married, their fun was fine, they
loved each other. And I was steeled,

sensing a bout of the old
Ohhh it's just . . .' Dean shrugged. Cor-rect, I thought,
and asked *It's just?* Another shrug.
*Could it be, just could, that here
I'm camp and it's okay, you're straight
and it's not?* A week after they were built
these dunny walls knew that one by heart,
knew it for bullshit. *Dean, you are tolerant
of everyone but you!* There he was,
needing those fish-net and suspender
accoutrements, but needing to meet someone
and hear, *Well aren't you sane, no
you really are!* 'And guess what kicked
it off? Call all this theory, another
Wal-special, but 'round that year
The Rocky Horror Show came prancing
into town; and seeing Dr Frank N. Furter
something snapped, getting dissolved into
a something-else that wonderful
he couldn't, probably wouldn't, almost
certainly shouldn't understand;
a something else not any mere abstract 'you'
but rather he, Dean, so simply did:
sex if you like or, even better, some part of it.
Benny, don't gape, I'd rather tell this much.
Been waiting for the proper time though,
it's taken longer than most that's all,
and no, I won't elaborate, that night belongs
to me and Dean, wherever, whoever, whatever
he is!'

    'Not bad,' Carrie laughed.
    'A good one,' Barb agreed.

(xv) Hannah

    Didn't she predict they would be here
and phoney? Hannah knew this type:
party upon party bloodhounding

for sensitivity or outrage;
that charm of certain/ uncertain androgyny;
the gay as cipher. *If it's not me tonight*
(and it wouldn't be),
it can't be any other woman
(and it wasn't).
She mightn't enjoy Lesbine company
but real dykes knew their bounds:
what they posed for was themselves:
This is us folks, from now you will adjust.
Not here. She knew these women,
how they'd coo their inane contralto
Good one, heh heh, good one
at last week's gag the next quip,
those inane tales from the cruise-life.
And what varnished these hags better than
a coating of *Heh, good one?*
Gaping they'd pant at any amount of
rumoured combinations: eyes turning to supernovas
as the details got programmed:
That went here and this went there . . .
daring to condescend on those she loved,
for true, she loved these guys.
That they were childish, unnatural,
was hideous of course, and one day
someone (her?) would have to tell them.
But tonight friends were hosting, Hannah was among
their guests and Mason would turn
embarrassed now, annoyed later.
Fuelled by *Good-ones,* antihystamines,
and PMT, an old grey battleship of
a hangover blazed home, to disembark
tomorrow. She might be angry but
remorse she didn't need;
and *fake, shallow,* their unending
et ceteras, all the stock words,
simmered down. Everyone noticed
but very few cared for ranting.

(XVI) Barb

  Benny, Barb recalled, never had
gay friends living here. 'Gays? My place?
Verboten! Seduced by temptation
for half an hour, followed by the bedsheet-
shuffle and morning-after guilt
on permanent display. Straight men,
straight women, gay women?
Liberty Hall baby! But the fraternity?
Nix.
  (At least till Wal: 'I'm feeling useful!')
  '... Neil,' Carrie was told, 'Benny's friend,
was living here. We'd this affair.
Love I suppose; but in ten months
I knew the when and how of stopping,
if not the why. Neil was renovating,
painting this and other places.
In this room, yes,
a fair few things were smashed;
I hadn't slept for days, with a son and husband
reminding me, if only they knew,
Neil wasn't where I was. Were we cowards
never to ask each other much?
We rarely did; but when I presented him
the opportunity *Ask me to live with you,
it's asking me to live again*
he stood there shrugging, shuffling.'
  Benny was away, the extension windows
hadn't any glass, two cans of supergloss
flew out to meet the fence,
and in the corner where, tonight,
the turntable stood poised for The Village People,
Neil sobbed.
  'What? Something like *fuck you*.
How limp and unoriginal I thought.
This'll be nearly over. One more
reconciliation, later.'
  An end of it and
a start of it: when she came back

they weren't exactly 'it' again;
but Benny returned and soon the 'it' was Wal.

(XVII) Carrie

'He's your friend Carrie?'
                              'My dearest.'
'Aren't you a nurse?'
                         She's sweet and now
for it, Carrie dared herself. 'Let's say
a nurse, let's say a call girl.'
      And sweet as Barb appeared, nothing was sweeter
than saying that: didn't floor her.
      'Let's say . . .' Barb spoke slow, a smile
increasing. 'How can I, could anyone, top *that?*
May I ask when?'
      'Not that often but today though.
I once asked someone what she did
like you've just done and, boy, *was* she!
I had a friend, every woman has a friend
who might or does.'
      Anyone that special must do something
even better, Carrie had thought, as if Amanda
would always be alive forever.
How could you invent her?
Whatever Amanda knew she wanted to
know it, only it and all.
      'How easy *Been meaning to ask you*
sounds; the easy's always crushed;
each time we met I crushed it;
just blabbing on with her and anyone;
thinking how courage always fucks
the future, that the unknown must be
the unknown and courage needn't be courage.
Still, I thought, *you must have secrets,
Amanda, name me one*, until
after another dinner yes I asked her.
Took home enough to re-believe:

infatuation, admiration, love,
what they might be and how, even,
to enjoy them if ever I grew up;
I wanted to join her; so I joined her.'
      How smooth it seemed to softly drop
on one you mightn't meet again
how you were occupied, one till six,
two days a week with extras
like today, if needed:
life in an Edgecliff cathouse,
its occupants and visitors: the artist
who gave her a painting; the cop
who somehow arrived at three,
each Tuesday; or the one who went o.s.
and wrote back almost love-letters;
wherever he was. Bar love
Carrie could take on offer anything
Dearest, the weather here feels like those days
I won't forget when we met . . .
and being top-shelf you're forever met,
someone's always riding up in the lift,
going through with it.
      'Four of them worked together:
a place in Surry Hills:
the owner was the prick of pricks.
Amanda had plans for an apartment.
She went to a financier, one of hers,
who'd lend for it; to the owner,
one of hers, who'd rent it out;
and to this cop, hers at the time,
who'd protect them.'
      Barb was laughing: easy, silly, strange
(and was it 'heroic'?); would the adjectives stop?
How great to be so ordinary
so anything less like a freak.
      'I'm a happy amateur, want it that way.
The girls think I'm crazy, but there's enough
to keep me sane . . . not recruiting, Barb,
never would, but come across and meet us;
you could always answer the phone.'

Something to say and be believed
or not believed? How to offer Carrie
a gambit in reply?
     'I mean ...'
and something in Barb's head escaped:
'How can anyone judge?
When can you say *Now I'm in control,
why shouldn't I be?*'
  (Benny was announcing liqueurs elsewhere.)

(xviii) Benny

  'Time for The Village People,' Wal was chiming,
'Benny!'
   'Hardly. Let's do the "Manhattan"
soundtrack.'
    But *Oh dear* ...
two tracks in Benny, Edward Everett Horton-
style, was baulking: hadn't Barb seen it
with Neil? Yet sensitivities being one thing
wasn't he being over-precious?
Given their grand tour of moviedom, that year,
what music remained? The love theme from
'The Battleship Potemkin'?
      Oh he was a brooder
and loved it. Benny could conjure those
despairing sighs if ever Leo guessed
his ongoing psycho-rummage:
'Don't say you're still onto *that*, or *that*?
Benny, detach yourself a bit,' as an injunction
thundered, 'ascend Olympus!'
And Benny might, but allow him, please,
this luxury: to retell how,
two refrains still wavered on
from his uni working holidays:
the said *'Like to stay back?'*
and unsaid: *So many guys out there
need this.*

    Sometimes, almost to tease,
the older man talked local footy
(he coached them).
'On training nights if it gets stinking wet
we'll strip someone, dump him in the mud.'
And Benny's eyebrows arched:
But since he can't tell anyone that
quite that way, don't be a prig!
Yet after leaving his friend and boss,
the silo foreman, Benny would turn
languidly defensive, smartarsed.
Pre-dinner drinks at Platitude Downs,
cornered with vintage cheer from
mother's sister's spouse: 'So, son . . .'
(a man on the land trying to stay relevant)
'what's the varsity of life taught us today?'
And being patronised, 'son' simply lied.
'Today uncle? Genocide.'
    Yet still he carted around that evening
in his skull, it was enough to close your eyes,
think of the Mallee, and wince 'Oh, Benny . . .'
heading for twenty years on,
'where'd you appropriate *that*:
"Hay Fever" at the Mechanics Institute?'
    That March/April/May when all he considered worthwhile
was someone unattainable (if doubtless likable)
a near-enough straight who, last summer,
appreciated him, a grown-up if you like,
Benny turned fodder for Leo pep-talks:
'Quit wilting! Just pour y' self into some jeans,
and go out!'
    So, when Barb left Neil
and Benny played Leo, that irresistible
jeans-line almost re-used itself;
though once poured, what?
(Months on, he suspected, someone had been found.)

(xix) Leo

'This tale,' Leo announced, 'is a profane sermon to fill
the hiatus before, and no doubt after,
we go: a saga of thwarted lust;
of a grand if distant friendship
(with whom I'm not exactly certain);
and of imagination: pure perhaps,
applied maybe. The story's mine
or, rather, ours . . .' Leo indicated M,
'and anyone else's; frankly the whole of Sydney's
up for grabs.' (Barb closed her eyes
to Leo's voice, purest Adelaide,
and tone, a raconteur's . . .) 'Now, advertising
helps . . .' (feeling she heard Don Dunstan,
somewhere). 'Frankly it's brought us, M et moi,
some of the nicest people. *We use
our imagination, please use yours and meet us.
Clean, discreet, the works.*'
Mason watched M, someone echoed from
that pale and oval face, her eye's
animated sadness.
                      'She gave her name,'
Leo told, 'as Margaret, Margaret Watson.
How wonderfully anon. Don't you feel you
went to school with Margaret Watson?
This one wrote from Sydney.
She lived in a North Shore P.O. Box,
her husband's work was sending them south
and they were experienced beyond description
(though she'd describe all right),
in fruitful human interactions.
A cheeky come-on, her first note
teased us. Sounds good, we thought.
From then on each of Margaret's letters scorched the last
we kept replying *Our lives are tame:
some dope, touches of amyl, who doesn't
nowadays? have friends over, make
new ones, bop on. Love us to meet,
we must sound like novices,*

maiden aunts . . . to her and whatever name
the husband had, Marvin or Mervyn,
something like Merv or something not.
By now we'd be having Margaret parties,
phoning friends. Doing much tonight?
Margaret! they'd cry, dropping all for
another grand recital.'

  Hushed and astounded, bemused or angry,
his audience stared at Leo who started
improvising, he'd make their evening
worth it.

   '*Hi folks* . . . *you know who and
Merv the Perve from sexy sunny Sydney* . . .
like that but to the power of ten.
*With a hubby hung like a hippo I'm still
randy as a rhino (y' like that?) Can't wait to
meet you both and all repeat all
your friends. Remember Merv's mate Claude?
Well last night him — and his supercock* . . .
leaden-foot erotica out of the crassest
advertising copy. And yet,
like earthlings who had chanced upon
beckonings from Alpha Centauri
we floated further into some
fantasy-universe (hers? his? theirs,
a computer's, God's, any combination of same?).'

  Benny and his elevated eyebrow
gasped, 'Le-oh!' The bullshit prosecutor was
breathing heavy. 'Say it ain't true,
allay my fears . . .' turning to M, 'Please?'

  'We're afraid so,' she smiled.

  'Well it hasn't happened to me.'

  'Or me.'

   'Or me.'

    'Or me.'

  'Wish it had,' sighed Wal.

      Hannah
played with rhubarb.

   'Pictures?'
Mason asked.

　　　　　　'To a point,' hummed Leo.
'Margaret and spouse? No.
But pleasant snaps of healthy young Australians?
Certainly. Nothing outrageous, barbecue
and picnic shots with commentaries.
This one's Karen say.
After I've gone down and turned her frantic,
Merv moves in. She's a hot wet honey
and insatiable. But this approximates.
One phrase though I've memorised,
it closed their opening note, quote:
There's little in the to and fro of
human love we haven't tried.
A good one, eh?'
　　　　'Maggie 'n' Merv! For godsake!'
This was Carrie.
　　　　　　　　'Bah! Humbug! Post Box Sex!'
This was Benny.
　　　　　　　'Then it imploded.
Letter five: *Sorry can't make Melbourne,*
now. She was (can you believe it?
I can't) pregnant! *Taa. Loved writing to*
you both. (Loved hearing from you Margaret.)
Bye now. Consigning her letters to
the elements we turned our spacecraft home.'
　　　Barb, though, plumped for optimism:
'Couldn't she, or they, exist? A bit?
Or does that make the story, well,
sadder?'
　　　Word by word,
line by line, Leo and friends had thought
her real. 'Shouldn't get so pregnant,
that's all. Such an organised swinger
wouldn't. Would she? Anyone know her?
Sound familiar? A rabbit
fitting the profile? fitting the fantasy?'
　　　'Love to have it,' Carrie laughed, 'but no.'
　　　'And we'd love to stake out
the P.O. Box,' M confessed. 'Join us anyone?'
　　　Hannah gulped.

(xx) Mason, Wal, Benny, Barb, Leo, M, Hannah, Carrie

        '. . . Of course! Of course!'
Mason, studying M, was recalling two or three
so-plaintive photographs. 'Carson McCullers!'
    'Who?' asked Wal.
              'Sorry, nothing.'
    So many friends I've had, thought Benny,
they seem no more than ashes now,
scattered from those endless blazes
scorching the wildside.
For those few wishing to return, there were
the many who would never trust, or risk,
an open house as simply as that.
    (Maybe, thought Barb, but come in/
get out! it's the same door.)
    And the older Leo grew how lesser 'jealousy',
'betrayal' mattered, hardly sounding
real words tonight, why dwell on them
chez Benny?
        'Are you two exes?' Barb asked Leo,
    'Next day he was . . . what year was
our one night stand?'
              'We stood?' quizzed Benny.
    Galloping away on a drug collection,
or whatever else could rock them
into the dawn (port? porn? poesy?)
they finished in contortions so improbable
only a God recovered from the sight
might tell them how.
    Hannah looked across at Leo, stared
and moaned.
        (Why'd that person ever bother?)
    'I just Ma-dam,' and,
as a cat prowls in slow motion, Leo
turned his mind to her,
'I just pretend that those I tell,
whatever I tell, might be amused;
that, if I'm worth their while,
they will enjoy themselves. Folly? It could be,

and certainly a risk, though some just might
appreciate pretending and, Ma-dam,
I'd never wish pretence with you.'
    Did she hear him? Bobbing the table
Hannah's face dropped slowly
(not designed to please: those who soon
snore off into dessert never do).
    'Tonight's too much for Han,'
her boyfriend heaved.
                    Hosting or guesting
had better ways, Leo knew, to crash with style:
bombed in a corner, say, pulsing with reggae,
that stetson over your eyes,
with muttered phrases from Nahum Tate
to Jimmy Cliff via Jean-Paul Sartre.
All thought of which gave benediction fodder:
how would it go? *Some evenings it gets so like
we speak another English tongue, if still ours.
Let it stay like that. Write it down? Why?*
Whatever these words meant they
held enough. 'Coming M?'

(xxi) Benny, Barb

    This bagatelle, considered Benny,
doesn't quite amount. (Did he have to
do do do what he done done done today-
by-now-yesterday, and mention Neil?)
*It's something you might enjoy though,
and important, because I need to say it.*
Two of his friends loved each other,
once, and somehow he, confidant, sounding-
board, resident Dotty Dix, got wringered
into the action. And that's the difficulty,
Benny discovered to himself,
in saying this so-simple something:
but, gulping in,
    'Neil knew Hannah, years back.

Met her here once, too and couldn't *stand* her.'
    Laughing, Barb believed it.

(xxii) Carrie, Barb

    'Wait, I'm out your way, Barb. If you can trust
someone stoned as me to drive . . .'
    Then Carrie moved across to Wal;
clutching hands they kissed and whispered spells:
gossip and affection, grown-up echoes of
playground crushes.
                  At the lights confessing:
'I must love Wal, some way . . .' she turned left,
'But Benny's, well, made for him and that's
all fine,' (and sighed) 'certainly just fine.'
Now her evaluations rose:
'How was that American? Low key
yet spunky eh? Hannah's hopefully forgettable
and those multi-level swingers, okay
who can preach, but weren't they beyond you too?'
    Carrie might live for hours like now
but Barb was awake enough only
to sound agreeable. Which, somehow,
roused her. What, she thought, would close tonight?
A tub of McWords *Nice meeting you?*
(*Eat in? Take away?*)
    If Barb wanted coffee with her, somewhere,
one day, Carrie gave a card,
naming her afternoons, how Rosie,
who did the bookings, was sweet
and messages there were safer, sure,
than any hospital.
               It could be a way
to tell *You helped make this evening . . .*
if only it was. But this tentative coffee,
tour of the cathouse, friendship . . . oh yes,
Barb felt, something could tally,
but when she arrived at deciding what,

exactly, tallied, it no doubt wouldn't.
 Reaching Barb's place Carrie held her hands.
Then squeezed. Barb sped inside.

(xxiii) Benny, Hannah

 Someone was moving on the couch,
he turned to see, puffy from collapse,
Hannah rise with *We're not over* yet,
Bennyboy a smirk of bleared aggression
hailing him.
   'Mason's left. Leo and M.
Barb with Carrie. All gone!' he chimed.
'Wal's teeth are getting scrubbed, we never
played his precious Village People and now,
like every nowadays, I'm dog-housed.
What will get you up again?
A different drink?'
    'Let's . . .' and,
as Hannah's word hung, he combed the cabinet
(*Let's out*, his psyche winced).
'Let's post-mortem. Your friend, he doesn't
like me.'
  'Leo?' (His back was to her,
mixing the inanest.) 'He *loves* you.'
  Prissy retainer props spoilt heiress, what
thirties screwball farce was this?
A Wal *yoo-oo* echoed from the hallway,
their neighbour croaked a reply, and Leo
was dispatched.
   'Where you get
those women?'
   'You've met Carrie,
I've mentioned Barb before. She and Neil? Remember?'
  'She fucked *him*?'
     'Jeez Hannah!'
His retainer's cool halted that second,
heated itself and rose steaming at her:

'They were in love!'
      'So was Maggie Thatcher, once. Benny ...'
Where would her mind-tour take them,
now? 'Why can't I wear a cowboy hat?
I feel so conformist. *You're a "character"*
they'd tell me as a kid.
Well straight women aren't meant to be
characters.'
      'And what men are?'
      '*Yoo-oo*, good night,' beeped Wal from somewhere.
      'Night,' she muttered.
            A siege was on; Benny,
weathering them before, relaxed:
time was his ally this morning,
little but a battery of wails would breech him:
though then he'd only pure, plain hope
to combat her tears. Hope the very basis of emotion.
      'Benny ...' no she wouldn't cry tonight,
'why won't women and I ... get on?
I had friends once. Remember
the Women's Movement? No upper lips were
stiffer since the empire sah!
How could you be a *character* with them?
That let down the team.
Know why I'm a fag-hag? Nothing's safer.
How could I fail *your* side?
Somewhere it's guilt, or gotta do with guilt;
we're all expected to be dykes,
child care and wheelchair access provided!'
      Excessive for his humanist demands,
'You're not ...' sighed Benny
      'OK not expected but it felt that way.'
      Looking at her how he'd love to cry:
Know what it takes to give a worried rave?
A good (let's hope very good) listener,
who won't stereotype, be stereotyped;
in brief one-too-fuckin'-much paragon
of counselling skills. But if that's what,
what's the end?
With tribes of hypocrite pastors, their

sanctimonious wifies, sprouting ping!
through the suburbs like a crop of herpes
any good fairy waving the poof!
of tolerance won't get them to disappear.
They thrive on us!

      Hannah, though, continued ploughing.
'Chubby, fair and sensual. Am I kind of
Edwardian? Haven't you caught me in bow-tie
and tails, fag-hagging queenie sing-alongs.
All the nice girls love a candle . . . /
I'll be loving you, sideways . . . sing-along,
bric-à-brac, Benny, why do you pooves
do it?'

      'We're smart enough, dumb enough,
there is no-one else.'

      'I've drunk well past enough.
Used to bail up dinner guests when I got
this full: *Her name's Doreen. Well spare me*
bloomin' days . . . Not tonight.
Mason's going home. I got to decide;
I don't want to decide. They aren't like us.'

      'Americans? Well we're hardly them.'
A sliver of guilt winced Benny:
that he could be so bland, if
tired and bland.
               It hardly mattered.
Hannah was veering:
'You've got to hear of Margie's ex.
Somehow that bastard . . . that bastard
bunched all the cords coiling through his life
into this tumour-knot then, slicing,
did it. Keith did it. That Saturday morning,
jogging in the fog, I found him
(all windows up, all doors locked)
out for the longest count, in Margie's car.
For a moment, Benny, the world contained
two people: one dead, one living: him, me.
Then it's me realising who and what's occurred,
it's me shattering the glass (there's little sounds
so much alive) and it's me screaming to a Canberra

that won't listen anyway (bloody fuck it won't):
I want to buy the papers, have a shower,
brew some coffee, spread the honey on my toast . . .
but here's the corpse of stupid Keith!
And weren't we meant to stay so calm!
When I wasn't, Jo never forgave me.
Wasn't calm for months. Didn't they get it?
I'd nothing else to do! Dead how many hours?
It may've been centuries by then!'
        Keith/Margie/Jo . . .
too tired to process the names she splattered,
(Canberra even) Hannah-pet, thought Benny,
it's getting towards four,
I dropped a hash-charged nervy seven hours
back, Wal's been acting enigmatic, and if
the rest was fun fun fun, Mark's bash is on
tomorrow night. Mason's delightful,
why not mention him and leave it at that?
  And, as if the hour if not her host
demanded, Hannah soon obliged.
'Sometimes he might be selfish, hasn't
the world's finest body, biggest cock; his face
can merge with so many others it's hardly
memorable: yet I forget that, if I ever think it,
because this guy has something which
the Margies and the Jos would never guess:
tolerance, intelligence, sanity.
And he's not a Keith!
It's tomorrow mate, round ten I'll wake
with the motherest of headaches,
plod Saturday, take a sauna, want sex
want sleep want a feed, get some of them
and try to decide not to decide.
I'll let myself out . . .' She wasn't
starting to go? Only irony and the dishes
remaining, the dishes could wait.
'You're a great listener, Benny: the best.'

(xxiv) Benny, Wal

    He tried undressing, succeeded, then
padded across their room.
Why did the dark move everything?
    'Benny?' Wal muttered, 'that better
be you.'
    'It's not John Holmes,' his friend replied,
'but if it is, enjoy it.'
    Benny found the bed.

LEO

for Robert Langsford

      I've a friend, guess this one's myself,
for effect though, please think he's a mate.
Any ambitions sir? Yes, to be a top shelf
cruiser, as if the earth might evaporate

tomorrow. A favourite memory? Hubbies puffing
homeward from a night-jog, an enjoyable task
done. He terms the business, not merely for nothing,
Free Entertainment in the Parks

(though what *they* may call it never escapes,
a pity).
        One evening on this *hi there* famous beat,
stage right, two truckies. Maybe he'll traipse
off with the taller, but . . . We've others, like to meet

our mates? And I, or my friend or was it his friend,
aaaanyway our hero blanches
as two, then another three arrive. Can't defend
himself. The trees would be as branches

and branches, twigs with these guys.
He can sprint, but if he made it
to his car there mightn't be time to . . . surprise!
'We only want some fun!'
                And they did:

fair dinkum fun. Just one thing
leading wherever one things head. Their caution, if slight,
remained, each kept nit by rote, all had their something
to contribute though.
                He licked the late spring air. The night,

the park and flowers had that much life!

For, with such a mass of willing beaux
to help what, at twenty-three, you want to try try
and try again, seven at one blow

as were, you better believe it! They had to be camp of course,
one or two maybe not. For seven 'normal' men
with just, you know, the need to horse-
round with themselves, no not often just now 'n' then . . .

oh dear!
       They tidied and headed to a flat,
he driving a boy who shrugged as if it was over,
it was nothing and, well, never done quite that. And *that*
was hard to accept.
              Under a full moon's spooky cover

tenants were putting out their bins.
'Come in sport. Never know when there's a party.
Always keep y' 'fridge well stocked with tins.'
And, talking of work or whatever, till 'We like you matey,

but tell us . . .'
        'Mmmm?'
              'What's it like being a poofter?'
Our friend squinted, had to shrug (but not like the boy had).
'. . . please. We're interested.'
                    It wasn't the time to smash off the roof or
improvise a lecture, or even to be mad

enough risking *You mean you don't know?* 'Life,' he mumbled.
'S'pose it's that. What's anything?'
    And, as if it answered more than enough the boy stumbled
up to turn the tele on.
             They continued drinking

till the taller guy, who'd convened proceedings,
somewhat finished them. 'We like you mate . . . serious.'
    Like? You've loved me as you've never *liked*. Any pleadings
otherwise are shit.
           Seven blokes delirious

with their game drank on.
                    'I'm meeting a friend ...'
                                        'Yeh? Catch yer'
    With those two hours' bemusing fol-de-rol
never forgotten, he drove off.
                        'Music to Midnight' had Satchmo
playing and singing one of his best: 'Body and Soul'.

Part 12

KIM 'SPACEY' LACY .... COMMODITIES TRADER
AND BAR OWNER
SOPHIE CROSS .... MERCHANT BANKER,
KIM'S LOVER AND BUSINESS PARTNER
KEVIN JOY .... DECEASED
NEIL 'GOGO' SPENCER .... KIM'S FORMER SCHOOL MATE
RAY 'FRENCHY' DONELLAN .... TAFE ADMINISTRATOR,
KIM AND NEIL'S ONE TIME FRIEND
'GRUBBSY' LEAF } .... SHIRE IDENTITIES
'STINKY' CONWAY

Mister Kim Lacey

With proud and daring characters there is only one step from anger against oneself to fury with other people; transports of rage afford one intense delight in such circumstances.
                      Stendhal, *Le Rouge et le Noir*

(1)

    Each time she entered Crazy Horse murmurs came stalking
Who's that smart bitch? What trouble does she want?
    Kim counselled patience: 'You're copping the brunt
of barflies, Soph, ignore them!'
                      No, let her do the talking:
'I mean, fuck clubs on vacation!
Let's give ourselves some limits, even lawyers aren't this bad.
Tell me Kim, what's it like being had?
What were you after: low-key property speculation,
a nestegg for your ego? Get out of The Horse,
it is both embarrassment and trash.'
    But always fancying himself like someone out of 'M.A.S.H.'
Kim turned sitcom: 'Whatever Hon sure of course . . .'
    No! What she saw hadn't even that novelty of con-artists, cranks.
These were worse: until this place Sophie never thought she'd meet
men so criminally dull.
                      Soon though she'd be found poised-on-her-feet:
for this friend of Kim's had approached one of their banks
(if it was even that) and they employed her: flowchart stuff,
which had you not even guessing how so much cash connects
with . . . just about the lot.
                    Better ignore it, better infect
yourself with simply living here: how, late afternoons, clouds, delayed
                enough,
began to give the city a scouring:
how you dashed, you always dashed, through the dusk
to change, then out to dine and back into the air-conditioned husk
of your apartment.

           At dawn, though, something was souring.
The executions, Sophie knew, had started; little evidence
was needed of that: like The Horse, cashflows, the rains,
killings went with the place; you weren't to imagine these men in chains
who'd never known (nor would they ever now) the essentials, the
                                 requirements.

(II)

       With a slug and a swig down the capsule slid:
it split, dissolved and swam to settle on the nub
of things: the appropriate part of Kim's brain.
                                       In the tub
Sophie was soaking.
                    Ahh money and the things you found you did!
Like flying into Sydney for a school reunion? Well if it can be done,
           do it, right?
The greater the riches the greater choice of whim:
and now you're a commodities trader . . . oh Kim!
       Yep, he knew *that's what I'll be tonight.*
Showing Soph where fifteen, twenty years back he'd thrived,
introducing Neil, Ray, whoever passed for peers,
maybe shout the bar a round of beers,
made good/ made bad this local had truly arrived.
Clothing store tyro/ greenery source/ guitar plucker,
no need for Kim's early careers to get re-itemised,
just dress yourself in legend (he'd wised
to do that from the first) and shed remorse for any sucker
dumb enough not to.
                    It tempted him to greet GoGo
like Spacey once had been: the ever-worldly mentor
Heyheyheyman still trying to find y'self a 'centre'?
       (But Neil still 'centring' himself sounding one almighty nono
Kim considered their long-time mutual mate, Tobe:
what a true talent; what a near to close-personal-friend;
what an income source; what an unfortunate end!)
       Then Sophie returned from the bath, wrapped in her robe.
With a make-up spectrum set to be dabbed on her face,
and her head turbanned in towelling, she looked too imperious
for Kim to admit *Where we going? Look honey, serious,*

The Shire? I'm half scared of the place!
Right now some things sure are a necessity he needed little convincing
to get us through the occasion.
Leaving their hotel
'Me?' Kim demanded, 'Outa mah tree? I'm outa the plantation total!'
    Surely his lady Soph wasn't wincing?
    But she was. For, the bloodstream awash with top-shelf
pharmaceuticals ('Men even stronger than me might cark it . . .')
a prodigal dealer was heading home to his first market:
just to make, re-make, a dickhead of himself.

(III)

    Yes there'd be a school reunion. And whoever
tracked down Neil told him a rumour was humming:
The Spaceman of all people yes that's right Lacy was coming.
But then everyone was. Where? Where any Shire get-together
worth the name assembled: 'The Oceana Room'.
GoGo must remember the cuisine: beefstrog, chook à la King,
cheese 'n' greens and even oooh yeah! something
for the vegos.
    'This'll be the night truly set to boom.
Plus . . .' Neil's informant verged on uncontained,
'"Luvtrip" have reformed and are rehearsin'. Hard!'
    Only a touch more phoning around remained
and Neil, volunteering, visited Ray. He'd turned a trifle fat.
'The Ol Space?' And Frenchy shrank. 'Give me a break!
The next time we meet is if I attend his wake.
Otherwise . . .'
    That surely (Neil stared) wasn't that?
But it was: 'Chrissie's been with him. That man is scum.
I can't I won't say more. Reunion? Reunite with what?'
And, in case his friend had forgot,
'Kim was never one more R. Crumb
furry freak y' know. Oh Go-mate no! Up north . . . Chrissie 'n' him . . .
and what he got that silly moo to do . . . *It worked! It worked!*'
    Donellan wasn't teaching 'I've been,' he put it, 'jerked
sideways into TAFE admin.'
Still, ex-chalkies gotta go some place.' He invested in wine,
was found chipping out of bunkers most weekends;

and yet they still mattered certain friends:
'Call us, we'll eat: you bring your girl, I'll bring mine . . .'
    So Kim who'd always conned, conned Chrissie? Well never
            doing the mainstream (weights
say, or a doctorate) you'd still to admire the way he must've whisked
her into his small-time trade. It sure bulged like a cyst
for Ray: once she'd seemed so safe, never enjoying his mates.
Little wonder now this TAFE high-flyer clammed:
What with Lacy prowling Asia for any stray Raelene or Suellen
then ending with your missus! Who could blame Donellan
for feeling, as Neil guessed, this touch unmanned?
    He wasn't finished though: 'Tell 'em, the gang, Grubbsy, Stinky,
I can't come. It's not the way things should've spanned
One day they might understand
Mister Kim Lacy's not another rinky dinky
boutique dealer . . .' But the facts, whatever they were, lay in traction
as Ray kept whining 'I'll never believe it!'
                Never believe what:
Chrissie sharing holiday time with Spaceman in the cot,
then bringing home her sliver of the local action?
Ray, Ray Neil wanted to do some shaking *She's your ex.*
Forget her!
    One day The Shire might hear things. 'Not from me but. No way
I've a position and Michelle to protect! My girl's a very decent lady!'
    A very decent lady? What had happened to Frenchy, the high school's
        Mr Sex?
    And yes it was, Neil guessed, just-this-side-of-tack
Some thirty-plus adoloescent risking her dash
or worse for gemstones, a hunk of hash . . .

(IV)

    Between his shoulders Neil felt this *Whack!*
    'GoGo! Great being back! Still live round here?'
    After all those years-under-alias Kim knew he was Spacey,
even Lacy, again.
            'Ah!' Neil corrected, '*Mister* Kim Lacy,
late of Mister Kim Lacy's . . .' there was a second's pause, 'Way Out Gear . . .
for Fellas 'n' Birds!'

                        'Two stores,' came the shrug,
'my youth did us on that. The old learning curve
had to start some place but . . .'
                                    And their chat swerved
into *Now!*
            You recreationally drugged?
Kim asked in as many words.
                            Neil smiled,
years back who wasn't? Then that fifth horseman,
the big grass nono, paranoia, arrived.
                                    'Of course, man . . .'
Spacey concurred and, seeing it all safe, he filed
the mate under 'loser' (being charitable 'straight').
Spencer the school ma'am deserved to be taught
enough of Kim's real world for his own good. To indicate
I've supplied sounded ambiguous, so careful with nights
like these, back in places like The Shire.
                                    Such alarms,
though, seemed disposable. 'Gemstones,' Kim discovered he'd said.
            Whilst 'Arms?
Ammo? Yeah Neil you heard correct. Danger? Well the Golan Heights
it wasn't but then what is?'
                        To always hanker
for the quick march of tomorrow's action (where schemes 'n' dreams
                were Kim's fife
and drum) had left him this rather dull man thinking he'd lead one
                amazing life;
for behind convention lay . . . convention! He was a banker
now, something like it (and then add lover, party-goer/giver, friend).
Today when 'crime' meant unpaid parking fines, dud cheques,
an occasional d 'n' d, weird enough (if you wanted it) sex,
all without a victim on earth, he be ready to defend
himself against that first cast and every stone:
'I look at conmen, pimps, thugs,
and see what I am not!'
                        And if tonight he'd returned, smug,
to some outer Sydney nostalgia comfort zone,
bring on such nights with all their incidental dross:
'Stinky' wasn't it who slapped on that much Brut you'd smell
him miles off. The past? There's nothing like it!

                                    Whose spell
went *Crrack!* 'Oh-oh, here comes Soph my lady, Sophie Cross.'

(v)

    Someplace o.s. Neil had married and, for a year,
he lived there. Back home, working for tradie-mates,
Sydney suited him. Try out other cities, states?
For what?
    They shouted him a beer.
   He was, thought Sophie, pleasant in such un-diversity:
had never tried the guitar, didn't act.
Left plenty of jobs but not once truly sacked.
Thought about a degree;
looked around of course, heaps of looking around.
Someone he'd loved was back home too: where she started.
With the spouse. Barb had given Neil a year of wit. Then they parted.
And, adding to the effect, he made a sound
approximating *At least I tried* . . .
He had gay friends but wasn't. On a kibbutz he'd tripped, twice;
and since then had rarely smoked. Name any drug it would stay on ice.
His father, who Kim might recall, had died
trying to rule the remains of his meagre kingdom, an end
just as it always had been.
    Neil's best excuse *I dunno . . . because*
had been his since age twelve. He was,
if such a man were required, Kim's oldest friend.

(vi)

    Though Lacy rarely needed the necessary debt
of mates.
    In a game with laws you'd never quite permit yourself to imagine
the best chance always entered from a tangent.
   There must've been hundreds that never knew what or who
    they'd met
'Businessman eh? Call us that as well.
Gemstones, matey . . . that and the odd bar for starters.
Always casting the next show but. We become partners?
Most kind Craig most kind. But gee why not, hell!'

There, easy as dealin'! No need to enter
negotiations with anyone this dinkum-straight and home-grown
as yourself.

(VII)

        Now, hemmed by people she'd never known,
inside some outer-Sydney reception centre,
Sophie thinks of how, on a terrace, once, sipping Bacardi and Cokes,
admiring an oncoming moon,
at the sunset end of a late summer afternoon,
another group convened.
                Then she conjures this: how the spokes
of evil (or whatever that is) are aimed at this place,
these people, to an hour as never before:
and this may look so clean, neat and civilised, sure,
but Kevin's here, there's Kim, and that halo of ringlets semi-circles
          your face
right Soph?
        And 'Right!' she wants to cry, 'Yes! I saw all that.
But now I'll be helping . . . helping the world!
     Never thought otherwise Kevin might reply *besides, how'd any good girl
ever expect a rat-a-tat-tat
from Mr Plod? You just met me met Kim and, if falling into it
a few of the more stupid things were done, you never cared what was schemed
or how. Right? Though now you care and want to be redeemed.
For a firm like ours swinging to the legit
would prove you such a tonic. As things stand,
with the world needing purveyors of good corporate health
who they'd be seems simplicity itself.
'Cross and Joy'? 'Cross and Lacy'? 'Cross and Partners'! Now that sounds
       mighty good*
And sure he's telling her *you never let me disappear, I allowed
myself. But Sophie thinks about me still
and I know why: there's never been a thrill
like lovin' Kevin Joy! And now she's doin' him proud:
she's seen this future: what could be greater
(with dinkum psyche wedding bonzer karma)
than Oz/Aussie/Australia as Boomerama
matand Ms Sophie Cross LLB, faciliator,*

set to facilitate such booms,
landing them where she wishes them to land.
    And even if life could pan-
out okay-easy from 198– to Dooms-
day, few hours would creep upon her
when she didn't think of Kevin: always bait, hook
and line enough to set her gasping *Look look*
call me sentimental but there must've been this honour
kinda of sorts, among whatever brand of rogues these Joy Boys were,
well some of them.
                And you'd to be one insensitive dunce
to ignore how she liked Kevin once,
or how of course he was pretty good to her.
    Money, though, had to be paid; a man needed to disappear
(who would've anyway). Scramble-brained, verging homocidal,
sweeping colleagues, friends, lover into that tidal-
surge of Joy (all risk/ no risk/ no fear/ all fear)
he was priming for disaster: his, hers, theirs: so beyond that fizz
of certain glamour which had been Kevin and Sophie
(each much much the other's trophy).
    Had been? No, she wished it, is is is!
Weren't certain tracts of life just plain invisible? Oh heaps!
As Kevin had 'vanished' so she'd never seen any actual 'dope'
(or whatever it was; for that matter every dollar note
she'd earned).
            Which gave her a power and yes, to admit it, the creeps.

(VIII)

    Now Kim was matching Neil coldie for coldie.
What exactly had happened this far into their lives?
Propping in one of their home-town's more acceptable dives,
a little out of place among ye olde
stamping ground's water-drawers and wood-hewers
they allowed themselves that form of expanse to go with after-dinner
                  mints,
brandy and cigars.
            Kim's refrain continued: the heavy hints
of certain drugs and guns, a sideline in sex tours.
    And Neil, knowing tonight had one task

(to endure this crash course in out-sleazing boyhood mates)
resigned himself: nobody grows, everyone just exaggerates;
Spaceman what've you really done? Neil hardly wished to ask,
bullshit having been Kim's life ('You may not believe this but
my uncle runs the Mafia no make that he's Johnny O'Keefe!).
    Now, with an occupation beyond mere *Poorman/beggar/thief*
Lacy was still wide-eyed for any upcoming mutt
who *Yeah mate yeah!* would wider-eyed
believe, well anything.
                  First I heard *That* now I'm hearing *This*!
Neil commenced to hiss,
though through it all still grinning like the father of some shotgun bride.
Until Kim came weighing in with memories, real memories.
Nostalgia take one! GoGo must recall how, grabbing a guitar,
he'd strum out a not too bad bar
of 'Classical Gas'; or (take two) the time they seized
all available kudos with that late-night raid
on Fatso, the newsagent.
                     Then, after reliving what had, or could have,
or not, Spacey turned coy: 'I mean
if y' wanna re-tread Shire celeb here's one ready-made.
And whilst we're about refashioning history
let's reintroduce the quid, the bob, the zac.
Gee fellas 'n' birds isn't it great being back!
GoGo,' he paused, 'if someone's giving a speech tonight he won't be me.
Let's face it, what could you have me say,
since no-one could possibly believe any of my truths?
Why not *Ahem: existing entirely on a diet of fruit loops
I have this hot line to the CIA?*'
    Neil stuck to grinning: with these deals-which-won-my-empire
                update
who'd think Kim he was, some latterday Biggles?
'I'm like you Space here for the giggles,
but next time this mob wants to reunite, mate,
I'll be heading off up the Birdsville Track.'

(ix)

        And Sophie was seeing how even this Neil, having enough
wouldn't consider the truth let alone the lies: it sure was rough

on old friends, success.
                    By now doubly jack
of the night (what was this Luvtrip attempting,
LRB out of CCR?)
here was her objective: Kim in a car
and back to their hotel, pre-empting
any further buddy bail-ups. Not that there'd been much.
This Neil aside (and he seemed press-ganged) and arc
of avoidance semi-circled Kim. Was the party to embark
upon some payback? Over what? In the double dutch
of recycled suburban teenage intrigue
Sophie, sensing nuances, inflections, knew words scarcely mattered;
just wheel in Mr Kim Lacy and they scattered.
        Oh why should she or anyone bother? Why beleaguer
herself with love? What love? Then with sex? What sex?
When she was charitable Kim was just a chump
(and she couldn't think of one better to dump,
provided it paid).
                    Well, forget him. She'd meet rich man X
in the city of Y, turn out a mum in her BMW,
picking up Larissa from after school care
(which, except it was Kim, may've been tonight). And no it wasn't unfair
to ask 'Neil, isn't it? So sorry to trouble you
but let's help get our friend into a taxi and home.'
(*It's the most I'll do given
he's just some 'business partner' now, hardly any reason for living.*)
        Men weren't much trouble. She held her own
(or rather it was who to hold it with that mattered).
        And tonight, she heard Neil (safe safe safe and dull) quiz-
out girls' names: *Liz and Monica, Chrissie, Louise*
and on on *Naomi, Hannah* the boytalk clattered
till it stopped.
            But Kim was concerned (from him it was indeed concern)
'Not here alone? Involved with someone aren't you?
A few of this gig's birds have survived. Gomate can't you
at least try?'
            'Now Kim,' she had to be firm,
'needn't be crass.'

(x)

        So, for his penance a yarn had to unfold:
'How'd I hear about tonight? Well an hour out from LAX
this fella coming down the ailse backtracks,
looks again and 'You're Spacey Lacy!' In my game getting told
who you might be gets risky; but, after a few seconds thinking
No it seemed okay admitting *Yes* to Grubbsy, Grubbsy Leaf,
insolvency troubleshooter, who's telling me it's his belief
this world sure was blab bb' blahblah shrinking.
(Gomate must remember the old Grub!) How this reunion, date and
                place, were set;
So how come I hadn't been traced? Well well well water
had sure flowed under the bridge. His daughter,
I think I have it right, played the clarinet.
        And after a few celebs he knows are named I swing in with mine:
                Craig Stubbs.
We own this bar together but whilst Craigo's heading down
(remember 'Horizon',
'The Family Network'?) I am not.
                        Leaf's eyes are on
me tight now: he's clicking things through, smart fella Grubbs
Mmm mmm he nods real slow *Of course of course.*
        Then Space told Gomate: 'Y' wanna know about today's Craig
                Stubbs?
*There was Stubbs Stubbs / Arranging body rubs /
At The Horse / At The Horse . . .*'

(xi)

        Even more some franchise lessee now than Senor Beegbux
who didn't know of Stubbsy now?
                        Neil did. How pips, pith and rind
were all he left behind
(if that); how, he baring his bum to all those countless wood-ducks,
it was bye-bye court injunctions, media bans, unending writs.
Just one more *The Big I Am*,
another loudmouth bankrupt was on the entrepreneurial lam;
(as if he cared!): for a Stubbs gag over brunch at Port Douglas

reached Geraldton for a dinner.
Say fellas wasn't he a winner
and, fellas, won't he be again?

(XII)

       One more mug less
never existed, Kim knew that, knew there'd always be the next.
Just work on your people magic, see how it gels
then flog it. For Spacey, if nobody else
growing up in The Shire, that had been near-written-as-text.
  But if this was the attraction
to land him back where the best parts of his career began
what was Kim doing hearing three emerging community leaders,
    emcees to a man,
blabbing through the high school honour roll?
            'Now for our missing in
    action . . .'
Stinky announced (still, if you got near, this aftershave freak):
'Hannah Little's out there some place saving this wide brown land,
Grubbsy has the odd swollen gland,
whilst Frenchy, err good one Ray, hardly wanted to speak!'

(XIII)

  'We just get here,' moans Kim 'and now Soph's set to go.
Well tell us quick: the dames, Gomate, the dames:
Hannah Liz Monica and need we continue with names,
what've they, what've *You* done Spencer? We've all that not so tiny
    something to show-
and-tell the world *I sure learnt a bit last night!* Ask whatserface,
Ray's ex about *Her* education. Pardon chum but no-one's exempt,
anybody can do it. Even her, Chrissie, our lamest attempt,
succeeded. For if living's a game, and you've the pace,
then my crowd must've played a coupla real blinders
those weeks months years when deals offered even dealers bliss.'
  Well how come then it finishes like this:
you offering yourself half-necessary reminders
that *When the true time comes you live it! You must!* Aah Kim
oh Spacey Oooh Lacy how come?

To which he might reply *'Being a hero?*
Being a villain? Where's the matter? When you've to zero-
out one more dodgy partner to survive, and then replace him,
it hardly happens except it has to. And that was My hour
when Was *or* Will *be never existed. Abolish every tense*
but Now! *and this turns your reward: an innocence*
as few could ever grasp. And if that is evil it is also pure:
distilled beyond potent. Plus what I'd do was mighty fun.
Oh Gomate trust you'll never know, but understand:
you meet enough folks you're sure to shake some killer's hand.
Hardly said, did I, I was a nun!
Listen to me! You must go after God! The rest is petty theft!'
  (And were he to be heard what would Kim receive: contemptuous
    disbelief?
Or, if he didn't mind his mouth, a smack in the teeth?)

(XIV)

  So for the ol' days (though few it seemed were left)
Kim, but only he knew it, went in to bat;
and bowling up names to himself 'Naomi! Hannah!' he hit 'em for six.
'Liz! Monica! Chrissie! Louise! GoGo! GoGo! Those immaculate chicks!'
  'And who?' cringed Neil, 'brung that?'

Part 13

CRAIG STUBBS	PART OWNER, CRAZY HORSE AND THE FUCFUC
'BIG OZ' OSBOURNE	WEALTHMAKER
DIXIE	WIFE IN HER TIME TO BOTH STUBBS AND OSBOURNE
ICEMAN SUPERBOOT THE MOOSE SHANE PRICE ADRIAN CROSS	FOOTBALLERS
KAREN	THE FIRST MRS STUBBS
KAREN'S FATHER	A GOSSIP COLUMNIST
DOUGIE	KAREN'S BROTHER, A BANKER
LAST GASP LENN MR BEERY HEART-THROB	WEALTHMAKERS
STEVE DODD	TOYOTA DEALER
GIBBO	COMEDIAN, SINGER-SONGWRITER, STUBBS' MATE
MR FIXIT	OF THE LOTUS PARTY
KEVIN KIM	BUSINESSMEN
DEEDEE LYONS	MEDIA PERSONALITY
MEG	JUST FINISHED SCHOOL
BERNIE	BARMAN IN THE FUCFUC
FELLA/HOTSHOT	CUSTOMER

STUBBSY: A SUCCESS

for Megan Jones, and with acknowledgment to Megan Jones, Tony Douglas, Gideon Haigh, Bob Peters, James Stewart and Richard Walsh

Money is a kind of poetry.

WALLACE STEVENS

By the end of the 1987 fiscal year the Group had achieved its objectives of achieving the long held critical mass objective of gross assets of $1 billion, operating businesses with a pre-eminent position in media and entertainment and resorts and leisure in Australia and a strong beach head in the United States of America in the same service industries.

CHRISTOPHER SKASE

... can't remember where we stood before that day,
the other mob though, they head the ladder.
And we are towelling them. Courtesy of Iceman and
Superboot they've caught footstep fever,
Cross hasn't time to be a show pony,
and even The Moose must think he's twenty-one
and talented again.   After every goal I knew
the cameras were back on Dix and me: it might be
one more simple Sunday arvo but this was Sunday's news:
all else around him may appear like bankrupt,
except these men: and they are playing for Stubbs!
Get him a sound bite, he'll tell you
*I knew there was a handbag team, Australia.
Guess what? It isn't us!*
          Then, by Wednesday,
with $tubb$corp stonewalling
and BoomCon still raiding like Genghis Khan,

a diversion: the latest squib of a beat-up:
my Stags were in revolt: trying to run two truths
We're still y' mates, Craigo and the even simpler
Sorry but, can't support you.
                        It had begun as an adventure:
a well-intentioned wealthmaker helping out his game.
From that day, if ever I'd the inclination,
I might try opening my mouth to yawn
Football? You must be kidding!
                    Gone were the days
of *Sure fellas sure, just put me down for the tab*
(the liquor bills, the escort fucks,
an end-of-season trip few of them deserved)
but then, as now, all they had to do was
win their mate his games and call him Craigo.
                                        Well,
he might've been staring straight in the eye of
Cyclone Ruin, that afternoon,
but some of the boys are waiting; and Stubbsy's never,
never that busy not to meet
his mighty Stags.
                    Then, as this 'deputation' seats themselves,
Pricey assumes how real livin' operates
and opens with 'Y' ratshit, Craigo . . .' and how
mug-players never count for much, but just
this once, I'm to see things their way.
'What else remains?' he asks and, keeping on
with his same bait-smile, gives a reply:
'Exile with The Moose to drive you round?
Oh Craigo whoopy-doo!'
                    But few can backpedal like me
so, after he's thanked, only a minute is required
to swing in with my final pitch:
'What you need Shane, fellas, are facts.
Aren't you in luck! I am the CEO of facts.
And I made Moose my chauffeur?
Well who got Superboot his KFC franchise,
bought Iceman's missus her manicure salon?
And, when two of you dived into that girl's pants,
who paid off her father and the cops? More facts?

More facts! Haven't we Stags won six on-the-trot?
Aren't the punters pouring back? Aren't we set for
boom mark two? No, it'll never be time to announce
This is as good as it gets but hey,
mightn't it be a start? Sure I never played a game,
but who of you has played my game, business,
anyone?'
    Then I told about business, not real livin' business,
but the gospel according to best practice shit-kicking:
you start with jealousy, blend in hints, innuendoes,
then make your wood-duck sell and sell and sell.
I told them Fella:
'Just look down the track and see, next month,
next year, a roadblock named Boomer Consolidated.
Once you hit that it'll be bye-bye franchise,
oo-roo salon, evening Inspector, these are the very two.
So when you're no longer treated as sportsmen,
but mere commodities, don't come crawling home to
$tubb$corp.'
    Try smiling, Fella; it's what I said.
Whilst you're at Crazy Horse something should amuse you.
Wouldn't be Aussie, male, let's guess thirty, if it didn't
right? I'll allow it: being so drenched in the place,
by now, Stubbsy's not the man to say where novelty stops
and 'just existence' carries on.
    Months after 'Sixty Minutes'
sprang us with, wouldn't you think, what went for
common knowledge, Aussie came stalking:
Him! you could almost hear them *Him!* (*Stubbs*! seeming
near impossible to say.) And then a few, well quite a few
of course, braved the idea and, with cheek or gall
or curiosity, came on in like Fella has.
    Though wouldn't you
call it 'enterprise'? I would. 'Enterprise':
what we've lacked or better never had until
a few years back. 'Enterprise': that ability to say
*This one's different, sure, but since it's different
deal us in, it deserves our best.*
    Can't say I invented the idea
but, round Fella's age, all I wanted to happen

I got to happen, too much sometimes.
                              At $tubb$corp
press briefings grew into the art they always should be:
so *Kickbacks?* they would lob and 'Don't live in Fantasyland,'
I might return, 'Sir Joe appreciates young folk like us,
young folk giving it a go, and we, you! should appreciate
Sir Joe.'
        But only an optimist could believe
that there amongst that scrum (and didn't I say sc-rum?)
someone wasn't too jealous, one fella might,
with understanding, nod *Mmm not bad, making something*
of himself, giving the wide brown land more than
it deserves.
        But that fella, Fella, was unlikely.
Try being Aussie and successful: all probables get
shaved back to possibles, safe possibles, safer improbables;
though take it softly, even then they'll never let you say
There's stale money: your mean, tight money,
and then there's my money: fresh money, money
that's breathing, that still can dream
                              And Fella knows
they'll never let you say that, best of all, in Melbourne:
Melbourne, where the top few thousand (who think the place
is made for them) are simply losers rich enough to treat themselves
as winners, celebs who are celebs because there's always
got to be celebs. Why should they (how could they) even consider
a *salesman* (too much the superbox, not enough of The Members)
in short consider Stubbs?
                    But if a salesman has it, someone else is
sure to want it; and Melbourne did.
                         As money is business,
business is the world, and a salesman has to make that money
make the world.
              When I started spruiking for Horizon
I jetted north half-to-all of Collins Street, the toughest of
the country's corporate cows. Old son,
I told myself, start milkin'!
                       And here's what I didn't say
Even though I've flown in you lot to listen
no-one's going to stride that extra mile to learn, are they?

But, since few can own today as I do,
starting now I know of two names you'll remember:
Stubbs and Horizon.
You are here so I can ask: name that last time
you or Aussie truly dreamt,
and then made anything of that dream.
So how's about letting your money live again
here at my beachhead to paradise:
Horizon-on-Capricorn.

      No, I never said quite that
but just began by aiming at their simplest pleasures:
how the rhythm of any Horizon day
began with brunch, a butler-serviced brunch,
whilst, at The Marina, Hover-Horizon
lay poised to skim away towards The Reef.
And I asked them to imagine it: a reef that holds
five hundred different kinds of fish!

      Great pitch, Fella?
Not quite, not if you're almost overdoing it.

   Someone in the front (arms crossed, legs out)
stifled a giggle or a yawn.
'Therefore,' came his sneer, 'we're being asked to invest
in brunch, butlers, a hovercraft and, by extension, fish.'

   He waited, certain that with him
I'd taken on more than even I might handle.
Which I had, except I was going to protect my pitch
the only way I knew: by making up the rest,
adding to that, then seeing where we'd landed.

   So I tried: 'You'll invest in people at Horizon,
the real livin' dollar . . .' and paused. They stared.
I shrugged and sighed:
'The Japs already have.'

      Well not quite yet.
So I improvised this Watanabe Corporation
direct from the Ginza. Heard of the ol' one-two?
Well introducing the new:
first play your Asian card, then follow through
But Aussie money never is as good as
Jap money, is it?

     No no no no came the panic,

we wouldn't say exactly *that*.
                              Of course they wouldn't.
            I'd known them and played them since I was
a tyro: twenty-three, heading everywhere
with a class fiancée.
                     Her old man was a journo,
who stewed these silly-buggers in his column.
Had I, he asked (raising a eyebrow,
quizzical-to-supercilious) had I heard how a former
Lord Mayor (the vascular surgeon/developer one)
bought off a union boss
(guess who if I wanted to, there'd be
no prizes) with a vein-job on the missus:
the moment she was wheeled from the theatre
concrete was cas-cading! Had I?
But let him tell me more being (quote)
Not just some crypto-pinko token-eccentric
but rather (quote again)
A clearing house for the safest, and not so safest,
gossip. There's one in every city, well
he was Melbourne's; which suited him:
the place was y' total amateur hour: hardly much,
correction almost nothing, ever got done. Did I know
what he would tell if he could really tell?
Why the after-hours drag queen banker
of course, the dunny-prowling prominent
back-bencher, the heiress who wasn't quite
daddy's little girl *and* their abortions but, but
This above all as Pudden his Latin master
told him *to thine own self* . . . I knew the rest?
Now *that* was art and he had traded art,
well the pretence of art, for the pay cheque:
find him every weekday night inside all those Jim Geralds,
tucked under the arms of all those Jolly John Citizens
training it home to Camberwell, Moorabbin.
It got him that much extra-jaundiced,
with his tongue so firmly in his cheek
Oi ave oo alk ike iss.
                        That eyebrow raised again,
the columnist peered towards the salesman

(wouldn't 'top' Melbourne love to do without us,
well they couldn't): 'Mmm . . .' he attempted,
then 'Know the only brain-fuel for this hour?
A single malt and neat. Your school Craig?'
(I named it) 'Really? That passes muster.
So who employs you?'
   I employed me: Real Livin' Toyota
of Brighton, Aspendale, Mitcham and Thornbury.
    'Mmm . . . you work in car yards?'
   If it had to be described that way
well yes: I preferred 'showrooms'.
         'Karen?'
Looking up he tried to focus and 'Marriage?'
he seemed to ask himself. Then 'Craig,' he answered,
'this is the Swingin' Seventies, must I give
permission? Stand between you two and your hormones?
As if I would! A topper-up?'
        Still, he supposed
that I had plans, that I wouldn't park his child
in some townhouse, breed for a bit
then scoot. Dougie, his boy, was also making money.
We hadn't met?
     Not yet. I knew his part of town;
one day I'd get there.
       How to remember Karen?
For little except that, after setting up a flat
(hardly a townhouse) we passed our time in marriage,
trying to, at least, enjoy it Three years in
I'd become a back number:
got informed (by her) she was fucking something
Unfortunately special (Karen's words)
I've often wondered what, of course,
though that night merely told her '. . . thanks, thanks heaps.
But just remember Mrs Stubbs, I owe you bloody nix.
Me, I'm off to watch *The Wild Bunch*.
Start the divorce!'
      Still, I might see her brother
at the footy *Good mates, Craigo? None better, Dougie.*
Those days, sloshing round The Piggy Bank
(an economist I think)

there wasn't much the columnist's son could do for
What's your business? What's your business called?
(Though Aussie couldn't do much more.)
         He'd a simple
Toorak life: wait for a week then, Saturday morning,
something might come together: out of the townhouse you stroll
into The Village, buy your papers and, over coffee,
hope to read about yourself.
       So when The Piggy Bank goes global
(or thinks it does) Dougie gets to run the wine club.
He does the doings so proud, six months on,
somehow, he heads their can-do arm
The Trust. (The *Trust*?) This starts him onto
big boy's work, Dougie style:
the wife's kicked out, the nanny gets installed;
to maximise respect and self-respect
a hair transplant is given orders
(they're refused).
    Still, arm a man
with a cache of affable clichés
and he'll pitch to the planet *Tell us your dreams*
my friends, we'll back 'em, back 'em to billyo.
Trust The Trust, our time has come.
        Then,
global spruiking done: 'Gee Stubbsy,
a lotta water's flowed under the bridge
since you were flogging ... Valiants? Well,
life's certainly a bit of give and take ...'
   Correct: just take from The Piggy Bank
and give it all to Craigo. There'd be no
greater wood-duck than you, taa Dougie.
For at The Trust every time was presents time.
    'What's he want to be when he grows up?
That fat man from the North Pole? He may be *your* mate,'
Last Gasp Lenny sneered, 'but Dougie's not immune.
Didn't we make that prick?
The Piggy Bank is pi times ratshit squared,
one perfect O for out. He even dealt with Heart-throb!
After flying Heart-throb down he's shoved in at The Hyatt;
then its dindins, a show, and getting fucked by

the very best from Poppets International;
just for a working breakfast!
Poor Heart-throb was so pleased 'n' shagged his signature
was automatic writing. Working breakfast? Wanking breakfast!
And yet . . .' Last Gasp paused, a puzzled smirk
creasing his Mister Moon of a head,
'who was lending who just what?'
        Now that beats Uncle Lenny. No-one was certain anymore.
Was Craigo? 'Fellas,' he told me like he always told me,
'Fellas gotta make their dollars, sure,
but vitamin dollars not hot dog dollars.'
So when I needed my vitamins, not just some stunning root
and an okay brekkie, call. Last Gasp could get vitamins
places even 'Big Oz' Osbourne didn't want to know
existed. The bottom of Bass Strait?
The bottom of his grandma's grave!
        One day
mightn't Craigo think of needing Lenny's EasyCred?
Oh Last Gasp, please! Wasn't my self-respect
in hock enough?
        'What's wrong,' he lobbed it tart,
'in making bucks? You scared Stubbs?'
        'Yeah mate,'
I volleyed, 'feverish!'
        Still, when betrayal had me
exiled here at The Horse, why not? I thought,
he couldn't do much worse than Dougie
(somewhere in Gippsland enjoying concurrent terms,
acquiring computer skills).
        Pity Lennie, too,
got packed off to a farm,
pity one more of his nags collapsed returning
to scale. But weren't these, he explained
after my call arrived, just details? Details
that wouldn't stop *us*.
        The Stags, by now, were poison:
but if I'd like Eight returned, or Horizon, or Dixie
(a new network, the next resort, another wife)
or, if I really wanted to skewer Osbourne/
aim another shot at Hollywood . . .

                                        'Anything,'
I told him, 'anything and my reputation.'
                                        And,
from his confines came an upbeat
'Craig wants, Lenny gets, everyone is happy …'
            Even from the jug he'd set up my return?
            Until he croaked on us it seemed possible.
            DeeDee sent this video: Last Gasp's funeral and wake:
and *Fee-lings* some infotainment tenor wails
wo wo wo wo fee-lings but all I hear
is Last Gasp beaming in from where he's gone
Bet you're missing all of this eh, Craigo?
            No more than you are, Lenny.
                                    And do I want to know
(and I know he wants me to know, even here
at Crazy Horse) the tale of Last Gasp's
last gasp?
            Sure, pitch it mate.
                        On day release,
halfway between prison farm and petrochemical site,
he pulls across for a trip to the gents;
never returns.
                His send-off looks
a near-to-complete who's who and how's how
of where us wealthmakers are right now:
Mister Beer and The Big Oz on bail,
Dougie and Heart-throb on parole, whilst the rest,
craving such kudos, almost wish they'd
some time to do.
                Bye, Last Gasp, czar of the buy-back fee,
with all of your mates agreeing
what a fat little prick you were,
truly, there wasn't a damp eye in the house.
You remember Last Gasp, Fella?
You must've met The Big Oz, everybody has.
But Heart-throb: the Futurex whiz-kid,
our matinee idol wealthmaker? Well think of this:
an apprentice Stubbs, as he did once,
pumping me for answers he already knew,
since I was the one needing the information

that here, well this side of the horizon, a new force approached:
the confident young man with his pretty wife (wife's cousin,
some gallery owner, an obliging actress, his second pretty wife).
Can't you hear the voice-over *This is the story of a man in love* . . .
with himself: those cheekbones, those curls, his tan
matching his eyes; which should've made for a film star
(acting as if he'd truly something, even if
few were certain what): this man who, walking in a door
at eight, always came out by nine owning
a cement company or a dog food factory or a chain
of bra salons; if owing more. Next month
something would be sold (salons? factory? company?)
having been churned through Futurex and out (bra companies/
cement factories/dog food salons). So who recalls,
or needs to, wants to, the mess that Heart-throb owned or
sold or didn't? By the time his hour arrived it was
over. Wanting to be news he finished as history.
  All of us did.
  Decades are remembered for their personnel:
name the thirties and you'll think battlers;
consider the forties, soldiers come to mind;
fifties, sportsmen; sixties, teenagers;
seventies, politicians; and the eighties, us:
Stubbsy and The Big Oz,
Last Gasp and Mr Beer,
Heart-throb and poor dumb Dougie.
        But never be a fool,
Fella, and stand between them (or anyone like them)
and a bag of cash (or anything like cash).
Instead, if you've the courage, join them for
(as Steve Dodd might've said)
A full meal of rich real livin'.
      Give Craigo
half-a-year, give Craigo half-an-hour, he'll be
starting again and guess what? Allow him,
he'd employ you.
     When Osbourne, the banks,
and any amount of governments proclaimed this-one-here
numero uno national wood-duck, I told this-one-here:
unlike his bosses, that flunky who arrives

to get you, Stubbs, who has the required gall
to think he'll bring you home, that man, at least,
deserves respect.
      It's what I said. Wasn't I correct?
Fella has his job to do, he's doing it near proud and,
even beyond that, since all Australia knows
I'm boltholed in at The Horse,
he's modest, isn't so full of Fella to think
he's tracked me down.
      This man knows his truth.
What's better said of anyone? Well maybe more:
This is the kind of fella I'd love to see
getting me results.
     So he's from . . . someone has to be from . . .
Cherrywood? Don't bother explaining,
doubtless it's like Bentleigh, everywhere else is and,
being Bentleigh, once, I can employ Cherrywood.
Believe it, I'm not that boneheaded Gold Coast
transplant of myth *Don't hire till you see the whites*
of their shoes! a slob on a sundeck.
      You work long hours? I work long hours! You know
we have to work long hours. And,
if you want me for your boss, sure, I'll play boss:
but this sort of boss: one who's boss enough to say
Enjoy, play it how you think it should
be played, create. Just ask my girls
(even over at The FucFuc and that's more
than a touch beyond the imagination):
they're freelance, consultants if you like,
and hardly 'mine'. That's how I saw them all
at $tubb$corp, how I'd like to see you.
Who wouldn't be the kind of boss who'll announce
There now folks, didn't I tell you,
wasn't it worth it? For you're no Boss
just being a boss for the sake of being a boss
(not even Osbourne went that far).
     You don't believe a word? Oh Fella, why?
Even if I don't, one day, I might. Like,
don't you want to dream how, soon, you'll say again
That is too beautiful that is too fuckin' beautiful

and it might be a day's work or a woman or even
a resort.
   I know that one, I know how,
under the spray Horizon lay
not merely constructed but, better, newly born;
only now I knew why I was flying:
only then was it possible to see
something so much part of me (yes,
part of Australia) and tell myself *See that:
it's mine* tell everybody else
*Come on over to Stubbsy's, see what he's given
the world.*
   And ditch that word
'success' (The Big Oz had 'success' and Last Gasp,
Mr Beer, even Heart-throb) for there had to be
a word that told much more, telling you what
Craigo and Horizon truly were.
       And there,
above Horizon, the sea and the rain forest,
I wouldn't just dare anyone to find that word,
Fella, the daring done I'd pay almost my life for it.
That sight went so beyond brunch and hovercrafts,
dreaming and 'success', by God, like God
I'd taken my chance: here was the Garden of Eden
re-run; if there was any blame send Stubbsy the blame!
We'd this most exquisite brolga-in-flight
for a logo; that bird was going to skim
the swamp of envy, dip in, snap up and
gobble enough abuse and accusation to sustain . . .
my lifetime? Lifetimes!
       Flogging Toyotas had been one thing,
the world was another. A client had suggested
the travel dollar: to look for something heading cheap
and going fast.
     Up past Rocky was a chain.
   Yeah, of four fibro motels
(noisy fridges, floral carpets and runny-eyed
ex-diggers managing in their somehow fashion):
'Take-Your-Time', 'Skippy's', 'Excelsior', 'La Vista'
By crikey, I was told, *big changes were bloody due,*

this part of the Sunshine State was waking up.
Yep, I couldn't tell them yet, it's 1974,
welcome to 1955.
Each man wore a similar grubby cardigan,
seeming to share the same wide-eyed,
if slightly sour, opinions (you felt the same
slow-fusing temper). They'd all flywires
that whinged when opened, just to snap too fast.
(And, no matter how long they remained
I'd want these doors oiled!)
    Anyone here actually in charge?
Ever thought how satisfying that can sound? Bet you have.
These words should be honed shrill, to the edge
of sneering, for fewer questions demand as
fine a no and fewer noes cut through as much.
What is power but being able to ask that
and, in your asking, answer it?
A fella can be referee, umpire, linesman and McEnroe.
    Ever thought how much which has to disappear
does, simply by a me, a you,
becoming boss, when the rest of them haven't the ...
let's call it 'art' to know
someone's got to be responsible;
hasn't Fella thought of *that*?
    And who taught me *that*?
Craig Stubbs of course.
But who taught him how to teach himself?
Steve Dodd. Steve what?
    All cities have them,
and he was Melbourne's. Selling cars and
employing men who had to sell
almost as well, Steve made that trade
into a profession, that profession into art;
everything that Osbourne and BoomCon think
they are but couldn't be, he was.
And Steve just flogged Toyotas.
His was a face which told you
Believe this man, he's got a decent product.
What's the trade cliché? Some flabby, florid,
pea 'n' thimble man. Well Steve was neat,

Steve had flair and that precision
which can measure how much push to give
per customer; and, knowing better, how
to listen. He smiled easily (but not
too easily) and the smile would tell
*Doing this service obligation-free
your neighbour's pleased, he's that kind of guy.*
Try naming any city that hasn't had
some embarrassment (who ought to be in war paint)
flinging his arms and barking
Have I a deal for you! No kid
ever did Steve Dodd impersonations.

       For a moment, out of school, I'd thought of
the army or the cops, but knew I was
to be my boss one day. So,
after selling shoes (and that lasted a week)
a mate mentioned how, over on the highway,
Steve was after talent. I knew cars,
liked people better, but money more than both.
Fifteen applied, one was chosen.
And the first rule I'd to know with deals?
Guess what *Enjoy it!*
You could put one over competition
(one thousand and one!) that
was business, always would be;
but never over clients.
Con-artists were discovered, never forgotten:
the word spread: for people simply wanted
decent cars, and we supplied them.
What we had to believe was what
they wanted to believe *She's a great machine,
you'll have a wonderful time.*

       A side of beef,
a jackhammer, a pack of cards, a flagon
of plonk, people went to shops knowing
what they wanted. Cars were subtler,
and we weren't exactly a shop, but anyone
visiting Steve Dodd Toyota wasn't just
admiring the duco. They wanted to be met,
doubtless wanted to buy: some car, one day.

Why not ours, now? Steve's job, my job,
was helping them decide, getting people doing
what they wanted, what they *really* wanted.
I was to remember that and, how,
for half an hour at least,
I was to be the company they kept . . .
but, well, why not a lifetime?
And if not this car why not, certainly,
the next? *Everyman's a mate*
Steve would say *until proved otherwise* and
One day, soon, they're sure to buy,
make certain it's from you. They won't regret it.
He made it fun. Steve made it like yarning
over your front fence whilst you hosed,
said it should be straight as that:
there wasn't any way a customer wouldn't be
your newest mate, couldn't become your best one.
I put his lines to work and
'Hey Stubbs!' I heard and '. . . boy genius!' and
'. . . you've hardly started shaving!'
A face was recognised: someone's elder brother
carrying a smirk as only an intern or
an articled clerk knows how
Where you going? Me? I'm heading: up!
So I got him talking. The subject:
what mattered most, himself; I gave it half an hour,
and then another; not having to prove himself
much more, he signed.
A month before I turned twenty Steve
had me running Aspendale where,
if I ever had the time, I dreamt of
partnerships and dealerships, becoming like him
the Rolls-Royce of salesmen, enjoying it now,
enjoying it always.
      I'd only known Steve for
eighteen months when, one crisp, brittle
Sunday morning, teeing off at Kingston Heath,
he sucked up air, moaned it out
and died. At forty-one.
He'd shown how I could look

any man in the eye and how, doing that,
would make that man this friend.
And he'd shown how agreement never was
enough, there had to be belief;
and how, like now or one day, you'll
just fall over and die.
                    The funeral,
Tuesday. From Wednesday I'd do anything
for anybody worth it,
for as long as the doing it took. Saturday week
after Radio Hit-Bound's match-of-the-day, I give across
Steve Dodd Toyota's D-o-g award.
Glad you got that one:
League, Union, Soccer, Rules,
maybe there is a code or two for Fella,
so he doesn't spend all weekend working on ways
to hit Crazy Horse, bag Stubbs and ship him home.
Bore you with this though: it's early July,
we haven't won since April, I've sacked one coach,
another's tried resigning and, in the mud, Moose
just flaps like a flounder. *Next year* I keep on promising
those who'll bother to listen *we'll melt him down
for glue, but till then* I demand *Mullins stays
and Mullins plays* trusting there's still a blinder
in him. There almost is and, for over half a game,
we're improving, improving hard.
                            Cut to the post-game
sandwiches-and-beer: I work both teams (players, officials,
whoever's been let in) moving my path to their full forward,
Cross; there he stands with Price, his mate,
and aren't I loving the idea:
a low-key ale with two of the competition's
biggest names. They're showered clean, flab-free lean and,
after the game we gave them, a trifle bruised.
Stay friendly, I advise myself, don't overstate the feelers
if indeed they're feelers, these men are smart, too smart
these two. And it tempts me to say
*Money? Sure I've made my bit, but don't tell me, fellas,
you earn s.f.a.* Of course I don't. Cross at his best
would be so worth anybody's bid I'd double it

and, if he wanted company, throw in Price.
'Adrian ...' my gambit's plain, 'Shane ... fellas well done.
Moose and his boys tried heaps of course,' (they didn't
disagree) 'but we're improving ... great game as always,
even with the conditions, great ... thought we had you
halfway through the third ...' though true I needed to confess:
'I'm not the one who's just spent two hours in
the Waverley rain, getting my brains scrambled.
I'm just an average punter ...' And then I pitch:
'How's your future shaping? Tell us how this sounds:
half a mil for starters over the next three years.
Life after footy? Glad you mentioned it.
Like the bush? I'll throw in a farm. Enjoy a beer,
your fellow man? How's a pub sound? Maybe you both teach,
Adrian, Shane? Ha ha ha ha buy you a school!'

    And Fella sees my joke, sees my joke's on me;
too much it was for Price (overrated talent,
out of the packs no more than a shitkicker)
Price is laughing, jabbing towards my breastbone with
'Stubbs, Stubbs, why should we contemplate *you*?'
'Much less,' his friend tries topping him
'your precious Stags.'

                No Adrian of course, of course not,
Shane. Later, offer half as much again,
where do they sign? Where I knew they always would:
under the $tubb$corp letterhead, where everybody else did:
two wives, a few comedians, DeeDee, unending wood-ducks
and a footy club. Look, I'd the cash once:
I could afford to say *Do what you'd like to be,*
better still but, do it for me and get paid:
wanna tell gags? Tell them. Wanna win premierships?
Win away!

        When was it the game turned national
and I acquired my team? I'd relocated West
but had I married Dixie Osbourne?

                           Anyway, last season
The Stags had headed to the cellar so fast
all I'd to do was knock on their door
and announce *Stubbs here I'm bringing The Moose*
and a few of his mates to save you.

                        And then
I thought of Gibbo. Since those days when Karen
and I hit The Flying Trapeze to see his act
(have him to our table, hear him shit
on everybody else) Craigo headed his fan club.
Wherever The Stubbs went the mate tagged,
their court jester, with all his *b'beep b'beep* and his
aaarck! aaarck!
            In private Gibbo's face has that wide-eyed,
gulping *gosh!* you know you'll have to play to.
But Gibbo phones me, not so confident:
'I'm not big-headed am I am I?
But, but what does Aussie truly owe me? Mate?'
My reply sits cooking: 'Best mates, Gibbo?'
'Craigo,' I could hear him shrinking, 'yes,
the very best . . .' But best or not what what
what was he *owed*?
                    'One juicy, don't-you-forget-it,
blowjob.'
        'Just that?'
                    'Uh-huh.'
Oh Craigo Craigo, can he quote me can he
quote me?
                'Much better: you still write songs?'
(He still wrote songs.) 'Well write my Stags a number,
then fly across and sing.'
                        'What me mate?'
'No no, Bob Dylan mate!'
*'I'm just a simple Perth boy, no big-noter, nothin' flash,
I like mah beer 'n' girls 'n' footy: straight.
But mah voice gets kinda lumpy, when a fella puts it this way:
The Stags are somethin' special, aren't they, mate.
Oooooooh
Givin' it a go, / For The Stags it must be so, /
Week in 'n' out they al-ways do their best.'*
Well, did I like it? Gibbo was puffing, entranced:
'We fly in Roddo for the first home game.'
        'Roddo?'
                'To launch it Craig, Rod Stewart, Craig,
I've met him . . .' (and off he sings like Roddo now)

'For this'll be the rea-son, / Each 'n' ev'ry sea-son, /
The cup 'n' flag are flyin' in the West!'
'Coffee Gibbo?' Showered in scent you could lick
from the air Dixie that arvo was strapless: her mouth
like a bucket of pearls and her blouse knotted over
that taut brown midriff. Coffee then?
      'Hey!' As ever
a Gibbo *hey!* meant yes to something and Dixie
(lovemaker, heartbreaker) *hey!*-ed back.
Okay okay Dix with The Moose? It kept them happy.
With Gibbo? Whatever she wanted this creep stood chanceless.
And sure, I'm democratic enough to say yeah well
Dix with Con at the Seven Eleven, but Roddo, *him*,
Rod Stewart?
      'Gibbo matey the song has sound:
Johnny Farnham, Johnny Rotten, we hire whoever
Except Stewart!'
          'No Roddo?'
                'No Roddo.'
But talk about buoyant: 'Try this then, Craigo (his voice
leering with the thrill)
'Oh we will overwhelm, / With Stubbsy at the helm, /
And who can beat that leg-end called The Moose?'
'Gibbo?' (you only ask this softly. The strumming stopped.)
'Gibbo, whose song is this?'
          'Mine?' he stared, 'yours?
Ours? Craigo?'
      'Moose isn't a legend. He's a thug.
He's over here to hit people.'
          'No legend, Stubbsy?'
'No Moose, Gibbo.' I'd never bought a song before.
      And never loyalty. Early one working brekky (strategies
to staunch another cash-flow) we had on G'day Aussie
with the sound down. And there, guesting, was Gibbo:
white shoes, blazer, tinted specs.
Don't I thought *don't overdo me mate*
for, as we beefed the volume he was announcing:
'Morning, Friends of $tubb$corp! And that means
all of you, Australia!' This time of day Gibbo
couldn't be so surely Gibbo, could he?

         You suckers, anyone is game for Gibbo, anytime.
Like the next guest: some principal dancer
up against the infamous Gibbo beeper,
the hawhawhaw of studio hands:
'Don't tell me you're … (b'beep b'beep) a horse's hoof?'
Did he say that did he say that? Probably.
And he'll arrive at Crazy Horse one day,
probably; all Aussie is sure to; everybody does.
         Just minutes after I arrive here
the local Mr Fixit comes by to tell how
welcome Mr Stubbsy is, Mr Stubbsy friend
of Lotus Party yes. And Elephant Party?
Mr Stubbsy always very good to everyone.
And that good. But must stay friends with Lotus Party.
I tell him make it simpler: call me Craigo
and 'Claigo …' gets purred. 'Mr Claigo Stubbsy
great fliend of Lotus Party. And how is Mr Moose:
girlfliend make him happy?'
                             Oh Fella,
I wasn't planning a retirement home,
The Horse was a dare investment: a minor stunt
to recall I owned.
                   Two bushweek businessmen,
Kevin and Kim, came with the place,
with Kevin (clipped, sardonic,
a someone it's best to let them win at squash)
just a man I met working-out in Singapore;
a master of minor plans (pet shops and gemstones
and caneware, The Horse and The FucFuc)
someone who wouldn't bother $tubb$corp
but, sure, someone giving it a go,
would I buy in?
                Then, one day, years back,
Kevin sells out to me and Kim, heads to Manila.
'At The Horse,' he told me, 'we've AP.
Over at The FucFuc, approximate AP.'
                                     Did Craigo get it?
Does Fella? Asian Pussy here, drag queens up the road:
call them my virtual girls: pre op, post op, ev'rywhere
an op op.

And still I'm asked:
'Mate, what *are* they?'
'Err different, mate?'
And yet, not so different for someone to shrug
Well, why not? heading off to solve the question.
They all return to The Horse,
just so slightly shyer *I've done that?*
blinking out of them.
Know that look?
I invented it:
like we'd be hearing *This way fellas!*
and all of us would eyes-right to the photo-journos,
smiling as only success can teach.
Know the *that* of *I've done that?* well
that had been done again: Horizon or
The Family Network, Dixie or The Stags.
And whatever the question all replies would be yes!
Yes! till the BoomCon blimp drifted by and Osbourne,
squinting in, lifted a phone. Now,
every evening, I'm fast-trackin' pussy plus
to boilermakers on Amex and the sproutings of a habit,
horny outer-suburban social clubbers,
backpackers ditched by last week's sweetheart.
Yes, this is Crazy Horse, this is Australia,
the rice trail starts here. Don't ask him for more
though, Stubbsy only runs the place.
Tell it this way:
Bern the barman over at The FucFuc calls up
one afternoon, how some old mates are
tracking over. And ex-wives? I thought, creditors?
Fella's crowd? No, it's end-of-season trip time
and here come half a dozen mighty Stags:
all led by mega-mouth himself, Adrian Cross.
'Thought you'd retired, Ades.'
And 'Marketing manager, Craigo,' I knew he'd reply.
'Still an aggressive prick as ever?'
'Never,' he confesses, 'but combative? yeah, sure . . .'
and how for a wealthmaker 'you make a decent pimp.
Must've flogged some great Toyotas.'
Only Cross, of course,

could try on that, the rest aren't exactly certain:
wanting to laugh, at who but? Everyone waits,
hoping I'll sweep it and everything aside. And I do. My way:
'These girls are girls. Just that. And they aren't mine.
No girls were freer. Adrian,
I owned you more, much more, than I own these.'
And Fella, even better I could still say it
whatever words I wanted still belonged with me.
When Craigo tells Gibbo Moose-o is no legend,
then Moose-o isn't. Own enough and words
can mean all you require them to say.
                              'Osbourne,'
I tried telling him once, 'we may as well start buying
the language!'
              The day before Eight was totally acquired
I'd this vision-of-visions:
me telling the home town every truth there ever was,
how I'd be owning their words.
                    My fellow Victorians,
I'm Craig Stubbs: you mightn't know it yet
but by tomorrow this channel you are watching
will be mine. And heard of that sensational
tropical resort half the world is visiting or
wishes they could: we hardly need to gloat
upon its owner, do we? Not Bentleigh's greatest son!
Well guess who heads a certain chopping block
of crocks that's hauled off half a dozen
of your very best due west? Melbourne,
all of $tubb$corp (The Family Network, Horizon,
my mighty Stags) says hi, come 'n' see us
when you want to . . .'cause, not only you'll want to,
you'll have to.
              How'd I acquire Eight? For starters
I'll be generous and thank a certain Gibbo.
One Logies presentation he baptises Eight
The Dag Network. And knowing Aussie for cruel-enough
I'd more than an intuition it would stick:
with daggy shows, daggier ratings, all their *gosh folks*
someone's gotta come last and Gibbo smirking
'I'm hardly y' culture vulture, hardly after class,

but aaarck *Eight*? Aaarck *Eight*?
And, as the audience cacked themselves ridiculous,
I could imagine dags: these old men in cardigans, watering
their gardens in the rain; *no* their wives,
tending pressure-cookered shanks; *no no* the daughter,
thirty-five but still at home with her Barry Manilow posters;
and *no no no!* the son with his greying duck's tail,
hot-rodding the Vee-Dub; and, even better, as Gibbo buried Eight,
I'd visions of fibro motels and Eight being mine!
      Next morning, heading to The Village, I ambushed Dougie,
asked its value and got its value: a morning's crap.
'Your language Dougie, please. I'm *buying* Eight!'
'But Craigo but, there's nothing left to buy.'
Not quite. They'd proud money, Eight, and I was set
to make it prouder.
      Dougie blinked: there'd been a hex
on Eight since ... couldn't even think of since,
Eight had always been hexed. Besides, they had connections,
connections meant white knights.
      'Oh white knights, black knights
and good night The Dag Network; doesn't The Trust believe
in class? Welcome The Family Network!'
So another big day in the life of Craig Stubbs, game-player?
Well one of many. Still, wouldn't it be worth it
hearing my wood-duck-in-chief, Dougie,
attempting one more joke *Better than flogging err Commodores
eh Craigo?*
      The Trust had pumped in our capital,
what more glory did he require?
      Bahrain or Bhutan, Birdsville
or Balwyn, who knew where the bucks commenced?
I never bothered to discover, only knowing how
they flowed into $tubb$corp and stopped where they
always do: with this one, the man still wishing
to dream.
      And had he dreams!
If a man's to own anything, I prayed,
(and let me be that man) *make it Eight*; knowing
as my board settled themselves that morning, Eight wouldn't be
the dags' much longer.

But 'Fellas, fellas,
before we start,' I teased, 'let's take a peek at what's
on Eight, at what we're getting.'
                    'On *Eight*?'
they wailed, 'we might want to own it,
but do we have to watch it?'
                    Indeed they did.
The mid-morning host sat in a prefab set:
he'd the shakes, it wobbled, and a catatonic guest
waved some gadget she was flogging:
it wasn't working, it never would.
                    Five years before,
one Saturday afternoon when nobody noticed,
it's rumoured Eight almost topped the ratings.
I have never tried believing that.
                    And
who had owned this parody? Parodies:
old crocks and their young crock sons:
Melbourne's finest.
                    I thought of Karen's father,
how he loved-to-loathe them,
and told the host, the quest and her gadget
*Time we carved up the carcass: preserve the best
but nuke the rest. Sorry Melbourne's finest,
1959 is over, you're in for a spot of downsizing:
we owe it to Australia's mums and dads and kids
to see that Eight's reborn and added to
the arch of excellence which is becoming $tubb$corp.
Bye-bye Dag Network, you're becoming my Family Network,
doing us Aussie-proud!*
                    Now I'd head-hunt.
Before my first (and only) date with DeeDee
(wishing to hand over one flawless red rose with
welcome aboard and hoping to say much more)
I itemised places, worldwide, to take her
(but she'd been there and everywhere else). Okay,
that night aiming for the intimate, the discreet,
it was to be just dinner; but when Craig Stubbs
dined DeeDee Lyons all Sydney knew:
well, something at least: they knew me or

they knew her or who I was or who she was and,
better still, what we were doing there:
till the restaurant became the town, and the town
became that gigantic leagues club I guess it
always is.
                  I was born to business,
and business must accept its public eye,
but with DeeDee in that town, that place, that evening
Don't we know him? public eyes announced,
he, ho ho, farted in the phone box.
                              Better readjust,
I told myself, readjust and learn, learn from The Ice Queen,
Celeb 101: How To Smile Like Tom Cruise And Control Your Life.
We do it which way, DeeDee?
                                      'At school you weren't,'
she asked, seeming to know my answer, 'a prefect?'
Nah Deeds, too much the loudmouth.
                                In Melbourne,
somewhere, she'd been one, of course,
and I shuffled through all appropriate places:
Merton Hall/St Catherine's/Firbank. No. *Big* no.
She was the Nineteen Seventy something dux
of Vermont High. Where, I got told, she learnt
'All my prospects had to be made by moi.
And you, Craig?'
                          Knowing she'd caught the $tubb$corp saga
(who hadn't?) but guessing she'd enjoy a re-run,
I pitched: scraping through Glen Eira Grammar,
flogging shoes for a week.
                            'Then the car yard...'
DeeDee baited.
                  I ignored her bait:
'Then the showroom, now The Family Network and,
even better now I'm employing you; and, knowing you
can stand the pace, employing Gibbo. Sure he's a maniac
but hey! maniacs stormed Gallipoli, we were built
by maniacs. I look at Deeds 'n' Gibbo and I see
not merely ratings but class, total.
Send one of the Chappells in to bat at the sports desk:
it's over: we *are* Australia!

       With DeeDee
you'd to be not merely duckshit smooth,
but duckshit pate smoother. But though I was,
why bother? I could've been some truckie
out of Longreach, and *he'd* have stood more prospects:
shot down and bagged for all the exotica
she thought he was.
      Eight did her in a doco.
Y' see it? Well remember this from the DeeDee doco?
How 'Any man in my life just has to be . . .'
and her sigh blends into a laugh, all overlain by
this hint of a shrug which confesses 'Well yes . . .
just that . . . a man. Love? Love for a Virgo's
mmmighty hard!'
     But she wasn't told
I want to employ you, I know you deserve it
for her star sign or her sex life
but because DeeDee has the most acceptable face
wherever she works; and our team had to be premium.
That day we started clearing out the Dag Network dags
I told my board: 'When Eight goes ratings ape
think Gibbo's Coast-to-Coast, but when we're
seeking trust, respect, think Newscope With DeeDee Lyons.
Ratings will never last without respect,
and, if you've a smart girl seeking that respect
Look you'll hear Australia telling itself
this must be true there's her there's DeeDee Lyons.
Fellas she'll make us and I'll do all to
ensure it.'
    Whoever the woman is I always have.
You name us, Fella, the least fashionable room
in any house. Correct: the laundry. Then imagine
this teenage party over twenty years back,
with young Craig chatting up (he'd call it
negotiating) a girl in the laundry:
she's leaning back so slightly to the trough,
above her the hot water service hums,
and what's she getting told? Probably how he
doesn't think he'll become a dentist or
an engineer (particularly a dentist) but how

*I'm rather good at flogging cars, new cars,
they're making me a bit of money.*
                         Some things
get overrated, and Fella there's been times
I'd relegate *sex* to that, times when I'd ask
what's this *Satisfaction*? Just a song.
Though, as a way to help position yourself,
'sex' if you want to call it 'sex'
walks in on time enough of the time.
Remember how it felt arriving at some turn
with your arm around this girl you met
at the previous party, and how, this time,
you weren't just asking the mates to be impressed,
but daring them to believe?
                         Sure I may've had
some plan in the laundry; then though we were interrupted:
this Bucky Beaver in a poloneck, who needs
so much to be a dentist he even gargles
as he speaks. This kid is checking us,
or rather her, Meg:
doe-eyed Meg from Brighton, doe-eyed Meg
from Brighton with the oblong earrings
yes guys just finished school . . .
And I knew what had to matter:
Mate he needed to know, *you can call me
shitburger or shitburger-with-the-lot, but I
meaning we will not be gatecrashed;*
and what still mattered more:
not even *Will this woman speak to me again?*
(let alone could I/can I fuck her)
but this: she had to realise how Craigo here
could offer, outbid and deliver more than
anyone just dropping by to inspect the goods.
You tell me what she (what you) preferred:
The Dental Students' Ball/The Combined Toyota Dealers'
Dinner Dance?
                         And, since I guess because I'm good at it,
Fella would pack her off with the dentists
wouldn't he? I'll guess again: try us on art:
offer Fella a Renoir nah nah he'll take the Pro Hart.

But who can blame him his watertight,
Cherrywood life? Fella can never make himself the fool
that Craigo has and, this arvo isn't he feeling great!
                                        Yeah well,
let's imagine this one: it is a mild summer evening,
yes in Bentleigh, and west down Centre Road I hoon,
over the highway into Brighton, with Thorpie rasping
the evening's anthem *Most people I know/*
Think that I'm cra-zy-ey-ey-ey . . .
So it's the dinner dance Meg? Sure Craig . . . though.
and there's always *though* she'd things, certain things
I'd better know: Meg was sortov going out with Rick
and was a Catholic, kinda. So? I smiled,
don't bring the boyfriend, don't bring the Pope.
Saw her a few times, and Fella tell you this:
Meg had these gentle tits that must've sloped
better than most in town, always keeping me guessing.
Quietly impressive (let's say that)
she was going to impress not the mates, the folks,
not even the bosses, but the bosses' wives,
who'd tell everybody worth it
Craig knows some really nice girls.
                        No,
Meg wasn't on deck to be undressed:
one day this Rick would return from
wherever he'd gone, get that under way; till years on
Meg looks up and there on The Family Network,
live from Wealthmakers 88, I'm welcoming the world
to Horizon. 'Not the Toyota Salesman!' Rick will hear.
'He took me to a dinner dance!'
                        Now, of course,
Horizon's keys are with some Taiwanese,
commissioners run The Stags,
Dix has scuttled back to Osbourne with what's left,
and Eight's been re-re-reinvented:
Network Oz, Gibbo headlining Coast-to-Coast,
live from the BoomCon blimp.
                        How'd Adrian put it?
Whilst the gag market remains a bull market
that little bastard lives in fuckland.

Well guess who phones The Horse? No, not Gibbo.
But day or night, somewhere on the planet,
Osbourne's drunk, drunk and demanding
isn't he the true-blue-dinky-di-est
corporate cunt in history, the biggest ever credit
to Down Under, well isn't he? Why stop at
media, at leisure (like Craigo did)
at newspapers and breweries, why stop at
universities? He was set to own everything
that was, is and would be. But, though the world's
most universal citizen was speaking, full time,
all the time, Oz was Aussie!
      Craig, I'd to tell
myself, you've lost. All those years (from Real Livin' Toyota
to Crazy Horse) you were an utter novice,
only in need of simplest rewards:
some mates, a wife, a network, footballers,
a resort...
    'And I'm heading highbrow,' Osbourne warns,
'got me a magazine, me magazine is *Playpen*,
Playpen Oz, and, for a treat, we're subscribing Craigo!'
And there, after the letters itemising blow-jobs
(real or imagined, received and, even, given)
among the obligatory coy cartoons
of blondes-in-the-cot, and just before the centrefold,
we've Gibbo's contribution: reheating whatever
$tubb$corp myths remain and topping them with
a sprig of gags.
     Now, on The Sunshine Coast,
refugees from Bentleigh and beyond are asking:
Stubbs? He tried to run The Stags. Yeah,
and didn't he tell their chairman of selectors
Listen prick either you play Mullins ev'ry
and I mean ev'ry game, no matter what,
or else we relocate.
If Perth can't accept my boys, they're begging
on The Gold Coast!
      Sounds great, Fella?
Sounds even better if I'd said it
(just remind me next time and I will).

And was he satisfied with even that?
asks Gibbo. *Of course not, but he loved it!*
Who needs Horizon, why bother investing in
the very best, when, as the man informs,
everything and anything sells?
Let's tell Fella this:
Stubbs simply didn't want enough.
Just one movie studio? Why hadn't he considered
half-a-dozen? Might've got somewhere.
   We slid into Hollywood, sighted First National,
bid, waited, tripled the dose and continued waiting.
Who'd that town think we were, BoomCon?
Don't know about you I wanted to tell
Southern California, *but we at $tubb$corp can aim
a show further than is ever expected and
(whilst all of you are dumb in your bewilderment)
like that dirty brown trout, we'll be in and
we'll be out: Aussie hotshots giving it a go.*
Just like you are Hotshot.
Except when was your last downside?
Still, I guess you must've known the feeling:
How, the moment your Gulfstream IV hits tarmac,
this much is telling you *A warrant's out!*
In the VIP lounge DeeDee confirmed it.
But *management fees?* It stunned me, tell us Deeds
and I'll pay and pay again. Who to but?
And nothing's more certain, she got told,
than Americans looking to their own and no,
I hadn't exactly bought First National or anything.
So make us laugh: give Craigo a BoomCon update.
   On television Osbourne was blitzing his way from debt:
comeback ninety-nine. All it ever seemed to show
were Aussies, sure in themselves,
for BoomCon: white-coated boffins held up test-tubes
for BoomCon; workers strode grinning from their building sites
for BoomCon; teenagers discoing night-after-night away;
diggers round a cenotaph on Anzac Day:
BoomCon: we're with ya total, Oz!
   At our Christmas bash (was it a year before or two
that my juggler cascaded continual dollar signs?)

'Saltin' it hard?' Mr Beer had asked, 'Young Craig?'
Please, I suggested, giving him a reality check,
congratulate the man who's just disposed of BoomCon,
walked away with Mrs BoomCon.
If he saw Oz tell him from Stubbs:
commiserations, he was fine as the next wealthmaker
for a wood-duck.
                Yeah yeah the boy was saltin'.
But now imagine you are saltin' too
(Hotshot's Volvo, his manor house in Cherrywood ...)
all in the name of Raelene Hotshot who,
one day, tells you *mine honey mine*. How might
a hotshot feel, how could he understand?
                              One arvo I'd flown
to Perth, collected Osbourne's wife: and though
he must've loathed me for it I knew this:
he loved the idea: for that man
not only understood my audacity, somehow
and even better, he adored the thought of Dix 'n' me:
that thought to which he added
Top it you prick? Sure, one day I'll top it.
All my marriage, all my life, I've been waiting
my ultimate wood-duck.
                    Doesn't gel, Hotshot? I was *it*!
And yes, there was still enough between these two,
enough which had nothing, and better still, the lot
to do with sex: Big Oz style power-sex:
how to obtain yourself a rival then
fuck him over.
           As if I would never do that!
'Well, in the sack ...'
in the sack with Dix I asked 'Oz life. In the sack ...
tell us ... what's he like?'
                      What was he like?
Let's say that, as in business, the hog
loved his grunting. As for the rest, oh Australia!
why haven't you the imagination?
                          Because he has it for you:
courtesy of renta-shrink and the bodgiest recall
this side of the amnesiacs convention:

untriable, innocent and free, the nation
loves him: in court or out of it
they'll always give their Big Big Oz one helluva
thumbs-up: he's our battler-wealthmaker
and all the world adores a fat boy
No no no it wasn't him what farted
his chocka, bag-o-lollies grin:
'Sorry fellas, love to assist The Commission,
but the specialist says I've, y' know, this battler's brain:
can't remember a thing!'
Oh Oz your memory wasn't always so refined.
'Stubbsy,' he asked once 'ever got it with . . .
The Ice Queen?' Osbourne had of course,
and, knowing who she was, I still asked *who?*
just to hear him pant out 'DeeDee!'
        And 'DeeDee!'
I repeated.
  And? he wanted me to ask. I didn't.
DeeDee? Women? I could afford to find out for myself.
I always had.
   Look there,
hanging above the Jack Daniels and some local rotgut:
well what does Hotshot think it is?
Just an enlarged snapshot, mounted and framed?
Maybe, but nothing's been as owned as how I own
that polaroid. It's Take-Your-Time,
the first of those fibro motels. A dump.
Like you DeeDee hardly knew what it was,
but unlike you she thought it was art; and wilted,
telling me *How prim-it-if! Yes how dom-es-tique!*
And how much was it? With six made,
one per boardroom, none were getting sold.
I wasn't heard: we were well into another of
madame's intellectual strip-shows: first, off with
her 'media' gear (only a way to earn a living)
next, 'business' (seemingly sexier, lingerie-style,
still not enough). Soon there'd be the essential,
nude DeeDee of the fine arts major.
The polaroid, she told me, wasn't art *exactement*
and yet it was and yet it wasn't and yet . . .

Did I see what DeeDee saw?
'Whatever you mean?' I asked. 'Well yes, but
then again, no . . .' and told her what the picture was,
how, yes, there was a kind of art in that:
the more I made the more it would be worth.
Take-Your-Time is only art now:
part of my imagination, as it should be.
Oh it had a manager when I arrived.
His imagination might've run a laundromat.
Wouldn't have risked him with even that.
I hired a grader to knock it down and,
scooping Take-Your-Time into a herd of trucks,
they carted it to some tip.
                    With nothing but land,
an overdraft, a dream, I could start $tubb$corp.
The night Wealthmakers 88 opened Horizon
envy dissolved into admiration, and even
the original corporate buccaneer, Mr Beer,
seemed a mite uncertain, a wistful not-quite
Mr Beer.
          'Be honest Craig,'
he asked, 'tell us my product's decent.
Isn't it?' (How'd Gibbo's song go?
The palate gets cleansed/ Life gets a meaning./
What would Aussie be/ Without it?)
'Make an okay drop,
don't I matey, don't I?'
                    Well he did,
or rather me being smartarsed:
'you employ the men that do!'
          He started smiling: 'Know how to keep butter
on our bread, eh Stubbs?'
                    And, for a second,
I must've seemed like Kim Il Sung, but
the party being mine, it was allowed. Then,
patting his shoulder, 'Matey,' I looked into his
matey bug-eyes 'Y' product's fine,
serving it aren't we?'
                    His smile continued:
'Never be too clever Craig. And cut back the trappings,

son. Hock, prison, exile, envy, ridicule, the grave . . .
just pick your wall and know that after you hit it
(and there's a wall for every prick on the planet)
what powers have trappings to rescue anyone?'
True business knew that wealth had to exist
without them; that they were girl's stuff.
So your latest woman needed diamonds, sapphires, pearls?
Do how he'd done it; buy an appropriate store
and borrow whatever, whenever.
       No,
he didn't advise often, Mr Beer,
only those deserving his respect:
not, for example, that peanut share-shuffler
Heart-throb: shoelaces and paper clips, his hit 'n'
giggle empire, that was Futurex, and
'Dare you to join the big boys, Heart-throb . . .'
Mr Beer croaked, loving the put-down.
Then he repeated *respect* twice and told me that
unless I'd been a liar (and running)
an index finger down a side of his nose) unless . . .
$tubb$corp was hung like a stallion!
'Look what you've made . . .' he purred, coming closer
than he had ever been. 'Craig, anyone can think
they own a brewery, or a network, even a footy team.
But a resort . . . Horizon . . . Craig . . .'
These words had to stop. They were replaced:
he was jealous as he'd never been, like all Australia
should be; it was like I had not a wife,
girlfriend, even a CEO he couldn't exist without wanting,
but a daughter, pure yet ripe, swaying down the aisle,
on my arm.
    Well Hotshot,
I've never seen Horizon quite like that,
doubt if I ever could, but thanks, I told him,
I know compliments; just the required fuel
for the speech I was to make.
        'Gibbo still here?' I asked.
Of course he was. 'Mind if I borrow a song, mate?
That beer commercial of your which goes
What would Aussie be/ Without it? Well,

I'd like to take that one step further:
what would Aussie be without *us*?'
It seemed they'd never thought of that,
but luckily the reality cancelled the nightmare;
and, after their nodding and muttering, 'Put it this way,'
I continued, 'there's a world out there and friends
I'm going to tell this world: take a good look
at these wealthmakers, world, because you'll see
not just Australians but Australia,
and not just Australia but Australia reborn.
Sure, we've had a few tough years,
but only whingers would bother harping on that (if you're
a whinger the times are always bloody awful)
and any present, by the way, can leave
because the spirit that got us through Bodyline and Changi
is back, and world you're welcome,
right here, right now, to come and enjoy Real Livin'.
We love our country, sure, there's nothing like it,
but being sentimental doesn't mean we're not tougher
than you wouldn't want to guess.
And I'll say this to all our governments:
stay off our backs and you'll be proud of us:
you better be, no you'll *have* to be because
when messing with wealthmakers any outcome's
obvious.'
      When she saw Osbourne 'n' Stubbs
can-canning with the leggiest of models
DeeDee hardly believed it: what were we today:
'Enemies?' she shouted, 'Rivals? Friends?'
'Call us,' Osbourne offered,
'average Aussies celebrating their prime,
what their prime can bring: beautiful girls,
intelligent women, things to make you sigh
Ain't real livin' grand!'
The night was made for it.
                    And, with nothing but
a few discreet lines, upstairs, not even Dix
distracting him, people-who-knew-how, for friends,
it was a nah wuz Gibbo: and did we want
his Big Oz song his Big Oz song his Big Oz song?

Oh I'm in love with the Big Big Oz/
And the Big Big Oz loves me . . .
Off his tree? Out of the fuckin' forest!
And 'Hey! Wealthmakers!' he roused us further,
'In 88 wadda wedoo? We . . . one . . . two . . . three . . .
di-vers-if-y!'
          'Take the prick,' Osbourne sneered,
'he's one of yours. And so is this . . .'
as my wife, his ex, scooted into the Horizon ballroom,
on her moped, throbbing to the Dixo theme
Th' minute y' walked in th' joint (Uh. Uhh.) . . .
Figure any combination of musos and
Dixie Cup, woohoo, would be up
wigglin' th' butt, I want it you get it
and the world goes round. Hi all hi all
the machine and me are raring so come on
Aussie come on let your hair down weeeee!
Osbourne smirked: 'Big was never big enough
for Dixie, Craigo. She hasn't changed.
She never will.'
      My pager called:
down south, Horizon Two, Bullshit-on-Tweed,
had lain quarter-done for half a year. 'So blow it,'
I rang through to the Friends of $tubb$corp,
'blow it into the old Pacific sea.'
                    And that was it.
My neighbour, who should've had a bath,
was licking slop from his moustache;
whilst behind us Australia tucked into
DeeDee's eye-fillet journalism:
'In an attempt to rescue his career,
a tired and emotional Craig Stubbs flew out
this morning, vowing vengeance . . .' Oh sweetheart,
oh oh, what manner of mind processes your lines?
Beside me the b.o. was thicker than
his soup-strainer, their owner checking
what truly mattered between that economy class
and this economy class.
             'Fuckin' animal!'
he breathed up through his teeth,

'should be down there, drowning!'
Slowly I turned, snatched at his lapels,
hearing 'Please!' the batsqueak of an attendant.
'Mis-ter Stubbs!'
     They moved him,
and I still mattered, just.
       As you will soon.
Can Hotshot take advice?
I'll tell it this way *Who's made the news tonight?*
I wondered *Dougie? Oz? Heart-throb? Me?*
No, it was Mrs Beer mark three,
our one-time Jacqui O, our virtual Lady Di. Hardly now:
she's borrowed a mouth from Carol Channing
and seems furious: 'Your bully boys!'
she cockatoos to her estranged. 'Call off your
bully boys!' Then, hammering her order home
'Heel 'em! Heel 'em!'
      Heel who?
Simple fellas with simple fellas' jobs to do:
turf Madam and all that is Madam's from
the Beer home, getting what's so rightly Sir's
returned to Sir.
     Too bad it has to be
on prime time (remember how she looked, recall
the sound?) too bad it always will be. No,
one more rich 'n' greedy dummyspitter is not
exactly dignified.
     Well here's a trick:
no hardly a trick, a tip that even if
you've no brains plus, will lead into
a trick: size up where the cameras are,
and then ignore them.
     Or better, let Craigo play your coach:
It's a warm and friendly summer morning,
let's say February at its most sensational;
digesting your coffee you march towards
the Royal Commission: today it's time for
Chief Investigator Hotshot's evidence:
the was and is of Stubbsy, the how and why
he's such a big bad boy. Listen but:

this striding-out (for what will be
your finest hour) has quit the past already:
it's playing in the future now, Hotshot's covered,
he's on prime time, he's never been ambushed
by Network Oz before, by reporters
set to turn him back into one dumb fella.
Keep up the laughter, Stubbsy's your media adviser now.
And why? Because you've a job to do, and I believe
in fellas having jobs to do, doing them well;
besides, when it comes to the networks, the press,
we're in the same team: what we know
they want to know. Ever been given the DeeDee
once-over? Never be mug enough to even offer
Later later sweetheart later or *No comment now
or ever!* You've only one defence: silence.
But why the reminder? Hotshot's smart,
he'll say his nix, he knows how Craigo bobbed up
constantly for years *Fellas here I am!*
         I could've used you.
For all his buttoned-down routine
Hotshot's smart as Stubbsy.
        I could've used you.
He won't be cornered like his boss
(well why not partner?) was.
      Inside,
somebody is lining up further wood-ducks,
somebody else is getting all the other loans
rejigged into infinity; whilst outside, Hotshot,
standing before every journo who's invited themselves
to $tubb$corp, is keeping his big trap shut.
Yeah, I could've used you.
And you found me instead.
       So? Do I look that seismic
with concern? Felli (and all his other fellas)
hasn't got me: he'll never *get* me. Still,
I've spilt him things (could spill him more)
I never would to Karen, DeeDee, even Dix.
Accept me for that passing host I am,
who'll never be so hard up to think
he deserves some true-blue, off-into-the-sunset mate.

Moose? Moose tried winning us games.
Gibbo? Gibbo made our laughs, but laughs and games are
anyone's; and, as only a mate can, Osbourne
fucked me round: but being everybody's mate perhaps
that's how he'll run the world.
Why not just give in and spend the evening?
No, not here, yet, we're hardly open. Come back
after some hours, say. The FucFuc though
is highly operational and, if the menu's hardly
Fella's fare, tell them in Cherrywood you only looked;
tell them nothing happened, nothing much. The drinks,
whatever else is tempting, they're on Craigo:
all you need's a voucher *This voucher entitles Fella (and all his
mates, never forget his mates)*
to whatever he wants as long as he wants it.
No?
Not even maybe? Fella you *are* difficult. C'mon:
over the road up half a block, just be Stubbsy's guest
this once and ask for Bern. Got it? Bern.
The FucFuc (no I didn't invent the name!):
catch it, if you're game.

GIBBO'S COAST-TO-COAST

My first thought was, he lied in every word . . .
   ROBERT BROWNING,
      'Childe Roland to the Dark Tower Came'

Get a few tall poppies and behead 'em.
And don't believe all rumours, merely spread 'em.
                              GIBBO *obiter dicta*

        Call it a triumph of self, a coup for style:
whether through charm, lies, certain PR guile,
accompanying et ceteras . . . whichever did it
one year he was barely considered,
during the next few none were so mateyed, mated:
each soap starlette over for the Logies seemed fated
as his, part of the prize: '79 / '80 / '81:
best new talent (*Wog Fun / Ocker Fun*);
best variety (*The Live Shows*); best sitcom (Aussie)
(*Rhmrhmrhm The Car Won't Start*)
                              Yet, what was he?
Besides this overability with songs, gags,
quite the mean of men: as he eats, he drinks, shags
whenever he can; respectable parents, a decent school . . .
        With this talent: getting his acts embossed on the spool
of history: a regular for those rounds of *remember when* . . .
as mostly the rich will have: 'Heehee I owned a network then . . .
funny man, Gibbo . . . knew his worth and could be bought
like anyone . . .' Then, as the reverie soars, 'Thought
our price had, if not an inbuilt loyalty component . . .'
And, whilst what could act for truth becomes the moment
welcome, even if you haven't twigged, to the biz
of moi, Gibbo: the he, the him, the his.
        Sure, like Hamlet, Othello and Macbeth
I'm flawed (if hardly heroic).
                    Even if the end's mere death
all my excesses have had, praise any lord,

their limits: don't jet me to the Betty Ford
yet; 'cause name a better (name a finer) boast
than *I remain national I'm still coast-to-coast.*
       Unlike that human beancurd Craig the bland,
broke in Singapore/ The Philippines/ Thailand,
muttering sheepish in one of his latest bars
a few dozen sorries and a gross of taas.
       But before rewinding this testament to Genesis
(when friends were truly friends and 'nemesis'
a big word you'd to look up) this minor task:
how to answer when reporters ask
'Weren't you two the apogee of mates?'
and 'There must've been midnight tête-à-têtes
that turned confessional *Face it Gibbo, I'm a jerk!*
       Well, given a life that was work and work
which was my living, from his all-purpose requisite gall,
to creditors primed to knacker him ball by ball
and wring off his dial that trademark smile,
I saw the lot.
              True, others prefer their Stubbs in exile
('Why should *we*,' some columnist brayed, 'want this offal
back?') Yet Crazy Horse (doubtless some brothel
variant) aside, what is he, pardon the déjà
vu, but one more Aussie holed up in South-East Asia?
And, though my heart has tendencies to wince
(for Craigo's scuttled and I haven't seen him since,
like those near-to-thousands who met him/ knew him
enough for a friend) any still wanting to screw him
(as if they could) ambush Gibbo, demanding his Stubbs-dope:
'How'd that cynic in you cope
with such one-dimensional bonhomie: *Hey man!* hurled
like a verbal frisbee?'
              Easy. Those days it was a *Hey man!* world.

       And now my mate's in heaps of trouble, folks.
He'll survive but. Y' want more Stubbsy jokes?
Know the difference between Craigo and a light
bulb? But face it, gags are cheap and to indict

a guy because he's broke, been near-to-charged, has split,
is criminal.
   And say, now that we've mentioned it,
(or should've) where's Moose-o nowadays? Employed for once:
it's almost real work and, if this stunt's
a touch weird, I hear reports how ve-ry nice
Moose-in' round can get, guarding the merchandise.
   For would you believe that Mr 'Borrowed Billions' Stubbs
is back starting-from-scratch with . . . body rubs?
But that's Craigo; that's business: having y'self sluiced
all points north of Aussie with Le Moose:
who, so adept at peeling off his shorts
when The Stags were yours and he'd a career, of sorts,
still remains loyal whilst all us lot prove dross.
And given the man's *I'll stick by ya, Boss*
he's hardly some toyboy languid on a sofa.
But . . . I mean . . . going into exile . . . with y' chauffeur?
   Yet had I Craig's number there'd be faxes, dinky-di/
true blue *Dear Cobber, the wide brown land says hi.*
Thanks for all the parties but here comes the post-fling
reckoning, Stubbsy, the reckoning?
After you served that cocktail of bad luck, blunders,
deceit and getting caught, just to run a joint ex-boywonders
shouldn't have to run . . . mate, please try the ultimate revenge:
a comeback which works . . .
   (Mine has. And that urge to binge
my woes on shrink/ journo/ barman/ even priest
has gone.)
   When friends prove, at the very least,
dickheads, we've a DMZ between sarcasm and concern
to negotiate: so tell 'em big boy's sorry, return,
cop something sweetish, start again. Which Craigo won't.
Only smalltimers copped the brunt
that should've been yours . . . and they were Stubbsy's fans,
once. Not for them *A man's*
gotta do and other clichés. All they've done since is stack rorts
and excess beside networks and resorts
then, playing historians, head towards a verdict:
judging as only those who've been flicked
away like fluff are able.

           Loving my gags, hiring Moose
or DeeDee, was that enough to cobble out some truce?
If I doubt it I have to. My savings sent
down the gully trap of 'management'
weren't I that month's wood-duck? You'd made a plague
out of friendship once too often, Craig:
and, if the sweet talking wouldn't stop, one fucker
named Gibbo knew the sweeter listening would. Near suckered
in again the clown bailed out; though taa you spiv
for the experience, that much he'll forgive.

☙

       DeeDee sends her best, she's recycling the era
into a two-part special that makes it clearer
where we (meaning you, Osbourne and the rest)
went wrong. There's an et cetera of experts plus guest
pundit me, giving the human touch.
With any remaining respect? Not over-much.
       And Deed's rapid quizzings, combined with a probing gaze
(shall I grill or fry him, bake, stew or braise?):
'Craig Stubbs, Gibbo, you're one of his closer friends . . .'
(had to have someone who is, or pretends
that way . . .) 'So, what's he like?'
                                   It wouldn't need much prodding
to dump the lot (cut to her measured nodding)
so I think: should we run this bland as he'd approve,
or hard like he'd admire? I paused, moved
to a synthesis: 'What's my verdict DeeDee? There's worse.
Always has been.'

☙

           No-one's seen her lips purse
quite as I have.
           Back when Gibbo was y' mecca
for dags, helping to digest their brekka
with gags, in she waltzes, with only me to guide her,
fresh from uni, DeeDee my offsider.
       'Just,' I take it easy, 'trust us as a mate, girl.'

(And what was I supposed to say?) 'Okay straight girl:
I crack the funnies, you just read the news.'
    Still she wouldn't bite, though she'd my kinda fuse:
non-existent. Like her or not
Deeds was all-woman, all-women did the lot;
or thought they should.
      As the girl blossomed
though, was princessed, petalled, possumed,
I marvelled, heart thumping rat-a-tat
Who else but Gibbo's responsible for that?
He *struck the match, that's how her blaze was lit.*
    Now, let's jump a decade and a bit,
with me on a bar stool. After two sips of Pernod
enter my once and future colleague, DeeDee Wonderjourno;
hardly Bo Derek, Bo Diddley or Bo Peep,
but played by the Ms Hepburn/Jackson/Streep.
    'G'day prickface . . .' endearingly gruff
like a whack in the balls 'never liked your stuff
but I can forgive. Here's how we make our monies
now: Je suis news, you supply les funnies.
Get it?' I got it, let this be her shout;
oh: and wit was in whilst sexism (you guessed it) out.
    I'll say it was. One network's lesser stunts
was shooting a DeeDee profile, but only once.
With a coiffure hers totally to choose,
not for this head the pageboy bob of a mere news
readeress, but a sweep of groomed mane
to, filly style, flick back. Though don't call her vain,
just confidence-on-a-package (close to a mil).
Who better then to toss any old pearl in the swill
and watch her public grovel? Oh slay me,
Deeds, you've come a long way baby:
sipping a coffee, visiting your old school;
then getting quizzed by a patronising fool
in whose *Ahh my dear* carriage
of questions rode the ultimate *you've rejected marriage?*
Well! Judge if he deserved this put-down sent and got
I'm no dyke but if I was so what?
Poor chap reddens, swallows, sweats and chokes,
adding 'badder' to the bad name of us blokes.

Ahh little beats that I-is-who-I-is-ness
of DeeDee taking care of DeeDee's business.
Pure distilled cool: no tantrum, hiccup, blooper,
was remotely yours DeeDee you old trooper.
   Like me by now she'd paid up all her subs
and dues: it just required one Mr Stubbs
to hire her: get Deeds co-hosting 'G'day Aussie'
with Gibbo.

࿔

    Oh she was premium! And because he,
Craigo, had himself a network, such class
seemed necessary.
     Pity *he* ended as little more than farce;
shame each evening the man went
closer, closer to schlockest entertainment:
one day calling for this National Ethics Code; being seen
the next, tree-planting (his bout of being green).
Might as well believe this Australia shrugged
*since tomorrow Craig the Rich Engine will4ve chugged
onto another track.*
     Then, with a flurry
of writs turning him into this middle-aged man in a hurry,
it's time to go; though loved or hated
but never ignored, something remains to be consummated
and DeeDee's clichés giving our heartstrings their kickstart
('The gender-specific straw which broke the state of the art
didn't come down in the last feisty shower . . .')
we saw '$tubb$corp, the Final Hour'.
And what of his brief, if recent, bout of ethics
now? I saw an artiste playing us for hicks:
back straight, chin up, chest out and like a man
face the music for a few sound bites, then scram.
Fawning one minute he veered into the stroppy
(bet she couldn't name a taller poppy)
then remade history: one solitary bloke alone
gave Aussie such a go: this man tapping his breast bone.
And if, next year, he'd be mythic as the yeti
(with $tubb$corp churned to corporate confetti:

no Craig no! Anything but the shredder!)
well tsk tsk tut tut boo hoo stiff cheddar.
           Somewhere a high-flyer was making tracks,
take down the dish, disconnect the fax;
hear one-time rivals (seeming to glide like ice-dancers
round Deeds) volley back their answers
even before the questions: Craigo the businessman?
industrious to the twentieth carat, the eighth dan:
asked much, gave more; the patriot? that bloke would kill
for Aussie; the partygiver? he was Cecil B. DeMille;
the spouse? mmmm tolerant . . . And the bankrupt? There's always
               some text-
book weakness that'll undo you . . . for some it's sex,
with others, money . . . and that prick had to screw him-
self senseless into debt. Ours! Stubbs? We hardly knew him.
          Oh they may seem tack, but such disclaimers
from closepersonalfriends sure aren't lamer
than most. Though, when a mate's sprawled on the ropes,
Gibbo'll stand by; at least that's what he hopes . . .

ò

          When young my women tended to be nursey
and I prowled St Vincent's, The Alfred and The Mercy.
Out went a daggy Wesley College urchin,
in came this groomed, ruthless, hardword merchant.
These were the days when Gibbo (what a yawn!)
would hurtle into driveways, parp his horn;
reversing just as fast. If I'd mates and this was par
for their course ('That Gibbo sure gave us a laugh!')
soon they'd be dumped. Better friends were mine
now: high-risk finance and interior design:
Craig and Karen.
                    I was this apprentice clown
(my self-styled brief to loosen up the town)
hosting a beer launch (one of the boutiquier pubs)
when a hand was offered: 'Craig Stubbs,
Gibbo. We don't just *like* your act . . . count us lovers!'
          And this pariah-to-be who'll grace a brace of *BRW* covers
(not to mention 'Corporate Crook/ Corporate Sook',

and 'The Bumper Stubbsy Gag Book',
– recall the ones about his IQ or better, sex life? ...)
was just-a-bloke that evening, introducing his wife,
enjoying himself. Not quite. It hardly remains a sport
when the rich enough decide to pay you court;
but how'd I know a rising robber baron
was shouting me drinks? So he smiles, introduces Karen,
says 'you had us out of it total jeez Gibbo jeez ...'
and (pausing to mouth *cheese*
at *Vogue* paparazzi) 'I'm getting known for mega-punts
round here, so when someone for once
does something worth it he's my mate and here's my card ...'
It hadn't been cut-price gags flogged by the yard
that night, but top-shelf humour and, better than most
he knew what Aussie needed: 'Laughs coast-to-coast.
Heard any lately? Too few too bloody few ...
Oh yes and Karen loved it too ...'
      Oh yes ahh yes ahh Karen yes well yes.
Say it this often who needs to second-guess?

      One evening, with this less-than-exactly-vague
urge to inspect the luck of lucky Craig
(etching a portrait of good lovin':
dinner warm and waiting in the oven,
what devotion!) I pressed his intercom:
'It's Gibbo, Karen, Stubbsy not at home?'
      No, Craig was interstate. I cleared a cough.
Interstate indeed, I'd seen him off.
But please come in, she deserved a chuckle.
'Much gag-work about?'
                  I shrugged this *fuck-all*
shrug.
      Minutes on her psyche's changing gears:
smiles have ceased, suddenly there's tears:
no mere sobs, a few drops from the odd duct,
but a full gush.
          (God she was all product,
Karen: firm breasts, long slim hips,

flowing lacquered perm, moist full lips:
a Charlie's Angel or a Carly Simon)
        You'd think a jokeman might have greater timin',
but subscribing to this neglected wife's agenda
posted my hands, which weren't returned to sender.
        'Please ...' came a sigh (perhaps a *not yet* please?)
My name said twice and her shoulders squeezed.
Lonely at Eight, it's just a weekday night,
'I like you Gibbo lots ... despite ... despite ...'
Her eyes were closed. 'Oh help me to be happy'
        Sure I'd help, with a foreplay snappy
to non-existent; which is I gather passion.
For Karen, too, was liked, in Gibbo's fashion.
        Coy as a nymph or randy as a satyr,
the bottom line seems, surely *Does it matter?*
But change *Me being me*? Bad luck I can't.
Tell you though what my affections aren't:
the see-through blandishments of one more glib beau.
'... trust me Karen-petal, this is Gibbo.
Mop the tears, please, I understand:
Craig is the future, Craig is in demand,
and it isn't *you* that has so staled your spouse ...'
(What help is logic, intuition, nous,
when free wills are on a collision course with fate?)
'So cut whatever's lost, and fuck his mate!'

        When life gets messy let me help clean the mess ...

        'cause life, then, was potent, needing a shot of mere excess
(Manets/ Monets, Lear Jets/ blimps) to hook you,
the tiniest line of hype to book you
into Suckerdom One with the rest of us, pegged
and squirming in admiration. These men were 'family' they begged
to be thought the get-real-ist blokes on earth.
And they got it. 'Thanks ... mmm, so what am I worth?
Think hard then treble it then treble *that* again.'

They were *who*, *where* was here, *when*
was now, they owned *how, why*? because.

🙦

      With a nation scampering to him on all fours
time, Craig felt, to leave the corporate ghetto
that was $tubb$corp and sponsor a 'Rigoletto'.
      'Bit highbrow,' Osbourne, first-nighter-in-chief
ragged me, 'eh Gib?'
      If public sarcasm was his brief
I'd be more subtle. 'Dunno, Oz, guess
this plot has parallels even today.' Wasn't I jester
to self-proclaimed risktakers and wealthmakers;
to those measuring office space in acres?
Mentors all! For this much I'd learnt:
enough power can turn what you weren't
into what you'll become: 'miners' shrewd
enough never to have 'mined'; 'brewers' who'd hardly 'brewed'.
Near illiterates mortgaging their tongue.
At least the gags I've told, songs I've written and sung
are mine; and, as Verdi shows us, no-one's feared
quite like the funny man.
      Osbourne sneered:
'Somewhat less than a gift-to-the-nation
isn't it? Craigo and opera? An aberration.
When he's done with their prima donna traumas,
all their "Götterdämmerungs" 'n' "Normas",
the blaze will shrink, all fire turns to ash.
Next year he'll find his level: Johnny Cash!'
I stared in reply, sent somewhat aback.
Him of all Australians to take a culture tack!
When Stubbs raided Paris, a Manet going cheap,
The Big Oz fumed, knowing he wouldn't reap
that day's kudos. Can't say his eyes commenced to shine
with the grief of *This could / should've been mine;*
but something started.
      Okay, in the divvy of spoils
Craig had got Dixie . . . but nineteenth-century oils?
      '. . . know as much about art as the next guy,'

he confessed 'You know much, Gib?'
                              'A bit.'
                                        'Great. Let's buy!'
So give your neurones a collective squeeze
and imagine some dilettante storming Sotheby's
with *French Impressionism Rah! Rah! Rah!*
           Well hardly. 'Jeez ... one lousy Ren-fuckin'-oir,'
he whined, 'and don't I feel an almighty bunny ...'
'cause you ain't got no Monet, honey.
Sorry to be the spoilsport Oz, but hell,
whoever has, whoever will?
           With one more tilt at destiny to tempt
him though, Osbourne would. Couldn't exactly pre-empt
his ignorance; for money just isn't enough.
'But come the unveiling, after our crash course in the stuff
you'll seem informed.' Quite quite.
'... well this here's the tricky bit: your's is a *Mo*net, right?
The *Ma*net's Stubbsy's.'
                     Sure sure, he'd get by
as he always got by: rough diamond clever
enough: 'Manet or Monet, well who/whatever,
there's these two painters, see: his, ours,
and his does people.' Whilst yours? 'Mmmainly flowers ...
and Aussie, he did them for us!'
                            Yes, direct from the heart
of 'Big Oz' Osbourne, authority on art.
Gah-gahed by '... brushwork', he'd '... bought genius again ...'
and sure his name obtained the fattest firms, the smartest men;
Sure, his was '... the very best in food, company, wine ...'
but 'Was ever a *Man* ... *Mo*net! more exquisite than mine?'
Given such wide-eyed corporate gee-whiz
was ever a good life more good life than his?
When y' champers is Krug and y' vases Ming
never! Not that these or anything
were ever owned by him or anyone except the banks
(probably). A nation, meantime, offered thanks.
           This shot is purest Oz: never a man to squib
posing (chef's hat to an angle, come 'n' get it bib)
he serves a stir-fried brunch fresh from the wok.
Another kid with toys, on loan/ in hock.

Oh how we loathed but couldn't do without
this paragon survivor of the rout.
'Stubbs?,' Osbourne grunted, though didn't exactly gloat,
just drew an index finger over his throat
(as if a hitman for the House of Saud)
and went on living. Miner, developer (above the crowd
yet of the crowd), communicator, motivator, brewer
(below the sewer yet of the sewer),
grand mega-vizier of the PR puff
(am I too soft, don't do him wrong enough?).
    Then, as a millennium closes, things further mesh:
'G'day Burkina Faso/ Bangladesh,
may I own (and even run?) the joint?'
    Though what's exactly yours is more the point
Oz; oh, how remiss, there's no such thing as debt
when Sheik bin Whoosits can flog you his private jet.

&

    Now, let's wrap our braincells around this one and grapple:
once Dix has had her hair trimmed in The Apple
she Concordes over with big yoo-hoos for hubby:
shagged out and snug inside their Mayfair cubby
(as a delicto heads uttermost flagrante)
wolfing some PA hardly over twenty.
    All repartee is never-to-be-forgotten:
'Over sixteen Miss Hogsbottom?'
        'Under sixty Mrs What-did-you-say-your-name-was?'
    Whilst, with snout peeking from his sheets, the cause
(this pink nude pudding of a Foo) the sleaze
himself sighs 'Now girls . . . oh please . . . oh please . . .'
    Then try this for an affair to disentangle:
our very own golden triangle:
Dix, Osbourne and his platinum Amex:
nothing like revenge to put the hex
on restraint: ''scuse I, won't waste your time
but these, these and these are mine
and this, this, this and even this.
Aren't opals tacky? They'll never become *you* miss.
Oh stay where you are, don't quit the cot
for me. Advice kiddo? Milk him for the lot!'

> With Osbourne at present totally dispatched
> his ex can't help herself, and gets rematched.
> (Though next to ol' Dix most men are bland as sago.)
> Still, shrugging *Why not?* she hustles after Craigo.
> Who's saving a treat to serve for the future bride:
> this mate-as-bonus, some Gibbo-on-the-side.
>
> Birds swirling into waves and out of coils,
> beneath them Dixie, gleaming in her oils:
> a coconut fug shimmering from their glow.
> I licked the air and titled this tableau
> (after my imagination did a scrounge)
> 'Plutocrat's Concubine Prone On Banana Lounge.'
>
> (If you're a mate, beware. Any breach
> will set me storming.)
>
> Soft growls replacing speech
> and her growling *Get me!* I moved to get her:
> the hour was prime, the view, well even better:
> mid-arvo seascape, near to pure Ken Done.
>
> Dix, glancing up bookmarked *The Power of One*,
> a warm contralto oozing from her throat:
> 'What soul! What art! My brain's about to bloat!'
> And, as she stretched (my member swelled in ripples)
> slipped down her top, presenting both her nipples,
> shameless enchantment!
>
> But why emote this hard?
> We're not re-making *Sunset Boulevard*.
> Indeed we weren't, we'd hardly make her room.
> I gulped an *Errgh!* for who was screwing whom?
> (Just who the sugar parent? Who the floozie?)
>
> To follow this: her vigorous jacuzzi.
>
> Now a spa with a naked couple on its hands
> is great for a bout of fantasy demands
> ('Come, suck this breast and this! why need we care?
> or 'Sweetest Gibbo, shave my pubic hair!')
> hardly that afternoon though. It was enough
> that she, with her marriage but tomorrows off,
> should set aside post-coital rub-a-dubs
> for the gospel according to the imminent Mrs Stubbs:

'You may not believe it but this girl has her code
just like Jesus all those years back: Dixie's sowed
a lifetime, now she's reaping. And the only dues
are due to moi.'
                    A bell rang. Delivering drinky-poos
came two bright workmen from the local cellars.
'Attend 'em pet . . . ready when you are fellas!'
With a hen's night demanding liquor by the crate
this Kombi load was poised to lubricate
Coral, Yolanda, Patsy, Sam and Midge.
'Oh Gibbo-darls, just whack it in the fridge . . .'
but, as she was saying '. . . a plain old-fashioned bitch
does wonders. I mean,' Dix turned franker, 'if you itch
then sscrrratch it!' So what err irritant was next?
She never paused 'Well dumpin' on your ex
for starts. If Oz 'n' me can remain chums
why not the rest?' I silenced any umms,
and bemused by the latest crop of retread singles
('. . . who hasn't had their blow-ups, blues 'n' bingles?')
I heard her rundown of the spouse pool, the partner mart:
someone's soul mate? Someone else's tart!

            Whilst patient Osbourne, myopic-devout
with his own mission, waits to buy Craigo out;
as if some deity (the market? fate?) demands
not merely wives but networks shall change hands.
            With soap 'n' talk, talk 'n' soap, each arvo grows
into an evening lathered with game shows:
tasteful as public dental flossing,
their aesthetic just this side of dwarf tossing,
till, something a little less than life, obeying these laws
even ockervision's finest must, the news on Network Oz
arrives.
            And we are hearing '. . . at today's $tubb$corp AGM
life sure was rough-house . . .' Eh? Eh? Ahem. Ahem.
What is this? Craigo's not so sleek, not so poker-
faced, and, voices off, cameras pan to some honest broker
chap (elderly, trim) lurching towards a mike:

'Nothing, investors, bankrolls this fourth reich,
since that is all this is: money and nothing!
Gentlemen . . .' His hands spread to signal *Knock all stuffing
from me, I'm a martyr maybe, but still a man!* Guards
pounce: back down and out with glass shards
they fall, through a door into the sport and weather.
Unlucky Craig!

                                                   ও

                   And lucky me: all strands bunching together
now, guess what heads the ratings? 'Gibbo's Coast-to-Coast'.
With up north (a touch more fortunate than most)
to play the squire I'd grabbed these few hectares
and started building. If I'd shares
(and I had) they'd be deep blue chip: hardly the junk
of $tubb$corp . . .

                                                   ও

                   or that erstwhile corporate punk
calling himself 'The Big Oz'. Whadda nom
de ego! As if we didn't know how some gladhanding Pom
straight off the boat started a paper round,
and how, a few decades on, the very same ground
half this nation's borrowings and savings
into the dust of debt: all propped by such fatuous ravings
as would embarrass the most low-life tabloid hack.
     Then, his ex returning, an airport paperback
replaces life: 'Craigo's smashed, Dix. And you are mine for good.'
     Scorched with revenge, everything is blood:
nipples swelling with desire, firm breasts cupped
in his paws, she's husky: 'Oz! Bankrupt!'
         Oh Australasia! Imagine this: 'Sweetheart it's over.
He's done precious. Y' one-time lover
boy's dead meat sex bomb.
                     Part farce/
part melodrama, the rich are our mirror and class
never quite making the listings nowadays
who needs the movies when you can gaze,

stunned, on what we're just not quite; and love it
as ourselves. And sure, if you tell 'em *Shove it!*
they'll be peeved, maybe, though just a minimal distressed,
perhaps.

❧

     Late one year, 'Coast-to-Coast' in recess
and any warm-up razzes for the latest motivator
earning me 'Call us sometimes' or 'Catch y' later'
(who better than corporate clientele
to wave their matey wands then crack the spell
– being boardroom bound, set to move and shake
with 'No-one's funnier ... hehheh ... fit to quake –)
immune to such condescension I'd to cop
(though still it's lonely hovering round the top)
and tired of playing a middle-aged Don Ju-an,
I needed a rest.
           On the Cape Leeuwin
to Cape York and return gag circuit, having to barndance
my way through months of one-night stands
(when every few hours your penis turns volcano,
laying you prone as if you'd swallowed Drāno)
I got driven to plainest speech (why pad it?)
womankind y' wunnerful, but I have had it!
        So, at the final $tubb$corp bash, knowing even a libido earns
long service leave, rager Gibbo turns
celibate for the evening and, nursing slow scotches
does what he's never done badly: waits, listens, watches.
        Hel-lo, touch before twelve enter The Moose and pow!
'He's so goose-bumpy!' gets overheard, 'I want him now!'
And operations commence: could this sheila/bloke/both
get Moose, well anything?
               A pause then 'B-b-b-b-bloody oath!'
(a wee beyond his depth? A fraction nervous?)
With thought of Shag-a-Stag (some gigolo service
I'd never start) and all those other nights featuring such weft
and warp of humanity *There we are* I sighed. And left
giving my life so far ten outa ten
and telling no-one.

☙

    But recalling how, back in the back-when
days, during that total taste erosion
Melbourne's glorious comedy explosion,
a legend birthed himself.
Its ease bewildered: with all the stealth
of a Clydesdale I'd found fans (deadshit-suckers
the lot) just aching to be slagged *You stupid fuckers!*
Whose gasps then turned to the nervy heeheehee of pigs
on-heat. Next, with a batch of brekky gigs
my career took aim at impotent/frigid, ockers/homos,
your folks/ my folks/ even me; engagements and promos
followed; remaining resistance couldn't but burst,
and fast-tracked into the court of Craigo the First
I'd arrived.
   (Enjoy the moral sweep of my journey?
This poem's been Gibbo's and it ain't yours Wearney!)

☙

  Oh, but, list to the investor's wail!
         Now, hark the yelp
of the bankrupt!
    Well I'd love to help,
me about as useful as an aqualung
in the Sahara.
    Achtung! Achtung! Achtung
hippies gays dykes yuppies punks dinks
and Aussies all: I leave with Gibbo playing sphinx:
our inheritance having already gone to unborn precision
honed 'Big Oz Juniors', so much for business.
         Now, television.
Given things have been the same since Yogi Bear
(or Logie Baird) I propose we start to prepare
for only more of it. A pitch of concern, a quota
of art, maybe; but more of it.
      With coda:
out there in Ozland lives a kid who'll make plenty
court-jesting for the Stubbs of 2020.

He won't be me.
   Down market and up; wait a minute, wait a life; what joke, what show, ever proved infinite with fortune and/or rating set to botch it?
   'Gibbo's Coast-to-Coast'? I'd hardly watch it.

Part 14

AMANDA .... BUSINESSWOMAN
SHANNON ⎫
CARRIE ⎬ .... TWO OF HER EMPLOYEES
WAL ⎫
BENNY ⎬ .... CARRIE'S FRIENDS
SHANNON'S BOYFRIEND
THE MAN WAL MEETS
LIZ ⎫
CHRISSIE ⎬ .... FROM AMANDA'S PAST
LOUISE ⎭
GARY .... COP, AMANDA'S FRIEND, CARRIE'S FIANCÉ
KOSTAS .... MOVING THROUGH
HANNAH ⎫
LEO ⎬ .... BENNY'S FRIENDS
CARLO ⎭
COBBER .... NEW ZEALANDER SHEARER
THE KID ETC .... TAXI DRIVER
SHELTON LEA .... PASSENGER
JACK ⎫
BERNIE ⎬ .... BARMEN
SHANE ⎫
ADRIAN ⎬
ICEMAN ⎬ .... EX-FOOTBALLERS
THE MOOSE ⎭

THE DOC	SPORTS PSYCHOLOGIST
SUSAN	SHANE'S WIFE
STUBBS	SHANE'S EX-EMPLOYER
BARB } CLAIRE }	SHANE'S SISTERS
ROGER	BARB'S HUSBAND
GIBBO	SILLYBUGGER

Making the world revolve (II)

Shannon, Amanda, Carrie

     Shannon knew that Queen Amanda's reign
had limits. 'Please,' she warned in her clipped NZ
mutter/accent (little in the world
exactly like it) 'she's playing favourites:
setting up the remainder and lying to their clientele;
watch it Carrie, you might be next.'

     But try to attempt an Operation Save Our Necks
and Amanda would commence to rain-
down the rhetoric: Carrie meant more than mere clientele,
didn't she know that? That and the A-to-Z
of human nature (worthy-madam style): how favourites
are necessary: since half the world's a man's world

some ladies kept this fifty per cent of the world
revolving that much better. Fair as the next
boss? Amanda was much more! Weren't they 'favourites'
just by working for her?
               Then charm reined-
in all misunderstandings (from the ABC of revolt to the XYZ
of surrender ... *And as for clientele:*

they just want 'class', that's why they're our clientele)
as this is a tough world, a negotiator's world
where 'Kerrys' had to interchange for 'Shannons' (like
Aotearoa doubling for NZ).
     'After me,' Amanda negotiated, 'there's only down. And what's
         next?
You work The Cross, smacked-out in the driving rain!'
     (Of all her fantasy-advice hardly one of their favourites.

Still, they had far more believable favourites:
e.g. Amanda's golden rule with all potential clientele:
don't expect some James Reyne,

he's certain to be a Russ Hinze: all over the world
beer guts and red bull necks
were queuing: from NYC via NSW to NZ.)

      Oh yes, and Amanda loving Carrie this needed to be said:
Sorry Shannon, being one I've learnt far more on 'favourites'
than all your guesswork, which amounts as next
to nothing.
      Lining up like clientele
such thoughts flew into Carrie's mind,
whirled themselves, then fluttered off.
               She looked out: rain

had started, clientele would be arriving in this rain.
    Ho hum.
         Not perhaps on World Y, Galaxy Z,
but here on Earth favourites were pains in everyone else's necks.

Wal

      That Christmas Eve all he wanted to hear
was *Oh Wal a tea service!/ a dildo!/ one more Village People LP!*
you shouldn't have!
           But Benny was back with his folks
in Adelaide, and Tony the heart-throb ditto, Dubbo;
whilst Carrie, who'd scored herself some shiftwork
had slotted him in for lunch, tomorrow *Chez the boss.*

      A few months back Wal had cruised 'Big Boss',
the very latest in club-bars: great atmosphere: you could hear
the lot and understand zero. So, with plain chatting hard work,
let alone chatting up, Wal went to pee.
When he returned they were 'Pre-sent-ing Mister Dub-bo
Nineteen Eightywhatsit! Tell me, folks,

isn't this one yummy?'
         'You're dating a *door prize*?' Folks
who cared for Wal (Benny, Carrie, even Kenny the boss

at work) were concerned. (Benny feigning the need to dab eau
de cologne upon one's temples, fearing that here
began yet another how-de-doo.
                        Except, Wal finding in a pea
brain and melon pecs Mrs Wal, it seemed to work . . .

A man, Wal

except . . .
        His name isn't his name and doubtless his work
(if he thinks it that) is something not to tell the folks.
His kind of cash is as easy as shelling a pea:
'So it's your place is it Wal? You're the boss!'
Then in the car, this Wal seems excessive: saying, almost to hear
himself, how they'll run off to Surfers, Cairns (yeah why not Dubbo?).

Pity this Wal is a bit like Dubbo:
something pleasant you just drive through . . . hardly work
at all, even if it had to be explained I'm not exactly here
for sex. Coming from decent folks
I gotta show you poofs a timeless lesson: who's boss
from A to Z via KLMNOP

and return. *As Wal gets hit again he starts pee-*
and-shitting himself Why did Tony have to be in Dubbo?
And the man's lips swell into boss
lips Yes *they mouth* Christmas gets lonely. *His work*
continues: lights off, curtains drawn, the folks
next door out; no-one to see, no-one to hear . . .

Amanda, Carrie, Shannon's fella

        'Forget your Ps and Qs,' Amanda demanded 'this isn't work!
your friend must've gone via Dubbo, Carrie. No-one, folks,
is a better boss than a madam. Do I detect *Here here*?'

With her head easing its stretch marks
of the past few nights there was plenty of rest
for the wicked on Amanda's patio.
        'Still no news
of your friend?'
    'Off west, searching for his lounge
lizard ... here today gone to Dubbo. That's Wal.
Even with loved ones at Christmas shit happens.'

  Which was mean. Friendship, she knew, never happens
through ticks and crosses, a toting up of marks.
Yet if the doorbell rang she wished to think *That's Wal*.
It never was and, prepared for an early night to rest
up for tomorrow's shift, evening found Carrie in the lounge,
waiting this year's variant of every Christmas news.

  (Wal chasing anyone but Tony would be news
to her, so why wasn't he here, or at his phone/Little happens
at things like this without him.)
       Spread across the lounge
Shannon's fella watched sport: the year's top tries, marks,
aces, sixes, holes-in-one. An interruption gave it a rest:
more on last night's slaying.
     Carrie shrivelled. 'That's Wal,'

she tried telling the fella.
    'That's what?'
       'That's Wal!'
she finally howled (Amanda arriving to his explanation '... a news
flash ... some dead guy ...').
     After she'd phoned Benny and the rest
Carrie had to stop. Sure, years after such a thing happens,
you might find yourself sighing *What a way to go, top marks*
but there'd never be, she sobbed on Amanda's lounge,

any more additions to the Wal-tack (that vinyl lounge,
those 3-D nativities) and no more hair that's Wal
(by Leo Sayer out of Harpo Marx).
    With the Pope poncing around, Amanda turned off the news.

Best love being efficient love she shrugged *It happens*
He'd given Carrie much, she might spend years waiting the rest.

    So 'Don't move' was suggested. 'You better rest.'
    Carrie agreed: 'But come over to the lounge
and hug me. I've a confession: it so happens
that when you met him you were to think *So that's Wal!*'
    Kicked-on by the simplest, tears began again. Within hours newspapers, leading with his face, would spray the town like blotch marks;

his friends waiting forever the rest of him.
                                'So that's Wal,'
Amanda murmured. 'Lounge back and soak in the news
as it happens. Full marks Sydney full marks.'

Benny

    'His wake,' and Benny sighed, 'wasn't meant to be *like this*!'
    (As if Wal had a message for all these rooms of pick-ups,
neighbours, workmates, friends and everyone he'd ever loved
*Sorry Benny, Carrie, Hannah, Kenny don't want to be gratuitous
Tony, Carlo, Leo, M, but you'll never get me
back again. I've gone a long way past mere dying.*)

'Sure,' Benny was saying, 'my friends have started dying.
But I'd have never thought *like this*!
Though Wal, I always warned, you must be careful. Get me?'
    (But a killer, playing at pick-ups,
thought he'd audition for God, God and so gratuitous
with it. And, if all creation loved

its Wal, the only way this maniac loved
was staring into his victim – anonymous, dying –
knowing life as so gratuitous.)
    Then Benny shot out his hand flat *like this* !
and swiped the air: 'Playing for rough trade pick-ups
he played himself for a mug. Please doesn't anyone get me?'

(Yet all they were hearing was Wal *Oh darls they'll never get me.*)
'That man merely had to glance at certain men and he just loved!
I know I know not all of them were pick-ups,
and he was only after a touch of Elizabethan dying.
But how'd that final night occur: *like this? Like this?*'
(And Benny's hand kept swiping. Gratuitous?

No, little was less gratuitous.)
'Please Hannah,' he motioned to their neighbour, 'get me
one more g and t? Where were we? Wal abroad? It goes *like this!*
If America was some guy aching to be loved
Wal would be the lover: He was dying
for it: their quaaludes, discos, movie stars. And pick-ups.

'*No no no!* Wal admonished *that's a ute. Pick-ups
are something else: magic, trouble, totally gratuitous.*
Sure were. Each time you cruised weren't you, in some sense, dying?
And yet only weeks ago you get me
out of bed because you've lost your key. How I loved the way you loved
annoying me. Why do you think *I carry on like this*?

'Because you really get me! Because, Wal, you were loved
right to that second someone smiled *like this!* When even "normal" dying
wasn't gratuitous enough; and you'd to meet your ultimate in pick-ups.'

Carrie

   But weeks of continual tears weren't practical
for Carrie: time lost, quite simply, was a life wasted.
   Though there was Amanda (her secular reverend mother)
dispensing what might have been a somewhat higher
kind of love: knowing how remarkable this was: to see
her friend still glowing over Wal, his life and passions.

   In that smorgasbord of passions
where, if you were ruthless — obliging/ meat-market practical,
there'd always be an inevitable *Da! Ja! Yes! Oui! Si!*
Wal couldn't say his time was ever wasted:

with a cock stretching higher and higher,
and all these guys to do the stretching, this was one mother-

load of outrage!
           Carrie, of course, promised not to tell his mother
how Wal was back being a serial cruiser with rough trade passions.
     'But I should talk,' she sighed. 'Tits and a fanny for hire!'
     And though caution was always counselled, being practical
never entered Wal's proceedings (until that night he was truly wanted).
     Amanda heard just once of his old lady;
she was more ludicrous than the Holy See;

if love were nourishment, hers was a packet of CCs.
There was no further mention of the mother.
     Or, telling of Adrian, Carrie would bitch how he'd wasted
months of her energy. Twice. And how she'd thought *Passions?*
If only I could forget them! Grow up and be practical!
     And how, one day with all his 'Hi ya everybody hi ya!'

Wal had arrived: an orderly who'd never climb much higher
(though, two hundred years ago, he might've run away to sea).
     Yet let's be practical:
Wal in his simplicity had never thought *This is one mean mother!*
I must have him! Or did he? Who really knew his passions?
Not Carrie, not even Wal.
              Oh you wasted

days figuring that one!
              And you avoided mirrors: telling how wasted
you'd become.
     From today Carrie could only rise higher:
Just to get up, there seemed no greater prize to seize.
Confusion, restraint, grief: there may've been other passions
but, like a baby screeching for its mother,
to sob your face off seemed utterly practical.

     Though passions weren't meant to be so practical,
and knowing she'd never again hit a higher C,
'Mother of God!' was howled. 'Am I wasted!'

Carrie, Amanda

   Carrie stayed at Amanda's. In the spare bed
for nights she dreamt of Adrian and Wal. They curled
around her like cables.
        'How about some music?' Amanda said.
'How about Petula Clark's "Colour My World"?'
(She was kidding of course.) 'How about "... ground control
to Major Tom"? How about some soul?'

   No, they'd pass on soul;
for Carrie was explaining how once she'd been to bed
with Wal: and it wasn't a matter of self-control:
they'd talked and hugged till, curled
into his arms, she finally slept. This friendship was the truest world-
apart she'd ever known: whatever one of them said

nobody heard it quite like the other. *Better left unsaid*
never existed; until his death when Carrie, soul-
searching for questions, knew all answers were nothing but the world.
     Now: will Amanda and Carrie finally make it to bed?
Admit it readers: since they met hasn't the prospect curled
about the psyche? Sorry, it's out of your control.

Though, with pen and paper, at my control
panel (that's a brain!) I'm working at it. That said
I haven't the remotest need to think Wow! This'll get their hair curled!
No, here's what you're getting . . .
        'Aren't we near enough to soul-
sisters?' Carrie asked Amanda. 'Let's go to bed.
I feel like you're the greatest woman in the world!'

   'In the world?'
(Her friend had never felt like having *that* control.)
'Please, just make me the greatest in my bed!'
   So they made love, great love. Enough said.
Real goosebumps stuff, from crown to sole.
   Later Amanda rolled a joint: stoking the filter she curled

the other end. Soon this leaf of smoke curled
off the number. Slowly it whirled
its way towards the ceiling, She stared, sold
on its pattern. *Tonight, if I'm in control*
of something rather nice, there's plenty which needn't be said
she thought, looking across the bed

at Carrie lying curled (sleep starting its control).
And yet a bedtime tale is always good for the soul.
    'Here's how I started my way in the world . . .' Amanda said

Monica, Liz, Louise, Chrissie, Monica's parents

    'In those days my name was Monica,
when the bad times were too good, the good times not too bad,
Liz was my best friend at Mary Immaculate.
(God I must've loved her!)
    Now here's what four of us would do most Saturdays: tart
ourselves up like Dusty Springfield or Abigail, for all the fellas to behold.

    And here's what they would behold:
Liz, Louise, Chrissie and Monica
being near-enough women.
    (Later Louise, no-one was less of a tart,
went off and got herself a baby. Too bad
the father was this prick, Kim, who dumped her.)
    Then Mondays we'd return to the Academy of Mary Immaculate,

once more getting the lowdown on Our Lady: her centre-piece, the
        Immaculate
Conception, was something I couldn't seriously behold.
Mary? Who in their right mind wanted to be like *her*?
    'Okay,' a nun ordered, 'look up Monica
in this dictionary of saints.'
    Who was? Too bad,
I've forgotten.
    Then I discovered St Mary of Egypt. What a tart!

She'd do me! Well not so much a tart
but this semi-reformed pro who'd one immaculate
way of working her pilgrimage to the Holy Lands. Too bad
the book fell open at that one! Rushing to Liz 'Behold,'
I cried, 'our patron saint!'
                        'My god, Monica,'
she gasped, 'how'd they let you read about *her*?'

      Liz, what would I've done without her?
I'd a mother who thought me the total tart
and this sleaze of a dad.
                    'You're Monica,'
he'd tease, 'because the name sounds so grown-up.'
                                        With me feeling
      immaculate
as shit getting told how behold-
en I was to both the church and him.
                                  He wasn't too bad;

at times; asleep. Too bad
he thought he was Hugh Hefner and all my friends especially her,
Liz, potential centrefolds.
                          Worse but, he didn't know how to behold
a dressed-up daughter: his eyes might explode but a certain tart-
ness honed his words: 'My but you look umm err immaculate?
Well I suppose that's easy when Monica's

y' moniker. Say mother, take a perve at her
and behold! What? She's no longer ours? too bad;
for that is one immaculate tart!'

Amanda, Gary, Carrie

      Amanda told her friend Gary, Gary the cop,
'You'll love her, Carrie's tough but sweet.'
      And the sex, if you'd to measure such things,
was pretty good, his best in ages.

Later, when her head lay on his chest, he asked:
'You really want to continue this kind of work?'

Well, since he'd put it this way, 'Work. Work
enough as yours.'
He flinched but, being a smart cop,
still guessed she liked him. Sorry he asked!
It's just he was addicted to all that's bittersweet.
And, with a certain chivalry straight from the Middle Ages,
he kept in mind those things

Amanda mentioned: these certain things
she felt a necessity to say: 'Make it work,
that girl's never had a break in ages.'
'You think I'm okay, Carrie?' As a cop
who knew you'd to take the sour with the sweet
he was edgy, fearing he'd drive back fuming *Well I asked*

for that one!
But 'Gary,' she laughed, 'You needn't've asked
I would've told you!'
In the rush of things
he knew there was precious little 'sweet'
(though who needed that) in being direct: 'Okay, after work
one night care to go out with a cop?'
Go out? She hadn't been out with anyone in ages.

The next evening they just sat and talked for ages,
each answering what the other asked.
He was divorced: 'My ex is a lady cop.
I'm thirty-six, into fairly simple things:
a house, kids, holidays, work
and you!'
She paused: 'Please don't move us into the Honeymoon Suite

not yet. This'll succeed toute suite
enough I guess. It won't take ages.'
Yet if his certainty that such an affair was set to work
chilled Carrie, slightly, that and how without being asked

love looked to be driving up, some things
Not just a client I'm falling for a cop

some things were happening which hadn't happened in ages.
      'Is this etiquette for the part-time working girl?' she asked.
And 'Cop it Carrie,' she replied, 'Cop this one super sweet!'

Kostas, Amanda

    Someone had gone and got his cafés fired.
So Kostas was quitting Melbourne. Moving up the coast
he phoned Amanda, got invited over.
                           Salads and mineral water
seemed the order of her Australia Day
with a small business theme propelling the chat (*their* variations:
      cathouse and gambling joint making them almost soul mates,

well that's how Kostas saw it).
                      Some mutual mates
down south (acquaintances she'd say) describing her had fired
the man's imagination and, balancing brunch variations,
looking out on the inlet, Kostas conjured this part of the coast
for something like a future base. Could he return (well before Anzac Day,
he laughed) if she wasn't busy? Back here to Pittwater?

    Now, who possibly, was turning Amanda to water?
A lean, balding, presumptuous Cypriot with dodgy mates,
that's who. Sure it still seemed early enough to nod g'day
and leave him be, but *The moment's arriving* she thought *when I'm to be fired
from my proverbial cannon again. How can I coast
through a life like mine surrounded by affairs, well their variations,*

and stay immune? Oh, there'd be inevitable mood variations
but what could be done? Take one Regulove daily with water/
She knew you had to be an island most times, that giving any part of
      your coast
to a man ran risks: since under his command the mates

were sure to land. Which didn't mean Amanda wasn't fired-
up enough to try. Mmmmm that'd be the day.

But nothing, she warned herself, ever exceeds Day
One and its joy of starting. Consider these variations:
sherries being served, an opener taking block, the kiln fired;
and lovemaking as the sun dazzled back at them, from the water.
      By evening, more than merely mates,
her head lay in his lap; TV on, night descended the coast.

      'Just our luck!' she wailed, '"Gibbo's Coast-to-Coast,
Summer Edition": name a daggier end to any day.'
      ('Me with stupid,' Gibbo pointed to himself, 'he 'n' me is mates!')
      When such gag attempts were more like bad cocktail variations:
rotgut, syrups, heaps of cream) who wouldn't prefer a decent book, a
      glass of water?
      Or Kostas? She aimed the remote control: 'Television, you are
      fired!'

      Next morning letters got fired to all Amanda's gang: 'Dear Mates,
it's me. Ever thought how sex, how love, hardly had variations well, since
      yesterday,
I've gone utterly to water; i.e. the entire Pacific hurtling into the East
      Coast . . .'

Carrie, Gary
for John Hawke

      And this was where Carrie's momentum led: what she wanted
      to say being finally spoken.
      She was telling Gary of Adrian, her prick
of a former boyfriend: a one-time king of Melbourne football.
      Oh yes the name was known, Gary even remembered the
      nickname,
but knew it very much her business,
like many things. Were Carrie and Adrian still 'friends'?

he wondered, still the ludicrous 'just good friends'?
No-one brought out Gary-as-decent-cop like her though: he'd never
    spoken,
never would, about Carrie and her love-business
(he wasn't that much of a prick).
But even if Adrian had merely given her a nickname,
he didn't want to know it.
                        Gary too had tried football,

his kind of football.
For six seasons The Tigers gave him reasonable friends
and the unimaginative 'Plod' for a nickname.
If a serviceable career his wasn't spoken
in the same breath as Coote, Tutty, Gasnier. But now, when any line-of-
    credit prick
can't wait to run a club, the game was just another business.

        Would Gary go into business?
Given how cops stayed the state's leading political football,
and each third workmate had to be an Internal Investigation prick
why not?
        'Who are my friends?'
such a climate got him asking. Somebody must've spoken
something, for Gary acquired a dog of a nickname:

which was to stick, the nickname.
        Adrian, Carrie told him, had gone into business.
Even now his was a name to be reverently spoken:
whole boardrooms were waiting to hug him, just like a football.
And who were these latest friends?
First off 'Big Oz' Osbourne, the nation's leading corporate prick.

(How she'd love to prick
any tycooon's ever-expanding bubble!)
                        And Adrian (whose nickname
wasn't Mr Magic for nothing) Adrian was often in Asia, making further
    friends:
these days it was called the merchant banking business.
        And no matter his code of football,

Gary couldn't stand him.
       Sometimes it seemed hours since the cop had
  spoken

(You could hardly think of him broadcasting the football).
     She thought of giving him Rowdy as a nickname,
   Not quite! 'We'll be more than friends!' he cried, 'not merely
      because of your pussy, my prick.
I love you Carrie!' And yes his heart had spoken. 'So. Let's get down to
   business!'

Carrie, Gary, Kostas

   When was Carrie's last time life had been so truly you-and-me?
For a while lovers had clambered aboard in files.
And though such an order lessened any menace,
now she commanded her ship of love; and the compass going with it
pointed true north.
No need then to hide love in cathouse or motel

(unless your preference went for a motel).
    Though she'd hear things: just-between-you-and-me
things: 'Until a few of us stepped in kids from way up north
were servicing half of this town. Then some prick shredded the files!'
He saw her cringe. 'Oh Carrie . . . your game's got nothing to do with it!'
    But there's always a tang to cop-menace

and sometimes she could near to conjure it: Gary-and-menace
springing a minor lag in some absurd slum-motel.
Keeping his charm, yet nasty with it.
There's you he'd announce *there's me and then there's you and me.
So which will she be fuckhead?* For Gary had little need of files
when west, south, east and north

lay wherever he turned. Or, better still, here at his North
Pole an entire world started spreading.
       But, since he'd rarely show his
   menace,

not to her, here's one for the happy-files:
the weekend they flew to Melbourne and stayed in an upmarket motel,
'The Corroboree Rex'.
                      And, on the bed, primed for a spot of you-
                  and-me,
all she heard were gags, cop-gags.
                      'Gary! Get on with it!'

she howled. 'Just get on with it!'
      He was always surprises. Like one day they drove north
to Amanda's where 'G'day Kostas,' he sprang on everyone, 'you and me
go back decades.' And he grinned wider than Dennis the Menace.
             Though it hadn't been decades since Kostas, paying off Gary in
             that motel
was told 'Sure mate sure. This'll never make the files.'

      An extortionist cop and a matchmaker madam never need files.
Only a knowing love of people. With that (plus the memory going with it)
they should've opened a motel!
Not that they would.
             Kostas kept moving north.
Whoever wanted to stay around Gary's hearty menace?
      As for the cop and the nurse (Amanda's ultimate you-and-me)

they went touring. Up north there always was that next motel.
      'You and me,' he explained, 'we'll never need files
on each other.'
             And Carrie just had to trust his love; and all that menace
             with it.

Carrie

             Yet there'd still be time to consider Adrian (when Gary, to her
             knowledge,
was elsewhere in Sydney getting crooks arrested)
for thinking of Adrian was hardly taboo,
and it would always exist,
this obsession.

Oh she understood why so many Aussies
loved Adrian: he was always making the news!

(He was made for always making the news!)
    Yet few if any had the Carrie-knowledge:
how Adrian sure helped to make her sick of certain Aussies/
certain men. 'Sometimes I'd love to see them all arrested,'
she told herself. Or 'I sure don't need *him* to make me exist!'
Then thinking of Adrian became ridiculous, near enough taboo,

but a common or garden taboo
made to be broken.
                    And she wasn't waiting for the News
at Five that afternoon. (Since someone decreed Wal shouldn't exist
she never had). TV was mere events, hardly information, never
                    knowledge.
Why there might be Adrian, a date on his arm (she'd have them arrested
too, these tanned, blonde, celebrity-Aussies).

    Of course here's how they saw Adrian, most Aussies;
how they looked on his affairs: little was wrong in a touch of taboo.
What would you have them do? Get him arrested?
For what? Taste? His past? Somewhere a News
Limited columnist might possess the required knowledge;
but she was safe: when it came to the celebritocracy Carrie didn't exist.

    Funny how being Gary's girl helped her exist.
Even if in eighteen million Aussies
I am alone, knowledge
tells me that falling for a one-time client, a cop, isn't taboo.
      This afternoon she did turn on the television. Leading its news
two men, some place up north, had been arrested.

But weren't two men always being arrested
anywhere in Asia? Why else would they exist?
(Since Wal had died all that Carrie heard about the world was *News*
to me!) Until now. Now with two men, Aussies,
expecting anyone would believe how certain drugs weren't taboo.
      'Fuckwits!' Carrie muttered. 'That goes against common
            knowledge!'

And here was just as pathetic a taboo: how you couldn't exist without your proper knowledge of the news.

Like how, today, up there (Penang? Bangkok?) two Aussies were arrested.

The Kid, The Baron, Mr A
and The Alien Await the Mini-series

for Shelton Lea and his poetry

       Cobber isn't listening; but worse he's never
even heard.
          Wouldn't you have air, just air, between
your ears to fall for bang-bang?
                  And now
the world is told two Aussies have been grabbed.
Well first: it wasn't mine, I was only sleeping
there that night; and second:
I'm the Australian. The other is
this fucked-out, bang-banged Kiwi shearer
who's tuk-tuked home to The Horse
for years and now this sorry sad young lad
won't tuktuktuk much more; not him;
not after his little pack of bang-bang.
        And still The Man thinks he's an Aussie?
      No, I am the Australian.
And what's that mean? He was a kind
who used to drive about and save, save
till he could hop a plane and get to do
all the average silly stuff that us,
the Aussies, do.
            But not too average.
I was at a beach in 'Lanka once,
sniffing it, sniffing anything. And,
as I see these silly kids there, spiking,
this little man, the tiny man, the nothing man
says 'Just over there please, there, there
with the kids, what do you see?
Like to catch some more?'
         Yeah catch some more and more again.
      'Yes yeah,' says nothing man, 'and more
and more. You couldn't guess,
your imagination wasn't made to grasp

how good that more shall be.'
                        'Oh can't I
nothing man?' I'm saying. 'Back home take out
this trade and couldn't you cull a dozen floors
off every second office tower?'
            He had to believe me?
I had to believe me!
                    Me who'd not done
anything wrong much (and, more likely, tried
doing some things I hoped were right) me,
who'd even got to tell Terri, Terri
my speed-freak hooker mate: 'Okay do it, do it
all the time, but check it and before you check it
check yourself.'
            I can listen though.
                            There was
that poet (who'd seen a lot and done
even more) but who, that night only wished
to just enjoy himself.
            Mid-week July it was and wet.
Up where Hoddle Street decides it can't go further
he wanted to cab it: Punt Road then on to
my way, The Junction and beyond.
            I knew who he was, had seen him places,
so when I'm warned
'Once you cross the river, brother,
your nose bleeds ...' I caught him.
            'The product, brother,
tell me something I don't already know.
Poem us a poem, poet, make our driving
worth it.'
            So *Could you* I'm asked.
Could I what? *Kill a dog with a hammer?*
Would you 'Go on,' I encourage. *Stammer*
when you crushed the skull of a child?
And I understood: although you might enjoy it,
the quieter living, as I do, here's the problem:
you come out mighty under-prepared.
And if you fought a man to death
with boots would you be beguiled

by his blood? So when you stepped
into that world beyond yours
what were you doing? *And when you've
stabbed and stabbed at your unfaithful lover*
'This way Porn,' they were meant to say,
'Come this way home to Mr A.'
They never did. Someone must've moved her.
*Would you feel mild and calm, like after
a bloody good screw* Now the poet talked
real talk, my talk! *or would you blubber
to insanity?* And this was even better:
the option. Weren't poets meant to supply
at least a few? *Some people do. Some people do.*
      And some are just like me, The Kid,
who, till now, has survived with style,
me, Mr A for Aussie-nothing-wrong-much,
just hoping for a quiet life with her,
his lady, Porn.
      But they'd moved her:
all of them: The Man and everyone: Lacy,
The Jeweller, Cap'n Midnight (even Jack?).
      Now they were moving me
and someone else they still thought was
Australian: him blubbering off his bang-bang.
      As we are leaving Cobber's place,
this last time, 'Know what this means?'
I asked him. 'What we're in for? What remains?
The mini-series. It'll have the lot:
Asia, us, women, a drug set-up, being stupid
and The Man. You're only worth
a mini-series now. Oh yeah, and in
the final episode guess how we leave the slammer?
And why us? Because this is what he does, The Man:
he tells his friends The Joy Boys/ The Non-bank/
(even The Horse?): *Oh sure business is on, fellas,
but hows about insurance?
Hows about a mini-series?*'
      Am I being listened to? Hardly.
Though an idea arrives in Cobber's mind and,
whatever else is there, he's enjoying it.

        'Mini-series?'
He needs information 'Who's playing me?'
  'Who? Doubt if we'll ever know.'
  Where we go
there's someone Australian, someone official,
and, since I'm to serve him things, why not
as entrée, my life?
     'Me?
Lived all over the place: Ashwood St Kilda
Ashwood Elwood Richmond Elwood Ashwood.
All over. And you? Cherrywood? What is Cherrywood?'

       &ae;

  But there's little remaining to add
when all you can say is
'I haven't done anything wrong much.' Or
'I trusted that shearer.'
     'That shearer,'
they tell him 'says he trusted you.
Bang-bang? He's never heard the word!'
   Then a local comes, saying words which mean
Get up, you're moving.
   Crossing this corridor, from one room
to another, the same is being done
to some schmuck in the opposite direction.
Then, as he glances, it's Jack who's glancing
in return.
   And both of them haven't time
to even gulp the other's way:
a few hours back The Man took over
all momentum.
    (And even then, by then,
since he'd been told how, back in Aussie,
Mr A was pining for his Porn,
momentum had been Lacy's. It was as if
Kim just flew you up to hand you over.
The Man and all his men need sacrifice:
it makes them feel good.
And that's how Lacy likes people: feeling good.)

Kim had called him. Kim had plans.
And if he was a sook *Oh Mr A the woman's gone
my good woman Sophie's gone and well
let's say I'm shifting stuff, some stuff, again*
he still could bargain.
                         'You want your woman
flying home to Aussie, Mr A?
Then pay a visit, do some work
and Porn-in-Aussie's your reward!'
           So Mr A becomes The Kid again:
bemused if interested; on flying himself
close to what might be the facts, The Baron;
or The Alien, just like he told Terri once,
checking it.
           'Work you say? And paperwork?'
           'Done.'
                   'What's it then?'
                                    'Blocks'
       'Just blocks?' (He doesn't even wait.)
'Narcs then?'
              Narcs are neutered and
all dogs are fixed. Someone to meet him?
There's always someone to meet their
Mr A.
       Except there's not.
       And, as he flies in it's breakfast time:
the town is off to work.
                        His work?
With one traffic light between here and
the North Pole getting to The Horse
takes ninety minutes.
                     Outside, rolling Drum
sits Cobber ('Remember? The Kiwi? The Shearer?');
this neat little pack is on his back.
       And The Horse is closed.
       'So? Stay at my place,' Cobber volunteers.
       Perhaps. But first they're trying Lacy's flat.
Vacant. Jack's hang-out? He must be away.
Porn's pad? Porn has moved.
                           Things have

started now, whatever they are,
he doesn't want to know. He'll have to though.
   What about Stubbs? Shouldn't he
be everywhere? Stubbs, it's understood, flew out
last week.
    Back to The Horse. Still closed.
   This ghost town stuff isn't his way,
the way of The Baron; it feels like
the way of The Man.
     And he needs to ask
another question: what's in Cobber's pack?
'Stuff,' the shearer smiles,
'What stuff?'
    'Only the best.'
'Do I have to stay a night with you
and your substance abuse?'
     Abuse?
Cobber is roused but roused sweet.
'I know my substances and this,' the smile
continues, 'this is tops. Bang-bang. Ever tried it,
Cob? Take some home we'll finish off
as millionaires! My place then?'
   It's afternoon. No Horse, no Jack,
no Lacy. He has to try The FucFuc.
That's open. Bernie Millar's just got up
and Bern knows nothing.
     Not even Porn.
Mr A got to find his Porn.
   'Why not the non-bank?' Bern suggests.
   They go (as if Porn would be there!)
but no-one's there; the non-bank
doesn't exist.
   'Yeah,' drools Cobber, 'Chicks,
I tell you mate, and bang-bang.'
   Bernie's called: 'Here's where we're staying . . .
So ask Bern, ask round, right round. And when the answers flock
to The FucFuc call. Oh, and it's still closed,
isn't it, The Horse?
    And Bernie
(so much for the one-time future vice king)

Bernie's numb: 'Jeez Kid, I dunno.
Haven't seen 'em much this week
J-J-Jack 'n' that.'
    'Tell the world,'
The Kid announces, 'I'm waiting.
Waiting for Porn in a room full of bang-bang.
What else does the world want me to do?
Oh, and of all the billions of humans, Millar,
why am I asking you?'
     Bernie but is
'In the dark mate as you are mate.'
   Then, with 'mate' in all its glorious combinations
and intonations such a Bernie-word, 'Bern?'
It must be asked,
'Weren't you *born* a dirty old man?'
   'No mate no,'
(he's answering another question,
always has) 'I'll ask.
First thing I hear I'll call.'
   'Porn or no Porn,'
Cobber's told, 'I'll leave tomorrow.'
He should've said that yesterday;
and, with little left to do, he sniffs
some bang-bang.
    Soon his sleep is Porn,
all Porn: how their love just grows, just grows;
how not last night, nor tomorrow,
but now, this very hour, she'll rap his door with
*Mr A I love you Couldn't stay away
hey let's go Aussie today . . . Mr A?*
   And still she's knocking. But Cobber's up
to let her in.
   To let *him* in:
much too early always much too early, The Man.
   Four of them are locals, another two,
just looking in, Australians.
   Can't you imagine it: there's this road
that once went somewhere?
Then it simply stops? Stops at nothing?
At The Man?
   Fuckin' bang-bang!

BRING ON THE GERONTOPHILES!

> *no I am not going*
> *to have you 'in' for dinner nor am I going 'out'*
> *I am going to eat alone for the rest of my life.*
>   FRANK O'HARA, 'Essay on Style'

      Not to eat, nor to sleep and surely not
to live, Benny never went home again.
Flying in from Adelaide he just strode his way
up Hannah's hall.   Next door police were combing through
his home. Benny though was safe enough:
there was no porn, few if any
marital aids.   Hannah was in hyper-Hannah mode
which, for once, was comforting:
'I'll bring in the cops. You are staying here.
They've taken Wal.'   She'd found him:
coming home from the lover's, just to rest a touch,
freshen up and head back to the lover's,
she waited for her neighbour. 'Pressies 'n' drinks,'
Wal had promised, 'drinks 'n' pressies.'
      Heading noon
and nothing like his custom built *Yoo-hoo!*
she went next door. The place was open.
Quiet and open.   The police tried hard.
Loss is nothing but loss and, as if it
were theirs, Benny eased them through
the questions: 'Was he my lover? A friend. Not just-a-friend
of course. A brother if you like.'
      He stayed at Hannah's.
On the news you'd overhear Wal's name
and, for a second, start: 'What has he done *now*?'

                                                ઢ

In Melbourne Barb had heard:
that bodyshape the footage showed,
wheeled into an ambulance, she'd met that man.
Though if it had been Bazza the Bankstown bouncer
where was the news in that, Australia?
But he was Wal, Wal the Annandale queer,
and throw in Christmas that made the killing
nation-wide. Plenty, sure, were wanting more.
       Barb wrote: 'I could send words of
a novel length, that wouldn't be enough.'
Only a week before she'd sent a card
'To Benny and Wal, thinking of you, Barb.'
which meant what? Now everyone was
thinking of them!

       On their property Neil and his girlfriend
gave him a holiday; and though he might
enjoy the bush Benny was never that much
of a hippy: besides, the fresh air gave him headaches.
       Carlo offered space and time.
Drama coach, ex soapie star, generous
with outrageous admonitions ('Employment isn't easy,
but if I can find it, work, and stay in work,
then so should anyone!') they were friends,
of course they were friends! with little in common.

       Benny was numb, Benny went into
character mode, as if all he could say to
Hannah, Barb, Neil, Carlo, and half the town was
Say neighbour, that's real neighbourly of you, neighbour.
He didn't want to feel a fraud, but he did;
he didn't want to rent out Annandale, ditto;
he wanted just to pull that place apart
and start on digging one of those childhood
all-the-way-to-China holes.

Then there was Carrie. Sure he'd said
'Please keep in touch' not expecting much
from Missy Fast Lane: she was Wal's friend,
she did the Wal things (well some of them).
   Yet, in their fashion, they were both
the widows, 'No two have shared our man
like us,' she wrote. 'Promise I'll keep in touch,
much love.'
    A few months on
he took her dining. True there were Carrie's
men problems, there had to be with Fast Lane:
an ex, visiting Sydney, wanted to see her,
but it was nothing, little-to-nothing,
though she was pausing a pause which might've said
Forget it! I told you forget it!
       Benny turned consoler,
he forever turned consoler: 'Carrie,
you'll always have men trouble. Why? Men,
don't you know *are* trouble, and you being you
just tells the world *I want love and I
want to love: love in as many forms and
combinations as I feel I can.* So love! So love!
What do you think I'm doing?'
    'I'm a nurse,' she offered,
'that's all now, a nurse. Oh yes and I am marrying ...
Gary's a cop.'
     'How dodgy a cop?'
    'The greatest cop in New South Wales!
Why not?'

        ଛ

    Once, when he thought Barb
might marry Neil, giving away the bride
sustained him for a fantasy. Now, in lieu of Wal
could it occur?
     So much was in lieu of Wal.
    And something had to be done. But it was what?
He'd never had to *do* a thing!
He had always ruled as Good King Benny:

encouraging, warning, being consulted.
    If there had been a gilded rule it was
When you don't know him well enough
never bring him home. Take it slow, Wal,
take it slow.
    That Benny should proffer!
On some weekends, ten, fifteen years ago,
he was a machine, a witty, courteous, honourable
sperm machine. Long weekends were worse:
by Tuesday you needed a holiday to recover from
the holiday.
    Then there was that Sunday
he took True Happiness of the past eight hours
to matins.
    And he twitted: Young Pick-me-up
just nudged and twitted.
They refused to see the other again,
ever again.
    'I'm not cut out,'
he told a shrink next week, 'to be
a father figure.'
    'And you,' the quack, bless him,
snapped, 'you have no say in the matter!'
    But, yes, like Wal as corpse.

    And yes now, very, very slow with it,
Leo was dying: possessed, as he would say,
'Of this fatal but unfashionable disease.'
(Though true no current ailment had any
greater fashion.)
    Exit one friend, exit another,
and if this might make him an increasingly bitter man
there had to be more, much more.
    Wal had been a careless, self-destructive fool
but he was also (and Benny plunged into it)
marvellous, just marvellous! Kitsch? Maybe,
but name him a better word.
    And if Leo loved his lifestyle

better than his life, he loved living, he loved people:
growing irises, poetry recitals, listening to Lully
and Marley, holding parties, if it had colour,
if it had words, if it had sound, if it had
the human race, this was Leo's monument.
Last Cup Day during his barbecue to welcome in
the blooms, his arm on M's, Leo staggered out
to his backyard, and his friends' applause.
'Few,' they got informed, 'are living quite like me!'
  And, if Benny got annoyed that 'few' were still
too many, all anger after that seemed arch and campy.

  No, let him be angry this way:
wherever you turned they were sticking-a-label
on it: like those colour supplements with articles
on the Queer Industry.
      'Queer?'
and Benny kept his temper steaming,
'I may be coital-specific but my love
goes everywhere. Still, if that is "queer"...'
And as for Industry with the Big I:
that was the morally uplifting world of
ants and bees: all fable.
  But labelling and labellers never stopped
the latest poofter bash gone wrong:
some brave coward doing in yet another
faggot. 'Oh they are sticking labels,'
Benny fumed, 'right up us.'
      Though fuming to himself,
knowing he shouldn't keep so damn restrained,
that a crisis delayed was indeed a crisis,
that soon he must get down to truly crying,
crack up in front of someone he was
falling for and blub for days
Wal Wal you stupid bastard Wal!
  Then get this miracle of a head job
which would be their industry, their business: him
and the man.

    Why was the human world
so tortured still with what was going where?
It was the *who* behind the what, the *who*
behind the where that mattered! Call it love,
call it looking for love, for something that might,
given luck or management, adding to the happiness
of being noticed, succeed.
       Except
no cruiser was quite like an old fool
cruiser: at forty-four Benny sometimes hit
those bars he thought he recalled, leaving
very very soon: and, if these were no great
sarcophagi, he was sure the mummy!
    Oh bring on the gerontophiles!

SOMEONE TO MAKE US FEEL HAPPY
(THE SHANE PRICE RECOLLECTIONS CONTINUED)

The homecoming

      Once, on a trip to Melbourne with The Stags
I caught up with The Doc.
          'So how's
their development arm?'
          I was their development arm
and 'Doc, I'm ratshit.'
          'Susan?'
    Susan was 'putting up'.
I knew it would be better if she didn't
have to.
      'Teaching suits you, Shane?'
    'Never should have left it, Doc.'
    He had a friend who ran a place:
its prestige, enough tradition and (co-ed for
a decade now) modern approach balanced, somehow.
      Besides, Doc's friend knew, or thought he knew,
what went for Melbourne-style prestige:
his staff contained '. . . five ex football stars
with brains.' If I wanted it
the alchemy of the Doc network would make me
number six.
        One of the five
recognised me: 'Each time we played you, Pricey,
Sometime this afternoon I promised myself
I'll flatten that slippery bastard. Never did.'

The nurse

      'Shane, I'm a friend of Adrian's. I think
he needs some help.' (Friday lunch hour, a woman,

phones our staffroom.) 'I must do something for him.'
       Which is, I thought, the Mr Magic way.
Name us whatever's new.
                'For starters though,'
I needed to be direct, 'if you are like,
anything like a journalist, hang up please.'
         'I'm not,' she tells, 'I'm Carrie, Carrie Larson?
The nurse? I need to see you Shane.'
       That nurse? The next best love of his life
but one, after his fashion? Oh I remembered Carrie.
      'That bitch,' confided Ades, 'does things to me,
yeah Shane, pretty ridiculous things!'
       And you, mate, don't have any input?

The jitters

      So what did I have to know of Adrian Cross,
merchant banker to the free world and beyond?
Up north someone's in trouble? Up north
someone's always in trouble.
            A few days back
two stupid Aussies (nothing's as stupid as stupid Aussies)
are happily shifting the feel goods;
now they're victims needing to be redeemed,
calling their product by another silly name
and blaming each other.
               That's what the north does.
I can almost predict his call
'Shane mate, can't you do anything about us?
Don't you know *anybody* now? If I/we/our bank
goes under it's because well you work it out
mate it's the current liquidity, the jitters
in futures you must know.'
              Mate it's because
you haven't any money left: who was it told me
'Swing into it, Dumbhead. The life of all time
starts now?' Hey Ades who was it?

The speed

   'Pricey', I got told when he entered the corporate bloodstream
'shouldn't you be trying this? It's infectious,
this is how we're meant to be.'
        And yes
I will admit its very speed was tempting;
I even imagined how, one morning,
another shy student is jogging to lectures;
that's until he runs into Mr Magic!;
by evening he's this hotshot investor loudmouth
ploughing the nose though half a K of premium coke,
hardly pausing to ponder *Now how did* this *happen?*;
besides, he has mates attending to all that,
mates have the time and *oh!* they'll guess by midnight
Wow! there he goes still making his unmistakable
way in the world, wherever he is; seeing how
when one big-noter stumbles on an even bigger one
and starts to hear those good hard words
which tell him *This man's so right this man is
speaking for me* the rest of us rarely know
the game that's being played.

The quicksand

      Unless you play
your own: that time The Stags (then, the $tubb$corp
entity, the club, not us, the team) were arsing-up,
I led a delegation to the great King Craigo:
part players' revolt, part final chance to tell
the man 'Y' ratshit!' and 'You might recall
my father, Stubbsy?'
     Should he?
  'Oh Craig, you wanted to be the hotshot
dealer of the decade, and Real Livin' Toyota
(Mitcham Branch) had trading problems, right?
You must remember Old Man Pricey!'
    Oh Stubbs remembered Pricey,

the other Pricey, and, casting for adjectives
reeled in, with a certain effort
'Understanding, your dad was, if I recall,
understanding.'
     'Why not just bland?' I asked.
  No, Stubbsy would never say it
that way, no.
    Which was a pity since
I knew my father and my father's bland.
   These are the times I adore:
watching it all go quicksand: times when
giving little fuckers like Stubbs *Just enough,*
till so much of *Just enough* turns *enough,*
then *More than enough.*

The magic

     And then
there's the aura which arrives with winning,
constant winning. When I was twenty-four
that season had it. Each Saturday evening
the Social Club bulged with every available
Mr Put-me-down . . . and my team-mates
flicked through their index of attitudes:
would it be cheek for some tonight, deference for others,
or *Hey there deadshits!* that look which demanded
Cultivate me!
    Primed since his pre-match lunch
an old solicitor was going bug-eyed:
'This is for Adrian . . . you were magic, boys . . .
and Shane, this one is yours . . .'
       Two wads
of snap fresh twenties 'n' fifties,
courtesy of yet another blissed out clown,
taa err thanks Mr Put-me-down.
   'Tell us Pricey,' Adrian loved tempting me,
'tell us we're not whores!'

                    Don't,
I thought, don't overestimate yourself.

The life!

            No, this is something I'd rather remember:
when us non-joiners join we mean it:
there he is on the videos of that flag, that flag
and that flag, taking his turn at the presentations.
'Number 39, consistency himself, Shane Price!'
            Consistency? There wasn't much left to do!
It's mid-June, and we've been slaughtered by
as many points as it would be saner to forget
(as if you'd be allowed!) and the coach demands
a pre-dawn training run. You want consistency?
Well set that alarm at four-fifty
just so you can answer the phone
ten minutes later 'Beat you Boss! Right on my way!'
            Or more consistency? I'm a bit older now,
watching the post-match meat mart, with Susan:
Footballers' Girls a whole generation of sweet things
falling over each other just so someone might ask
(behind their backs) 'What? Her? Rooted half
the club. Where you been mate?'
Then every week each sequel 'Footballers' Girls II'/
'Footballers' Girls on Ice'. Oh those coke lines!
D-cup centrefolds! First-class returns to name-your-
nirvana! Brother was that the sportsman's life!

The lounge suite

         That was? Well let me recall a dozen tins of Vic,
two packs of Marlboro Red, and Tuesday, after training,
'Cop Shop' with some mates.
                        These were events
I wanted to happen and they were happening:

I'd finished propping in that sleepout at my folks'
and growing up, had bought myself this flat.
Somewhere in the Eastern Suburbs I taught Catholic kids,
hoping to think they thought ace things
about their Mr P. But Tuesday night was always
the mates' night: three in a dump though one
(and he was picky) had bought this vinyl lounge suite,
direct from the Salvos, just for 'Cop Shop.'
        They probably haven't left the place (and no-one
would know if they had). That's the great thing
in consistency: why should you be noticed?

The girlfriend

                              I met her
at the Social Club, she was a team-mate's sister,
but Susan, a legal secretary, twenty-four,
had never heard of me.
        A boyfriend having dumped her
she was wary, wishing never to be dumped
again.
        Sunday I took her driving:
told her there wasn't anyone around.
We met again that week and Susan heard
how, if she had a boyfriend dumb enough
to ditch her that was a problem, his; not ours.
God I was moving fast with *ours*!
        And I was wanting to say:
*Look I'm twenty-seven, I'd like to share lots of things
very, very soon . . . and even more
I'd love the idea of looking at you forever.*
        She'll always get me saying the most
outlandish things. Like, one morning,
after she was dressing, and Susan knows how
to dress herself: 'I can hardly wait,'
I blurted out, 'to see your tits again.'
                'And me?' she asked 'Suppose I am attached?'

The Heaths

      Soon I had to take her to the Heaths.
But Barb was gardening whilst inside Roger
compiled the Collected Works of Roger Heath.
      So Uncle Shane took his nephew, Sam,
into the park for a kick-to-kick.
All children deserve love: wives, husbands, girlfriends
boyfriends, they need to earn it.
                        And Roger,
needing foundations for such a love,
studied, worked and organised his family:
arranging and caring for both wife and son.
Any trouble was that kind most families have:
one they'll never know they're having.
                            One day,
I suppose, Barb will read something, somewhere
(no doubt she already has) and, for all their years,
the Heath years, a book is telling her:
This is the way he's treated you: yes look, look,
you've been cheated, you've been disempowered!
(or any one of half a dozen mangles
of the language) which might, of course, be true
except: what has ever been so simple?
                          Look Barb,
it won't take much to admit *You don't say!*
but your husband is, was and will be
one moody but honest bastard:
honest but selfish, selfish and moody again.

The lovemakers

      Susan in *Do it!* mode:
often to finish sex she likes it
this way, we both enjoy it this way:
after she's come she'll stagger to a wall,
spread her legs and tell me *Do it!*
      And it's the easiest thing I'll

ever do; and I might say I always wanted
women to be this easy, but when I met her,
Susan, I met them all.
            Why am I telling, whoever I'm telling, this?
Women, my sister Claire once said
– at least the ones she knows –
talk of little else. 'It's easy,' says Claire,
'even men should try it!'
Sorry Claire, this is what men are for:
Marlboro Reds and VBs, the odd vinyl lounge
and 'Cop Shop'. Oh, and winning games.
            And no, after Susan I'd hardly spend
my Tuesday nights the way I had;
and no, after Susan the off seasons were
hardly spent at home.
                        Do it, she urged,
let's save and do it:
The Grand Canal or the Khyber Pass,
the Taj Mahal or the Scrovegni Chapel!

The decision

            When The Stags, or at any rate Stubbs,
offered me the package I told her
it was *ours* ours to decide.
            We decided all right:
Craig Stubbs came where on the *BRW*
Rich List: tenth? fifth? third? He would pay
like few in the game were likely to.
(He might even buy me a school!)
            I was thirty. How old is thirty? In footy
it's as old as the number of games you have
remaining.
            Oh, and the sex that night,
after the decision: any good?
            What do you mean after?

The works

        After the kids had started their weekend
I chatted in the staffroom for an hour
then walked to where I'd suggested:
'The Forest Lawn'.
                Yes that was her, Carrie the nurse.
      'Up north,' I offered 'you wore this
quite extravagant skirt, remember?'
      'And you,' I was reminded,
'you got this migraine.'
              'Not from the skirt.'
    'Not from the skirt.'
              'Adrian?' I asked.
    He'd been to see her. Funny how
Carrie was about to leave her flat
and set up at the boyfriend's townhouse.
Gary wouldn't freak: an ex arriving
and that, he wasn't jealous (that was
guaranteed) but rather, rather protective?
      'We work so well together . . .' she confessed;
leaving me to get a grip on 'work';
and yes I could've told her:
a game, sex, a trip, kids, a job, love
when I say *It works so well*
I can't imagine anything better.
      Carrie sighed. 'So well together.
I can't, I won't have it spoiled, ever.'

The planet

    Adrian?
        He'd flown into Sydney
with half a dozen men on his agenda,
plus Carrie.
        There was a bank:
a something-like-a-bank bank,
and this bank had given Stubbs a job,

and Stubbs had given Adrian a job
and (Carrie was sure there must've been a shrug)
it had to work, it had to.
      He was speedy.
Adrian was stuffed but speedy.
   'I've seen a few drugs,'
Carrie was in natter mode, 'and here
were any number of them. But his seemed worse:
He couldn't stop. He could never stop.'
    Clients were needed. His gang from the old days:
weren't they all businessmen by now,
and didn't Shane still know them?
    What, our team-mates?
          She supposed so.
   'Well I might meet a few
but what would be the drum?
How this if-indeed-it-is-a-bank bank
is backing ex-bar owner/ex-ex-billionaire
Craig Stubbs, and through him our Mr Magic,
for what? Ades needs clients? Stubbs required
wood-ducks, right? And guess what? As ever
it's supposed to work!
Couldn't he have come to see me, me
and this old gang?'
      She'd asked him that
but *Melbourne, Carrie? Nah, not the Melbourne karma
this time round.* 'He's paying me though,'
she added, 'flying me down and paying me
to ask you.'
     'He's mad,' I added too.
'Business gets attempted in a thousand ways.
Now, part reverie, part intrigue, part practical
joke, all Mr Magic: make this
the thousand and first: send the ex!'
    And if he'd come?
    So I imagine the ballpark figures,
the trade-weighted indices, the shelf companies
on islands half the size of the Glenferrie Oval.
And no, I thought, when I want gibberish,
gibberish that might at least help save me,

I'll be off to church.
                    'Carrie,' I hoped she'd
listen, 'I mean, round and round the world
these nostrums hurtle and it's just one planet!
Just one planet! I mean,
if we were trading with outer space, perhaps . . .'

The cynic

          Here's what was premised:
as if I was to conjure for Carrie or the world
some explanation, disclaimer, obituary-in-advance.
But, as a coach might find himself
after his team disintegrates, I stonewalled:
'Yeah, well, Adrian . . .' line-in-the-sand stuff.
          No I would tell her little. Why?
There wasn't much to tell: hardly anything on
him she didn't know.
          'So,' I veered, 'our great god Craigo's
resurrected? When old man Price had a few
bad weeks over at the Mitcham branch
$tubb$corp never resurrected him!
A bit of fishing, a bit more of drinking,
it might scrape by as Real Livin',
but living?'
          The cynic tabulating
how happy we're to be, I'm good at that.

The game

          'Ades?' I asked, 'what don't you know?'
Tell you one thing though: distract him enough
Mr Magic could be mighty slow.
That first February, with the coach dividing us
for twenty-five minutes of his traditional scratch match
(Protestants versus Catholics and the rest)

Cross was on Price.
                      'The name is Shane.'
I tried to shake his hand, hassling how
'The name is Shane and yours, show pony,
yours?'
          Too bad I aim for where the ball is.
          Too bad he coathangers the air.
          Too bad my pass sets up another goal.
          Too bad whatever-the-name-is sprawls
onto the oval.
          I grabbed his hand and
hauled him up. 'Shane Price!'

The men

          Then there was The Doc, our sports psychologist:
a little man who wrote on 'men'
and how they're 'men'.
                  We need to humour them,
don't we? But his questions were answered and
I liked him.
          As my guest at a coterie function
'Who's that,' he asked, 'with your friend Cross?'
          Why did consensus always take Adrian
for my friend?
              But who was that? That was Gibbo.
And who was Gibbo? Someone overacting the sillybugger?
A friend of Stubbs? A hanger on?
All of them Doc in one shit cocktail:
the total put-me-down: any amount, fellas,
that tab is mine.
          'Doc eh?'
and Gibbo didn't have to pause: 'What's up? What's up?
Name us your latest giant step for medical science.
What are we curing today, the clap? the clap?'
          'Doc's got this thing about us, about "men"'
Adrian wanted to explain. 'Geez Gibbo mate
not like *that*, like how we tick.'

'Tick?' Gibbo knew no 'tick'.
'Doc baby, these guys must never *tick*! Kick perhaps
but meatheads all, especially Pricey.'
         And on and on:
put him down for something better than that!
   Look Doc, I wished I could say,
want to know about *men*?
It's reckoned Gibbo shouted half The Stags
to the choicest pick of Poppets International.
In his apartment! And all he did was watch!

The moose

   Or maybe Doc should've heard The Iceman:
'Fuck that Moose! The other night
he got so out of it he ended up in drag. In drag?!
Ever treated y' self to seeing Moose-o in drag?
Won't tell you how but then we met three queers
and Moose, who thinks he's somehow in disguise . . . is recognised?
Ooh mate, "Three cheers," the poofters cry, "for Madame Moose!"
Big guys, real big, bigger than us
and so we give three cheers.'
       Or how,
that time at Gibbo's '. . . stoned not quite good
but certainly proper (I know it's not your carry-on
but Pricey let's get this right, right?) there's Moose:
pizza slice in one hand, whilst his other arm's
around this not too classy scrubber, and in that hand's
a tinny?! And a joint?! Moose-o, well,
he tries to get some pizza in his mouth.
He doesn't mate he doesn't; the sheila gets it
in her hair?! Well do you mind mate
do you fuckin' mind! There's women who leave
and women who never will; well not for a while
and she is going ape, real ape, saying
(and get this) that if he respects her
Moose'll get that pizza right in his mouth

and let her go. Poor Moose. This scrubber's rat bait.
She'll keep but.'

The love

      'Gentlemen,' Stubbs was saying,
'I've an announcement. But you all know my announcement:
let's make him welcome, Australia's greatest sportsman
Mr Magic, Adrian Cross!'
Then, after the Stag-coterie had glistened and swelled
in the sheer coup of *We have him!*
'Fellas . . .' (Stubbs was smirking and the smirking told me
Y' know, Shane, I needn't say any of this)
'Fellas, who said footballers can't think? Meet
Professor Pricey! Beware but, he's sensitive:
you must know the type: once the season ends
he'll get a beard, grow the hair and head off
to Italy or India!'
      Who else, I wondered, gorged themselves
on such delight?
          The answer was easy.
Little in life, almost nothing in art,
matches that winner-deadshit Giotto's Judas.
Oh for a jet direct from Stag HQ
to Padua, just to revisit him! Has anyone else
(even Craigo) ever had this power to look
with such a love his prize in the eyes,
receive such love in return?
      'Well, who'd ever believe that Mr Magic
was set to strip for The Stags?' Stubbs
rubbed it in.
          And Adrian rubbed it back:
'Any time for you Craig, any place.'

The future

      To get the remaining piety dispensed with
all I need to do was tell the brother-in-law
'Sell out? And you wouldn't Roger?
A living? Make a living? It takes three
easy steps: get a manager, get a contract,
get me cash. All the living I require will follow.
You can't "sell out" to the future!'
      I still can't accept I said it.
Where did I think I wanted to work?
Real Livin' Toyota?
      (Though what was Roger's beef?
He barracked for Carlton!)

The marketplace

      When my sister Claire told me
'A boy, I'm really seeing this boy!'
'Yeah?' I asked, knowing she loved it
blunt, 'So what's his team: Pies, Dons, Dogs,
Roos, us?'
      But whatever the us the game
our game was going national.
              And national
meant, for Cross and Price, The Stags.
      I played two seasons, Susan had our baby.
I reached three hundred games and then retired.
      'So Pricey what you doing now?'
      'I develop The Stags.'
            'Shit eh?
How'd you like it?'
           'Pays the bills mate.'
      Which is enough but I mean
don't you ever see me after one more afternoon
of Stagball, badgering the team 'Right fellas,
another chorus, just for the cameras one two three
Giving it a go/for The Stags it must be so

Just for the cameras? Whoever needed
supporters now?
  Visiting Melbourne I dropped in on The Doc.
 Men, Doc? Haven't you worked it out yet?
Men are stuffed. Oh and another thing
the world needs male bonding like it needs
another round of 'Giving It A Go'.
 'So what's it like Shane, developing
The Mighty Stags?'
    'Developing one more mighty
dodgy arm of the $tubb$corp debacle?
Developing my Aunt Fanny!'

The rumour

 You never know how much a private life
is private, until it's public.
   As if I never knew that!
Though if some handle it and some can't there's
others, me for example, who need never bother.
 At school of course rumours rarely halt,
but I like rumours.
 Did you play footy sir? Who for?
Never heard of you I'll ask my dad.
How many games, six? A few more
How many goals? Ever get reported?
What kind of player were you?
Look at the videos: more ferret than dinosaur.
Anywhere the ball decided to be
that's where they wanted me.
Why aren't you asking about Mr Magic, son?
 Because, being twelve, son has hardly
heard of him. That's right ask dad.
 Play with anyone famous?
With me mates.

The confession

      All gush 'n' cleavage (though
for a while I enjoyed my time with her)
'You mightn't think,' Carrie was explaining,
'I'd finish this way. If indeed I've finished.
But Gary's a cop! I'm set to live with
a New South Wales cop!'
                    He was laconic,
I got told and, even more, a ridiculous softy
('Like you are probably, Shane.')
and even better, someone to make her life
a success.
      'I'm more than just another
plucky little whore. And Gary knows it.
Gary 'n' Carrie,' she seemed captivated by
the clang, 'now who contrived *that*?'
      As if she'd never thought of this a giggle
bubbled over. Staff friends were on watch:
this hardly seemed a Price-type situation,
and I agreed.
      And I was near-set to tell her
You've had a few boyfriends; now you want
to settle down. And you're doing all of this
later than some? It doesn't worry me
except my showstopper had to get in line
for hers.
      'You know I wasn't made, my mind
just wasn't made, for plain enjoyment of one guy.
Not until Gary. It wasn't Shane, there had to be
so much more, once.'
      Well what did I think?
      I thought that we had only met
a few years before, although I also thought I'd heard
of her.
      'That night!' she sighed
'with my skirt and your migraine!'
      'And *them*,' I urged, 'remember them?'
      'The hippy lawyers!'
                  And, as the bar

received a chorus of 'Yeah! The hippy lawyers!'
we'd something in common; and I could see why,
if next to himself by the length of the Milky Way,
Adrian liked her.
             'Things occurred that night.'
As if she thought I wasn't there she told me:
'Yeah, I went back to him.
Later I went to my room so as
at least next morning them, the lawyers
might have to guess. Weren't they stupid!'
What were we doing there?
       'A property boom was on.
Ades thought I might invest in a swamp.'

The absolution

       'Okay cops exist Carrie. I met one once.
Perhaps he's yours. And I'm looking at a decent woman
who wouldn't be here if she wasn't.
But I want to tell you there's no promises.
I cannot say *I'll see what I can do* because
even if I could, I wouldn't.
Adrian Cross, Craig Stubbs and their
Blankety-Blank Bank? Why should I bother
treading into one more swamp?
       Oh and you've never been with the same guy twice?
A few more? And you think yourself ridiculous?
Ever been a development officer?
For The Stags? You haven't?
Then Carrie you're reason itself.'

The guess

       Dreams do very little.
Let him who has the biggest dreams
keep on dreaming. As long as I've been

looking at events *This time* Australia
has never stopped telling itself *this time*
they mean it: a Craig Stubbs, an Adrian Cross,
they're really going to do it. These fellas here
will be that success we want them to be.
        Well Carrie,
I can't say what he was like in the cot
but if the sports star
finished as
little like a sports star, this businessman
(and I'm guessing easy now)
will end as nothing like a businessman.
Why? He hardly is one. Mr Magic?
He's the fella who was fed the balls, given
the words: the lad who keeps the ladies thinking
Now, what must he be like under those shorts?
the celebrity who makes the investors tell themselves
Yep, I'm going to trust this lot!
        Adrian fronts; he always fronts.
The first to be loved he's the first to be
clobbered: someone to make us feel happy.
Good for Adrian!

The message

        So Mr Magic's fronting $tubb$corp mark
ninety-nine; so some bank's unravelling,
a bank like Australia has never known till now;
so Ades is heading centre stage once more?
Guess what? I never knew he'd left it.
        Sure he was a colleague
but I've only had how many mates?
Those friends I met for a drink most Tuesdays
after training (bearded, anonymous, little need
to be a part of anything much,
just like their mate would like to think he was)
them, my sister Claire, my wife Susan.
        Sometimes, wanting to prove the maniac

I'm not, I'd love to tell The Doc
'... all that bonding claptrap means
they haven't got the guts to fuck each other!'
But a Pricey tantrum's hardly one of those.
           Besides, next month at the Social Club
there's yet another premiership reunion,
to which we'll go, Susan and I,
doubtless to hear some message from the Caymans,
how Adrian 'Mr Magic' Cross, is thinking of you, fellas!

The drift

           'Tell you where I stand: if anywhere,
here's where: surrounded by these dull,
consistent people, in good suburbs, in
good streets, in good houses; and if they'll
hardly be my mates well I've played for them,
sometimes I might even vote with them.
No-one, true, really deserved their comfort,
but none of them have set me up,
they aren't Stubbs; they never could be
Mr Magic; and I'm no wood-duck.
           Now I teach their kids.
And Carrie, if this is cautious living
then long live the cautious life!
           But, for a number of afternoons
we were the measure of things:
the chance to have a few plus million people
tell each other *Oh yeah that was the year
they won it; or them or the other crowd.*
There are worse ways to order the memories
of a city; well, I was a part of it.'
           If there was a drift I reckoned she
was getting it.
           The Forest Lawn kept filling;
it wasn't getting late but, since a headache
had commenced, I said it was.
                     'Yeah,'

I concluded, 'no hard feelings Carrie, yeah. Let's leave it there.'

Part 15

NEIL	INTO REMINISCENCE
SAL	GALLERY OWNER
THE MENTOR	BOOK LAUNCHER
DEEDEE	INTERVIEWER
KIM	REMAKER, SOMEWHERE
BARB } DAVE }	VIEWERS
CARRIE	BRIDE
GARY	GROOM
CARRIE'S MUM	
BENNY	FRIEND/EULOGIST
AMANDA	FRIEND
CLAIRE	GIRL FRIDAY
BESS	SELF-DISCOVERER
GEOFF	BISHOP
LEO	DECEASED
HANNAH	SENATOR
KARL	INTO REMINISCENCE
CRAIG	REMAKER, EVERYWHERE

THE EX FATHER-IN-LAW
DOUGIE
DIGBY 'GIBBO' GIBB OA
OSBOURNE
DIXIE
STEVE DODD .... FRIENDS AND
FELLA/HOTSHOT   ASSOCIATES OF CRAIG'S
JOY
LACY
THE MOOSE
ADRIAN
SOPHIE

PHIL ....SMALL BUSINESSMAN

'THOSE WERE STRANGE DAYS STRANGE DAYS INDEED!'

**Neil attends the launch of
'The Collected Poems of Toby Nicholson'**
for Cameron Shingleton

     'So you knew Toby then? Back then?'
At Gallerie Matrix, which she owned,
Sal asked Neil 'How come we've never met?
I met Kim of course. And Kim did it,
didn't he. He was, I mean, the one,
enough of the one?'
                Yes he hardly told her
*Toby was his first celebrity client,
so for a while Kim was a part of it.*
     'And where, Neil, are you living?'
     'Down south in a valley, Sal.
Most summer nights we turn off all the lights
and stretch out under the stars.
What else do I do? Coordinate the local
civic fathers' Getta Kidda Job campaign
and play bush reggae with my girlfriend's band.
Toby would've loved our place.
It wasn't he just stayed penned up
in Paddington, waiting for Lacy *every* day.
He moved about.'

     The Mentor would launch the book:
this wasn't Sal's idea but Toby's mother's.
     'Fatty's still around,' Sal sighed, 'he won't stop
being around.'
               After the bamboo flutes
had improvised, The Mentor rolled his sleeves:
'To business, all, to business!'

Oh bring on The Spaceman, please,
for a few bars of 'Classical Gas'!

&

But where was Kim?
Surely Go-mate knew
Lacy was the stuff of docudrama now:
What would ever bring him here?
    And yet, if it were theatre,
Youth Festival Theatre, Kim might prowl in
with cigar, moustache, nose, spectacles, and
'We know who that is!' the audience would tell
themselves, 'and that's not Groucho Marx!'
                                Except,
there was no greater disguise for Lacy
than being Lacy: he would simply point
to number one with *Me?* and Kim would turn to
just about anyone he wished:
What have I done? What have I ever done?
I'll tell you docu and I'll tell you drama:
I wasn't there, I was never there.
I mean where are we GoGo:
back in The Shire?
                      But Spacey (Neil would love
this answer) *has anyone from our suburbs*
been quite as famous? The Shire?
That's where, if things improve or don't,
Mayor Donellan will dedicate
the 'Spacey' Lacy Memorial Shooting Gallery.
    That might've paused him.
Too bad I've come to Toby's launch and all
I think about is you, Kim.

                Too bad The Mentor
was primed to do the launching and all he thought
about was ... cherishment? 'Wherever you be,
Tobe, cherish this, cherish the moment!'
    Which was but a start of it.

There'll be, guessed Neil, another half an hour
of Mentor!
       He wanted to be drunk,
not just drunk-drunk, but that kind of offhand
dumb-drunk Toby was when first they met,
queuing at the punchbowl:
that kind of adolescent-drunk
with always three tales to tell:
how wasted you were, what you did and
how you got away with it.
He'd never get that drunk tonight,
but aware of what he wanted done
Neil shuffled through the crowd and reached
the doorway.
       At the other end of Matrix
The Mentor sweated to his task:
'We are growing old, Tobias, old.
Not you son, no, not you . . .'
       Close to half Neil's lifetime back Toby
who, for all his dinky arrogance knew
what should parade and what should never,
Toby had told him:
'Mentor shmentor, that poof just deals The Word:
hard to soft then back to hard again.
Deals it, but nothing happens. Y' see Mister Neil,
we're supposed to do it to him! And no-one will.
You know why? Too fuckin' ugly.'
       With only one occasion now
(this one, this one) there'd be little use
in waiting. Twenty minutes into the elegising,
this one, when it occurred, would be for Toby.
       And before Neil knew he'd done it,
he'd done it.
       'B'lukb'luk b'laaaak!'

On the television special 'The Joy Boys File' Neil talks to DeeDee Lyons about his school mate Kim 'Spacey' Lacy

  A big-noter? Yes I've thought that too.
But doing what you'll say you'll do
requires a finer skill. And Kim sure knew
even that special brand of Spacey bullshit
needs its follow-through. His motto?
Lay out the meat then await the flies.
  And, though Kim's kind never needs friends
for life, just allies for the occasion,
truly you could enjoy the man.
  I'm not expecting a postcard, but if one came
I'd frame it. A big-noter's smallest touch?
Maybe. But we'd been mates, he still thought
of me and I'd be charmed. For when you're Spacey,
Spacey with those dreams no-one else believes,
what else remains but charm?
  And, since it all seems to have happened,
that's a great tale you're running DeeDee:
how, starting from 9 Banksia Drive
a less than secure groover joins the Messrs Big.
  Did The Spaceman ever need a life plan?
Who needs honey when you own the hive?

Barb watches 'The Joy Boys File'

  Once she adjusts to the idea, the fact,
that it's him there, Neil, answering fatuous-
celebrity DeeDee Lyons, all Barb can think is
'Wow, now how'd they track *you* down?'
  Though she is shaking,
hoping that Roger and the children
won't walk into the room, for if they do
This man she'll have an urge to admit
*Sometimes I still think I know this man
better than any man.* And *Intensity?
You want intensity? Then spend a few days*

observing us 1970/ '80/
some date.
  This 'special's' such a self-important show,
one that knows all its history has
close-to-the-lot: the far too mortal games
of grassing and counter-grassing, a bank which never
seems to have been one, two minor couriers
blaming each other, the bargirl bar,
the trannie-plus bar, an un-named implicated
businessman who's vanished, the scything energy
of Kevin Joy and his eliminations;
whilst, in the studio, behind her, DeeDee,
is a wall-length blow-up of Lacy:
alleged drug boss (if not deceased then surely
on the run); that or an old school chum.
  For much of its time, of course,
this program's made-for-a-TV-special truth
asks that each word shall qualify the last;
as if one screen of gauze is placed
before another, till all a watcher is allowed
are shadows; and that they, Kim Lacy
and his Joy Boys are nothing more.
  Not quite.
After the fuzzed flip-flop assessment of Neil's
loyalties ('Who am I to judge what
Spacey was? Am I allowed to say
"a plausible prick"? Well I've said it!')
everything turns to a teenage mailbag of
school snaps: the young proto-dealer
and his mate, the man that one day Barb
would love to tell *I knew I'd see you again;
though not like that!*
  It's a middle school form photograph.
  'That's me,' points Neil, 'and next but one
to me is Lacy' (who could've been
a brother of Barb's and one of her brother's friends).
Two of the four tallest boys, the group symmetry
leads to them.
  'Big grins,'
the photographer must've advised, 'c'mon big grins.

This one's for the grandkids!'
                            None of them,
however, has that kind of vision, yet.
                            Except,
out-staring the camera (they hope for all existence),
Neil and Kim are smirking; Neil, because
the exercise is ritual, a minute or two of high school
ritual: the silliest thing they've made us do
since the last one. Kim, though, smirks just a little
more: as if he's seen what he'll become:
The Shire's most famous son.

Watching 'The Joy Boys File', Dave Price collapses in his extension

            Five years after their divorce what made Wynne
still trot around to play at Mrs Mops?
That same urge keeping Dave full-as-a-goog
tonight and every night: the way it is and,
if there's one more heart attack to go,
it always is.
            Since the last one
Wynne had added to her works a hug
and some advice: he mustn't live alone.
            And he mustn't though, tonight, out of such slops
as make for television, he was glimpsing it:
the final David Price crusade:
to memo such powers who thought they were powers
Just find where these peanuts live and bomb it!
Or turn me onto them!
                        Pie-eyed a man might be, but,
as anger swirled into and out of his heart,
Dave had never been fitter. Though his legs were
hardly steady; and why was he starting to vomit?
            His body introduced Dave to the floor.

Carrie marries Gary
for Diane Black

       Benny took Carrie to the airport. Her mother
having flown Business Class 'With all them captains of industry . . .'
Benny sensed that till the tension broke
and he, Carrie or both of them cried
Stop! Stop! Stop! such inanities were ceaseless.
                                           'I like it,'
her daughter got informed 'how your fiancé's not about.' They drove
               away in silence.
       But Benny, who fancied he'd a way
with ladies, was primed to woo the mother.
(Besides, offering her his guest room and needed to.)
        'I like it
here,' his guide to Darlinghurst commenced, 'the one true industry
round these parts is coffee drinking . . .' words so bland they cried
out for *That, and a touch of sodomy!* (This idea plain broke

him up!)
           The old bat loved Benny's place: 'Well you're not broke,'
she sniggered and sent her girl away.
                Carrie visited Amanda, they talked of sex, of love, then slightly
               cried.
By now they were such friends, Carrie and 'Reverend Mother'
(as she never tired of calling her).
                             But after the sex industry
what remained but love? Often she lay awake and asked
(between me, myself and I): *Like it?*

and the reply always returned *You reckon I like it!*
       Some pal of Gary's, one who would certainly never go broke,
paid for both wedding and reception. It was an industry
keeping up with the old girl: two glasses in and she was away!
'So Benny, the rumour is you *lean* . . .' But it was useless to snap *Mother!*
(not when you'd been embarrassed since birth) to have cried

that once was to have cried
a thousandfold.
               'Marriage?' as Gary smiled his good cop smile

'Yeah I like it...'
Amanda, Carrie's after-a-fashion mother-
figure was telling her 'This is where your luck is. Go for broke
and fold those other men away.'
Yet it would be a strange industry,

this contained, ambiguous cop industry.
Okay, she doubted that Gary had ever cried,
yet like some lead in 'Neighbours' or 'Home and Away'
he was caring, reliable, fun: and this had to be acknowledged *I like it
like that* . . .
Nattering broke
her reverie. Guess who was going on about the wedding dress? Mother,

still slaving-on in the mother industry:
'She near broke my heart the way she looked but I like it
I really do.'
Benny gave the bride away. Amanda cried.

Claire faxes her ex

Well hi there Pookie!
Name the only girl to ever call you *that!*
So this must be guess-who again!
Even better, guess-who'll be heading your way soon.
Our CEO is facing burial under the business ethics code
and needs me, number one girl CP, that's who,
to help in digging him out.
(Though it isn't me
who sits on the boss's knee, Pookie,
Pookie the poet, I've too much respect for knees!)
Would *you* give women's magazines the time?
I doubt it. However, if you do, all you need see
is one of the latest headlines
GO ON REALLY GIVE YOUR EX THE AXE.
Which ex? The fella before you and the bloke
before him and the man after you and the one
after him? I'll only say, Pooks, you're the big ex,

you going on with those supportive things
about me and my body, how women shouldn't bother
with image; I recall your words, don't you?
'As long as she isn't a slob, as long as she
carries it well.' Mind you, who dumped whom
for Ms Anna X Icke?
                    Say Pooks, guess who's turned
out a treadmill gym bunny? Redder and sweatier
three times a week she pounds, one more ludicrous
plump girl; whilst high on the monitors M'sieur Oohlala,
the mid-morn cookery czar, flips his crepes
and giggles at Australia.
                    Afternoons it's worse.
Direct from Narcissiana USA,
the chat show cretins. I've worked *them* out!
Either they've lost something or they've found it
again! That's all America is!
                    I've a great boss,
each day we start before seven and,
over twelve hours later, leave. With all that time
Girl Friday combines with gym bunny!
                    Some bunny!
I'm also smoking again. Keep this up
I'll finish as that sort of mum they send outside
to puff in the carport.
First though I must meet someone for the dad.
        When I was younger (and sometimes even now) I thought how
striking out on my own seemed much too foolish.
Then looking at my parents, my sisters
and their husbands, convinced me
I'd no other game to play.
        So, when the ethics circus comes to town,
watch for me, there! by my CEO!
doing it right, as I've done so often. Even if
the result's another win for Ms Icke.
                    Oh ex,
you're forgiven. If I can forgive me and the way
I still appear, I can forgive anyone.
        You there in your TAFE,
teaching whatever you teach (my sources only supply

the slimmest details) since you've been tracked down
— even after these years — I dare, I double dare
you write me something: not about me about *us!*
Go on Pookie, you're the poet!
                                        Claire

Bess Cattermole comes out (after her fashion)

      I'm sure you know, Geoff, there's a women's karma,
and your mind can grasp with more than a decent guess
how lesbians, without a deal of drama
are spouting nationwide like watercress.
      And though amongst The Sisters I'm Roxanna,
here's what happened to your partner, Bess:
at Camp Sappho (how can one begin?)
she regained more than just the child within.

Oh it was great! With heaps of naked swimmin'
and, need I say it, mutual masturbation.
      Please Geoff you'll have to realise men aren't women!
      Though this I'll add, heart thumping with elation:
I never wed some dominie or imam,
Australia's not a theocratic nation.
We have such honest, humanistic goals.
      As has life amongst the Cattermoles.

Our daughter tops Environmental Studies,
our son can handball, kick with both feet, and mark.
And both have gotten used to mother's buddies,
though such viragos are surely set to nark
near to a synodful of fuddy-duddies
(not you of course, their laid-back patriarch:
through all of Christendom they couldn't pick a
broader-minded, even-handed vicar).

      It's not as if I've joined some kind of sect.
      I cherish how your concern easily ployed,
saw me through countless days of feeling wrecked
with PMT. Geoff truly I've enjoyed

our ironic give 'n' take of intellect
(a pleasant way to keep this girl stay buoyed).
   But 'sex'? With 'men'? I'd rather be sprayed with mace!
   Trust this doesn't hurt too much, Your Grace.

Le jour sur la plage de M. Pengilly
for Darrell Hilton

   If not my final journey
my next will start one pleasing, early autumn afternoon
at Largs: warm sun, cool breeze, low tide.
   See you there:
and dress me in a light, white cotton suit
with, why not, some too-red pocket handkerchief.
   No tie? No tie.
But certainly an attendant Panama; and paramour;
and paramours; and friends seeing me into
   my deckchair; the hum
from Lady Gowrie Drive being enough to let me know what
the world has been, what, apart from *mes amis* I'm leaving.
   Even with the traffic
and the few obligatory seagulls, this should be all peace.
Music might be nice, but what, and played by whom?
   (Not Bruckner for starters.
When I return as some fin-de-siècle Viennese
then Bruckner, one day, maybe.) But indecision will occupy hours
   (*L'apothéose de M. Lully?*
'*On ne peut pas toujours avoir ce qu'on veut*'
de M. Jagger?) and once the choice arrives
   logistics follow. Please,
at my stage of existence who needs further
logistics. No: no music. Let's just commence a magnum:
   something crisp if not too parched
and, in deference to the parochial, South Australian.
Then imagine this: halfway through the celebrations
   (these must be celebrations)
I'll raise my flute in final toast, some distance
toward the heavens. And let it fall . . .

Anglo-Catholics for friends: Benny Hull at the requiem mass for his friend Father Leo Pengilly, St Peters, Eastern Hill, Melbourne (an extract)

      After the laughter (there had to be laughter)
and all the murmured nods, what remained for the mourners
but to concur with this beefy yet handsome,
middle-aged counsellor?
                      Benny continued
'And what were Leo's last words?
Faggots, friends, are tough! Boy was he correct!
Born, acquired or made who in their right mind
would slog through his proclivities
unless they were patently what they were?
Well there's but one measure of life and that *is* life.
How glad I am we're mortal! How glad I am
for all ... for all ... no no *Because of*
our friends' excesses (compassion, wit and downright
horniness, none of which he knew could save him)
Leo made me hear and see and think
(even if I thought *Leo, Mon Vieux, just grow up!*)
He made me love!'

At Leo's funeral Neil recalls one of the first times they met

      On a warm and blustery
late August Sunday we strolled by Luna Park
hoping that the air could repossess
those hours lost from the past few nights.
      So where's Benny?
Further down the bay, visiting a great aunt;
as Leo tells me all about Sydney, *his* Sydney:
how you could cruise down every street,
smile at anyone and ask *Your place or mine?*
which may have been half a dozen metres of Vaseline Valley
though hardly The Shire or anywhere else.
      Yeah Sydney, I reply,
knowing all I want to do is get back home to Barb

(enough of a home, the home of my heart);
and, since everything about the time and place
seems Wistful Inc, Leo shall be told.
  And the reply?
'Love 'em by all means love 'em, but after that,
Olympus, Spencer, just ascend Olympus! Be detached
as Zeus!' (Or, why be modest, Leo Pengilly who
admits it himself!)
    'Surely that was meant
for entertainment? Benny is later asked.
   'Yes,' he sighs, 'a movie, *Carry On Faggot*.
  Leo was always losing things, or else
giving them away: bicycles, hard hats, handcuffs,
paintings, his latest contact addresses; 'Spencer,'
he was always saying, 'will there never be
an occasion we won't meet stoned?'
   Over the next few years
the time of day he gave would never stop
growing; except for largesse he laid
nothing on me.
    Going to 4/9
ought to have been a part of
everybody's life.
    I liked him.

Neil tells himself Twined to their mean, both agony and bliss,/ Memories are mainly made of this

   Just before heading abroad I'm with Benny and
half a dozen others; we're walking home to Leo's
after a local dinner.
    And the dope, the drink,
the company, so breach my arsenal of invective
that through the St Kilda streets
I'm shooting adjectives: hoping one day they may crack
onto their target: Roger Heath.
     (Today
they still rain back as nouns, verbs,

everything a language thinks it is:
King Rog the cool the dry the *Il Supremo*
of his little desert kingdom.)
        Then, that night, I finally salvo
Aren't you hearing me Heath, aren't you hearing me?
And, since he couldn't, he wasn't.
          Now, given a decade,
I try conjuring my current attitude. And find, amazed,
I'm just arriving at jealousy, learning
to hate him.
    That night in Melbourne,
not that Barb knew, my words were hurled
on her behalf. Though what she'd seen in him
I must've missed, since how could I be
less envious: her paragon of moderation
had stymied little, blocked nothing, had made us
free agents. With a career and family so firmly his,
such actions were hardly Heath's.
        Besides,
what family and career were mine?
      Whatever we love, I tried to self-explain,
whatever we love is temporary;
no matter how long it endures such is the nature
of affection. Even the slowest, most simmering
of affairs (a possibility I must've considered
though never acted upon) are a merest exercise,
one if it succeeds finds our hero giving a lifetime
to ... to ... to ... hyperbole!
        Well guess who's
jealous now? Heath could give up his wife,
didn't but he could. I couldn't.

Senator Little rehearses lines for her first press conference as Parliamentary Leader, the New Progress Party

(i) Private Hannah
    With due consideration to my claque
(who see yours truly as some caped crusader,

in equal portions Gandhi, Greer and Nader)
the scorn and moral fury of their flak
(for all that it exhilarates) distresses.
Luxuriating in the present hour
we're not (repeat it class) are *not* in power;
never will be, Misses, Mesdames, Messieurs.
      I am my oldest, most acknowledged fault.
In need of copy? Well Heeeeers Hannah!
Senator Mouth, the tabloid's crunchiest manna,
the dinkum true blue's most endearing bolt.
Yes, self-depreciation is a form of skiting.
      (A headache builds, I crave a decent sleep.
Leave a message when you hear the beep.
Or drop a line, we'll answer you, in writing.)

(ii) Public Hannah

      Sisters and brothers of our Australian press,
presume this day as the reason for Hannah's birth.
      And sure she had some estimate of her worth
but what's been the oddest compliment? (Go on, guess!)
Being described, since she tends to bluster,
as 'This somewhat left-of-centre female Kennett'.
      What do girls like her bring to the Senate?
Nothing boys like you could possibly, Buster!
      Off stage, if stressed, when found she's tending to blub,
then our Shire girl gets on the phone to mother;
or craves appropriate actions from her lover.
(This finds them steaming in a vigorous hot tub).
      Now though, to out-blitz all previous Luftwaffes,
it's Operation Charm: there's nibbles, finger food, drinks.
      The Senator listens, she feels, she loves, she thinks.
Later she'll introduce you to the staffers.

Karl recalls Hannah

      There she goes again, still waving her arms.
Don't say she's on about the seventies! Once more

the seventies! Wasn't that when Mr Whitlam turned into
Gough?
 What else? The student conference.
Sometimes it's still a decade which seems
all student conference. And what did ours have?
Jaundiced activism and a certain private mischief.
 'Are we,' she asked, 'moderate radicals or radical
moderates?' (Young men like me were growing used to
such gradations. We answered them with *Mmmm*.
Great word *Mmmm*) 'You've seen the motions,'
Hannah demanded, 'proposed a man, seconded a man.
How about a woman moves one?'
 So I went 'Mmmm',
and 'No guessing the woman . . .' and 'What have you
in mind?'
 A lot more than arm-flailing,
although such flailing helped.
She even took on the nutty professor of
revolutionary logic, the great Blume (part show trial
prosecutor, part messianic rabbi) took him on
(with Hannah logic, not that I was certain it was logic)
took him on and won. She must've waved the arms
(though this was diversionary) but here was a woman
speaking, which, about this time in the conference,
began to *really* matter.
 Beating the Blumites was like beating your folks:
the Spirit of Generation stamping its foot to tell the world
'From now on I won't be doing what *my* parents did!'
 In the most worthwhile sense we were amateurs.
I'd no idea what we thought would happen.
I'm still not sure. For a while there, after we'd got to
where we were heading, all I could think was
Power? What, me/us, power?
 In bed I gave way to
ambitions: 'Premier,' I told her, 'I want to be
Victorian Premier. It's enough.'
 'That'll be nice,'
Hannah conceded; then nattered for forty minutes
about her mother: how really, if she knew about
all this, she'd be good, quite good, about it

(Hannah was sitting up and waved her arms
over the bed); how mother was large in local government
('Yeah,' I agreed, 'such things have their place');
and yes next time, although she'd never done it before
mother was voting Labor for sure.
      'Oh,' I offered,
'that'll make a difference!'
Yes, there she goes, still waving her arms.

Karl recalls Dave Price

      Reffo boy, Glen Eira Grammarian,
little pleased me more than being Australian.
Smartarse, cynic, connoisseur of The Colliwobbles,
I knew all the disappearing brand names,
every *coo-ee!* ever uttered.
      I had parents.
They sat in their East Brighton living room
waiting for a dozen clocks to chime,
hoping that their only child
would bring them in a Rachel or a Leah,
and he would, if they were Aussies,
with boyfriends.
      I took everything this homeland offered:
the bushwalks, the near-to-mighty Maggies,
our rock 'n' roll and no-one else's,
the girls and all their
*Put one over me and I'll put more than one
over you* return of service;
and then, at university, my friend Lindsay,
his family and father.
      Dave Price had the slick kind of
quiz-master double-take just right for
those Australian films they never made
when they should have.
He loved singing, arm-wrestling, the shuddering
dreadful magic of easy listening,
and cheap red wine. He hated waste,

all Liberal governments, being contradicted
and the effeminate.
He was one furious drink driver.
He called me Bunyip. In 1972,
during the greatest election ever 'Bunyip,'
I was asked, 'why is the party of "the individual"
the party of mindless conformity,
and the egalitarian party the party
of the messiah?'
In 1943, somewhere in the islands,
he saw a head blown from a body. All he added was
'You don't know what else those animals did . . .'
or in elaboration 'I won't tell, I will never tell.'
In 1969 he announced
'Everyone tells their old folks to get stuffed.
And where's that got them?' In 1971
he considered chucking it all and
throwing in his lot with Chairman Mao,
for a minute.
   I've told many about him
and 'Yeah, yeah,' all have said
'I had a teacher like him. Only one, mind,
one was enough.'
   When we met
his self-pickling was already under way.
When he died three of his four children
hadn't seen him for a decade.

At the marina (Kim Lacy speaking)
for Bill Pitt

   The Spencers? They were a loaded family! Though Neil
    confessed
it was his Old Girl's money and not exactly spent.

   That chump deserves a fax.
     So where you reckon I am, Go-mate?
Begin by making a version of The Shire,

but one that spends, one that is truly making it.
Our marina, I keep getting told, ranks second most

exclusive in the state,
though 'second', you can guess, is hardly 'most'.

And so we're working on the rankings.
This, GoGo, just has to be The Shire with balls!

    I bet his father moves that same sauce boat
around his dinner table, announcing how *Here!*

here! would've been him, the boat, had he made
Kokoda.
    And *This!* I used to think,

rolling their pepper shaker hand to hand, I'll make *This!*
Mr Spencer, you leaning back in the carpark of

The Pacific Inn, a few choice ounces of leaf 'n' heads
waiting in your boot to make you rich as I am.

    I was detested! Though for what?
Unlike his sons I was trying to work,

to work it so The Shire would bloom!
    When I told Donellan what my shops and stuff

were making, all Frenchy said was 'Jeez, if you're that rich
what are you doing here?'
    He almost understood, except

this was my market and these were my mates,
    Money? Isn't it what you do with it they hate?

    I asked Kevin once 'So what did he do your father?'
'Carpet sales,' snapped his reply 'and yours?'

Soon as I told him Kevin's face was slit
by its long Joy smirk. 'Kimbo,' his head was shaking,

'Kimbo, my old man *slaved* for pricks like yours.
Which is why I don't.'

    Maybe you should've, matey. You might've been loved
just that bit more and got to survive.

    They love me where I've landed. A touch quiet
during the day I mix with little but the sea and sun;

I'm starting to enjoy my lady even better, keeping clean
and learning how to stay retired.

Some evenings but, I tell my neighbours how I owned and ran
'Aussie wide, fellas, Aussie wide . . .'

Real Grouse Jeans for Blokes 'n' Sheilas.
    And all the marina loves it! 'Listen,' they cry,

'Listen, listen, get him to say it, that one that one,
say it again buddy!'

    Accents never were a strength (though, by now
the tan, the ponytail and Dolphins cap

sure help. Them and a nose job). For it has to be faced:
I might be whoever I say I am but

down deep, down mighty deep, who wouldn't love
being 'Spacey' Lacy, The Shire's first Kid

to flog way-out gear for fellas and birds.
    Sometimes you must stay true, however true, to something

Craig Stubbs recalls or talks to just about everyone

(i)   He imagines 'public opinion' in the words of his former father-in-law, the gossip columnist

                        Stuff those glib howls to remain 'even-handed',
justice? It's no longer a matter of 'when',
whatever he had he'll never have again.
We'd love to get him back, but where he's landed
is good enough for us: no closer, that far.
When $tubb$corp sneezed guess who caught the cold?
At Crazy Horse all the staff got told
'Just keep him exiled *your* side of the bar.'

(ii)   Dougie
for Laurence White

Who gave out credit like a tart with sex?
Our Dougie.
To $tubb$corp, BoomCon, Futurex?
Just Dougie.
Who revved like a dozen outboard motors
each morning as he hit his quotas?
'I knew Craig when he flogged Toyotas!'
Taa Dougie.

'Y' wanna spin in my Lear Jet?'
Gee Dougie.
'It's faster than an Exocet!'
Yep, Dougie.
'Next week, next month, err next year fellas,
the market will be buyers? Sellers?'
You'll get more brains in trainee tellers
than Dougie.

'It's time to snatch, or dump, some shares . . .'
Now Dougie?
'Ditch the bulls? Umm back the bears?'
(Wow Dougie.)
'No really mate . . .' Well if you must,
but we'd rather know who put The Trust
through one part boom to nine parts bust:
ooooh Dougie!

(iii)   DeeDee

      When television knew no greater morning
(that day we raised the Family Network awning)
I met an old hand, this was the old hand's warning:

'Sure spend your cash, it's effort you shouldn't waste.
Oh bake it solid, combined with a decent baste.
But never overestimate Australian taste.'

      Yet wishing to flog the natives more than beads
I signed up Gibbo, concurrently with Deeds,
to double act as first and second seeds.

      Then once we'd traced all interlocking webs,
and charted how opinion flows and ebbs,
I learnt that art of packaging my celebs.

      Still cold-turkeyed? A little more than pissed
the other night? Sprung on your latest tryst?
Transform it via a $tubb$corp publicist!

Have fifty beaux been sluiced-on through the gratings?
Weren't there hints of splits, patch-ups and matings?
Please, Ms Lyons, forget 'em; look at the ratings

of a not exactly 'next door' kind of lass/
ingenue with a certain languid sass
and brains to spare!
      Oh DeeDee weren't you class!

Bring the scroll forth, give it an unfurl!
Their laureate, our thoroughbred, my pearl!
No, not bad for a breakfast weathergirl.

(iv)   Gibbo

      Like pissing into a gold leaf dunny?
That's probable when Aussies think you're funny!

(v)   The Osbournes

    Back again with your comeback King?
Oh Dix, I could never blame you! Craig was
such an amateur: who wouldn't wanna go
where the BoomCon blimp goes, or rather went?
    But if that wealthmaker
your first and third husband still can't tell
his Monet from my Manet … and even that
would be okay except his was never his:
not a cent got paid and oh, Oz,
that payment sure is happening now!
    So, how conjugal can she get, Dix?
It's a pleasant drive out to The Farm, I guess,
once a month a barbecue's allowed; and,
given the choice who you would prefer
(what seemed that extra-better for
the Dix image, an exile or a felon?)
'I'll be that good girl guide I am'
all Aussie heard, 'and stand by my felon.'
                                Sometimes
it's very easy to be a woman, and though
wealthmaker-wives are suffering, every day/
every way these troupers look their country
right in the eyes and announce 'It hurts, how
it hurts, but I believe in him. My man is
bearing up so I bear up. As for me,
aren't I the most innocent lass in the world?'
    Crap Dix, you were as guilty as Lady Macbeth.

(vi)   Steve Dodd

    That Sunday lunchtime of the saddest,
strangest day I'll ever know 'Craig mate,'
I am being told, 'it's all ridiculous but Steve
is dead!'
    I head
to the Brighton showroom: not even twenty-one
I figured how we'd always work together.
But now, with his staff more than two-thirds

gone on shock and wine casks, and no-one,
no-one wanting to be in charge 'Steve,'
I keep on saying 'you may be flat out
on a slab some place but you have more
real livin' still than anybody here.
From now, whatever I'm to do I'll lead
or, better, do it by myself.'
    And I'm still like you Steve:
a giver not a taker. So imagine this:
how I gave our nation a network
to watch, a team to be proud of,
a resort to visit.
    And the only chorus to be heard?
Put him down put him down put him down!
Well nothing has worked less.
Sure with new players, new shows, my team,
my network, may be simply names by now.
But Horizon? Whoever thinks they own it,
has to understand for all Australians that's
still Stubbsy's place.
    So Steve, imagine:
me asking you to join the Family Network board,
inviting you to be my guest in the $tubb$corp superbox,
booking my mates into Horizon's Steve Dodd suite.
    Or even better, this:
later, with our womenfolk, sipping the greatest-
ever chardonnay, and easing our knives
through simply the softest steak.
Not one care, not one remotest care . . .

(vii)   Fella

    Hey Hotshot,
weren't you conned! They never needed Fella,
they merely sent him out to stake The Horse
and let themselves look good. Stubbs?
Old son, hadn't you been informed
he's innocent? All that was bunny-digging
with bare hands: worthwhile enough except
since they've done it all their lives

the bunnies dig it faster.
    Why can't you be like me?
Why can't you believe beyond
the neat, well-loved predictable of Cherrywood?
Of course you had to do it:
you were born to make that report,
give your evidence. But after that?
    Soon in Cherrywood bland autumn will wind into
blander winter. And what'll remain?
An ever-wistful knowing that
if you'd arrived with Stubbsy on your arm
nothing would've made you more Australian.
    For Fella hasn't got his Fella,
just a few footsloggers in the smack army,
the idea of a bank that hardly existed
and memories of botched potential.
Can't you do better than these by, say, July?
    Me? About then I should be buying Aeroflot.
So there, Hotshot!

(viii) Joy and Lacy

    Who were you pricks?
Still in Manila? If indeed it's Florida
how goes Florida? You may be
part of that fine print we're warned to read
but, who were you pricks?
    So sorry Kevin, Kim
– I owned some joint with you by accident
– we shared the same bank
– the sort of people after me are after you
– we all know how to vanish.
        But gemstones,
caneware and a bar? Fellas,
I'll tell you who you are:
two popes of shonk. You never meant
for anyone to think *This crowd's legit*
all you wanted put around was
We're so small who'd want to touch us?
        I mean,
who were you pricks?

(ix)   Moose

   Amongst the Poles, Hungarians and Czechs
are refugees from BoomCon, Futurex:
'St-Stubbs?' they stutter, 'wh-what are you doing *here*?'
   And though he thought it best to disappear
would Craigo let you down? Fuck man!
You were his Stags' greatest ever ruckman:
So Moose, what's left of Crazy Horse is yours.
   They're most flexible, the locals, and their laws
which, with a cash flow, can be put to use.
   Yet somehow I imagine you, The Moose
with, on your lap somewhere in all of Asia
a bargirl propping, or maybe she's a geisha.
   But, though you like her, it's 'Honey please not now.
I'm off to view the fleshpots of Cracow.
Craigo says that town is stacked with dolls!'
   Fly over mate, I'm sure you'll love the Poles!

(x)   Adrian

   ...but until I'm dead
every year is ripe for *This time this time*
this time.
   Now,
try and explain again what's 'venture capital'.
   Sorry Ades, the nothing you can't even grasp
(let alone the nothing you do) means
you only head my charm division.
   But never tell me Mr Magic's
re-making himself, I'm re-making, always re-making
you 'n' everything.
   It was a merest curtainraiser,
$tubb$corp. Australia, mind, helped to get me
learning: run onto a ground with
y' Dougies, y' Osbournes, y' Heart-throbs.
And what'll bring the game undone?
Need I inform Mr Adrian Cross:
too much show pony finessin'.
      Europe?

whatever it is, any part of the place
hardly mattered till now. (Aussie?
That was last season and another crowd.)
   Mate, we're wanted.

(xi) Sophie Cross

   . . . Oh yes we're wanted.
This isn't where I thought I'd finish,
because I haven't finished.
     And Sophie,
all we'll say of Mr Joy and Mr Lacy is
Some of us are scum and some are not.
(Even you had to work for them.)
Go anywhere today and even the most
innocent of wood-ducks will brush against
smack cash and coke cash, anything but
real livin'.
  Steve,
my first and only boss, he always said
'Real lives do real livin', *our* livin'.'
He was my education.
There must've been schooling (Glen Eira Grammar
wanted to make me something)
but what happened? I leave the place
smart enough to be a shoe salesman.
My second job I'm working for Steve Dodd.
My third is making sure I and the market
work for me.
   And we needn't tell you this
but let's: when you are in the market
there's just two rules: people count
and make sure those with power are told
Your job is letting men like me prove it,
prove we're right.
   What was the Stubbs mystique?
Craigo made it! What's his follow-through
mystique? He'll make it again!
   That bank, your bank, son of the non-bank,
whatever one of them you're working for

they must know it's simple-getting-simpler.
In some places power isn't just what it was.
Hey! Power's saying *I don't exist,
and even better I've never had to.*
You must know how I began:
with four fibro motels that had to be
carted away: it's like that:
everything is space now, space adding
to space. And this is a man
who loves to build and loves to give.
There may be more but building and giving
isn't that enough?
     Let's back him!

Sophie (continued)

... two/three times a day
the bank, our bank would seem to circle
one more potential client, pleading for their benefit
*Sure you have a good life, but want an even
better one?*
   In that city, those days,
we were awash with trust
in the joy of accepting just what we were told.
So you can understand how, as now we have a client,
Craig Stubbs, we had a client, Kim Lacy.
Didn't you think that first time you met him
This is a wonderful man or, if you didn't feel so,
couldn't you excuse someone who did?
   I had him as my client, friend and lover.
We'd meet for work, eat as friends,
and then come home to recommence as lovers.
Oh I was thinking *Kim, make a fool of me,
get me to coo 'what are you doing here big boy?'*
It was the stuff of magazines,
each time he spoke with his
Take me/ leave me/ oh by the way never forget me
charm, Sophie, that stars-in-her-eyes

pragmatist, would leap to the controls:
'Sure let's eat, then let's return to my place!'
                 He flies out Monday but flies back Friday.
Weekends were playing it sexy, playing it light.
I needn't really but I'm saving up
all that is best in me for Kim; Sophie is
feeling good about herself.
                           This man,
he's no Christian my Zen karate thug,
nor Captain Quiche the milksop ex,
nor Karl, all big black beard and having
too much his own way. No,
these could be my eyes I'm looking into.
    Keep it light I'm urging *Keep it light*
though now I'm dazed enough to guess
We think so much the same!
When Kim cries *Yeah!* don't I cry back
Yeahyeah! and doesn't he reply
Yeahyeahyeahyeah!
                     Deep enough, y' know
it's turning deeper: every day more memories,
more plans.
           Our past is starting to truly matter,
our future refuses to wait.
        Until the big until.
        He has a business partner flying in:
The Aussie end of their gemstone/caneware trade.
'You'll like him,' I've been told
'he may be cynical and rough but no-one's
straighter. A great catch for your bank.'
        And Kim's partner/
our future client/the big until is Kevin Joy.
        In remand, the first time I meet
this little loser-loner 'Miss Cross . . .
he's saying '. . . it's not me now but. Not horse.'
Why am I believing him? Why don't I answer:
I know all this to be lies, because you, Mr Joy,
the elder son of a small-town carpet salesman,
just happen to be rich.

                        And yet
if he's only the master of his one-syllable defence
It's not me now but I'd met,
had even loved, worse men.
                        But there
that afternoon in Crazy Horse, the moment
he arrives all I can see is their careers
spreading, just spreading out.
                        Drugs? How else
can anything like that exist, but overlap?
It overlaps with gemstones now,
with caneware, bargirls, innocence,
yeah yeah heaps of innocence!
            'Couldn't forget you Soph,' Kevin Joy confesses,
later. 'You helped the daggiest of ex-crims in
Australia. But now,' and so begins his mantra,
'We're gemstones, gemstones, gemstones . . .'
(*Yeah* I want to ask, *Not horse?*)
'Do I have to sing it?' he continues,
'the clean ones, darlin' we're the clean ones?'
Well at least he is. There's Kim though,
and Kevin Joy's demanding;
'Stretch your eyes Soph, really
stretch your eyes . . . can't tell can you?
It isn't me now but it's Kimbo.
Don't you know he's usin'? Not hugely but
yet usin'?'
            Inside me something is squealing for release,
and I'm telling myself
'You really know these guys now. And
knowing them you are in it in it in it.
Well, no matter the buzz, the extravagance,
Kims' eyes, yours, all that light 'n' sexy
way he made you feel till yesterday . . .
this is lies this is lies this is lies.
Don't be in it!'

Digby Gibb OA addresses the Darling Downs Small Business Association's annual awards night
for Jan Stumbles

   On the Outer Barcoo where churches are few . . .
not so not so!
     As Pastor Wellbeloved
my spiritual adviser keeps saying:
If the Good Lord recommends Billy Bloggs sheep dip
(and he does he does) friends, you better buy it!
   Now the hugest hand for Billy, the pastor,
and that big big fella without whom Queensland
would be zero: your mate 'n' mine, God!
          Church?
Do I go to church? Who me? Rabbi Gibbo
the Mad Mullah of Maroochydore?
Is the Pope Hungarian or what?
       The funnies?
Sure they made me packets, Coast-to-Coast,
but the funniest thing I ever did
was to warehouse four hick radio lemons
for Craigo Stubbs. How'd he know one of them
would blossom into BUSH-FM
the home of sweet sweet country sounds?
   Stubbsy? We would've had a gentleman's agreement
except: how can you with some bankrupt barfly
who hasn't got the good old Aussie g 'n' d
to come back home and say he's sorry.
   As for moi,
what did Liberace say?
'You know that bank I cried all the way to?
Hehheh . . . I bought it!'
       'Queensland?'
as all my Southern mates were telling me,
'Queensland? Monday one day, Sunday the next!'
   Okay, okay, y' wanna Southern joke?
How you circumcise a Tasmanian?
Hit his sister on the back of the neck!
   Yes I said that! Yes I said that!
But, Darling Darling Darling Downs I am also

saying this: here's to the man who's dipped his wick,
                                    done the trick
                                            and made it stick.
(There's nothing more Queensland than a Southerner
who's changed his ways.)
                      With heaps of kisses
                         from his missus
                         guess who this is?
Small business persons! Looking us right in our eyes
with his very own basic Queensland values
none
      other
            than
                    your small (but every day in every way
getting bigger 'n' bigger) businessman of
the year!
        Wow 'em,
                Phil-baby!

The Darling Downs Small Businessman of the Year speaks his mind

        Dear friends, here before you's a buddy
with a face that's all sweaty 'n' ruddy.
        I'm more than you think
        after too much to drink
in the tired and emotional nuddy.

Still, my rating for bullshit is nil,
I've the way and the requisite will.
        So cancel those frowns
        for here, Darling Downs,
is the gospel according to Phil:

be you black, brown, white, puce or vermilion,
in this world cast of six thousand million
        since Adam began it

there's one rule for the planet:
some steer but most sit on the pillion.

Yet with passion I urge every driver
from Kattamatite to Kaniva:
      working women and men
        just need guidance. (Ahem!
Let me cough and then clear some saliva.)

Don't take your staff too much to task,
I've a better approach (need you ask?):
      less stick and more carrot!
        My, what excellent claret!
And you say that it comes from a cask?!

Now they'd hardly recruit me for Mensa,
yet I know that's a mighty brain cleanser.
      But since *you've* paid the piper,
        and this piper's gone hyper,
well he better conclude his cadenza.

In the Great War we'd Monash and Jacka
(though today requires different yakka).
      And when dealing with freaks
        take this tip from the Greeks,
just say *Fuck off ya stupid malacca!*

I've a bald spot a few fading tatts.
Though my hobby remains crackin' fats!
      With this sexual rhoomba
        now danced in Toowoomba
I'm still young, so I'm joining . . . the Nats!

Part 16

BERNIE MILLAR	ON THE RUN
JACK	AVOIDING TROUBLE
THE KID ETC	JACK'S FRIEND
DAVE	DECEASED
WYNNE	EX-WIFE
KARL	FRIEND
BARB	OLD FLAME
DOT	DAUGHTER
NEIL	IN TOWN
KIM	FROM THE SHIRE
THE SERGEANT	FROM SEATTLE
JULIE	FROM BLACKBURN

THE HORSE!

        Then Bernie Millar finds they've framed The Kid:
and it won't be just the jug/nick/slammer
to concentrate the mind of Mr A,
but this: how he'll be flying through his life now,
straight to the end of it.
                        Everyone was disappearing,
everything was closing.
                        After they commenced
to run their town the Clean Government Party
didn't need them/ didn't want them.
Bernie had hardly slept last night,
but it was lucky how, today, he was late for work.
From across the road he saw them: all the boys
and all the girls marched by the cops
out of The FucFuc.
                And he stood back:
eyes, brain and heart, particularly heart,
working out the end: this silly Aussie in
late late middle age, whom everyone on that strip
knew, watching it.
                Back at The Horse, The Horse was closed.
The Bank, he'd never known where it was.
And Jack?

                                     ❧

        'What are you?' someone (a friend of Stubbs,
perhaps?) asked Jack.
                        'Facilitator, mate.'
(A good word that, it near meant anything.)
                'You recall The Kid?' facilitated Jack.
'Well this is him, Bern. Except they say he's
Mr A.'
        And Mr A what do he say?
'Yeah. First time I met you Millar,
what was my option? Potential bum boy for

a rockspider.'
            Him there with his arms all over
his local girl, so very pleased with being
Mr A. And what does Bernie do?
Tries hard to tell the truth.
But soon as he whines 'Aww kid . . .' he knows
that this won't work. 'I just wanted me
a bitta fun. Nothing serious. But look here . . .'
'I'm looking', mutters Mr A.
                        '. . . if y' wanna take
that attitude (Mr A he shrug) 'well I'll just leave.'

&

    In every town, like Bernie's as a boy,
they have 'em: that teacher who has no control,
that teacher who, surely, has too much;
the extra hearty stock and station agent;
the alky piano tuner, the King Dick dropkick cop;
the minister who calls you 'laddie',
each in his quaint-stuff way y' local
Bernie Millar.
            Who was hoping, that day in St Kilda:
'I know my certain kind of boy: isn't he
one of them? won't he turn out one of us?'
Oh it was a club, really. It was
like The Horse but better.
                    And when years on it fell,
just like The Horse it fell:
The accused, Bernard Millar of very little fixed address
was today found guilty. In sentencing Judge Fuckhead said,
my how he said 'Society, Millar, doesn't need men
like you!' But Millar shrugged, it had been a game,
tell him something new.

&

        They're gone, taken or gone:
Joy and Lacy, Stubbs, The Kid, his woman, all gone:
their Crazy Horse, their bank, Bernie's FucFuc;

Jack of course has done what any true facilitator
does best: simply backed out and out
until he stops appearing.
      All gone,
and Bernie's thinking *They'll get me, get me*
for the nothing I did and the everything I didn't.
And, truer than anything he has ever thought,
this stops Bernie. Then *No!* coming up elated
No! Don't tell Killer Diller Millar he's done
nothing. Go on! his orders follow through
Go on and do something!
   He's never wished for anything more in his life,
and starts preparing.

   Where's Jack? Wherever, Bernie's talking to him:
'Stay away. If you want to know
what can save your life (and name us anybody
sane that wouldn't apply to) even though it's closed
stay away from you-know-where.
Sure as we've been mates for thirty years
I'm warning, Jack, tonight I'll be making such a love
as only I would wish it made. Tonight The Horse
and me, I'll be torching both.
        Oh and if you see
The Kid tell him from Bernie: Mr A,
he's not a bad fella, just easy to facilitate.'

   It'll be one of 'those decent things'
that people who think they know about
'those decent things' consider heroic and applaud:
all that's never been in Bernie's bag.
   'I never should've worn that purple suit,'
he's recalling 'nothing made me more the pimp.
But really ... what job was that?
I used to sit in the same fake wood panel office,
a kero heater going most of the year,

doing my sums, answering the door.
How'd I know they were under age,
weren't they Asians? And then I'd ask the cops
Could you tell? So I'm walking along,
minding Bernie's business, when I'm found in a purple suit
doing a quite ridiculous job. Sure, sure,
I should've known more but can't you tell?
I'm disgusted too. Look I'm no bouncer
and the cops sure come at that! but dinkum,
a pimp? That door you just came through:
I opened it, but I do bugger-all!'

    So they name him 'Bernie Baloney'
and this time Judge Fuckhead he say
'You again, little man, you again?'

    Little man? From now on, no.
          Bernie, they'll say asking,
Bernie Millar? Didn't he ... let's see ...
he must've poured that petrol in a circle
round himself and stood there, shaking,
with the last thing he would ever own:
a FucFuc matchbook.
      'Hey Kid,'
I ask him when we're alone
'Like a nice, refreshing glass of Coca-Cola?'
The Kid sure knows there must be a joke,
he'll have to grow a bit before he knows
what joke. (There'll be an even better gag
when Bernie calls the cops.)
         Of course The Horse
was closed. It wouldn't open again.
And, in the dark, the petrol merely added to
all that tang of departed flesh the place
seemed heir to.
    So I tease him:
'Why weren't you laughing, Kid?
I mean, how much older than you am I?
Laddie must have done a spot of this before?

And, nothing ever working again, The Horse
would've been dark.
> *All the weeks before Bern's been thinking*
> *'Better or worse I have to do it. I simply must!'*
> *Even rolling into a church or two hoping God*
> *might be around; God's never found.*

      It must've been, it must've been then that,
with one of 'those decent things'
(who else could hardly imagine)
the universe of Millar reached its limits:
God was set to be discovered.
                        He tore off a match,
a little FucFuc match and struck it quick.
Burn Bernie burn!

BUNYIP AT DAVE PRICE'S WAKE

(i)
       In the extension the function warmed to its task.
       Karl though, for months now had felt under threat.
       'And are,' his old mates Lins and Dottie wanted to ask,
'yuppies your target?'
                Amongst others mmm you bet!

'... although they're minor vermin, little better than mice.
Instructing us to trim the fat, to tighten the slack!'
(Was Karl becoming his generation's Dave Price?)
'These new men and women!' he snapped, 'rich kids in black,

wallowing us around their mean bouillabaisse of spite.
Where all is market who wouldn't be nervous?
Call it, if you could be bothered, Thatcherite;
when the public's abolished where's the need for service?

Yet we get told there'll be a surest bliss
in some ever-adjusting reduction of scale.
Who'd have guessed government would finish like this?
Who knows the where, the why of the next fire sale?

Melbourne, however,' Karl was salvaging something, 'it's still my base.'

(ii)
       'Well hi there!'
                He turned and wo-ahh!
In the doorway grinned the most familiar face
of Barb, Barb Heath, the one-time Little Goer.

       'Yes indeed,' thought Karl, 'not unexpected. You *were* my lover
and, ten years on from that whirl-
pool, why shouldn't I twitch like some troppo colonel over
this *Damn fine specimen of a girl!*

But where was 'him', that innocent party, the spouse, Rog?
Why over there: middle-aged man with a beard.
      Thus trapped how could our hero weave 'n dodge?
      They were meeting much as Karl might've feared;

if he'd wanted to. Not him! And a series of 'Hi!'s
were forged as his response: 'Longish time/little see.'
      Karl wanted to look Barb right in her eyes
with *What, three times together? Who you/me/*

us? He wanted her in an empty room, held from behind,
So he could lie *Still think lots about you.*
With that idea an erection started to unwind.
Oh enjoy the beast! For I've lived a decade without you,

you and that summer we were as kids in a cubby
(till, playtime over, we howled *This isn't bloody fair!*)
One day he'd love to tell the hubby
Truly I liked your wife, Heath, so there,

it happened. I'll let you conjure the passion:
any wife and I made a most unsuitable brew.
Yours though was a fun more than after the fashion . . .

(iii)
      Looking at Karl Barb knew he knew she knew

how right here, in Uncle Dave's extension
(the patio, the bay windows, the seagrass matting):
it took but one extended glance, an ambiguous mention
of who-knew-what and adrenalin cascaded.
                         They'd kept chatting.

But for all her wide-eyed cheek this girl was dazed;
and shaken with the sweetest of choices: will we or won't?
      And even today this got signalled, whenever Barb's eyebrows
           were raised:
We sure know something, Karl, that the rest of 'em don't!

(iv)
        (And later, watching Heath and the Little Goer go,
Karl, lining up for his ta-taa kiss,
felt it superfluous to add *Barb I'm sure you know
we'll never stop meeting at events like this!*)

(v)
        '. . . please Karl,' urged Dot, let her elaborate:
'no kid ever thinks their folks as ever madly
in love. Ours don't. But Karl I'll tell it straight:
Wynney and Dad had soured, soured badly.'

(It made Dot angry to even consider a fib.)
'. . . after those years when thankfully she'd the pick of him,
Mum, too old to discover Women's Lib . . .'
Dot was pausing hard, 'Just got sick of him!'

(Him! Karl knew, the my-way-or-no-way, too full o' beer
Dave Price.) 'Of course I'm sad my father's dead
but Wynne,' Dot was firm, 'she'd had it beyond here . . .'
and raised a hand, flat, well above her head.

(vi)
        No families Karl knew put the heart on full display:
you got a curse? then please contain your curse.
He'd only caught the mine host Price, always at play:
'Bunyip! One more beer! And quick!'
                            Till better/worse,

like all the neighbours, one-time workmates, friends,
Karl too had been dispersed in the Last Great Price Crusade.
But this, they should've guessed, is another way a life ends:
you shed your worlds.
                He thought of that sign-off Dave made

every evening: 'End of transmission! I am off to bed!'
and wanted to suggest to the son, his friend, 'Call us Lins'.
But, the day jading him, left with what remained, unsaid.

(vii)

        Owning her unit this place was hardly Wynne's,

now; but *She* the in-laws had resolved *deserves a break:*
let's comfort (or something like it) the former spouse.
And set to do their best they assembled this wake
for an angry man who lived alone in his weatherboard house.

Yet, with her new life starting why bother to learn
whatever had made him such a sad, petty czar
(shellshock or some other Repatriation term)?
That had been his life, not Wynne's.
                        Now out in the car

Dot waited, cried and hoped her mum might hug her
soon. What a stupid afternoon! Where lay the remotest good
to even think *He wouldn't see us in years moody bugger*
and when he did . . .
           Sure, Wynne understood

his enemies were to be made, and even kept. But then,
to supply both their arms and ammunition,
not *That* set David front row of this land's most difficult men.
      Sighing she left his place.
                    End of transmission.

LOVELIFE (VI)

Barb and Neil (iii)

      Neil was in Melbourne attending a funeral,
he called up his old flame to check out her scene.
      She was delighted and jumped at a meeting,
before he'd fly out from Tullamarine.

Her heart was kickstarted, it wouldn't stop thumping
with part what had happened and part might've been.
Then she panicked: if Neil has a touch of the cold feet
won't he run off to Tullamarine?

      His toes though were warm, for the past urged his ardour,
put it down to nostalgia/ the odd wayward gene.
And as for their 'sex', all he did was imagine
a jet taking off from Tullamarine.

      They met at Brunetti's. Recognition! Adjustment!
(They'd both put on weight i.e. neither was lean.)
      So Barb broke the ice with 'Australia's best coffee!
There's sure nothing like *this* at Tullamarine!'

      So, how was Roger? (Not that he knew Roger.)
      Her shoulders were shrugging like *See what I mean?*
Their marriage still worked though, small-scale if functional,
more like Moorabbin than Tullamarine.

Still the family had grown with strapping twin daughters.
Her son was an adult now, long past a teen;
who'd dropped out of uni to work on an oil rig
(and she'd driven *him* out to Tullamarine!).

      'Well I have a girlfriend,' Neil turned confessional,
'all decks should be cleared Barb, best to come clean.
We live in the country, where she runs a bush band;
and one place she'd loathe would be Tullamarine.'

And then there was Benny, Barb sure had liked Benny
(who may've been gay but was hardly a queen).
Well Neil had flown down with Benny-and-partner,
who'd gone home that morning via Tullamarine.

  'Can you imagine the tricks they get up to?'
Barb interjected '. . . err, mighty obscene?
They must be a circus, though we wouldn't try them:
those Mardi Gras specials from Tullamarine.'

  So both, as you've guessed, coincided in basics,
they still voted Labor, though tending to Green.
  But he looked at his watch, as time ticked, insistent,
onward and onward to Tullamarine.

  Then, coffee over, a quick browse at Readings;
Carlton just glowed in its bright autumn sheen.
And Barb was determined she'd drive him to Tulla
(that's Melbourne, you're dead right, for Tullamarine).

  Though this inner-Barb was advising her outer:
Love's still an addiction, might have to wean.
Here's not the first junkie going cold turkey
twitching and sweaty at Tullamarine.

  Before they drove off then Neil watched his ex-lover
give a touch o' th' lippy to complete her smart preen;
Whilst out on the freeway thoughts turned generational
(through Essendon, Niddrie to Tullamarine):

'Back in the days of Cyril and Cecil,
Nancy and Stella, Gladys and Reen,
no-one on earth made their love quite as we would,
when cows grazed their full out at Tullamarine.

'Or think of my parents Elwyn and Ronald
(what is your mother's name? Noelene?):
retirees on super, scooting to Surfers,
whose raunchy weekends start at Tullamarine.'

    . . . yes we still feel the same Neil noted amazed, and
no woman that I've met was less a machine.
It's great and it's ghastly we'll still love each other
long after I've boarded at Tullamarine.

All else is a bagatelle sent to distract us
(if within there's a battle near internecine).
    Then he noticed a signpost, it stopped his reverie:
MELBOURNE AIRPORT (TULLAMARINE).

So they took a deep breath for the final encounter
(one round remaining in their magazine).
Who cared if the airline were Ansett or Qantas,
two adults were kissing at Tullamarine.

    Then an idea occurred (though the thought gave her shivers)
which verged on the dodgy yet wouldn't demean
to publish a book, obscure in its self-help:
How To Farewell Your Ex From Tullamarine.

Some women would chortle, some look abandoned,
a few might be blasé, still others would keen.
Barb took on all four modes as Neil taxied past her.
Full throttle then lift-off from Tullamarine.

Jack's Progress (ii)

Something, anything and it

      Jack's being taken home. One day the news and press
will announce his name and add 'bar manager',
early sixties, late of where he's coming from;
how he's being looked after. Right now,
either side of him, protection, government guaranteed:
fucknuckle and stumblebum. No, he insults them:
in the weeks they stalked him, his kind of check out/
their days of making a life of it
(neat Crazy Horse with a FucFuc chaser)
these ultimate cleanskins never did much.
He's going to tell them of Kim
(but his, not theirs) Young Kim Lacy,
that Sergeant from Seattle and how Jack
just facilitated.

                    ❧

          'Have you friends?' the Sergeant
asked, 'Kids like you?'
                    'Kids?' Kim Lacy
was a touch annoyed. 'Jack is your friend,
Sergeant, I am Jack's friend and me, I have this
wide variety of friends; take GoGo for example,
but GoGo's straight; except he has this friend . . .'
(don't tell him it's that word again!) 'this friend
called Tobe, Tobe the poet and his lady, Sal;
Tobe may never meet you, Sergeant, but you and me
will make him very happy. Why not?
Kim would soon have friends and, why not,
just like Tobe.
            'Talking of friends,' the Sergeant laughed,
'this black buddy, like me on R and R,
ends up on your Gold Coast? With this sheila?'
(Sergeant is very pleased with 'sheila'.) 'This sheila

who informs him just as things are set
"Baby, I'm a man!" And my black friend
he just looks up, smiles and says "Man, woman,
I've come this far for who-the-fuck cares.
Do something, anything and it!'"
    Now that's a friendship!
    What would it take to stop the Sergeant from Seattle?
one chop to the windpipe?
        But this man was professional,
no doubt with friends equally professional.
You betcha.
   He asked:
'In your part of Sydney, Kim, people get killed?'
   Only road hoons and their victims.
   The Sergeant knew better: 'Down there,
more can happen, baby, than you think.
Come on, can't it Jack? Remember sweetheart,
even your suburb's most simpering of grannies
is *this!* he snapped his fingers 'and only *this!*
away from *that!*' He pointed to the powder.

        ∾

  'Kim was scared and, gentlemen, Kim
was loving it. Y' know,' (they needn't have asked)
'I once met everybody's favourite drug czar: Joy.
He seemed worried that day, quiet.
I like to think I might've spooked him . . .'
   Ahh, save it for the Commission, Jack.
Then tell them of him and Kim and Jungle Jim,
of The Jeweller, Cap'n Midnight, Sophie Cross
(even dumb ol' Craigo) and your mates Bernie
and The Kid.

        ∾

    Who,
with less than months remaining
(and only lawyers and relatives permitted)
received a visitor: me playing at Uncle Jack.

        Still with that skewed passion for facts
he was reading almanacs.
Self-improvement? Anything by now improved
something. *The lot!* he looked with eyes demanding
Before it's done I wanna know the lot!
I have to!
        And, though they were slowly
preparing his end, it was to be trusted
he could tell things.
        The Kid of course went smart,
and he proposed a pact:
his words were his life: hang him you hanged
your information.
                They passed it along
and never returned.
                    'But Jack,' he asked
'you know what I like? How I'll never spill,
not now, but how you will.
You've seen the life, you know what it's like:
how, in my cabbie days, when something
was in the boot I'd be rehearsing hard
I'm on a call . . . it's a delivery . . .
this shmuck is a clean shmuck, no-one
sets him up . . . he must endure!'
        And then I thought:
not even fate possesses the malice
to set my friend with gs and gs of bang-bang
(enough of whatever stuff he thought it was
to prime the old fella for an unending tour
of Fuck City). Of course,
if that is what you're dumb enough to take
for spot-on dinkum oil, sorry,
but in these lands there's one sure mistake
never to be made and, since few forgive
the next white sucker, grieving shall be reserved
for higher animals.

                    ෴

          In the plane now
Jack is telling how he's resigned, how
it's their way and has to be done:
there will be a room: they will walk
his friend in and wheel him out.
          And these men with Jack
they have to understand: that God of coincidence
he's a malicious God: 'I've already had one mate
executed: Kent. And here's the worst thing Kent
or The Kid did: they met. I was there and
Bernie was there that unrepeated blink 'n' miss it
night of No-hopers Inc.'
                    So please,
since only he's survived, appreciate how such deaths
and lives can roll something into nothing
and back into something again.

                    ಬಿ

          Yes even my mate Bernie.
          Let's not add the crisp splat! of coward!
to unproven rockspider/presumed grass/failed pimp/
mediocre friend; any end to such a life, you'd say,
has to be some improvement. Well yes and yet,
given the chance, I'd order all Australia to queue
at his body bag. And here's why:
setting himself to finish his way,
with such defiance only a no-one ever achieves,
Bernie Millar torched The Horse and bye-bye Bernie,
blazed with it.

                    ಬಿ

          One history over, another
has to commence. So Jack's telling how,
it was rumoured thirty years before, someone
set up Kent; how someone/something as similar
set up The Kid; how Bernie (as if his life
was aimed to just that moment)
set up himself. And, since only Jack remains,

these men with him would get cooperation:
just to make a home for him and his facts
(facts which being sinewy-strong, rope if you like)
were ready for use.
      Is one of his escorts Maltese? Could almost pass as black.
With 'Nearly there . . .' he slaps the back.
'Welcome to the truly big time, Jack.'

Julie

    Soon as I was seized that was when
(I call them what's going on in the back bar*)*
the dreams commenced.
        This may start
as just another question but, knowing there is hardly
any answer, it plods into statement
why do I want to dream about *you?*
And note not her but you *(you could never be* her*).*
    For I've heard what has to be your voice
again, its soft/sour English whine
smeared with just the tang of whatever class
your mother thought advisable to join;
I'm dreaming of you, Julie, because you'd understand
this is the man who never knew
when to stop: he stops when he dies.

    From its nozzle the air shoots cool and clean,
for distraction there's an in-flight magazine;
and like a child he's bagsed the window seat.
    Beyond the clouds there's such a dazzle
to the sky (it ought to capture him as he awakes);
but it's another of those dreams that, for days,
keep on asking *Still remember her?*
that continue such a haul on Jack.
    Oh yes, he remembers Julie
(her moist young skin, that tight bun of long hair

unravelling just for him). Yep, even in dreams
she's still worldly-if-worshipful, eager to learn
much more: fifteen and jail bait.
      Why can't dreams, of all things, update
the girl? She'd be, he pauses to calculate,
forty . . . forty-one . . . and asks *Could I even
love her now?*
      And yes, will come the sigh,
just like the last time;
and though there's dumber things Jack's done,
little that he's lived will ever say this much:
It simply had to happen!
      (*Oh yes* he knows he
has to ask *if I had caught Denise
messing and messing hard, would I have
auditioned that for an excuse? But then
I was in Brisbane, wasn't I? That's nothing like
being in Melbourne.* It wasn't him dumping Denise
beside Queen's Lane, it wasn't Jack telling his woman
'You'll never do this again!'
      For years that killing made him unavailable
to anyone but kids. 'Bern,' he'd tell his mate,
'it's tough in the world. Kids need protection.
It simply has to happen . . .')
      Has to until
Julie's mother shipped her home to some place
with an ugly name he's forgotten.
      It's forgotten
too, if he ever knew, where they might've met.
Though he still knows how the choreography was set:
Some friend/acquaintance had a younger sister,
who hated Jack but had a friend; she was Julie,
and he, sincerely hoping how, one day, he might show her
music, writing, art, took Julie back to where,
over a mattress on the floor, he heard her
tell all she wanted to occur:
a magic which would turn any moment
into such a forever only a dream,
decades on, could tell him *Yes it has!*
Well something approximating that.

                            For years Jack knew
how Bern and the rest would ask themselves:
'What had he ever seen in that one?
Given her age, a mind of sorts, but a body which
had hardly reached its destination ... easy pickings?'
No-one bothered (more probably dared) to ask him;
or even cared to.
                    And here,
for all who enjoy melodrama unadorned,
are a few lines of the mother's version.
(Jack learnt them well.) *This man,
if he must be termed a man
is tampering* Remarkably bland word that
but nasty, let it pass
*tampering with my daughter
who's sixteen and only just. He's thirty-five
which sounds only as it sounds.
She's been minding his gun. She says they're in love.
But I am her mother and we
are going home!*
                Only after that
and a few months of Dear Jack correspondence
came Bernie's consolation: 'Cold, mate.
That girl was very cold ...' And though this
hardly helped, Jack knew of few who'd ever guess
the Julie kind of passion, kind of love.
'Bern,' he replied, 'we were pure cream and I
never felt stronger!'
                        But Julie was young,
young meant predictable, predictable went with years,
those years were all war and hers was a very angry front.
Soon with her letters *Red Mole* got dispatched,
and/or *The International Times*,
visions, she believed, still denied Melbourne,
Victoria, Australia; or, if she'd little care
about that place, at least to help sustain Jack's future.
            'Taa,' he advised, 'for truth as you see it ...'
            Twelve thousand miles/ten days away *No no no*
her letter bristled in return *much much better,
the truth! the truth!*

If he felt challenged, old,
Jack conceded she was always set
to drift from him; though even on his
tolerant terms couldn't she be thought,
if not hardline, well enough, sometimes?
  And, if her mail continued, Jack,
surveying what girls remained, continued the work-through.
That's when Bernie (no-one was understanding quite
like Bernie) got even more precise: 'Ooh you animal!'
  After Cambridge (was it during the commune or squat?)
Julie became a Trot:
seems to have met somebody else; never wrote.
  Better dream about it all one day
Jack never remembers thinking, though he did
better make it something.

Melbourne, early April, the early nineties

  After they took him, his suitcase and the bag
from the plane, the men drove Jack towards
the city, telling how, since he was special,
they'd booked him three days worth of room
(still better, suite).
  When he mentioned expenses they knew about
expenses, and urged: not to worry, charge it.
Now he wasn't to leave the building,
and they'd know if he did, but
given the hotel's precinct why should he:
Jack could have anything come to him,
just charge it.
  Stopping at the first floor the hotel recommenced
at the thirty-fifth; now, nine floors beyond,
this pale tired man, late middle-aged,
stooping more than he should
(whose beard if once like stringybark was patchier)
unpacked his bag of correspondence, receipts,
cassettes and a video.
Sum total evidence, Jack gave these to the men

thinking *You've been human this far, was it
worth it?* and got thanked. No they couldn't
stay for drinks. His colleagues possibly, allies
probably, but certainly never friends,
the men were hurried but smooth with it,
needing to return to the office, girlfriend, wife:
'So mate, until tomorrow …'

&

These were Jack's friends and more recent friends.
First, Joy: all amateur. The one professional thing
he did was kill; so someone had to do it better.
Stubbs: after owning all he did
to finish with Crazy Horse and The FucFuc, poor Craigo,
should've stayed with the Toyotas. Jack had hardly
enjoyed his type but, by then, Stubbs was ripe to like.
Sophie: little is obvious as the ambiguous.
She would go everywhere, finish up anywhere.
Bern: only luck he ever had was
Jack for a friend.
The Kid:
more like a son at times, a relic of
those Denise days (or were they the Julie days?)
any event the Des 'n' Iris days, even that poor deadshit
Kent days.
And Kim? What had been his latest motto?
*I've got to get strong/alive again/some kind of
career planned.* And he was scared of the lot,
so driven by the rush of being scared.
Oh do a public service, Jack, ditch him,
get yourself a legitimate old age! And yes
he was willing, so totally pleased to help.
What, after all, gave that much power?
Facilitating. Being behind the bar at Crazy Horse:
where he had watched The FucFuc teevees
watching Kiwis watching them back; American operatives,
suspected veterans of *The biggest game to date*
(and whatever *that* was it had to be American);
and beyond them, these: the sincerest of straight-

faced failed con-artists as only Aussies
could produce; unless they were these locals
(who might be any locals):
a VP of the Clean Government Party,
that army captain linked to National Renewal
(with politics, like anywhere, all boardgame, why care
which was elephant and which, water buffalo).

                              ಌ

      Today, by six, forty-four floors up and
looking south, Jack saw evidence of how,
with its orange-to-brown, mist-and-pollutants
dusk shades, the afternoon must have exploded
above St Kilda Road;
and his look returned to the suite.
Sure I'm in power, but who's run off with
the Gideons? All that approximated reading matter
was this fantail of brochures.
                       And what spread
themselves through three pages of
'High Rollin' Melbourne'? Girls girls girls and
still more beautiful girls. But Jack preferring
the cynical, phoney, antiseptic, yet beyond that
honest, 'escort', called for one.
      '. . . since I'm a good listener, someone with stories.'
    At Poppets International Katy was understanding.
'A student?' she volunteered. 'Kishi's a student
but a real dish.'
        'Well no-one over twenty,
make that twenty-five . . .' and though
there might be 'sex' he'd rather 'love'.
Did International Poppets get him?
            'At Poppets International,' Katy sing-songed '*yes-we-do!*'
    Now he didn't wish to be confused but would she
understand him if . . . yes Katy would, go on . . .
'Well here's what Kishi has to wear. Who says?
I say and I'll be paying to say. So Katy: smart jeans,
a pleasant blouse, a jacket, and if it's leather
even better. The girl's relaxed? Well so am I and so

is she again, I'm on the forty-fourth floor; and she's
to be my guest. Right? Right? So tell her we'll
be heading down to dine . . . call me a public servant
of a kind, your taxes at work Katy . . . Oh
and could this Kishi stay until tomorrow?'
  Before it arrived Jack already heard that
dingdingding of Katy's 'Yes-she-can!'
             (Tomorrow!
Didn't you love the pure and total idea of it?
Yes, let's invite tomorrow now!)
  'Give Kishi half an hour?' asked Katy.
  He gave his name as Jack, hung up, lay down.

Acknowledgements continued:

Definition of 'suite' reprinted from *The Concise Oxford Dictionary* (10th edition, 1999) by permission of Oxford University Press. © Oxford University Press 1999.

The lines from Frank O'Hara's 'Essay on Style' are from *The Collected Poems of Frank O'Hara* and are deemed by Random House, Inc. to be in the realm of fair use, and thus no permission is necessary. We thank them and their Alfred A. Knopf, Inc. imprint.

The lines from John Forbes' 'Drugs' and 'Ode to Cultural Studies' (the latter used as a chapter title) are from *The Collected Poems of John Forbes* and are published with permission of Len Forbes and the John Forbes Estate.

The line from T S Eliot's 'The Old Gumby Cat' is from *Old Possums Book of Practical Cats*, published by Faber and Faber Ltd.

The line from Wallace Stevens' 'Adagia' is from Wallace Stevens' *Opus Posthumous*, published by Faber and Faber Ltd.

The line from Billy Thorpe's 'Most People I Know Think That I'm Crazy' is published with permission of Mushroom Music Publishing.

The lines from Robert Graves' 'A Slice of Wedding Cake' are from *The Complete Poems of Robert Graves* (1996) and are published with permission of Carcanet Press.

Not only is the poem recited in Part 14 by Shelton Lea, the actual poet is Shelton Lea; thus poem and poet appear with permission.

Since the music for 'The Stags' Song' was notated by Alan Murphy it seems only right that he should be named composer to Gibbo's hideous lyrics. Thanks Alan.

Every effort has been made to contact the holders of copyright material, and the author and publisher would be pleased to hear from anyone who has not been properly acknowledged.

The Lovemakers was supported by many people during its writing (1986-1999) but none more so than Luise Huck and three of my poet colleagues: Pi O, Gig Ryan and the late John Forbes. I wish to thank all who stood by me in my quest for publication, in particular my agent Fran Bryson. What you are holding is a result of her loyalty, thoroughness and patience and their admirable risk-taking.

www.ingramcontent.com/pod-product-compliance
Lightning Source LLC
Chambersburg PA
CBHW021712300426
44114CB00009B/106